Gdańsk

Gdańsk

Portrait of a City

PETER OLIVER LOEW

TRANSLATED BY JESSE C. WOOD

OXFORD
UNIVERSITY PRESS

OXFORD
UNIVERSITY PRESS

Oxford University Press is a department of the University of Oxford. It furthers
the University's objective of excellence in research, scholarship, and education
by publishing worldwide. Oxford is a registered trade mark of Oxford University
Press in the UK and certain other countries.

Published in the United States of America by Oxford University Press
198 Madison Avenue, New York, NY 10016, United States of America.

This book is a translation of Peter Oliver Loew, *Danzig: Biographie einer Stadt*
© Verlag C.H. Beck oHG, München 2011
English edition © Oxford University Press 2024

All rights reserved. No part of this publication may be reproduced, stored in
a retrieval system, or transmitted, in any form or by any means, without the
prior permission in writing of Oxford University Press, or as expressly permitted
by law, by license, or under terms agreed with the appropriate reproduction
rights organization. Inquiries concerning reproduction outside the scope of the
above should be sent to the Rights Department, Oxford University Press, at the
address above.

You must not circulate this work in any other form
and you must impose this same condition on any acquirer.

CIP data is on file at the Library of Congress

ISBN 978-0-19-760386-4

DOI: 10.1093/oso/9780197603864.001.0001

Printed by Integrated Books International, United States of America

The translation of this work was funded by Geisteswissenschaften International – Translation
Funding for Humanities and Social Sciences from Germany, a joint initiative of the
Fritz Thyssen Foundation, the German Federal Foreign Office, the collecting
society VG WORT and the Börsenverein des Deutschen Buchhandels
(German Publishers & Booksellers Association).

Partial costs of publishing of this book have been generously provided by
the City of Gdansk and the Urban Culture Institute.

For Laura and Cornelius

CONTENTS

Translator's Note ix
Acknowledgments xi

Introduction: A Space of European Memory 1

1. Amber-Gold: Shedding Light on Prehistory 4

2. Green and Blue: Fishers, Merchants, Dukes, 997–1308 11

3. Brick-Red: Danzig as a Part of the Teutonic State, 1308–1454 24

4. Wheat-Blond and Rye-Brown: Danzig's Golden Age, 1454–1655 45

5. Fading Hues, 1655–1793 84

6. Prussian Blue: Fall and Rise in the Nineteenth Century, 1793–1918 114

7. Against a Red Background: From the Free City of Danzig to the Second World War, 1918–1945 145

8. Variations in White and Red: Gdańsk, "Fairer than Ever Before," 1945–1980 184

9. Kaleidoscope: Into the Future with Solidarity and the Discovery of New Pasts 212

Epilogue: Why Gdańsk? 242

Appendix: Names of Places 245
Notes 251
Selected Bibliography 259
Index 265

TRANSLATOR'S NOTE

From the early fourteenth century through the end of the Second World War, the city's population was overwhelmingly German-speaking. This is also true for many of the towns and cities in the vicinity, as the whole region known for some time as Royal Prussia, though subject to Poland for centuries, was largely inhabited by German speakers. As it traces new localities that are introduced during this period covering more than seven centuries, this book accordingly uses the German versions of their names, with their initial appearance followed by the corresponding Polish name in parentheses.

Conversely, for the period following the Second World War, as the population became composed almost entirely of Polish speakers, this book uses the Polish versions of place names with a parenthetical reminder of the former German names following their initial appearance. The reader can consult "Localities and Topographical Designations" in the appendix for the German and Polish names of these localities side by side.

In cases where a place name has an accepted English version (e.g. Warsaw, Vistula, Lodz, etc.), this book uses that form. The translator has consulted Merriam-Webster's list of geographical names in making these decisions.

This book generally uses direct English translations for the names of Gdańsk's districts, streets, bridges, gates, and other landmarks, because for the most part, such names in the city's historical center were translated directly from German into Polish after the Second World War and retain at least the approximate meanings of their German counterparts. In the relatively few instances where the Polish name does not correspond with the German, the text uses an English translation from either German or Polish, based on the historical period in which it appears. "Streets, Districts, and Other Landmarks" in the appendix provides the reader with the German and Polish names for all of the English translations.

ACKNOWLEDGMENTS

Eminent German and Polish historians have occupied themselves with Gdańsk. Their names emerge occasionally in the following pages, and a selection of their most important writings is located in the bibliography. My book owes its existence to all of them, and not least to those who are still living, researching, and writing, and who have broadened my knowledge of this city, in which I myself have spent many years. Thus, I thank them, as well as many colleagues and friends, Oxford University Press for the initiative to take on this book, and my family—not for the first time—for their patience.

Gdańsk

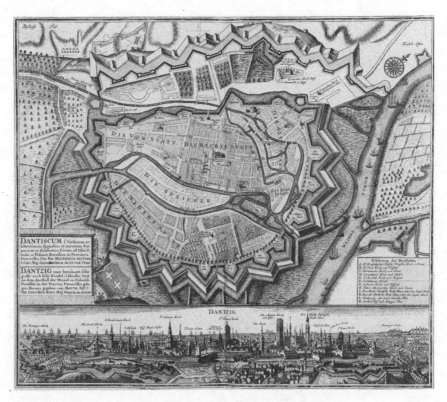

Map of Gdańsk, ca. 1730 by Matthäus Seutter. Wikimedia Commons.

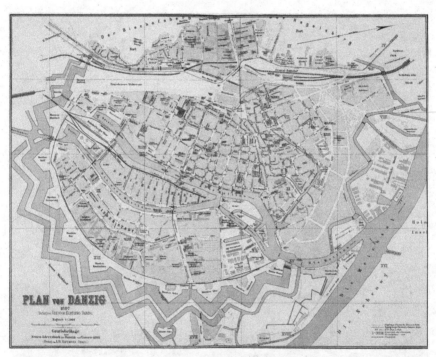

Map of Gdańsk, 1897. From https://www.polishancestors.com.

Introduction

A Space of European Memory

It is the city where the Second World War began and where, a half century later, the first domino toppled in the collapse of the Soviet empire. The images of Gdańsk in the twentieth century are manifold: Westerplatte, Polish Post Office. The Free City of Danzig. Strikes, revolt, Solidarity. Destruction, escape, and exile. Resistance, reconstruction. Lech Wałęsa, Günter Grass, and the drummer Oskar Matzerath. Naval artillery, the raised fists of the workers, smoking rubble. 1919/1920, 1939, 1945, 1970, 1980/1981—dates when the city wrote itself into world history. Hardly anywhere else in Central Europe so comprehensively embodies the upheavals of an entire century. As if focused through a magnifying lens, the modern history of the continent glares harshly here. It is the history of a tattered century.

Gdańsk's twentieth century did not, however, merely produce new historical symbols; it was also a period in which the city's older history was constantly reflected in the present. The liberal intellectuals of the Independent Self-Governing Trade Union "Solidarity" positioned themselves within the tradition of the early-modern merchant citizens. Communists wove the history of class struggle into Gdańsk. Nationalists styled the city at times as a stronghold of Germanness, at others as a loyal Polish port. Crusaders' den, fortified city, a people proved by affliction, Prussia's splendor, bastion of liberty—in increasingly rapid alternation, the sequence of images constructed through the ages has superimposed newly defined topicalities onto the city's past according to each respective present, spawning narratives employed to most effectively legitimize political claims or satisfy contemporary needs for identity.

Such a polyphonic recounting of these many histories inevitably plays an essential role in the representation of Gdańsk's past. Depending on which glasses the historian wears, the colored slivers of historical fact shift as in a kaleidoscope, bursting the old patterns and forming new connections. In the beginning was—a bishop? A German? A Slav? A Prussian? A village? A duke? Amber? Commerce? Clay and sand? In the end was—a symbol? A political organism? A regional society? A tale told by many voices? A fiction? An entirely ordinary city?

Of course, there is no answer straightforward enough to satisfy any ideologically motivated historiography. Thus nationalist-minded historians in the early twentieth century were unable to explain certain aspects of Gdańsk's history in a way that fit their constructed projections of the city's identity and past. German historians intent on proving the inherent "Germanness" of the city could never quite explain, for example, why the fifteenth-century city of Danzig, with its overwhelmingly German population, would rise up against the rule of the likewise "German" Teutonic Order and happily subject itself to the Polish crown. Soviet and Polish nationalist historians would find themselves at similar pains to distort, smudge, or simply ignore events that belied an unbroken core of "Polishness" running through the city's past.

This book will present frequent examples of such retroactively superimposed narratives on the city's history and identity, illustrating the importance placed on particular aspects of local historical culture in the efforts of the respective civic elites to recall the community's past to the minds of their contemporaries in order to construct legitimacy or establish identity. History has been utilized to provide comfort and evoke pride and at the same time to create scorn and envy. History was and is ever-present in Gdańsk.

Gyddanyzc, Kdanze, Danzk, Danczik, Danzig, Gdańsk. Again and again over its thousand-year history, this city of many names has been besieged and coveted by emperors, kings, tsars, and dictators; a subject, sometimes loyal and sometimes defiant, of regional dukes, Teutonic grandmasters, and the Polish crown. As a proud Hanseatic city, it attracted visitors, merchants, and permanent residents from all across Europe, becoming a remarkably diverse early metropolis. It languished under Napoleon and later embodied an attempt at a novel, post-national solution in the aftermath of the First World War. Germanic, Slavic, Baltic, Teutonic, Polish, Prussian, German, National Socialist, Soviet, Polish again. And through it all, Gdańsk has developed its own identity, a *genius loci* forged not only through the city's multifaceted and turbulent past but also from its occasional rediscoveries of that past from beneath a nationalist and totalitarian whitewash.

Gdańsk is a city that asks many questions but also has answers at hand. And one answer has always satisfied inquirers, regardless of their nationality, and is still valid today: Gdańsk is fascinating. Gdańsk is incomparable. Its development has followed a logic entirely its own. Beyond all doubt are the city's colors: the brick red of the churches and towers; the green of the region's forested hills and lowlands; the blue of the sea and the soaring skies; brown grain, golden amber;

and once again red, the Gdańsk flag. As these colors have accompanied daily life here for centuries, they also characterize each chapter of this book.

Yet this book does not consist merely of colors and memory. It is a history of Gdańsk, the biography of a city, and thus a treatment of concrete historical processes and developments, an examination of economics and society, politics and administration, architecture and art. Here the overabundance of history means there is so much to relate, and yet so little can fit within the pages of so slender a book. Individual destinies, traditions, comprehensive insights into the everyday life of times past—all of these must unavoidably be shortchanged. The multiplicity of narratives and completely divergent interpretations of this city can likewise receive detailed treatment only periodically. Fortunately, this also means that for many years to come, Gdańsk will remain a place well worth engaging for scholars, enthusiasts, tourists, and the city's residents.

1

Amber-Gold

Shedding Light on Prehistory

In the morning sunlight after a stormy night, when the restless waves sweep onto the beach, you see it flashing here and there, golden and warm, if you pay attention. Between shells and drying kelp, there lie little nuggets of an enchanting material: amber. You gather them in your hand and examine them up close: they gleam, they glisten. For thousands, millions of years, the sea has washed them ashore, here along the Gulf of Gdańsk.

The Amber Capital

St. Mary's Street in Gdańsk is a timelessly beautiful place. In hardly any other location does one so strongly sense the majesty of this city; in hardly any other place does this "Venice of the north" seem so profoundly warm and homey, so genuine. In front of and on the *Beischläge*, the ornate terraces so representative of these old townhouses, jewelers who have dedicated their craft to an extraordinary material display their wares. The light falling sharply into the narrow street makes the honey-colored stones glow mysteriously. Framed in silver, fitted into a brooch, crafted crudely into necklaces or exquisitely into cogs with full sails: it is amber, *Bernstein, bursztyn*, Baltic gold, to which Gdańsk owes its unmistakable luster, its fame, and its wealth.

Today, Gdańsk is a stronghold of amber workmanship, proudly calls itself the world capital of amber, and adorns itself with an amber museum, an amber altar, and amber's positive reputation. Amber is said to promote "a sunny, carefree life," yet at the same time foster a "tradition-conscious" mindset and help "carry inherited values into new eras. Amber leads to flexibility and spurs creativity."[1] Some may believe this while others do not, but the gold-colored stuff certainly connects the present with a distant past when the city did not yet exist.

Traces of Rome

Forty to fifty million years ago, the amber trees bled in Northern Europe. Resin flowed from the bark and collected at the trees' bases. Sometimes an insect fell into the viscous mass and died. As the water level rose and the Baltic Sea came into being, the forests sank and the water's currents carried the solidified resin clumps along, primarily into the area where the waves today crash against the coasts of the Gulf of Gdańsk, the Vistula Spit, and the Sambia Peninsula. Coated in sand and stone, the resin slowly transformed into amber.

As pieces of stone-age jewelry demonstrate, amber was already valued many millennia ago. In the Bronze Age, the Baltic gold was coveted merchandise, evinced by a golden ring with an amber gem excavated in Greek Mycenae. In classical Greece as well, the "petrified honey," as they called it, was counted among sought-after luxury goods.

Ancient Rome had an especially great demand for amber. Trade relations between south and north intensified, most notably overland. From the middle of the first century BCE, the "Amber Road" (or Via mercatorum, Merchants' Road) connected the Baltic Sea with the Mediterranean centers of civilization. This was no transport route in a modern sense but merely a road traced through fortified locations such as Kalisz, Opole, or Vienna. In addition, it is likely that the Romans themselves hardly ever traveled northward to the sea; rather, the trade—which, apart from the durable amber, surely comprised other products, such as furs—generally took place through further resale. Trade in amber was most active between the first and fourth centuries CE, as attested to by, among other things, the large findings of ancient coins in Central Europe. The trade stopped during the migration period beginning in the fourth century.

The Baltic coast not only served as a source of raw materials; since the Neolithic Age, amber was processed and worked here as well. Found on the beaches and mined inland, it served local artisans as a material for jewelry production. In Pomerelia, the region along the lower course of the over 650-mile-long Vistula River and the Gulf of Gdańsk, traces of human settlement can be found dating back to the tenth millennium BCE, when the glaciers melted at the end of the last ice age. The question of who they were, the people living here in prehistoric times, has stirred scholarly imagination for centuries. Yet even though the land around Gdańsk has occasionally yielded remains of ancient cultures, scholars for a long time had to depend on scanty written records and, above all, conjecture. The Danzig councilman Johann Uphagen was especially knowledgeable, or at least imaginative, in this regard. Based on ancient and medieval authors, he "proved" in his *Parerga historica*, published in 1782, that Goths had founded the city of Danzig in the middle of the first century BCE. He also maintained that the Phoenicians had made it as far as Danzig, as illustrated in Greek legends: Uphagen claimed that the river Eridanos, into which the steeds of the sun-chariot toppled Apollo's son Phaethon, is none other than the little Radunia that flows past Danzig.

Through systematic collection and excavation, the number of archaeological finds has increased since the end of the nineteenth century and led to further theories; yet authors have always managed to draw quite divergent conclusions, depending on their respective national ties. Pomerelia had indeed been settled by both Germans and Poles, as well as the West Slavic Kashubian people, and as modern nationalisms emerged in the second half of the nineteenth century, the task of scholars was often to supply evidence for political claims on this land and the legitimacy of its rightful affiliation with Prussia (or, respectively, Germany), and later with Poland. Such nationalist disputes were not limited to prehistory; they also informed the interpretation of all historical epochs.

Even long after the Second World War, German prehistorians strove to produce evidence that a "Proto-Germanic culture" lived here, indicated by "distinctly Germanic characteristics" in their grave forms and pottery (face urns).[2] On the other hand, Polish research argued into the 1980s that the entire area between the Elbe and Bug rivers was ruled in the first millennium BCE by the Lusatian culture, so named because the first archaeological findings particular to this culture were discovered in Lusatia. Polish historians argued that this was a "Proto-Slavic" culture, evinced by its uninterrupted settlement and material culture. They maintained furthermore that in Eastern Pomerania around 500 BCE, an "Eastern Pomeranian culture" that produced the urns emerged from the Lusatian culture. All later cultures also identifiable based on these archaeological finds, Polish research concluded, naturally belong to "several different Proto-Slavic population groups."[3] German research denied the existence of Proto-Slavs and claimed in turn that the Vistula region had been settled "long before the Slavic invasion... by Nordic-Germanic tribes," Goths in particular.[4]

In any case, it was undisputed that the region along the lower Vistula, like large parts of Europe in the fourth and fifth centuries, was caught up in the whirlpool of mass migration. German scholarship was prepared to concede that the Germanic tribe of the Goths (including the Gepids, so named by the late-antique bishop and historian Jordanes; he counted them as a people among the Goths who were living in the Vistula delta) withdrew from Pomerelia by the sixth century, and Slavs moved into the territory thereafter. Polish scholarship insisted on the continuous presence of Slavs (and potentially also of several Baltic Prussian tribes) in this region and played down the Germanic importance.

Contemporary scholars are more cautious and generally remain skeptical about whether any conclusions based on pottery and other finds can be drawn about the ethnic identity of the peoples who produced them. Thus it will likely remain unexplained whether the large boats discovered in 1933/1934 in Danzig's district of Ohra (Pol. Orunia) were built by "a Nordic tribe based in our land"[5]—Vikings, possibly—or whether they were "Slavic war boats," as is written today in the Archaeological Museum on St. Mary's Street, where one of the vessels is on display. While a temporary Viking influence along the Eastern Pomeranian and Pomerelian coast is unquestioned, Pomerania and Pomerelia have been occupied by Slavs at least since the seventh century while the Baltic Prussians settled east of the Vistula delta. In any case, it was as a Slavic locality that Gdańsk would enter history at the close of the tenth century.

Between Sea, Forest, and Marsh

The region around Gdańsk has arisen and been shaped by three elements: the sea, the surrounding forested hills of the Gdańsk Heights, and the delta in the Gdańsk Lowlands. Up until the late Middle Ages, the Vistula delta was a marshy region crisscrossed by numerous waterways. The largest delta distributaries were the Gdańsk Vistula on its way to the Baltic Sea, the Elbląg Vistula leading to the Vistula Lagoon, and the Nogat, bending further upstream to likewise flow to the lagoon. These distributaries washed up little hills to the left and right, while a strip of dunes extended out along the Vistula Spit bordering the lagoon. The beaches continued north of the Vistula's mouth in a long arc up to the sea cliff of Orłowo. Between here and the Vistula estuary, a narrow strip of flat land extended from the beach and then rose into a chain of hills to the Baltic Uplands, a terminal moraine landscape with numerous valley cuts and lakes. Upon climbing to these heights, one would see in the distance the broad curve of the Gulf of Gdańsk, bordered on the left by the little finger of the Hel Peninsula and on the right by the delta. Here, on a number of deltaic lobes at the Vistula's final bend where the Motława River flowed into it, there would arise first a fishing village, then a fortress, and then a city: Gdańsk.

Incidentally, some things have changed here over the past thousand years: the Vistula delta was drained and made arable long ago. The Vistula Spit became the edge of the mainland as the river created a new mouth for itself. And stretching close to twenty miles along the bay lies the sea of houses in the "Tricity" of Gdańsk, Sopot, and Gdynia.

A City with Many Names

"Danzig" is not a readily decipherable name in German, nor is "Gdańsk" in Polish. For this reason, people have always wondered about the name's origin.

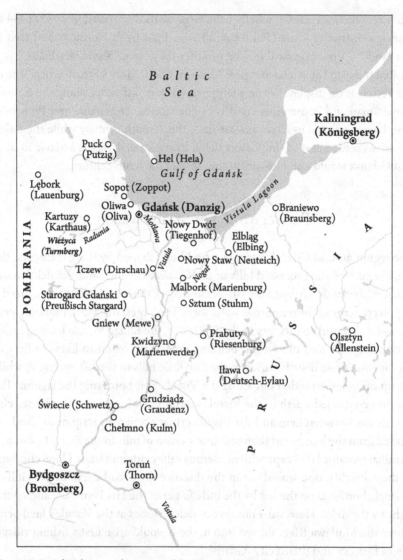

Figure 1.1 Gdańsk arose along one of the Vistula River's large delta distributaries into the Baltic Sea, in a region long shaped by swamps and countless waterways and thus well protected from dangers presented by enemies and weather.

Already around 1500, the humanist Conradus Celtis wrote in his *Vier Büchern Liebeselegien* (Four books of love elegies) that the Goths had founded Gdańsk and named it "Gedonum."[6] The legend of the city's Gothic past stirred up general fascination for centuries and even lingered at the end of the eighteenth century. Johann Uphagen claimed to see the name "Danzig" in "Gothiscandza," a designation that Jordanes coined for the region, and the Danzig scholar Christoph

Coelestin Mrongovius supposed that the name originates from the Danes and derives from "Danz-Wyck" or "Danes' fort."

As is so often the case, however, the vernacular would not content itself with such theories. Already in the first half of the sixteenth century, a chronicle written by the Dominican monk Simon Grunau tells the legend of Prince Hagel, who oppressed the people in the fishing village "Wiek" from his castle on Hail Hill (Germ. Hagelsberg), which rises west of Gdańsk's town center. Later, numerous local poets would adapt the legend lyrically. In 1833, Wilhelm Schumacher began the tale thus:

> There, where walls high and proud
>   Cover the mountain's crown,
> Once stood, built of shoddy timber
>   A castle, the dread of the land;
> Wherein dwelt, as the legend tells,
>   A villainous miscreant
> By the name of Prince Hagel.[7]

But the fisher folk devised a plan to rid themselves of the tyrant. Hagel opened his gates as the townspeople approached his castle for a dance (Tanz) in the prince's honor. Another poet, Eduard Ludwig Garbe, recalls the tale's end:

> And when the castle gate opened,
> The crafty men rushed forth,
> And slew Price Hagel in his keep
> Along with all of his servants.
> And as Lord Hagel beheld his fate,
> He cried, as they seized him:
> "Oh dance, oh dance, how thou hast betrayed me!"[8]

In memory of this event, the village Wiek was henceforth purportedly called "Tanz-Wiek," which became "Danzig" over time. Of course, this is little more than a nice story that served to make sense of something unintelligible.

Modern scholarship has also long disputed the meaning of the name Danzig/Gdańsk. For some, it was seen as a "Germanic regional designation,"[9] while others claimed the name was of Old Prussian origin. Many others, Germans as well as Poles, regard it as "doubtlessly Slavic."[10] The city's earliest mention in the biography of St. Adalbert, which appeared shortly after the martyred bishop's 997 visit, is of "Gyddanyzc." Spellings such as "Kdanze" or "Gdansk," since 1263 also "Danzk" and after 1399 "Danczik," have appeared over subsequent centuries. Today, linguists act on the assumption of a Slavic origin. Accordingly, "Gdańsk" means as much as a place located "on the Gdania River," where this Gdania could allude to the present-day Motława. This too, however, is mere hypothesis. The past yields no further insights into the matter, as is the case with many other aspects of Gdańsk's origins.

2

Green and Blue

Fishers, Merchants, Dukes, 997–1308

Steel-gray, metallic blue, azure, bright blue or dull powder blue, cyan; glistening, glacial, gruff, raging, frenzied, mellow, and cheerful: it can be all of this, the sea along the city's bay, but you hardly see it—really only from the towers, from the hills, and, of course, from the beach.

The forest sweeps up over the hillsides, spring green, fir-tree green, oak green, musty dark green, black-green, and brown, arranged across lush, grass-green valleys, meadow-flower green, bees-buzzing green—it can be all of this, the chain of hills along the city's sea. You can see them from almost everywhere.

Brightly lucid and brightly green, water-veined and partitioned, early summer crop green and clover green with cows, willow-pale green (with the red patches of villages)—it can be all of this, the flat delta. You can only see it from the hills and towers, or standing on the city's edge, from the ramparts of the Lowland Gate, from bastions bearing names like Jump, Wolf, or Bison.

And above it all the soaring Baltic sky.

These hues have colored Gdańsk since its beginnings.

One Thousand Years of "Gyddanyzc"

In 1997, Gdańsk celebrated the millennial anniversary of Bishop Adalbert of Prague's passage through the city on his missionary journey to the lands of the Baltic Prussians. The city is mentioned for the first time in the biography of the martyr, who would be slain not many days after visiting this place: Gyddanyzc. The members of the city's administration who had organized the 1997 event declared, "A pride in their own history, beginning one thousand years ago with Saint Adalbert, enables the citizens of Gdańsk to look self-assured to the future."[1] Gdańsk commemorated its 1,000th birthday for months with street festivals, concerts, markets, exhibits, historical spectacles, and in local and international publications. Newspapers and broadcasting companies from all over the world reported on the freshly spruced-up Baltic metropolis that had so deeply entrenched itself within the history of twentieth-century Europe.

For the local population, however, it was more than just an anniversary. It was the first opportunity since the political reversals of 1989 to express a new municipal identity. After the enforced blandness of the communist years, when everything was to be exclusively Polish and conformant to the Soviet system, the people could finally recall the multifaceted past composed of German, Jewish, Kashubian, Dutch, Scottish, and many other histories. Enlivened by a spirit of place that spanned the eras, the new city fathers and mothers considered themselves worthy successors of erstwhile Hanseatic council members with stiff ruff collars and wrinkled brows. For old Saint Adalbert, the city commemorated its millennium with the construction of a giant, rust-red cross on Hail Hill behind the city's main railway station. Illuminated at night, the cross bore far-reaching witness to the city's historical heritage and Christian identity. The vista extending from here reaches deep into the countryside, beyond hills, delta, and sea, and far into the past.

A Bishop and Quite a Few Surprises

Bishop Adalbert (Pol. Wojciech) was a pious man, if not always happy. Presumably dissatisfied with the twists and turns of fate when he had to leave Prague after political conflicts in 994 or 995, he wanted to dedicate his life to a mission among the heathens; in March 997, he arrived at the court of the Polish duke Bolesław I the Brave, presumably in Gniezno. He then resolved to travel into the lands of the Baltic Prussians. Accompanied by a number of companions, he rode to the Vistula River and then traveled by boat to Gdańsk, where he arrived on April 8 or 9. The martyr's biography, which appeared in 998 or 999, stated: "[The bishop], however, first visited the stronghold [or city] of Gyddanyzc, which separates the Duke's vast realm from the sea."[2] The bishop baptized "many hosts of people" in Gdańsk and afterward trekked onward to the Prussians, who killed him on April 23. He was promptly canonized and his mortal remains transferred to Gniezno, where they are still revered today.

These meager details are the only written reference to Gdańsk for the next one and a half centuries. They contain not only the location's name but also the clue that it was already a larger settlement (*urbs*) at the time and belonged to Duke Bolesław's state. But how had Gdańsk come into being?

For a long time, documents and topography were the only sources that yielded information on the city's medieval beginnings; systematic excavation was not possible in Gdańsk's densely developed historical area. The city's destruction at the end of the Second World War, when around 90 percent of the historical structures in the central districts were lost to combat and conquest in 1945, had the side effect of making large-scale excavation possible. Beginning in 1948, Polish archaeologists first focused their attention on the supposed area of the early medieval castle complex in order to conclude unequivocally that a large Slavic community had already developed there before the influx of German settlers. Other parts of the historic city center were partially examined over subsequent decades. Extensive new research became possible in 1987, when investors were obligated to finance salvage excavations before beginning new construction in the city center areas. This not only yielded an abundance of new individual finds but also provided enough partly unanticipated insights that the early history of Gdańsk appears in an entirely different light now than it did only a short time ago; new dating methods like dendrochronology and carbon-14 dating have been critical for the discoveries. As a sufficient investigation of key areas in Gdańsk's Main Town and Old Town districts has not been feasible to date, however, this reassessment of early medieval and medieval history is not yet complete.

What is clear is that the amount of settlement activity in the region of present-day Gdańsk rose in the late eighth century. Where the smaller Motława flows into the larger Vistula a good two and a half miles upstream from the Vistula's outlet into the Baltic Sea, a number of island-like hills provided protection from enemies as well as good anchorage, both for river boats and deep-sea vessels. The location also presented the opportunity to control trade on the Vistula, which offered an invaluable advantage at a time when transportation of goods by land was very arduous. Less advantageous was the regular flooding, particularly with the snowmelt in spring, as well as in the marsh regions located farther east. Over the centuries, though, dike construction and drainage projects were able to mitigate these dangers.

The earliest archaeologically verified traces of settlement came from excavation in the cellar of the Main Town's proudly looming town hall, where wooden houses were built after 930. Yet the actual center of early medieval Gdańsk was probably the castle located at what was then the influx of the Motława into the Vistula. Until lately, scholars assumed that this castle had already existed by the end of the tenth century and served as an official residence for members of the Polish Piast Dynasty. But more recent dendrochronological analyses have dated the earliest sections of the castle wall and residential areas to the period around 1060. Consequently, older notions that the formation of Gdańsk occurred around 980 at the initiative of the first historical Polish ruler, Mieszko I, require reconsideration at the very least. Was the first castle located in the area of the present-day Main Town, or perhaps on Hail Hill? It is not even clear anymore

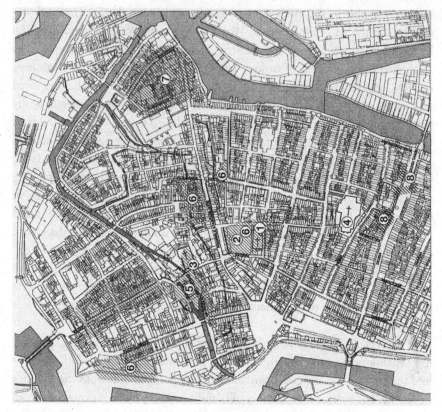

Figure 2.1 The centers of settlement in early-medieval Gdańsk, charted here against the backdrop of the early modern city, have become clear only in recent years.
1: current Church of St. Nicholas; 2: St. Nicholas' Church in the twelfth century; 3: St. Catherine's Church; 4: St. Mary's Church; 5: Great Mill; 6: verified extent of the city founded under German town law within the area of the present-day Old Town; 7: castle; 8: traces of the settlement in the present-day Main Town. From Henryk Paner, "Archeologiczne nowinki z Pomorza Gdańskiego," *Archeologia żywa*, No. 2 (32) 2005, page 7.

whether this castle survived up to the beginning of the fourteenth century, when the knights of the Teutonic Order conquered Gdańsk and built their fortress there; so far, the most recent verifiable finds from the castle area point to the middle of the twelfth century. Even though more recent timber remains may have since decayed, the ground beneath modern Gdańsk still has surprises to reveal.

Excavated after the Second World War, the typically Slavic complex of castle and outer ward (*suburbium*) measured approximately 6.6 acres and offered space for 2,200 to 2,500 residents. It was protected from enemies and high water by ramparts of wood and earth, reinforced with rock fragments and stones; these

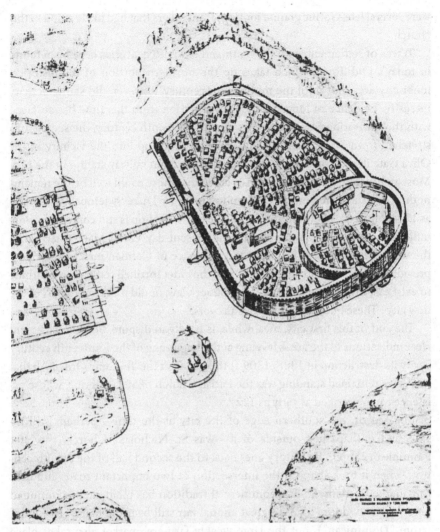

Figure 2.2 Reconstruction of the early medieval castle located on an island in the Motława in the twelfth century. Adapted from Andrzej Zbierski. From Edmund Cieślak, ed., *Historia Gdańska*, vol. 1 (Gdańsk, 1978).

earthen walls were up to sixty feet thick at their base and were presumably up to thirty feet tall. The planked streets of the residential area extended radially from the single gate located on the settlement's western side, from which a bridge led over the Motława to the mainland. The settlement was densely developed with small dwellings. Based on excavation results, members of the castle garrison presumably lived here with their families and alongside the ruler's servants, who worked as smiths, wainwrights, saddlers, potters, and fishers. There was also likely a stone church in the castle. Its foundations could not be located, but there were several late-Gothic granite footings from pillars that had likely stood in this church.

Traces of settlement from the tenth and eleventh centuries have been found in today's Old Town, which takes up the northern portion of the historical inner-city area; not until the mid-twelfth century, however, did settler activity intensify. Evidence of long-standing construction from this time has surfaced with the excavations of various sites. In the thirteenth century, the settled area stretched from St. Nicholas's Church in the south up into the vicinity of the Oliva Gate in the north and the location of the main railway station in the east. Most archaeologists and medievalists agree that these could well be the remains of the city established under German town law by Duke Swietopelk II as early as 1224, but more likely around 1263. The city's location is still contested; some indicators point to the area surrounding present-day Wood Market, farther to the west. This town was primarily the residence of German merchants. Had a previous "ducal" city already existed? Did the older fortified settlement continue to exist east of this new city under the Lübeck law, or did it become a part of the new city? These questions still await answers.

The end of this first city, meanwhile, is hardly in dispute. Scorch marks and clear indications of the area's leveling at the beginning of the fourteenth century verify its destruction in 1308/1309 at the hands of the Teutonic Order. All that may have remained standing was the Parish Church of St. Catherine, whose existence can be verified as early as 1227.

Located on the southern edge of the city at the time—perhaps still inside, and perhaps just outside of it—was St. Nicholas's Church, the later Dominican church. Its history goes back to the second half of the twelfth century, when it took shape at the intersection of two important roads and next to a market settlement. The commercial tradition has incidentally continued here: not only does Gdańsk's great annual fair still bear the name "Dominic" (from "Dominican"), but the large weekly farmers' market also takes place here. The city's Market Hall, which still exists today, was erected in the place of the run-down monastery at the end of the nineteenth century. When this covered market recently underwent extensive renovation, archaeologists had the opportunity to dig in its interior, with sensational results. They found nothing less than the oldest foundation walls of the city—the base of a single-nave Romanesque church, erected before 1190, which possibly served as a parish church at that time. This church probably burned down around thirty years later during a Prussian raid, and its remains were then granted to the Dominicans by Duke Swietopelk.

The modified reconstruction was completed by 1235, but this second Church of St. Nicholas fell prey to the Teutonic Order's destruction of Gdańsk in 1308/

1309. Its replacement was later built a little farther south, where it has stood to the present time. The foundations of the two earlier Romanesque churches, incidentally, can be seen as part of an impressive archaeological presentation in the Market Hall's basement between fish and meat stands. In 2006, to archaeologists' surprise, excavations adjacent to the Market Hall and St. Nicholas's Church revealed a Romanesque vaulted cellar from the later thirteenth century, now visible for the public to see.

In the early Middle Ages, not much stirred in today's historical city center located in the Main Town on present-day Long Street and Long Market, as this area was too swampy and reedy. Although there is evidence of settlement from the tenth century, a more intensive development (although of a fairly small area) can be verified only as far back as the twelfth/thirteenth centuries. Was this perhaps a "kontor," a foreign trading post for Hanseatic merchants from Lübeck who had obtained the right to build a fortified site in or near Gdańsk in the late thirteenth century? Yet specialists today doubt whether such a kontor was ever even built. Written sources and archaeological finds only confirm a major urban settlement in the Main Town as of the early mid-fourteenth century.

By this time, though, there was already a long-established, flourishing center about six miles north of the city: the Cistercian Monastery at Oliva (Pol. Oliwa), founded around 1178 or shortly thereafter as an endowment from the Pomerelian duke Sambor I. It grew rapidly and a century later possessed thirty-five villages, which would prove a source of future difficulties for Gdańsk.

Slavs and Germans, Fishers and Merchants

For the most part, the inhabitants of the early medieval fortress were likely Slavic and ducal or royal officials, along with their families, knights, and a large servant population. Many fishers and artisans living outside the fortress were probably also Slavs, most likely Pomeranian peoples (Kashubians), who spoke a language closely related to Polish. The presence of German settlers (*coloni*) has been established as early as the 1220s. It is likely that the earliest of these—Lübeck merchants and surely skilled artisans as well—had settled in Gdańsk some decades earlier. There were also Baltic Prussians.

Above all, Gdańsk owed its wealth to the Vistula River. Beginning in the thirteenth century, the transport of heavy cargo such as grain, wood, and lumber products like tar, pitch, ash, and charcoal intensified along this critical trade route. Boats brought fish and salt upstream and later imported goods from Flanders and the Rhineland as well. Major land routes led west through Starogard and Świecie on to Gniezno and Poznań, as well as through Słupsk on the way to Szczecin. Somebody traveling east into Prussia would be ferried across the Vistula near Tczew.

Beginning in the 1220s, Gdańsk was an important destination for Hanseatic trade ships, mainly cogs from Lübeck, for which a new harbor was created a little way up the Motława. The trade in goods in Gdańsk grew rapidly, which increasingly integrated the city firmly into international trade. Archaeological finds of Byzantine and Persian silk, Flemish and English cloth, and Saxon and Rhenish glass all confirm this upswing, through which the city soon became a prosperous community. Along with grain and wood products, returning ships carried honey, wax, hides, furs, and—of course—amber and amber products. The import and export tolls were extremely important for the ducal finances, but they also aroused a desire among neighboring powers, such as the margraves of Brandenburg and the Teutonic Order, to control the city for themselves.

Beginning at the latest around the turn of the twelfth century, Gdańsk was a significant center for artisanal production. A hundred years later, it was, for the time, a large complex of settlements with an estimated 3,000 to 4,000 residents, maybe even up to 10,000. The transformations in the population's social structure are indicated by the changes in their diet: whereas they mostly ate meat from wild animals in the twelfth century, they were already breeding animals for food with increasing regularity in the thirteenth century—these were mostly pigs and chickens, which were often kept in pens directly beside the houses.

Smiths and amber workers were of great importance to skilled crafts in Gdańsk, as were cabinetmakers, carpenters (almost all houses were made of wood), shipwrights, potters, weavers, tanners, millers, bakers, and representatives of numerous other trades. The city's Archaeological Museum displays numerous finds verifying this. The food supply was largely secured by the fishers who cast their nets into the flat waters of the Vistula delta and in the coastal regions of the Gulf of Gdańsk. Meat and grain for the constantly growing population came from areas immediately surrounding the city. As early as the tenth and eleventh centuries, agricultural areas from 5,000 to 10,000 acres were needed to provide for the population, and shortly thereafter, foods had to be imported from more remote locations.

Also playing an important role in economic life were the markets, such as the annual St. Dominic's Fair (beginning most likely in 1260) as well as permanent markets like the fish market and a market located near the Dominican Monastery. Alongside sailors and merchants, the rural population drawn to the city filled the taverns, which pleased the duke, who held an interest in the sales and could develop his state with the revenues. Incited by the growing trade contacts, the public placed an increasingly high value on education. Accordingly, a "teacher of children" named Gerwin appears in one of the few written sources from before 1308.

Shifts in Sovereignty

The political history of Gdańsk and its environs prior to the thirteenth century have left only faint outlines. At the close of the tenth century, the locality belonged to the Polish duke Bolesław the Brave, as revealed in the biography of St. Adalbert. But history will most likely never yield an answer to the question of when the region became Polish. From the mysterious *Dagome iudex*, a historical document about the first historical Polish ruler Mieszko I in 990, we gather that the land's borders ran east from the Baltic Sea to the lands of the Baltic Prussians; hence, the area around the mouth of the Vistula belonged to the Polish state. It is possible that the young state incorporated Pomerelia, including Gdańsk, between 970 and 980. Yet already in the opening years of the second millennium, the pagan Slavic tribes shook off Polish-Christian rule in an uprising.

Stretching between the Vistula's estuary and Greater Poland's center of power around Poznań and Gniezno, the immense marshes and forests complicated control of the area. The Polish duke Władysław I Herman had to learn this painful truth in 1090/1091 when he embarked on a campaign against Pomerelia but was unable to hold it. On their way home, his troops burned down the Pomerelian fortresses, possibly including Gdańsk's.

Władysław's failure did not dissuade his son Duke Bolesław III the Wrymouth, who set out in 1116 to conquer Pomerelia and subdued the region in the subsequent years. He placed the province under the ecclesiastical control of the Diocese of Włocławek and appointed a delegate as regent in Pomerelia. The first regent whose name is known was Sambor I, who in a charter from 1188 designated Gdańsk as his castle. His possible predecessor Sobiesław I is only known from later sources. Sambor, who most likely belonged to a local dynasty, even called himself *princeps Pomoranorum*, or duke (ruler) of the Pomeranians—but not *dux*, which was reserved for Piast rulers. The Duchy of Gdańsk possibly ranged from Łeba in Eastern Pomerania to the Vistula.

It is not easy to discern all that happened in and around Gdańsk in the thirteenth century; rulers switched too often, and the political coalitions are too unclear. After Sambor's death in 1207, his brother Mestwin I took control and strove for an ever-greater autonomy from Poland. Self-assured, he bore the title *princeps* in Danzk and extended his area of influence far to the south. His oldest son Swietopelk II, who began his rule in 1217, exploited Poland's fracture into smaller principalities to lead his state to self-dependence; already in 1227, he was using the title of *dux*, duke of Pomerelia.

A new player emerged at this point. At the invitation of the Polish duke of Masovia, the Teutonic Order firmly established itself in the Chełmno region south of Pomerelia in 1230 in order to Christianize the pagan Prussians. The powerful monastic association soon became entangled in disputes with Swietopelk, not least regarding the highly attractive earnings in Vistula commerce that was always increasing Gdańsk's significance. For this reason, as the opposing sides were negotiating peace in 1253, the Order was especially intent on asserting customs exemptions for its own goods in Gdańsk's harbor. Gdańsk had developed into a prominent city under Swietopelk, who had founded a municipal entity and established the Dominican Order there before he died in 1266.

Shortly after Swietopelk's death, a war (again over Gdańsk) broke out between his sons. In 1270 or 1271, Mestwin II was able take the city from his brother with the support of the margraves of Brandenburg, to whom Mestwin owed allegiance. The Brandenburgers had no intention, however, of withdrawing from this wealthy city with a sympathetic German population. New conflicts that would cost many people their lives, this time between the German and Slavic inhabitants, loomed on the horizon. Only with the aid of Bolesław the Pious, duke of Greater Poland, was Mestwin able to restore his rule over Gdańsk. He ordered the city fortifications torn down and confiscated the property of German burghers, although he sought a compromise with at least some of them. The city was able to retain its autonomy and quickly recover, although Mestwin's sympathies lay seventy-five miles farther south along the Vistula at Świecie Castle, where he spent most of his time. He had Święca, a royal officer, handle the affairs in Gdańsk.

The Teutonic Order was meanwhile becoming more powerful to the east, and it made no secret of its desire to gain a solid foothold west of the Vistula. To safeguard the land, Mestwin (who as yet had no male successor) bequeathed all of Pomerelia, in case of his death, to Przemysł II, duke of Greater Poland. Thus Przemysł came into his inheritance in 1294, and his 1295 coronation in Gniezno as king of Poland meant Pomerelia's return to the Polish state. At the beginning of 1296, though, the king was murdered in an attempted kidnapping at the hands of the Brandenburgers, who, like the Teutonic Order, still desired Gdańsk and Pomerelia and had hoped to force Przemysł to relinquish the lucrative province.

Władysław I "the Elbow-high," Przemysł's successor as duke of Greater Poland, seldom came to Gdańsk, whose citizens made use of the weaker control to expand their influence at the expense of the Oliva Monastery. The powerful Święca family also determinedly extended their influence within the region. Renewed adversity was in store as the Bohemian king Wenceslaus II came to power in Poland and thereby in Pomerelia. This time, the rulers of Riga tried to exploit the unstable situation by heading across Pomerania toward Gdańsk; only the Teutonic Order, at the request of Wenceslaus, was able to stop them. Although the Order left the city in 1302, this would only be for a few years.

Wenceslaus II died in 1305, and his son Wenceslaus III was murdered the following year. Yet another aspirant emerged with hopes for ruling Pomerelia: the bishop of Camin in Pomerania (present-day Kamień Pomorski). But the margraves of Brandenburg took exception and deployed their army, burned Camin to the ground, and occupied the Sławno region. In the meantime, Władysław I had again returned to Poland, reestablished his reign, and installed a new magisterial governor named Bogusza to oversee Gdańsk. Nevertheless, the situation remained unstable. Disappointed by Władysław, the Święca family turned to the margraves of Brandenburg for help; in turn, the margraves sent several hundred knights and in September 1308 stood outside the gates of a Gdańsk well disposed toward them. They soon entered the city and began besieging the castle held by Polish knights. Since Władysław was busy in southern Poland, his governor Bogusza asked the Teutonic Order for support. As agreed, the Order's knights reinforced the exhausted Poles in the castle. At the same time, the Teutonic troops marched from the south toward the city, whose citizenry was predominantly loyal to Brandenburg's occupation. Soon perceiving that the Order was in no way disposed to returning the castle to them, the powerless Polish knights were forced from the stronghold after a few battles. They withdrew from Gdańsk or joined with the citizenry and Brandenburgers entrenched in the city.

Conquest and Temporary End of the City of Gdańsk

Campfires burned around the city in the late afternoon of November 12, 1308. The Order's forces had already tried to storm the walls a few times and were ready for a renewed attempt. What happened in the subsequent hours would enter history as the "Gdańsk Bloodbath," although historians have disagreed on the details ever since. Were there up to 10,000 killed, or only a total of sixteen? Was the city leveled or just lightly damaged? Was the Order a brutal instrument of Germanization, or was it "exercising political prudence" to enable "a splendid and great future" for Gdańsk, the city under its "sheltering care"?[3]

In a new interpretation by the Gdańsk medievalist Błażej Śliwiński, the Order launched a renewed attack on Gdańsk in the evening hours of November 12, scaled the ramparts, and poured into the streets. The knights of Brandenburg and Pomerelia—supporters of the Święca family—as well as many Gdańsk townsfolk resisted frantically, but they had no chance against the Order's warriors swarming the city. According to later eyewitness accounts, the crusaders spilled so much blood in the spectral glow of the burning houses that dogs gathered to lick it up. One of the defenders had fled into the tower of St. Catherine's Church but was discovered and put to death.

The victors knew no mercy and killed many knights and citizens. When Rüdiger, the abbot from Oliva, arrived on the morning of November 13, the streets were strewn with corpses. Even if he could not prevent the executions, he was able to hear the confessions of a number of knights sentenced to death, as well as bring sixteen corpses to Oliva, where they were interred next to St. James's Church. In all, probably fifty to sixty knights and an indefinite, yet large, number of townsfolk lost their lives. Over the course of the following months, the Order would take possession of all of Pomerelia.

The events in Gdańsk quickly drew widespread attention. According to a papal bull dated June 19, 1310, the crusaders murdered 10,000 people, including many children. Witnesses of the incidents in Gdańsk were questioned during a 1312 trial in Riga between the local bishop and the Teutonic Order, and trials between the Teutonic Order and Poland, which would not stand for the loss of Pomerelia, took place in 1320 and 1339. While the representatives of the Order strove to downplay the extent of the "bloodbath" and thus only conceded the deaths of fifteen or sixteen Pomerelian knights, numerous respondents—some eyewitnesses and many others who had not been present—spoke of *strage magna* (great murder or bloodbath), *strage maxima* (greatest murder or slaughter), or even *abhominabile strage* (abominable/damnable murder).

For a long time, German historians placed great trust in the Order's assertions, arguing that 10,000 dead would have simply been impossible in a city with barely that many residents, and maintaining that the lives lost could have only been between sixty and 100. While many Polish historians since the Second World War have accepted this, Błażej Śliwiński has compiled significant evidence that there very likely was a "bloodbath" with an appallingly high number of victims—even if not as many as 10,000. According to Śliwiński, such a slaughter would not have been a rarity anywhere in medieval Europe, and the crusaders and their auxiliary troops wanted to retaliate against the populace for siding with Brandenburg. Due to a lack of source material, there will probably never be ultimate certainty.

Another key debate has focused on whether Gdańsk was destroyed in 1308. Erich Keyser, a hometown hero in Danzig and city historian in the interwar years, quickly relegated any corresponding tales "to the realm of legend."[4] But an attentive reading of the available sources has allowed for different conclusions. Paul Simson wrote shortly before the First World War that Gdańsk's residents not only destroyed the fortifications at the insistence of the Order's highest officer in Prussia, the Landmeister, but also tore down, "of their own free will, the houses."[5] Also suggesting the city's destruction is the fact that not a single town charter exists from before 1308. But only the results of excavations after the Second World War yielded certainty. In addition to the archaeological investigations in the area of the early medieval castle, much more recent excavations of the Old Town reveal an interrupted urban development at the beginning of the fourteenth century. After the fire in the Old Town, the rubble from the houses appears to have been quickly leveled; a number of years later, new streets and foundations for new buildings were installed on top of this layer of debris. It is possible that a few corners of Gdańsk were spared and remained inhabited, but most of the residents likely left the city; some former residents of Gdańsk were verified in Lübeck shortly thereafter.

A number of factors suggest the city's destruction. For one, the Order wanted to discourage Brandenburg from any future attempts on Pomerelia and the influential port city Gdańsk. Additionally, Gdańsk was an economic rival of the Teutonic Knights and Elbing (Pol. Elbląg), which had until then been the Order's most important port. Finally, until the end of the 1320s, there is no longer any trace of commerce in Gdańsk.

3

Brick-Red

Danzig as a Part of the Teutonic State, 1308–1454

Certainly, bricks can also be ugly: black with soot, gray-white with pigeon filth, scabbed and cracked, scarred. Yet when the sun shines and the morning light touches the mighty walls of St. Mary's Church, when Gdańsk's towers, gates, and walls begin to glow, then the bricks come alive. The past comes palpably near. Your hands glide gently over the crannied red. You feel the city's warmth, the charm of age. These towering brick giants are delicate, of a fragile beauty, and yet strong at the same time.

A Misleading Memorial

In 1967, the city mothers and fathers of Gdańsk had an idea: they would honor the upcoming anniversary of the 1308 "Gdańsk Bloodbath" with the construction of a memorial remembering "Poland's loyal guardians" who were murdered by the Teutonic Order. At the same time they wanted to pay homage to recent history, as stated in the call for proposals for the memorial: "Hitler's camps and crematories were equivalent to the crusaders' crimes. By reason of its political significance and contemporary relevance, the martyrdom of the Polish population in 1308 merits enduring commemoration."[1]

The granite monument, eventually unveiled in 1969, portrays a battle axe difficult to discern as such, its blade stuck in the ground. The side facing west bears the inscription: "1410–1945—Tym co za polskość Gdańska" ("To those who fought/enlisted/fell for Gdańsk's Polish spirit"—the title has multiple meanings); a Polish knight from 1410's momentous Battle of Grunwald as well as a Polish soldier from the Second World War take up the central section in the monument's engraved ornamentation. On the eastern side are emblazoned the words: "1308—Rzeź Gdańska" (Gdańsk Bloodbath). On the narrow northern side, there are three more years ("1454, 1466, 1939") recalling Gdańsk's defection from the Teutonic Order during the Thirteen Years' War (1454–1466) as well as the outbreak of the Second World War. In short, the monument is a typical product of an era in which Polish national historical narratives, cultivated since the nineteenth century, of insurrections and enduring martyrdom, of defiant pride and German-Polish enmity, all coincided with war, official antifascism, and the steady need to legitimize possession of the formerly eastern German and henceforth western Polish regions.

The monument still stands in stony admonition on Old Town Moat Street, directly adjacent to the remains of the Main Town's medieval town fortifications. Not far away, the brick monstrosity of the Order's castle stood long ago. At times an auburn gleam flits across this desolate spot, to which only few visitors wander. That's probably just as well, because the "Gdańsk Bloodbath" of 1308 is not exactly suitable as a modern national imputation. After all, it was not the Polish citizens who were fighting for their "Polishness," but rather predominantly German townspeople, alongside Brandenburg's troops and Pomerelian knights who had turned against the Polish regime, all resisting the Teutonic Order. But nobody wanted to view the matter in such clarity after the Second World War.

Order and Citizens

When it obtained possession of the city of Danzig in 1308, the Teutonic Order was already more than a century old. Founded at the end of the twelfth century in the Holy Land, it quickly developed into a mighty monastic fraternity of knights. But its Middle Eastern property, concentrated around the city of Acre in the Kingdom of Jerusalem, soon no longer satisfied the brethren. Sponsored by Hohenstaufen kings and furthermore favored with a speedily increasing number of land grants in German regions, the Order rapidly became a powerful economic and military organization under the leadership of Grandmaster Hermann von Salza. Thus, the Polish duke Konrad I's petitions for the Order's help in subduing and christianizing the dangerous Prussians in 1225/1226 found a receptive audience. Not many years later, the militant monastic brotherhood received the area around Chełmno on the Vistula River and readied itself to enter the Prussian regions, which it would go on to conquer within a half century. Conflicts arose with its neighbors Lithuania, Poland, and Pomerelia, ultimately leading to the Order's conquest of Pomerelia in 1308. In controlling the Vistula's course to the sea, the Order had now secured its territory to the west. It was not by chance that in 1309, the grandmaster and his most important assistants, the *Gebietiger*, relocated their residence from Venice to a castle located just thirty-seven miles southeast of Danzig in Marienburg (Pol. Malbork). The mighty castle on the Nogat would become the center of what was, for the circumstances at the time, a modern and tightly organized political entity. The Teutonic State was subdivided into "commanderies" in which convents, each occupied by about a dozen knight-brethren and priests of the Order, exercised power under the leadership of a commander. Danzig also became the seat of one such convent.

Although the Order had largely destroyed Danzig in 1308, the suitability of a city at this location soon became apparent: it could secure the Vistula estuary and control trade on the river; it possessed a good harbor and was well suited for productive industry; and it proved to be indispensable for the recently commenced drainage and improvement of Danzig's islet in the delta. The Order's rulers must have soon decided not to impede the city's reconstruction, although they also carefully watched the quickly growing mass of houses and, through regular interference, kept the citizens from growing too comfortable.

Castle, Cities, and Fishing Settlement

Danzig's spatial expansion in the fourteenth and fifteenth centuries is richly complicated. The Main Town arose next to the castle along with the Old Town and the Young Town, not to mention the many suburban developments. The Order's knights probably first occupied the old Pomerelian castle on the island located at the time at the Motława's influx into the Vistula, most likely beginning with the construction of a new castle around 1340. Of this castle, which was destroyed in 1454, only a single image is known to have existed: in the upper-left corner of an oil painting that disappeared out of Danzig's famous Artus Court at the end of the Second World War. The picture shows an impressive structure on the Motława with bastions and a tall central tower. With this edifice, the fortress in Danzig was likely counted among the Order's most notable citadels, even after the main current of the Vistula shifted toward the north in the second half of the fourteenth century and the castle was thereafter located "only" on the Motława.

Minor remains of the castle's outer wall, including battlements and parts of a square tower, remain preserved today, built into a number of residential buildings. Excavations have brought some foundation walls to light, but they nevertheless do not encompass the entire area of the complex. The castle presumably consisted of a trapezoidal main building with corner towers and a tall central tower. This building was surrounded by a moat, and there was one— or perhaps even two—outer baileys likewise protected by moats, across which bridges led into the city.

For over a decade after 1308, there was probably no commercial activity worthy of mention in Danzig, as merchants from Danzig do not appear in the city of Wismar's customs tariff schedule until 1328. This was likely also around the time that Danzig's urban development received a boost. The center of construction activity was not, however, the earlier city center, but rather an area to the south coterminous with the Motława: the Main Town. Houses appeared here, at first in a somewhat disordered pattern along a few roads leading to the Motława. Even today, the four major residential thoroughfares stretching to the river— the first being Hound Street, the second comprising both Long Street and Long Market, the third called Brewery Street, and Bakers' Street connecting with Holy Spirit Street to make up the fourth—are slightly crooked. Construction activity began a little later in the marshland to the north of Long Market.

After some time, the Order apparently decided to grant city rights to the newly emerging borough. Grandmaster Ludolf König issued a document based on the Chełmno town law in 1342 (to be amended in 1346 and 1378), which defined the area of the Main Town and also provided guidelines for the construction of St. Mary's Church in addition to the city walls. Their erection began promptly, and a wall measuring up to twenty feet tall with many towers and gates encircled the flourishing community within just a few years. Parts of it still exist today.

The municipal area between Hound Street and Holy Spirit Street soon proved to be too small. Beginning in the 1340s, the city expanded to the north toward the castle and into a marshy area first requiring drainage before gaining the designation of the New Town. Yet after only twenty years, this urban space was also no longer big enough, and what would later be known as the Old Suburb began to grow south of the Main Town.

Even early on, builders in the Main Town were interested in the land located across the Motława. From the Cog Gate at the end of Long Market, a bridge led to the river's other shore; the Cow Bridge soon appeared a few paces to the south. Numerous storehouses, a slaughterhouse, and an ash yard and tarring yard were built here, across from the Main Town. As a result of the New Motława, a canal that had formed by the close of the sixteenth century, this area became Granary Island. Bit by bit, the suburb Long Gardens emerged east of this warehouse district.

The area of the older Danzig destroyed in 1308, dubbed the "Old Town," possessed no city ordinances or privileges until the late fourteenth century; it is possible that the Teutonic Order did not want the main access route to the castle to lead through a densely populated borough. This area increasingly developed into a kind of suburb of the Main Town where artisans and merchants lived and often practiced agriculture on the side. The Old Town experienced a boom only after a canal rerouted the Radunia River, which had originally flowed into the Motława, into the Old Town area between 1338 and 1356; the rerouting was instigated by the Order to capitalize on the river's current. Here, next to a large mill owned by the Order, arose in the following decades a copper working plant, grinding shops, an oil mill, a tanning and fulling mill, and a sawmill in the Hakelwerk (Pol. Osiek), a settlement directly outside the castle. The Order retained possession of the Old Town and reserved its right to select the region's occupants, for whom it made property available in exchange for monetary payments and feudal lands known as socage. This did not even change when the Old Town received city rights in 1377.

If any continuity existed with the time before 1308 in Danzig's area of settlement, it was most likely in the few streets of the Hakelwerk. Slavic (and likely Prussian) fishers from the former fortified settlement, to whom the Order granted the right to fish and gather amber, moved here after 1308. The German name Hakelwerk "refers to a simple fortification made of hacked shrubs and hawthorn brushwood,"[2] also used to protect the baileys of other Teutonic fortresses. Polish was spoken here until the beginning of the fifteenth century.

With the following decree, Grandmaster Winrich von Kniprode founded a new city district in Danzig in 1380:

> We, Brother Winrich Kniprode, grandmaster of the Order of Brothers of the German House of St. Mary in Jerusalem, in accordance with the counsel and will of the *Gebietiger*, grant and give to our faithful Lange Claus and Peter Sandowin our city, the Young Town of Danczk, and to its inhabitants and their posterity all enduring Chełmno rights and laws.[3]

The Teutonic Order's aim in creating the Young Town was to generate competition for the Main Town after the latter's quick development. To this end, the two men commissioned with the locality, Lange Claus and Peter Sandowin, parceled out a region along the Vistula River northwest of the Old Town and the castle. Since the Young Town was destroyed after 1454, its exact location is still unclear today; it is assumed to be beneath the present-day Gdańsk Shipyard.

Under the Order's attentive regulation, the Young Town was completely incapable of such a dynamic development into a major trade center as the Main Town had experienced. Even thirty years after construction on the Young Town had begun, some of its building sites were still unassigned and would remain so. More productive and vested with much greater privileges, the Main Town was obviously and disproportionately more attractive to immigrants than the community so closely administered by the Order. Yet the Main Town still regarded its smaller sibling as unwanted competition and took advantage of the first opportunity, in January 1455, to have the Young Town torn down.

The People

Danzig's development in the fourteenth and fifteenth centuries was meteoric. At the close of the fourteenth century, an average of 172 new citizens were migrating annually to the Main Town alone, often with entire families. Including residents without citizenship, over 10,000 people already lived in the entire urban area (comprising the Main Town, Old Town, Young Town, Hakelwerk, and Old Suburb), and that number was likely twice as high by 1430. As a result, Danzig had quickly become, next to Lübeck, the largest city on the Baltic Sea. Even the plagues and famines that repeatedly beset Danzig could not curb this growth.

The immigrants who acquired citizenship, at least in the Main Town, were almost without exception native German speakers. About 25 percent of them hailed from within the Teutonic State itself, particularly from the city's immediate vicinity. Almost as numerous were those emigrating from northern Germany, followed by settlers from central and southern Germany. The portion born in Poland accounted for less than 2 percent, and even in this group were many Germans, though admittedly some Slavic sounding citizens' names were present in the late-medieval city. Even so, with a possible exception in the Hakelwerk, the urban vernacular was German and most commonly a Low-German dialect, in which many municipal decrees were even composed. Presumably, though, parts of the sub-bourgeois class were of Polish-Slavic descent—such as apprentices and journeymen, service personnel, day laborers, and dockworkers—as well as beggars and prostitutes. This symbiosis between a German middle class and a partially non-German lower class (albeit one that always quickly assimilated) remained the norm for Danzig until well into the twentieth century.

The population of the Main Town underwent a rapid social stratification, but there was still great potential for social mobility. Somebody like the long-standing mayor Konrad Letzkau, a native of the village of Letzkau (Pol. Leszkowy) in the Vistula delta, thus found the opportunity to become a wealthy citizen and merchant as well as hold the highest civil offices. Already in the fourteenth century, however, a civic elite was steadily emerging, consisting of a few dozen families whose representatives held most of the municipal offices. Everybody who was anybody owned a house on Long Street or Long Market, valued chivalrous virtues, and became a member of the Brotherhood of St. George. This fraternity built its assembly hall, the Artus Court, in the second half of the fourteenth century on Long Market. Though first reserved for a small number of particularly wealthy citizens, the meeting place whose name recalls the legendary British king and his Round Table was already serving wider public circles by the end of the century. A fortune of twenty marks was sufficient to gain access, unless one was a craftsperson or a retailer—in such cases the doors remained closed even to the rich. People met there in the evening as well as on Sundays and holidays after lunch, drank beer together, and conversed; occasionally the men invited women along to enjoy music and dance. Danzig's merchants from that time proudly wore a sword and often a valuable adorned belt that carried their signet ring along with their money.

By no means did Danzig live on trade alone. A visitor entering the city at that time would be more likely to believe that skilled workers dominated the scene. The streetscape was characterized by tailors, shopkeepers, shoemakers, bakers, and particularly brewers—there were no less than 378 representatives of this craft in the Main Town alone in 1416.

Given the numerical preponderance of artisans over the ruling class of merchants, it is no wonder that conflict arose repeatedly throughout the city's history. After some initial unrest in 1363, about which only limited details exist, open disputes erupted in 1378 when a protest was led by influential brewers who bristled at the grandmaster's allowance of beer from Wismar to be imported into the city. The rioters' goal was to improve the civic position of the craftsmen and their representation in city government. With the Order's help, though, the city council quelled the rebellion. The old order remained in place; a number of the rebellion's ringleaders were hanged, while others—including Hermann von Ruden, the brewers' spokesperson who came from an established city council family—were able to flee.

The Administration

Danzig's Main Town was ruled by a council composed of members of the mercantile community. It was subdivided initially into the executive "sitting council," comprising the mayor, his deputy (who generally alternated each year), and twelve councilmen who usually officiated for life, as well as the "common council," or the patriciate's representation. The council, whose two bodies merged in the fifteenth century, administered municipal property, supervised construction, and regulated skilled crafts, security, and market development. The city's regulations were stipulated in a book of statutes entitled *Danziger Willkür* (Danzig law); its first draft was likely issued in the fourteenth century, but the oldest preserved edition is from around 1440. A court of arbitration composed of the mayor and councilmen oversaw compliance with these provisions.

The council additionally saw to the maintenance of ecclesiastical buildings, administered the patrimony of the church, and appointed the court of law. The court's lay judges began to gain increasing autonomy in the fifteenth century and established themselves alongside the council ("First Order") as an additional legislative body ("Second Order"). These two orders were restricted to

Figure 3.1 This seal of the Main Town, used into the second half of the fourteenth century, depicted a symbol of mercantile success, the cog. bpk/20030792.

members of a few mostly intermarried council families. In all matters of civic self-administration, the Teutonic Order had reserved numerous ways to exert influence on municipal proceedings; this increasingly displeased the Main Town, whose elites were naturally familiar with cities like Lübeck, which enjoyed much greater liberties.

Symbols and symbolic acts carried great meaning in the Middle Ages. It was therefore no trifling matter when, in the fourteenth century, the Main Town changed its official seal, with which all of its important documents were certified. It initially continued with the seal from the pre-1308 Pomerelian city, a cog with crow's nest and breastwork sailing toward an eight-pointed star. By 1368 at the latest, though, there was a new seal depicting two crosses arranged vertically. A symbol of mercantile independence thus gave way to a representation of the Teutonic Order's rule over Danzig. The city also adorned its gates with this new token, and it remains on Bakers' Gate today. But if the Order believed that these means would be sufficient to bring the city to long-term compliance, it was soon disappointed. Now a member of the prestigious Hanseatic League, a powerful trade confederation made up of cities and guilds along the North and

Figure 3.2 Two crosses signified the Teutonic Order's suzerainty over Danzig. This has been the recognized crest since 1368 and can still be seen today on Bakers' Gate. After 1456, the Polish crown was added to it. Dariusz Kula/fotokula.pl.

Baltic Seas, the assurgent and self-reliant Main Town developed its own political ambitions and would openly defy the Order for the first time in 1410.

In comparison with the Main Town, the Order took a much harder line with Danzig's other two other civic entities. Artisans played a seemingly greater part in the administration of the Old Town, which would suggest a low number of merchants living there. Since the Old Town's city archives disappeared at the end of the eighteenth century, though, this cannot be stated with certainty. In any case, the Order intervened substantially in city affairs. Guild statutes could only be issued with Teutonic consent, and the Order individually taxed all artisans and homeowners, whereas the Main Town paid a lump sum. The other city seals depicted the patron saints of their respective parish churches: St. Catherine in the Old Town and St. Bartholomew in the Young Town.

Wood and Salt—the Rise of a Trade Power

The conditions of Danzig's economic development changed decisively in the fourteenth century. At first, they were anything but good: the Teutonic Order's takeover had left the city's immediate surroundings suffering, the city itself destroyed, and its inhabitants scattered to the four winds. Economic stimuli were lacking not only in the city's vicinity but also from afar, since Western Europe, plagued by war and pestilence in the first half of the fourteenth century, was mired in economic and social crisis. The Western European economy recovered in the second half of the century, though, and the demand for grain and wood—the Baltic region's chief exports—grew steadily. High-quality lumber was necessary for shipbuilding, and grain was important for rapidly developing cities in the Netherlands as well as England. The basis was laid for an increasingly tighter economic interdependency between Central Europe and its periphery.

Located at the Vistula estuary, Danzig seemed foreordained to satisfy this demand. For one, the trade routes were favorable, and due to economic changes in both the Teutonic State and in Poland, there was a sufficient supply of desirable goods at hand. The Order's systematic draining and settlement of the Vistula lowland allowed farming and increased the food supply necessary for the growth of Danzig itself. Also, the city benefited along with all of Poland from the political stabilization enjoyed during the long reign of Casimir III the Great, who ruled the kingdom from 1333 to 1370. The large profit margins that became available thanks to the enormous price gaps between Western and Eastern Europe drew all sorts of interested parties: local merchants, the Teutonic Order, and foreign traders from the west as well as Poland.

In the 1330s, large numbers of merchants began to settle in Danzig. They developed extensive trade connections, both in the immediate vicinity as well as with the hinterland farther up the Vistula. In the early fifteenth century, Danzig's trade with Poland overtook the competition of both Thorn (Pol. Toruń) and the Order, first in Masovia with Warsaw at its center, and later in Greater Poland and in the Polish capital Kraków. Grain was hardly traded at first, and products from Poland consisted primarily of logs and timber, potash and tar, occasional wax and honey, and hides and furs. The goods were rafted to Danzig at high water in the springtime, when navigating the Vistula presented the lowest risk.

The merchants turned their attention not only to the city's backcountry but also across the sea. These efforts were facilitated through substantial contacts with citizens of other Baltic cities that many current Danzig residents had left. The sense of developing comradery with the cities in the region was bolstered in the Hanseatic League, that great union of cities and merchants stretching from the Netherlands to the Baltic, from the Rhine to Kraków. In 1361, the Main Town sent a representative to a Hanseatic assembly in Greifswald for the first time, and beginning in 1377, it almost never missed a Hanseatic Diet. Gdańsk slowly overtook Elbing and Thorn as the leading Prussian Hanseatic cities as the inland Thorn lost its role as an important intermediary in trade with Poland and Hungary, and Elbing, whose harbor in the Vistula Lagoon was only accessible in a roundabout way through the Strait of Baltiysk, also fell behind. This is quite apparent based on revenues from the poundage levied on imports and exports beginning in Prussian Hanseatic cities in 1389, which amounted to somewhere below 0.25 percent of the merchandise value: in 1396, Danzig earned 375.5 marks through this toll, while the other cities brought in a mere 151 marks combined.

The Hanseatic League offered merchants outstanding possibilities for buying and selling goods—for example, in Scania, the southern part of Sweden belonging at the time to Denmark, where massive schools of herrings lived off the coast. The Hanseatic League enjoyed unique privileges here: beginning in 1368, Prussian Hanseatic cities owned their own branch offices in Scania, where herrings were salted and packed into barrels. The preserved, salted herrings were counted among Danzig's most important merchandise and were a source of revenue for many citizens known as *Schonenfahrer* (Scania-farers). The London office, called the Steelyard, was also a crucial hub for Danzig merchants bringing wood and wood products to the Thames (including the English army's famous longbows).

The Netherlands was still far removed from the later significance it would attain for commerce in Danzig. But in the first half of the fifteenth century, trade with Holland intensified; the Dutch brought salt and textiles to Danzig and increasingly herrings as well, since the schools gradually relocated west from the Sound (Øresund); they also purchased wood and grain, the typical exports from the region. The Netherlands thus presented growing competition for Lübeck and the Hanseatic League's other "Wendish cities," especially since the Dutch generally outpaced Lübeck's merchants by opting to take the more dangerous sea route through the Sound. Within a mere few weeks in 1443, no less than 120 Dutch ships arrived in Danzig's harbor. While Sweden was not far away, trade developed at a much more unhurried pace with the northern kingdom, which exported fish, furs, animal fat, and horses to Danzig.

Lübeck was fundamental for Hanseatic trade, especially since into the early fifteenth century a large portion of Baltic trade goods was transshipped here to be sent on to Hamburg via the Trave River, the Stecknitz Canal, and the Elbe River. Among other things, Lübeck delivered Lüneburg salt to the Baltic region. Portugal also became a more significant trade partner, since its demand for ship timber grew as its imperial expansion brought new, profitable goods flowing into Europe.

Merchants in Danzig were often simultaneously active in wholesale as well as retail trade, and there were as yet no pronounced specializations in particular areas. One important form of trade was the collective ownership of ships, which pooled the associated risk. Around 220 ships likely sailed under the Danzig flag in 1422, and there were perhaps as many as 600 by 1450.

The Teutonic Order took part in trade alongside the middle-class merchants. This was the domain of the two *Großschäffer*—the Order's chief mercantile officers seated in Königsberg (present-day Kaliningrad, Russia) and Marienburg—who dealt very profitably in grain, flour, wood, and amber. Beginning in 1388, the large Prussian cities protested regularly to the grandmaster, since the Order was exempt from the poundage toll and was also able to procure a number of other (not entirely fair) advantages. On the right bank of the Motława in Danzig, the Order constructed great loading facilities and warehouses across from the fortress. In 1410, these stored (alongside large amounts of rye, wheat, and oats) anchors, millstones, steel, Spanish iron, ash, Flemish salt, flour, peas, copper, barley, niter, saffron, canvas, caraway, almonds, raisins, sugar, spices including coriander, anise, nutmeg, ginger, and canella (white cinnamon), garments, Dutch and English cloth, paper, and more. Yet Danzig's merchants also had a further cause for discontent: many of them were indebted to the financially liquid *Großschäffer*.

Danzig's development into a significant trade center brought many foreigners to the city. On the one hand, the city served as a transfer site and sales market for Poles who mainly purchased wood and forest products here, but also luxury goods, fish, salt, and cloth. In addition to middle-class traders, nobility often came to Danzig with the lumber rafts and river boats to oversee transactions. Western European merchants also found their way to the Motława in droves, and many English traders even settled here with their families. They took on a large part of the textile trade, bought wood in Poland and Lithuania, and commissioned the construction of ships at Danzig's shipyards. A part of them settled in the suburb of New Gardens on a dike, which resulted in a street that today still bears the name English Dike (Grobla Angielska). But the native merchants felt threatened, which led to a systematic curtailment of their English colleagues' rights.

While large transactions were made directly with regional merchants, the Main Town also held weekly markets where both the local population and visitors came to buy goods. These were held on Fish Market, Long Market, Hay Market, and Holy Spirit Street. St. Dominic's Fair, which attracted visitors from near and far to Danzig, took place at Wood Market and Coal Market every year on August 5.

Brewers and Bakers

Skilled labor also played a significant role in the growing city's economy. Danzig's upturn in the fourteenth and fifteenth centuries led to thriving local crafts, and its narrow streets and yards echoed with hammering and sawing while bearing the scents of malt and dyes. Artisans produced for the city's needs but also for the Prussian and Polish backcountry. Richly abundant raw materials like wood favored a number of woodworking trades, while other trades suffered because large amounts of craft products, such as textiles, were imported from Western Europe. For its part, the great flow of trade encouraged branches like ship construction or breweries (since it was nonperishable, beer was the most important drink for ships' crews). As historian Maria Bogucka has estimated, Danzig's brewers likely filled around a quarter million barrels annually in the mid-fifteenth century.

Although the bulk of trade in Danzig was intended for transit, diverse crafts were still able to develop within the city. In 1380, for example, there were representatives of at least the following professions in the city: butchers, smiths, weavers, shoemakers, tailors, crate makers, tanners, peddlers, belt makers, bakers, coopers, furriers, breeches makers, shopkeepers, and bag makers. Many professions, including the sixty-eight documented bakers and forty-nine butchers in the Main Town in 1416, primarily supplied the local population. Others, such as masons and carpenters, kept busy due to the city's constant growth. Other artisans like goldsmiths mainly produced export goods.

As was typical for the time, the skilled workers mostly organized themselves into guilds, some of whose complex functions included assuring quality training, fostering relations with municipal bodies, promoting social and religious life, and caring for widows and orphans. Since the guilds regulated the number of exams given to obtain the rank of master, many journeymen never had the chance to found their own workshops; like apprentices, they often led very modest lives. Many guilds had their own altar or even chapel in one of Danzig's churches.

Constructing coasters, cogs, and also (beginning in the fifteenth century) modern deep-sea vessels or hulks, the shipyards were among the larger production facilities, as was the Teutonic Order's Great Mill in the Old Town with its twelve (later eighteen) waterwheels—a positively staggering amount for the time. The Order also possessed a mint, sawmill, and tannery in Danzig, all of which yielded good profits. Lime kilns and brickworks (the largest of which belonged to members of the Old Town's city council) provided the ever-increasing amounts of needed building materials.

Wars, Rebellions, and a Momentous Murder

It took a while in the fourteenth century before the young Danzig could take part in "high politics." One important step was the Main Town's involvement in the Hanseatic League, an engagement that entailed great benefits as well as obligations. This became apparent for the first time in the 1360s as the League took action against Denmark, which was threatening to disrupt the cities' trade. Danzig joined the other Hanseatic cities in enforcing a poundage toll to raise the resources needed to wage a war, and the city would take part in the League's conflicts time and again for decades. In one instance, it supplied troops for the Hanseatic occupation of Stockholm (1395/1396); in another, it provided 140 soldiers for an expedition to Gotland (1396). In 1398 and 1404, many ships from Danzig's Main Town joined an armed fleet supplied by Prussian cities and the Teutonic Order. Their target was again Gotland, from which the privateers known as the Victual Brothers were enjoying the support of Mecklenburg in their efforts to terrorize the Baltic Sea.

By allowing them broad autonomy and placing few demands on them in the fourteenth century, the Teutonic Order had greatly promoted the development of many of its cities. The Main Town was therefore able to act independently as part of the Hanseatic League. In contrast, the Order granted the Old Town and Young Town significantly fewer liberties. Yet in time, both by encroaching upon the city's rights as well as through its own economic activities (which the populace in Danzig increasingly viewed as competition), the Order also increased its efforts to partake in the Main Town's rapid boom.

In anticipation of a great conflict with Poland and Lithuania in the early fifteenth century, the mighty Order again demanded Gdańsk's support. War broke out in August 1409. In June 1410, after a long truce, the Order's commander in Danzig led a contingent of mounted citizens, mercenary sailors known as *Schiffskinder* (ship-children), and enlisted foot soldiers, totaling 300 men. They joined the Order's army and were utterly defeated by the combined Poles and Lithuanians; even Ulrich von Jungingen, the Order's grandmaster or supreme commander, lost his life. The Danzig banner—two white crosses against a red background—fell into Polish hands and was suspended alongside many others in Kraków's Wawel Castle, where it still hangs today.

Under Mayor Konrad Letzkau, the Main Town initially remained loyal to the Order and even sent 400 sailors to bolster its forces in Marienburg. As more and more cities and regions denounced their Teutonic allegiance, however, Danzig's population followed suit; riots in the city resulted in the murder of many mercenary soldiers returning from the battlefield where they had fought for the Order's armies. Then, as the city council learned that Elbing's New Town and Thorn had already submitted to the Polish crown, Konrad Letzkau was sent to the field camp of the Polish King Władysław II Jagiełło outside of besieged Marienburg to announce Danzig's defection from the Order as well. In a charter passed on August 5, 1410, and amended shortly thereafter, the pleasantly surprised king granted the Main Town six villages previously under the Order's rule, as well as fishing rights, earnings from the Great Mill, rights to free grain export, the prospect of free trade in all of Poland, and more. In this way the Main Town decidedly realized its ambitions for greater autonomy. On August 8, the citizens solemnly honored a royal emissary, and supporters of the Order in Danzig were expelled or even executed. Only the Order's commander would not yield and refused to leave the castle.

Yet the tide turned. Władysław abandoned the siege of Marienburg in mid-September 1410, which gave the Order the opportunity for a counteroffensive that led to the recapture of numerous cities. The Main Town hoped in vain for Polish support, and at the beginning of November, it ultimately had to pledge fealty to Heinrich von Plauen. The newly elected grandmaster ruled with an iron fist, but was initially well disposed toward the Main Town's elite citizens.

The Main Town maneuvered to save at least part of the privileges received from Władysław, refusing military aid requested by the Order and—even after Poland had accepted the Order's retention of Pomerelia in the Peace of Thorn on February 1, 1411—protesting a capital tax with which the Teutonic Knights sought to improve their severely stressed finances. The situation came to a head amid dogged negotiations, and the Order applied pressure on the Main Town, which armed itself and reinforced its fortifications. The Order's commander in Gdańsk summoned Mayor Letzkau, Arnold Hecht, and two additional councilmen to the castle for negotiations on April 6. What occurred over the following hours and days would for centuries occupy imaginations in Danzig and give rise to chronicles, poems, novels, plays, and history paintings. In 1866, Otto Friedrich Gruppe began his poem in this manner:

> Do not go, spoke Lady Martha, do not go, husband!
> The Knights are wroth with thee, go not to their table!
> And should not my weeping stir thee, remember thy children,
> I sense it is of no good—do not leave us orphans!
>
> It was Lord Conrad Letzkau who spoke: Dear wife,
> I will go, and worry not for my safety.
> They wish to offer peace after years of enmity,
> I go, for not to go would be cowardice.[4]

Lady Martha's forebodings proved right after all: Letzkau and two other councilmen were murdered in the castle. Only after days of uncertainty in the city were their corpses finally delivered and entombed to great public sympathy in St. Mary's Church, where a ledger still commemorates them. The citizenry was dismayed, but the Order achieved its goal: the humbled city was ready to concede. The council had to pledge its renewed allegiance to the grandmaster; the citizens paid a large fine; and the Order secured for itself greater influence in the city's affairs, where it hoped to diminish the patriciate's role and strengthen that of the artisans.

Yet further ills still loomed. Weakened by enormous war expenses, the Order minted newer and quite inferior shillings, whereby prices rose and the operators of the Danzig mint soon incurred the populace's hatred. Discontent increased further when the artisans again lost influence in the city council, and a revolt broke out on June 18, 1416. The rioters plundered the city hall, destroyed the mint on Hound Street, and robbed a number of patricians' houses. Mayor Gerd von der Beke and numerous councilmen fled to the Order's castle. The artisans could not savor their victory, though; at the Prussian Diet in Mewe (Pol. Gniew), Danzig's representatives had to agree to the arrest of the instigators, and when Grandmaster Michael Küchmeister held a trial shortly thereafter in Danzig, those found responsible for the revolt were sentenced to death, while others were exiled. Patrician rule was restored, and the wealthy city once again had to pay a large fine.

Danzig Grows Up(ward)

Danzig grew not only in breadth in the fourteenth and fifteenth centuries, but also in height, resulting in brick towers of many secular and religious buildings stretching into the clear Baltic sky. As an expression of bourgeois prosperity and self-assurance, they also served as a symbol of power directed against the Teutonic Knights residing in their castle as tensions increased between the Main Town and the Order. Time would tell to whom the future belonged, though. While the castle has long been destroyed, almost all of the medieval towers still rise above the sea of houses today.

Danzig's most significant sacral structure is St. Mary's Church, begun around 1343, initially (until 1360) as a basilica with an unusually long high nave and low side aisles. Shortly thereafter, its walls were raised, a transept was added, and buttresses were integrated in its interior to convert it into a hall church. This construction was finished in 1410. The imposing interior was now almost 350 feet long and about 135 feet wide, larger than almost any other brick building north of the Alps. Over the following decades, the church interior was partially vaulted, and a tower was added by 1466. The tower's squat shape led to many legends and speculation: some said that the Order would not permit a taller structure; there was also talk of Tullatsch the giant, who rested on his journey by sitting on and compressing the half-finished tower, after which further construction on it ceased.

Beginning in 1344 and built concurrently with St. Mary's, the Main Town's second large church was built for the district's northern expansion, the New Town. This structure, St. John's Church, was also too small before long, and by 1377, construction had begun on a much larger three-nave basilica to be mostly completed by the mid-fifteenth century. It is unclear what remained of the Old Town's thirteenth-century parish church, St. Catherine's; in any case,

Figure 3.3 St. Mary's Church has towered over historical Gdańsk for centuries. This was the view in 1900. From Herder-Institut, Marburg, Germany.

it was also heavily expanded and altered beginning in the mid-fourteenth century. Its characteristic exterior is from an even later time. A low, three-nave hall church dedicated to Peter and Paul was begun in the Old Suburb near the end of the fourteenth century, followed by many more: St. Barbara's Church in Long Gardens; St. Elizabeth's, a hospital church, and the sailors' Church of St. James in the Old Town; the Church of the Holy Spirit—another hospital church—in the Main Town; and numerous churches outside of the Old Town and in the Young Town.

Additionally, there were several monastery complexes. After the destruction of 1308, the Dominican Church of St. Nicholas was rebuilt and supplemented with a number of convent buildings. In commemoration of St. Bridget of Sweden, work began on the Convent of St. Bridget near the end of the fourteenth century, with an initially single-nave church, which received side aisles over the next 120 years. Eventually, the Franciscans settled in the Old Suburb in 1419.

This large number of religious buildings resulted not only from the existence of the various municipal entities (Main Town with New Town and Old Suburb, Old Town, Young Town), but also from the overlapping interests of the middle-class, the Teutonic Order, and the Diocese of Włocławek, to which Danzig belonged. Moreover, these structures were a symbol of the city's extraordinary wealth such a short time after its (re)establishment.

Sooner or later, a city developing as boldly as the Main Town would need to acquire a fittingly prestigious administrative building. In 1379, construction on a large town hall commenced on the site of a small precursor building at the western end of Long Market. Master Heinrich Ungeradin, who oversaw the construction, also had a tower in a Flemish style placed on the building. The town hall contained the city scales; chambers for councilmen and lay judges, as well as the city treasury; a chapel; and an archive room called "Little Christopher," whose gothic murals were uncovered after the Second World War. Located in the immediate vicinity on Long Market, the Artus Court was also expanded during this time.

The city wall that had stood since 1343 surrounded the entire Main Town with sixteen towers to facilitate defense. One gate led north to the castle, and three more led west, including the Long Street Gate, next to which the imposing Prison Tower would later stand. There were initially only three gates in the south. A number of prestigious entrances to the city were created approaching the Motława; of these, the Holy Spirit Gate, the Crane Gate, and St. John's Gate still stand, if quite altered in appearance.

A port city naturally also required harbor facilities. Accordingly, the Main Town significantly updated its loading equipment, deepened the waterways in the Vistula and Motława, and ultimately built the Crane Gate on the Motława in 1443/1444; this mighty edifice comprised two round towers, each of which was a hundred feet tall and between which the builders assembled a crane powered by a waterwheel. The well-fortified Crane Gate, which intimidated even the Teutonic Order's commander in his nearby castle, served to load and unload particularly cumbersome goods as well as to install masts in ships. Today, with its prominent silhouette, it remains one of the city's most iconic emblems.

The largest secular building from this time is the Order's Great Mill, whose exterior has been extensively maintained by the city. Erected at the end of the fourteenth century on the spot where a former structure had burned down on Granary Island along the Radunia Canal, it ranked as one of the greatest commercial buildings of its day and remained in operation as a mill until 1945.

Most citizens lived in timbered or framed houses until the end of the fourteenth century; brick townhouses, some of which have remained preserved to the present, appeared only after the turn of the fifteenth century. Whereas the wood houses were very simple structures, the brick houses boasted layouts of greater complexity: offices, workshops, or commercial spaces were located on the ground floor, while the residents lived upstairs. The soggy earth Danzig was built on did not encourage deep cellars, so basements extended above street level, and stairs and small terraces provided access to the houses' front doors. As ornate steps and railings were added to them over the course of the early-modern period, these developed into the Beischläge, the elaborate terraces so characteristic of Danzig.

Art and Everyday Life

Already in the fourteenth century, works of art enjoyed great esteem in Danzig. Drawing on influences from not only Prague but also Flanders and the lower Rhine regions, native artists soon attained such a high standard that even Henry, Earl of Derby (later known as King Henry IV of England), purchased two paintings on the Motława in 1392. The most significant platforms for artistic activity were naturally Danzig's churches, foremost among them St. Mary's, whose chapels were adorned with the work of the artist's guilds. Visitors can still view many outstanding Gothic works of art here today, including the *Schöne Madonna* (Beautiful Madonna) in St. Anne's Chapel, whose loveliness deeply impressed contemporaries and was the source of numerous legends. It was supposedly an assistant potter, falsely condemned to death, who created this stirring work in his cell. Profoundly moved, the city council spared his life.

The Catholic faith was an uncontested part of public and private life. Relations with the bishop living far off in Włocławek were not always harmonious, and in 1414, Danzig residents destroyed his stone house on Bishop's Hill to the west of the Main Town—although this action was instigated by the Order. Still, religious conflicts were largely reserved for Danzig's future. Active congregations in the city, including the mendicant order of the Dominicans— the "black monks"—were as much a part of the town as the charitable activities of the Christian hospitals. Churchly and religious ceremonies (worship services, baptisms, weddings, funerals, processions, and holidays) were important elements in people's everyday lives.

Education was by no means a matter of course. A school at St. Mary's Church is documented as early as 1350, and other churches soon added their own schools. Boys learned basic Latin, writing, reading, and arithmetic, while the Bridgettine Sisters instructed the girls. Anyone wishing to pursue further education attended universities like Prague, which twenty-seven students from Danzig attended between 1376 and 1409. Erfurt, Vienna, and later Kraków and Leipzig also attracted inquisitive youth who largely returned home following their studies and found employment in the city council or religious institutions.

Much remains unknown about the lifestyle of Danzig's population in the fourteenth and fifteenth centuries. Nevertheless, recent excavations have supplied archaeologists a good deal of new material to aid their careful investigation of the period after 1308. The wealthier citizens ate fish and meat, bread and salt, vegetables and local fruit, and they drank beer. Even wine and tropical fruit like figs and grapes were present on special occasions. Social associations played significant roles in everyday life, for instance the Brotherhood of St. George and the guilds, as well as the marksmen's fraternity, which artisans founded in 1354.

The Final Years under the Teutonic Order's Rule

The Order's politics toward the cities and regions within its state had changed after its decisive defeat at the Battle of Grunwald in July 1410. Whereas Grandmaster Heinrich von Plauen had attempted to engage the citizens more meaningfully in political matters, his successors strove to maintain the old ways, and necessary reforms, political and otherwise, failed to come about. Yet the Order's economic prospects dwindled at the same time that those of the city sharply increased, resulting in a shift in the balance of power within the Teutonic state.

Danzig's Main Town seized this opportunity to extend and assert its rights by passing its own laws without consulting the Order and successfully reducing the Teutonic influence in the city council. The rapidly expanding city's increasingly professional administration facilitated this, as the Main Town was employing growing numbers of clerks, laborers, guards, and other functionaries, as well as clock keepers, cowherds, and swineherds.

In matters of "high politics," Danzig had to navigate between loyalties to the Order and to the Hanseatic League. This sometimes led to problems, especially when the Order's designs conflicted with those of the powerful league of cities. In a new conflict between the Hanseatic League and Denmark in the 1420s, for instance, the Order's grandmaster took the side of King Erik VII and compelled the Prussian Hanseatic cities to remain neutral. After some time, the Hanseatic League and Denmark made peace, yet without the repeal of Denmark's Sound Dues that Danzig had hoped for. New conflicts arose when the Order sided with Holland after the Wendish Hanseatic cities, under Lübeck's direction since 1438, attempted to forcibly check Dutch commercial expansion into the Baltic Sea. Danzig's trade suffered here, as well as in a 1449 conflict with England, especially due to privateer attacks on Danzig ships.

Additionally, hostilities between the Order and the Polish-Lithuanian Union had by no means ceased. The Main Town took part in wars in 1414 and 1422, as well as 1431, when it contributed many hundreds of armed soldiers. On September 1, 1433, the confederate armies of Poland and Bohemian Hussites attacked Pomerelia and struck camp outside of Danzig, yet the bombardment of the city was abandoned a few days later, with the attackers withdrawing to the south after destroying the Oliva Monastery.

Like all of Pomerelia, Danzig suffered greatly in these wars, particularly because war always severely impaired trade. In light of the general discontent with the Order's rule, Danzig united with other cities and nobles located primarily in the western Prussian regions to form the Prussian Confederation in March 1440. For Danzig, the most important matter was initially the repeal of the approximately twenty-year-old poundage tariff exclusively benefiting the Order, as well as the excessive fees in the Great Mill. A first attempt to abolish the tariff failed in 1441/1442, partially due to differences within the Prussian Confederation.

Danzig's civil representation received new life when, beginning in 1450, the newly elected grandmaster Ludwig von Erlichshausen tried, with the diplomatic support of the holy roman emperor, to restore the Order's power and break up the Prussian Confederation. For its part, the Confederation made its own appeal to the emperor and achieved a court hearing in 1453. While Danzig's city council continued to act tentatively, a large portion of the citizenry displayed a hostile attitude toward the Order and its ongoing arbitrary rule. Thus, when the court in Vienna ruled against the Prussian Confederation, demanded its disintegration, and promised further repressions, the city was in an uproar. Would they ever cast off the Teutonic rule? The choice became clear to seek protection, once again, from the king of Poland. In January, representatives of the confederation visited King Casimir IV Jagiellon, who received them sympathetically. The Prussian Confederation denounced its loyalty to Grandmaster Ludwig von Ehrlichshausen on February 4, 1454. Citizens of Danzig seized the Great Mill the following day, and the Order's commander in Danzig surrendered the castle to the Main Town on February 11. Yet another thirteen years and a costly war would pass before "Royal Prussia," the area of German-speaking Prussia henceforth subject to the Polish king, would be claimed from the Teutonic State. As part of a great kingdom, Danzig would see unimagined opportunities for growth in the coming centuries.

4

Wheat-Blond and Rye-Brown

Danzig's Golden Age, 1454–1655

Sweat, dust, flies, chaff. The crop has to dry. Panting, the Polish rafters—"flisaks"—shovel on the Vistula's shore. The sun glimmers in the heat. Only dry grain fetches a good price. The grains fly blond and brown through the air, the land's yellow-ripened hoard. Wheat and rye. Rye and wheat. The crop has to dry.

A refreshing breeze blows from the sea. Already the flisaks look forward to evening. Józek has his fiddle with him, Włodek a flute; soon they will dance, sing, and—if it cools down—fall into a muffled sleep on their barge.

And the city waits, there, beyond the river's bend. The merchant Hans sits up late, looking over his books and counting: wheat and rye. Rye and wheat. Debit and credit. Tomorrow the barges will come, loaded blond and brown, and soon the money will arrive, and everything will work out. Now he too goes to bed.

Posterity Regards the Year 1454

It was a development with far-reaching consequences when Danzig shook off the rule of the Teutonic Order in 1454 and became subject to the Polish crown. As so often in Gdańsk's history, explanations for this have varied greatly.

On February 23, 1754, as the city of Danzig, still belonging to Poland, solemnly marked the event's 300th anniversary, Friedrich Klein recited an ode in the revered Academic Secondary School:

> O Danzig, this boon, granted by Poland,
> Even as a new seedling was delicious to thee:
> How much more fully must thy people savor it now,
> After three hundred years of shelter under Poland's wing![1]

The city council thanked him for this work with 200 guilders. In 1854, the city—by then part of the Kingdom of Prussia for some time—would have all but forgotten the anniversary, had a local paper not somewhat belatedly commemorated the event. Still in favor of the city's late medieval decision, the paper declared: "The Teutonic Order's banner, stained by so many crimes, thus fell forever from Danzig's walls exactly four centuries ago."[2] In 1904—by which time Danzig belonged to the German Empire—the city's transition to Poland was denounced as a "disastrous step ... by which it seceded from the Teutonic Order and Germandom," a misstep that had "bitterly avenged" itself.[3]

Half a century later, Gdańsk was again Polish and celebrated the anniversary with the motto "five hundred years of liberation from the crusaders' yoke." Leaders at a festive meeting of the city parliament managed the feat of succinctly interlacing late medieval and recent history in communist-Stalinist and Polish-nationalist interpretations of the story:

> Poland dealt a mighty blow to Prussian reactionism in the fifteenth century by returning Gdańsk, with the city's armed support, to its mother country. This same reactionism, in its new form of Hitler's fascism, was completely annihilated by the Soviet Army's strength of arms. Only now has Gdańsk truly become a free city.[4]

In 2004, after another fifty years, this interpretation was also long obsolete. The democratically self-governing city celebrated this anniversary by launching an annual multicultural "Gdańsk Festival" that vividly commemorates the city's passage to Poland and the commencement of its golden age with historical processions, theater, and concerts.

Thirteen Years of War: Sacrifice and Privilege

Difficult years ensued once the Prussian Confederation detached itself from the Teutonic Order and submitted to Poland. For the crusaders, nothing less than their state's existence was at stake, while in case of defeat, the Prussian cities and nobles who had broken off had to fear a fate similar to Danzig's in 1308. The war between Poland and the Teutonic Order would last thirteen years with shifting fortunes for both sides, and many hundreds of Danzig's citizens and many mercenary soldiers recruited by the city would lose their lives in battle.

At the war's outset, Danzig celebrated great successes and took a number of Pomerelian cities into its possession. It also unsuccessfully besieged the Order's fortress in Marienburg, had to accept bitter defeat near Konitz (Pol. Chojnice), and looked on as the Order's army approached the city walls in January 1455.

Danger was averted, however, by a successful sortie launched by 1,400 citizens. The city's financial power paid off in 1457, when Danzig participated in the purchase of the Marienburg fortress from the Order's long-unpaid mercenary soldiers there. The exploits of Danzig's privateers in the Baltic Sea also brought some relief; in 1458 alone, thirty-three ships from Danzig were actively raiding, waylaying any ships they could find putting into harbor in the Order's ports. The Order recovered somewhat and once again stood outside the city walls in 1460. Further cities in the area fell to its armies over the following year. Since trade on the Vistula River persisted despite all hostilities, however, Danzig had sufficient means to actively participate in the Polish offensive in 1462; the victory in a major battle north of Danzig was largely credited to the city, whose soldiers made up nearly half of the Polish army. Following another victorious battle in the Vistula Lagoon, it was only a matter of time before the financially lifeless Order submitted to the inevitable and ceded Royal Prussia to Poland in the Second Peace of Thorn on October 19, 1466.

While Danzig had suffered a great loss of lives as well as financial costs during the Thirteen Years' War, the merchant city also gained a tremendous deal of power. In the first town privileges he granted to Danzig on June 16, 1454, King Casimir IV quickly made generous concessions to the city, and these were greatly expanded on May 15, 1457, when the monarch paid Danzig a visit. The charter begins with the words, "In the name of the Lord amen."[5] Danzig, which had come to the king's aid "with steady loyalty and firm courage,"[6] received an enormous piece of land amounting to approximately 386 square miles—more than the holdings of Lübeck, Hamburg, and Bremen combined. This area included the Vistula Spit, a large portion of the Vistula-Nogat delta, Praust (Pol. Pruszcz), Ohra, and many more villages in the vicinity. The city had permission to fill all of its own secular and ecclesiastical offices (except for the priest of St. Mary's Church); the king was not allowed to build any castles within approximately eighteen miles of the city; and Danzig could mint its own coins, control the Prussian coastline in Eastern Pomerania as far as Elbing, and import goods from Poland and Lithuania without restrictions. The sole royal dignitary in the city was the burgrave, hardly more than an honorary office appointed from the ranks of the councilmen. Additionally, Danzig's various cities—until then independent entities—were united under the umbrella of the Main Town, with only the Old Town maintaining its own civic rights. "Occurring in our city Danczke on Sunday, as cantatas are sung in the holy church, after the birth of Christ our Lord one thousand four hundred and in the fifty-seventh year."[7]

Thus bolstered, Danzig quickly became the most powerful city on the Baltic Sea, the largest city in the Polish-Lithuanian Union, and an economically and culturally flourishing hub whose bloom would last two hundred years.

Destruction and Expansion

The Teutonic Knights had barely left when the citizens dismantled the Order's castle, which would never again serve as the seat of any ruler nor restrict the city's development. The area around the former castle remained undeveloped into the seventeenth century. The Young Town's days were also numbered. Out of fear that the Teutonic Order could use it as a gateway to Danzig, the Main Town had its unwanted younger sibling torn down in 1455. The Young Town's residents moved into the northern section of the Old Town, where they built new homes; this transition was not very difficult for them since floods had frequently plagued the Young Town area anyway.

As most of the tall church towers were completed by the end of the fifteenth century, Danzig grew outward rather than upward. This development was shaped, for one, by the massive expansion of municipal landholdings directly adjacent to the previous city limits. Hence, suburban settlements formed over time below Bishop's Hill, although most of these would later be burned down in the face of hostile sieges in order to impede attackers' access to the city. The granary district on the Motława's right shore likewise changed in appearance and became an island by the sixteenth century following the construction of a new river channel, the New Motława. As the population further increased in the first half of the seventeenth century, the new district of Lower Town was created southeast of Granary Island.

After 1454, the wealthy city of Danzig was less protected than before. The Teutonic Order's center of power was still nearby in Marienburg, after all, and Poland's royal court mostly stayed in distant Kraków. Changed external political circumstances forced the city to invest in its own defense. Because of its wealth, Danzig was able to maintain the newest standards of military technology. With the old medieval city walls soon proving outdated, the construction of new, mighty fortifications commenced around the city; these would be completed in the mid-seventeenth century. Beginning in the first half of the sixteenth century, builders—largely from abroad—oversaw the construction of a ring of ramparts embedded with towers and gates, with corners secured with bastions. Initial construction took place primarily on the city's north, west, and south sides. Operations intensified after the events surrounding the siege of 1577. Finally, on the advice of Italian specialists, a ring of fortifications also arose to the east and northeast, until a powerful, serrated rampart ultimately surrounded the entire city. Only Danzig's many towers and highest gables rose above the green walls sparsely interrupted by gates.

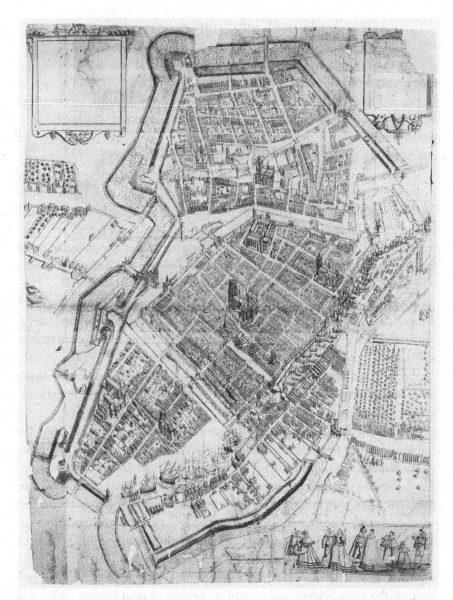

Figure 4.1 Around 1600, Danzig was a European metropolis. Dominated by the mighty Church of St. Mary, the sea of houses stretched from the bustling Motława harbor (*right*) to the city's fortifications. This picture, only recently discovered in Sweden, is attributed to the Gdańsk painter Anton Möller. Riksarkivet Stockholm, SE/KrA/0406/25/044/013.

Trade and Craft, Sources of Wealth

Danzig existed between worlds. Located between land and sea, between the Slavic and Germanic world, it was also between Europe's center and periphery. In this position, the sixteenth-century city became one of those intersections that brought about the "modern world-system," the dawning globalization of economic life described by sociologist and historian Immanuel Wallerstein. The conditions for this were supply, demand, and transportation.

While still dominated by raw materials, the spectrum of goods offered in Danzig changed in the mid-fifteenth century. Initially, wood and lumber products like ash, pitch, and honey from Eastern Europe's vast forests continued to come from Poland, Lithuania, and Livonia to Danzig and farther west. The main transport route was the Vistula, yet Danzig merchants also collected goods by ship directly from harbors like Riga or Åbo (present-day Turku). Furs from Novgorod, Livonia, and Finland were in particular demand.

Over time, grain pushed to the forefront of exported goods. Beginning in the second half of the fifteenth century after a period of stagnation, economic development gained new momentum in the strip of Central Europe stretching from Italy to England across southern and western Germany, eastern France, and the Netherlands. No longer able to internally meet their food requirements, major cities in the west, particularly in a region as largely urban as the Netherlands, sought new sources.

At the same time, Poland's socioeconomic system underwent a change. The nobility was able to further increase its influence in the state while expanding its landholdings at the expense of the middle class and farmers. The so-called *Fronhof* system emerged, a dense network of large noble estates, many occupying just a few acres, with others taking up several hundred or even over a thousand, which were either personally administered by lower nobility or counted among the large landed estates belonging to upper nobility and generally leased out. Bondservants performing their corvée carried out duties on the manor, which reduced costs and enabled substantial expansion of acreage. In the late sixteenth century, the manors could sell around 40 percent of their harvest on the free market, which usually meant shipping it to Danzig.

Even if only as a hub, Danzig was decisively involved in the development of this system, which offered large profits to all involved (apart from the peasants); nevertheless, due to the lopsided preference given to grain-producing nobility, the system also weakened Poland's societal and economic structure. With over 50,000 residents in 1600, Danzig naturally depended on the influx of foodstuffs, but the majority of grain that arrived in the city continued on to the west.

The Netherlands dominated this trade. Their prevalence in the Baltic Sea, where they soon outpaced the Hanseatic League and Danzig merchants, had been growing since the fifteenth century. A few statistics illustrate this: near the end of the fifteenth century, 30 percent of incoming ships in Danzig were from Dutch territories. Just a few decades later, they made up 50 percent, and in the second decade of the seventeenth century, no less than 70 percent of all ships passing through the Sound came from homeports in the United Provinces, mainly in Holland and Friesland. The large demand for Baltic grain lasted until the beginning of the First Northern War in 1655. For over a hundred years, grain made up three-quarters of the value of all goods exported from Danzig across the Sound; in 1625, this amount reached as high as 83.6 percent.

The Netherlands' proficiency was key to their success. Their modern vessels, the fluyts, could transport mass goods much more cheaply than the Hanseatic cities' dated ships, and the highly developed Dutch trade methods—credit, exchange, risk sharing across multiple shipowners, an extensive network of overseas trading establishments known as factories—were consistently superior to the capabilities of the merchants in Danzig and elsewhere.

In the Netherlands, the Baltic grain trade was considered *moedernegotie*, the mother of all trades and the basis for the nation's wealth. Four out of every five storehouses in Amsterdam were filled with Baltic grain, more than two-thirds of it from Danzig. Entire economic sectors in the Dutch metropolis depended on grain, such as the breweries, the shipbuilding industry, and the manufacture of bricks, which were carried to the Baltic as ballast. Yet scholars dispute the Baltic Sea's significance for the Netherlands' development. While Immanuel Wallerstein assessed it as "key to the success"[8] of the Dutch, Jonathan I. Israel has downplayed its importance, arguing that it was predominantly speculative, of interest only to smaller merchants, and, having facilitated only small gains compared to transoceanic activities, it was by no means vital for the Netherlands.[9]

Rye and wheat were not the only trade goods that made their way through Danzig. Cut and uncut high-quality wood for ship construction was still important throughout Europe, albeit decreasingly so. Rembrandt painted on oak panels delivered to him from the Baltic. Yet Danzig's hinterland had even more to offer. Between 1579 and 1588, the ledgers of the customs post in Weißenberg (Pol. Biała Góra), where the Nogat branches off from the Vistula, registered the downriver shipment of a broad range of additional goods, including malt, Hungarian plums, pitch, ash, wax, dye, beer, wines, iron, steel, scythes, lead, alum, copper, meat, cloth, ceramics, gingerbread, and much more. In the other direction, apples, plums, honey, fish, whale oil, bacon, hides, furs, beer, wines, iron, salt, pepper, lemons, cloth, metal goods, and other items were transported upriver.

Due to its great importance as a preservative, salt was, for a long time, second to none among the seaborne goods imported to Danzig. Since the salt mine in Wieliczka near Kraków could not yet meet the large demand, salt was imported from Lüneburg and, to a much higher degree, from the great saltpans on the French, Spanish, and Portuguese Atlantic coast. Fabrics overtook salt at the beginning of the seventeenth century. Iron, lumber products, and various crops came from Sweden, and herrings remained sought-after merchandise.

Although the Dutch had acquired great significance for Danzig's maritime trade, they could not seriously endanger the local merchants' standing. This was largely due to the privileges secured by the city in the fifteenth century, which not only guaranteed freedom of trade in the Polish-Lithuanian Union but also stipulated that all goods brought to Danzig first be made available for sale locally, while prohibiting non-citizens from trading with each other within the city. The manner of trade nevertheless changed. At the beginning of the sixteenth century, many of Danzig's merchants still conducted maritime trade; by midcentury, around 180 ships flying the city's flag passed through the Sound annually. This number would decline rapidly under the pressure of Dutch competition, partly due to the situation in Danzig, where merchants could in fact forgo the higher risks of maritime trade, since huge quantities of raw materials floated almost automatically down the Vistula, and resale alone promised large profits. Scholars have critically discussed and, to an extent, attributed this tendency toward passivity and the resulting dependence of Danzig and its enormous hinterland to the rapidly modernizing and industrializing centers of the west as a type of colonialism.

Yet Danzig's merchants were not entirely passive. Some of them continued to load ships to France, Spain, and even Italy in order to pocket better profits in times of high demand for grain or timber. Venice, for instance, initiated a regular, direct trade relationship with Danzig around 1600, through which Venetians came to the Baltic, while citizens from Danzig traveled to marvel at the proud Serenissima Repubblica. Companies in Danzig had representatives in many ports; these local agents, called factors, sold goods on commission at trading posts, or factories. Still, beginning in the 1620s, these activities receded in the face of Dutch competition. Around 1640, there were already close to fifty Dutch factors active in Danzig alone.

Trade dominated not just the economy in Danzig but the entirety of public life. The continually growing harbor buzzed with activity. Sailors, stevedores, merchants, visitors from afar, market women, and Polish nobles all bustled about. In 1583, 2,230 ships entered port; though there were fewer ships a half century later, they were larger. In addition to these came Vistula barges and rafts, small and large, vessels occupied by rowers called either *Flissen* or *Flissaken* in German (from Pol. *flisak*, "rafter"). They arrived in Danzig en masse, primarily during the spring flood, but also in autumn after the harvest, often in large assemblies supervised by an estate manager. For the approximately 400-mile trip from Sieniawa on the San River to Danzig and back, travelers needed to allow ten to twelve weeks. For ships carrying grain, before arrival in the harbor at Danzig, the grain was thoroughly tossed with shovels to aerate and dry on a designated area of the Vistula shore called a *Schörappke* in Danzig's Low-German dialect. After the freight was unloaded into a storehouse, the larger boats traveled to the Crane Gate, where the masts they had brought along were inserted, so that they could sail back home. Some types of boats were dismantled in Danzig and sold for lumber, such as the *Komeggen*, which resembled crudely timbered floating crates.

Charles Ogier, who stayed in Danzig with a French legation in 1635 and 1636, documented the vibrant life in the harbor:

> For many hours I observed the most diverse ships in the canal flowing about Granary Island, both those that sail on the sea as well as those that travel on the Vistula. It is pleasant to watch: the entirety of Vistula commerce comes from Poland on ships with rather flat bottoms, upon them a host of villagers bound to their labor as servants for their lords, pushing off these long and broad barges. . . . The Polish noble both

Figure 4.2 It was peak period in Danzig's harbor when Agidius Dickmann published this woodcut in 1617. River boats and rafts brought grain from Poland, which Dutch merchants eagerly awaited. Here a river barge with a lowered mast passes the Green Bridge as a merchant ship rests along the Long Bridge (*right*). From Zofia Jakrzewska-Śnieżko, *Gdańsk w dawnych rycinach*. Wrocław (1985), image 12.

commands his ship and goes himself to the merchant in Danzig, to his storehouse, which is often subdivided into six or seven long bays and is made up of just as many floors. The area that these storehouses take up may well approach that of the entire city, and the people, in astounding crowds, bustle everywhere in the streets and their intersections, especially in summer. . . . At the same time, while Poles and people from Prussia carry these sacks of wheat into the storehouses, the Dutch are already present with their ships, skillfully and carefully carrying the wheat away to ship it into the entire world. They did not come here with empty hands, for they purchase these gifts of Ceres with abundant gifts of Bacchus, which they bring from France and Spain. This wine then travels with the Poles up the Vistula to Warsaw and Kraków.[10]

Danzig's trade was not limited only to the Baltic Sea and along the Vistula. The nearby backcountry delivered great amounts of wood, grain, and all other sorts of foods for the large city. Metals came from Sweden, as well as overland from the south, as did spices and other luxury goods. Additional long-distance trade routes led to Silesia, Greater Poland, and Pomerania.

Commerce was a gold mine for Danzig, with the city's grain merchants averaging profits of 30 percent of their invested capital in the first half of the seventeenth century. Quality timber brought in even more, and trade in fabrics and herrings was also especially lucrative. In cases when Danzig merchants put forth the effort to export their grain or wood as far as Spain or Portugal, the substantially greater hazards (potential ship impoundment and risks involving currency and exchange) were overshadowed by prospects of returns exceeding even 100 percent.

Danzig was of prodigious importance for the Polish economy; in the late sixteenth and early seventeenth centuries, three-quarters of Poland's entire foreign trade passed through the port city. This dependence, both of Danzig on Polish grain and of Poland on Danzig's harbor, would prove highly detrimental for both when the demand for grain later fell in the west.

Commercial sectors besides trade also developed in Danzig. From the beginning of the sixteenth century onward, the city's trade balance was very positive. With much higher exports than imports, foreign buyers often paid not with goods they had brought with them but with money. This led to a great accumulation of wealth available to the public sector. For this reason, merchants in Danzig were mostly also bankers, and if they had built up a large fortune, they happily withdrew from active trade and dedicated themselves to finances (as well as managing their large estates). The city's burghers thus lent small and large sums, supplied credit to Prussian and Polish nobles, and even repeatedly helped monarchs out of financial difficulties.

Organized in guilds, skilled crafts continued to flourish. The brewers set the tone at first, before their significance decreased in the seventeenth century, and the mills developed into large-scale operations. Additionally, over 200 shops in the city worked leather in 1526. Butchers and bakers kept the people fed. Only textile businesses initially had a hard time, since imported materials dominated the market; but this venture became successful following the immigration of Dutch textile manufacturers. After 1600, more than 6,000 people made a living producing materials and clothing.

Masons and carpenters kept busy upgrading public buildings and maintaining the city's fortifications, but they were also involved in the construction and expansion of private homes. Brickyards and lumber mills within the city and its vicinity provided builders with the needed materials. Amber workmanship experienced a great revival, once the Teutonic Order's monopoly on the "Baltic gold" had been broken. The Polish nobility's luxury consumption, mainly in the seventeenth century, allowed skilled craft professions to thrive: goldsmiths, metalsmiths, and amber turners were renowned for their creations and were commissioned from afar. Brewers and dyers were often rich, whereas tailors were frequently as poor as the proverbial church mouse. Glass, metal products, furniture, soap, paper, needles, nails, weapons—there was hardly anything that was not produced in Danzig. The city became the largest manufacturing center not just in Poland, but throughout the entire Baltic region.

Ship construction reached its peak in the period following the Thirteen Years' War. In 1462, when the massive French caravel *Pierre de la Rochelle* shipwrecked outside the city, local professionals had the opportunity to thoroughly study modern construction methods, which fostered ship production. By the mid-sixteenth century, scores of ships were being constructed in Danzig and partly exported; even King Henry VIII of England bought two large caravels here. No fewer than 130 shipwrights were at work in 1526; outfitting the ships supplied many more people with work and bread. However, the heyday was soon past. By the mid-seventeenth century, scarcely a single ship was launched in Danzig.

Danzig Seeks Its Place

The status of Danzig as a subject of Poland was unusual, and it has been the topic of frequent discussion. For a long time, the city abided by the conviction that it was subject only to the Polish king and called itself a "republic." Danzig would frequently complain that the institutions of the Kingdom of Poland and (later) the Polish-Lithuanian Commonwealth—particularly the parliament (Sejm)—claimed undue rights in the city. German historians in the nineteenth and twentieth centuries adhered to this interpretation and even termed early modern

Danzig a city-state, a "free imperial city." To support this view, they posited that Danzig had fostered its own foreign relations and provided for its own defenses. Yet they neglected to mention that the city quite consciously kept its legitimate position vague and—depending on what promised to be more advantageous to its own interests—at times presented itself as a loyal member, and at others in open defiance, of the Polish state. Polish historians have also long grappled with this ambivalence and the city's skillful political maneuvering. While they could never sufficiently stress how devotedly Danzig had stuck by Poland, they had to either arduously explain or conceal the numerous exceptions to this rule. In any case, Danzig consistently kept its distance from the German Holy Roman Empire. Upon receiving an invitation to the Diet of Nuremberg as early as 1456, it declined on the grounds that it was a part of Poland, a stance it would maintain for a long time.

Rich and envied, Danzig was—along with Elbing and Thorn—the only major urban civic center in an enormous countryside dominated by aristocracy. Added to this contrast were linguistic and, beginning with the Reformation, confessional differences. From this vantage point, the city welcomed every opportunity to strengthen its position and tenaciously defend its rights.

Such differences also affected relations with the estates in Royal Prussia. The province's cities and nobility had common interests, which they discussed at parliamentary assemblies called *Landtage* or *Tagfahrten*, but disagreements arose soon after 1466. The monied people from the city had a mind of their own, as illustrated in the so-called Shaveling War (Pfaffenkrieg) of the 1470s, when Danzig insisted that a local cleric, and not a Pole, occupy the bishopric of Ermland (Pol. Warmia). Relations between the city and the Prussian nobles, who had willingly integrated into Polish aristocratic society, were sometimes problematic, as in the years when the marauding Mattern brothers wreaked havoc in the regions around Danzig.

Georg Mattern had worked in London as the factor of a Danzig merchant and had quarreled there with a shipper from Danzig over soggy and moldy linen. Mattern and two companions then thrashed this same man upon encountering him outside of the Artus Court in Danzig in 1492. Banished from the city with his honor injured, Mattern found support—first among the petty nobility in the area, and later with the Teutonic Order—and began robbing Danzig's councilmen and merchants. He avoided repercussions until he was finally hanged in 1502. Shortly thereafter, his younger brother Simon followed in his footsteps, gathering a large number of adventurous petty nobles and their bondservants to cause chaos in the region, kidnap local citizens, and even attack Danzig itself and set fires in the city. Again and again, he found support among the Prussian estates, who resented Danzig's autarkic policies. Eventually, Danzig's mayor Eberhard Ferber took forceful measures, obtained the king's consent, and hunted down Mattern despite the nobility's resistance. Ferber had some of the nobles in league with Mattern executed, and he ultimately caught the bandit chief himself. But before anybody else could take his life, Mattern committed suicide.

It was with notable distrust that Danzig regarded Poland's political ambitions in the Baltic region, as these endangered the city's economic and political interests. At length and partially alongside the Hanseatic League, the city implemented its own plans, which consistently focused on protecting trade to and from Danzig. Against this backdrop, increasingly substantial conflicts of interests also arose within the Hanseatic League. Initially, Danzig was still a very involved member of the League, for example, in its naval war against England beginning in 1469.

Danzig re-equipped the large French caravel that had shipwrecked in 1462 and sent it under the direction of a council member into the Baltic, where it, alongside many other ships belonging both to the Hanseatic League and to private owners, went on raids as the *Peter von Danzig* (Peter of Danzig). This required great effort, because the ship leaked incessantly, and the crew had to operate the pumps constantly in stormy weather. Bernd Pawest reported: "We pumped the night through and could not prevail, and the longer we pumped, the more water we took on, such that we were in great worry and distress."[11]

In 1473, the *Peter von Danzig*, after its sale to private investors and under captain Paul Beneke (who had previously taken the lord mayor of London captive), captured a galley sailing from Sluis to London with an extraordinarily valuable payload. The ship's crew and owners were thrilled at the great booty, and the shipowners donated the most prized item, Hans Memling's grand altarpiece entitled *The Last Judgment*, to the chapel of the Brotherhood of St. George in St. Mary's Church, where it hung until the Second World War. The painting's origins were forgotten for centuries; only in the mid-nineteenth century did newly discovered chronicles yield the information. Paul Beneke, a native of Danzig, was thereupon styled a "German naval hero," and supporters of the kaiser in the German Empire, the Weimar Republic, and National Socialist Germany would regard him as an embodiment of Danzig's fortitude in the continuous face of alleged Polish threat—even though Beneke had never fought against Poland.

While Danzig displayed solidarity with the rest of the Hanseatic League in the war against England, more and more disputes arose over subsequent decades: Danzig supported the trade and financial empire of the powerful Fugger family, with whom Lübeck was at odds; later, Danzig did not participate in Lübeck's battles against Denmark in 1531. Although Danzig actively contributed to the Hanseatic League's 1557 reforms and in the course of the reorganization became the chief city of the League's Prussian section, the days of a middle-class league of cities appeared numbered in light of the rise of the great powers. Yet due to long-standing solidarity, Danzig still took part in all Hanseatic diets until 1669.

Danzig played an active role in Poland's last war against the Teutonic Order from 1519 to 1521, although this had more to do with the Teutonic State desperately struggling to secure its national future. Following minor conflicts, the Order had successfully influenced the emperor to impose an imperial ban on Danzig in 1497 and to renew it in 1511, before it was ultimately lifted in 1515. In the end, though, this benefited the Order as little as the war itself did. Danzig placed 600 mercenaries at the royal army's disposal, strengthened its fortifications, and felt well equipped for the still dangerous foe. Near Frankfurt an der Oder, the Teutonic Knights had brought together a mercenary army of 12,000 men, who marched east, turned north to sidestep the Polish army at the Vistula, and set up their camp outside of Danzig at the beginning of November. Nevertheless, the bombardment of the highly fortified city lasted only two days before the army pulled back empty-handed. Danzig's ships harassed the Order on the Baltic over the following year; privateers were also busy, and the Order's grandmaster was forced to realize the hopelessness of the war. He would pay homage to the Polish king Sigismund I the Old four years later and convert his state into the secular, Protestant Duchy of Prussia.

Protest and Reform—A Great City in Upheaval

Danzig was a metropolis. Already among Europe's fifty largest cities in 1454 with its approximately 20,000 residents, it would grow much larger still: 35,000 people lived in the city and its suburbs at the turn of the sixteenth century. A hundred years later, there were over 50,000, and the count at the height of Danzig's development in the mid-seventeenth century was roughly 70,000, a total that the city would not reach again for another 200 years. Around 1650, there was no larger city between Amsterdam and Moscow; even Hamburg and Prague were smaller. Danzig's appeal was so strong that even the immense loss of life in the great plague epidemics could hardly curb the city's growth: an alleged 20,000 people perished in 1549; 15,000 lives were lost in 1564 and again in 1602; and 9,000 died in 1620, as did another 11,000 thousand in 1653. Other illnesses frequently raged in the city as well, although their tolls were not so terrible.

At first, the social stratification remained the same after 1454. The patrician families pulled the strings and were at pains to keep to themselves; they appointed all councilmen and lay judges, withdrew into their magnificent homes inside and outside the city, married among themselves, and convened at exclusive venues like the Artus Court.

The middle class consisted of diverse large- and small-scale merchants, shopkeepers, and artisans. While some owned stately houses, a great number rented meager dwellings and, like many journeymen, had to toil between thirteen and seventeen hours daily. Due to these significant differences, the various groups within the citizenry often pursued entirely opposing interests; yet all of them looked down on the poor classes made up of impoverished skilled workers, day laborers, fishers, peddlers, prostitutes, and beggars.

When taxes increased sharply at the beginning of the Thirteen Years' War, the common people's latent discontent with the patrician-appointed council spilled over. Accusing the council of financial obliquity, the citizens also envied the great profits the war brought to the patriciate. Under the leadership of wealthy merchant Martin Kogge, parts of the citizenry rebelled in autumn 1456 and enforced the election of merchants and artisans to the council. Yet when the costs of war likewise compelled this new council to raise taxes even further, Kogge appealed to the royal governor in Prussia for the council's dismissal. The governor reacted promptly, though not as expected, ordering the execution of seventeen insurgents, including Kogge. The patriciate was again able to exercise its unrestrained influence in the years that followed.

The next catalyst for social unrest was the 1517 collapse of the city's finances, presumably following mismanagement of municipal funds by prominent patrician families. By means of "forty-eight men" (mainly merchants, as well as some guild aldermen), the people enforced a reform of the financial administration and its supervision, though this did not lead to any reduction of taxes. Because of new wars and upgrades needed for its fortifications, Danzig soon required even more money, and as tempers again came to a head, the council had no other option than to concede greater rights to the "forty-eight men."

It was under these circumstances that the first news of the Protestant Reformation reached Danzig and met a warm reception, primarily among the less prosperous citizens. By 1518, the monk Jakob Knade had converted to Lutheranism, and in 1522 Jakob Hegge preached vehemently against the Catholic hierarchy and the existing social order. The people's resentment was directed not least against the egomaniacal mayor Eberhard Ferber, who like other patricians had adopted an aristocratic lifestyle and decisively resisted any oppositional currents. Even Ferber's exile from the city and the confiscation of his fortune failed to assuage the situation, with looting and ultimately riots against the Catholic Church breaking out, particularly against its various religious orders.

The ideas of the Reformation ran rampant in the aftermath and, intensified by social tensions, led to repeated conflicts with the Catholic patriciate and the city's Catholic institutions. In January 1525, renewed unrest ignited when supporters of the radical movement revolted in response to the Franciscan Alexander Svenichen's attempt to preach in St. Mary's Church dressed in his monastic habit. While the protesters' leaders were arrested, a large crowd marched through the city the same day to seize the town hall and topple the council. For many hours, armed supporters of the council faced off against rioters on Long Market until the council had to yield and accept the demands. These ultimately established the Reformation in the city, restricted the monasteries' power, created fairer jurisdiction, prohibited usury, abolished all taxes, and democratized the civic administration through the general election of the council, lay judges, and all officers.

Yet clashes of interest arose immediately. Whereas the poor adhered to their radical positions, the wealthier citizens feared the city's complete disorganization and pursued compromise, successfully changing the council's demographic makeup to the satisfaction of the masses while simultaneously ensuring the hegemony of the propertied classes. Additionally, the citizenry took an oath of loyalty to the word of God, the king, and the city. Yet stirred up by radical clergymen, the public still would not relent; churches were "cleansed" of their images and altars, and weapons were distributed. To restore order, the new council dominated by skilled laborers personally asked Martin Luther to send moderate preachers to Danzig, who arrived soon thereafter.

Meanwhile, King Sigismund I took action and demanded the immediate restoration of the newly superseded social and religious order. Given the monarch's imminent forcible intervention, representatives of the old patrician elite, rich merchants, and the new council agreed to placate the king by inviting him to come to Danzig himself to establish order.

With a retinue of no less than 3,000 people, Sigismund traveled to Marienburg (to Danzig's horror) in March 1526 and made his decorated entrance into the great port city a few weeks later. The king personally led the investigations, and numerous agitators were arrested and ultimately decapitated by sword in July. The monarch proclaimed the Statuta Sigismundi in June, which regulated the relations in the city and would largely endure through the following centuries. Sigismund appointed new councilmen and lay judges, the majority of whom belonged to the old elite, and ordered the institution of a "Third Order," which would represent the people. The Third Order was to consist of 100 citizens named by the council; these consisted primarily of merchants as well as the aldermen representing the four main crafts: smiths, shoemakers, bakers, and butchers. The Catholic faith was reinstated, but since even the patriciate had largely embraced the Reformation, the city of Danzig in reality became a Protestant city. Lutheran preachers were soon active among the remaining Catholic priests, who mostly spent their benefices' earnings outside of the city. Shortly before he left Danzig in July 1526, Sigismund also confirmed the city's existing privileges.

Ships and Statutes: Tensions with Poland

Immediately after taking the Polish throne in 1548, Sigismund II Augustus also confirmed Danzig's privileges. His reign took place in a period of the Reformation's expansion into Poland and Lithuania, of state reform and centralization, and of historical events around the Baltic Sea. Russian tsar Ivan IV Vasilyevich inaugurated a lengthy struggle for command of the Baltic when he invaded Livonia in 1558. Between 1563 and 1570, Poland (including Lithuania) and Denmark found themselves at war against Russia and Sweden; this did not please Danzig at all, given that this conflict was quite detrimental to Baltic trade. Particularly bothersome to the city's merchants, however, were the privateers equipped with Polish letters of marque, who used Danzig's harbor as a base for hunting enemy ships. The privateer captains and crews often hailed from Danzig themselves, and more than a few merchants invested in privateering, since they had to cede a mere 10 percent of their spoils to the Polish king. The burgher Paul Glasgow, for instance, owned shares in twenty-three privateer ships. Because the privateers substantially impeded shipping, though, nations placing special importance on commerce (for instance, Denmark) reacted irascibly and repeatedly confiscated Danzig's ships.

Greater unrest formed in the city when the king, who was determined to improve Poland's chances in the war by assembling a fleet of his own, established a naval commission he hoped to set up in Danzig. The city's anger boiled over, which several sailors from a privateer ship had to learn when, after leaving the harbor in search of food, they attacked and robbed Kashubian marketers. The council immediately had eleven privateers arrested and shortly thereafter decapitated. Nailed to the High Gate, their heads purportedly hung for two years to deter further crimes.

Sigismund Augustus appointed an investigative commission, but, to the king's outrage, the commission arrived at Danzig only to find locked gates. To avoid the worst, but also to secure Danzig's interests against the backdrop of the impending national reforms, the three mayors of Danzig (Georg Klefeld, Konstatin Ferber, and Johann Proite) made their way with councilman Albrecht Giese to the 1569 Diet of Lublin. They stood trial and were convicted and imprisoned for the execution of the privateers.

A new commission dispatched to Danzig under the direction of the bishop of Włocławek, Stanisław Karnkowski, sojourned in the city for four months beginning in 1569. As was so often the case, the city offered to pay compensation and was ready to cede half of the port charges and anchorage dues to the crown. Yet the commission would not let the matter rest there, and in March 1570, it announced the Statuta Karnkoviana, a new constitution for the city with the primary objective of increasing royal power. Mayors and councilmen would henceforth need to swear an oath of loyalty and oath of office to king and kingdom. The constitution furthermore decreed a stronger artisan presence in the Third Order.

Danzig protested. In 1570, the city sent a large delegation to the Diet in Warsaw, but they were unable to accomplish much, and the king confirmed the statutes, albeit with reservations. He also required the city's representatives to beg his forgiveness on their knees. At the beginning of the twentieth century, city historian Paul Simson called this: "A moment of deepest humiliation for them and their city. . . . In its entire history, Danzig had to date never experienced such deep abasement as on that day."[12] It may well have truly felt this way to Danzig's proud citizenry, but from Poland's perspective, it was a decisive step toward unification within the state and elimination of unwanted special rights enjoyed by the powerful city. Nevertheless, Danzig would still manage to have its way between 1577 and 1585. The imprisoned dignitaries sent from Danzig were incidentally released in 1570, and the construction of a royal fleet in Elbing was shut down upon the death of Sigismund Augustus in 1570.

For quite some time, people in Poland and Lithuania had been dissatisfied with the dual kingdom's lack of a constitutional union, as only a personal union bound the two nations. A much tighter integration—a real union—was prepared. In the course of the kingdom's unification and centralization, Royal Prussia's special privileges were also to be annulled. Despite heavy opposition among the Prussian estates, as well as in Danzig, where they feared both a retraction of their religious freedom and increased Polish interference in the city's internal affairs, the Diet in Lublin enacted the complete integration of Royal Prussia, which until then had existed as a protectorate of Poland, into the Polish-Lithuanian Commonwealth in March 1569. Many German historians labeled this "brute force and disdainful breach of law" on the part of the crown.[13] What Paul Simson wrote in his thorough history of Danzig concerning the Polonization that took place in Royal Prussia's rural regions was unfortunately a widely held view in the German east at the turn of the twentieth century: "Polish filth and illiteracy took over everywhere."[14] The splendid, "clean" city of Danzig was represented as a German island surrounded by surging Slavic floods, and modern nationalism was retroactively written into early modernity, a period when languages and mentalities, confessions and loyalties could be disputed, but notions of ethnic superiority were still unknown.

Danzig Stands Up to the King

With Sigismund Augustus, the last Jagiellonian king on the Polish throne died in 1572. The newly enacted elective monarchy presented Polish and Lithuanian nobility in particular with the chance to expand their rights at the expense of the monarchy during interregnum periods and through negotiations with claimants to the throne. Supported by its economic power, Danzig also sought to take advantage of these situations. Sigismund Augustus had barely died when the city refused to perform its obligations stipulated by the Karnkowski Commission until the fulfillment of each of the crown's promises as well as the reversal of recent injustices.

The city persisted in this attitude during the election of 1575. Danzig supported the Habsburg candidate Kaiser Maximilian II, who was sympathetic to the Protestants and who, the city hoped, would not meddle substantially in local affairs from distant Vienna. But two days after Maximilian was elected, another segment of the aristocracy also elected his opponent, the Transylvanian prince Stefan Báthory, who immediately went to Poland and was crowned on May 1, 1576, in Kraków. Impressed by Báthory's initiative, most of Maximilian's supporters quickly changed sides; only Danzig did not, in a gamble to secure the best outcome for itself. In September, Stefan urged the city to give in.

Events unfolded rapidly. To begin with, public opinion in the city was by no means unanimous. The wealthy councilmen had successfully kept the rest of the citizenry from positions of influence since the turmoil of the 1520s. This small group of elites, consisting at the turn of the seventeenth century of about thirty families, not only controlled the city's finances and established "a subservient society ruled by patrician families"[15] but were also Danzig's most economically powerful citizens. They were so prosperous, in fact, that they became less and less inclined to earn money through trade, preferring instead to mimic the lifestyle of Polish nobility. Around 1600, approximately half of Danzig's ruling class owned feudal farm estates.

Emboldened by the Karnkowski Commission's policies against the aristocracy, merchants and artisans in the Third Order demanded stronger involvement in the city's administration, but the council excluded them. Along with the brewers, the butchers were particularly active this time. Embittered by the marked decrease in revenues after the council's order that meat be priced according to weight and no longer at the butchers' discretion, they closed their shops at the end of 1575 and attempted to cut off the city's meat supply. The impending shortage led to the arrest of over eighty master butchers who spent a year in prison.

Báthory, whose demands Danzig had refused, had meanwhile imposed a ban on the city and sent his troops into its vicinity. Agitated by the peasants who had fled there, Danzig's fevered citizenry pillaged the city's three monasteries, accusing the nuns and monks of collusion with Báthory. Negotiations with the king continued, but the council was unable to carry out his demands, which would have amounted to a payment of 300,000 guilders, half of the anchorage dues raised in the harbor, and the surrender of the city's heavy cannons. Persuaded by the merchant Kaspar Göbel, who declared they would not pay the king a single penny, the guilds and soon thereafter the Third Order defied the city council's attempts at reconciliation with the crown. Accusing the patricians of weakness and treason, the people rejected the demands, even after news of Maximillian II's death cemented Báthory's place on the throne.

Báthory had also had enough by this point. He arrested Mayor Konstantin Ferber and the councilman Georg Rosenberg, who had brought him the bad news from the city. The king cracked down on Danzig, prohibiting trade with the city in favor of Thorn and Elbing. His troops and mercenaries caused great turmoil in the area; a war with Danzig seemed inevitable.

The populace reacted with further riots. The mob went to Oliva and attacked, plundered, and destroyed the opulent monastery with its art treasures, then forced the council to promise the citizenry's involvement in the city's financial administration. Enraged by the impending threat of war, the absent trade, the heavy financial strain, the billeting of thousands of mercenaries, and the council's reputed machinations, the people appeared capable of jeopardizing the patriciate's domination.

In its preparations for war, the city had recruited mercenaries, reinforced the fortifications, and strengthened the Weichselmünde (Pol. Wisłoujście) Fortress at the Danziger Haupt (Pol. Głowa Gdańska) headland, where the Vistula's Gdańsk and Elbląg branches diverge. But following months of inaction, the hired soldiers and parts of the city's population grew impatient and sought conflict. On April 16, 1577, without bothering to petition the council beforehand, approximately 10,000 people, about 3,000 of whom were soldiers, marched toward Dirschau (Pol. Tczew), confident of victory and anticipating rich spoils under the leadership of the recruited Colonel Hans Winkelburg von Kölln. Waiting with his troops near Liebschauer (Pol. Lubieszowskie) Lake, however, Polish commander (*hetman*) Jan Zborowski easily routed the attackers from Danzig after a short battle. Twenty-five hundred Danzig combatants died and almost 1,000 more were taken prisoner. They also lost all of their cannons and many wagons and weapons. The council, which had been against the excursion, could renew its authority in light of this defeat, and it once again took charge of organizing the city's defense.

Báthory commenced besieging Danzig in June. He fired on the city for weeks with numerous minor skirmishes breaking out between the warring parties, but he was ultimately at a loss against the outstanding fortifications. Supported by Denmark, which had sent a fleet to the Gulf of Gdańsk, the city defended itself desperately. A Polish attempt to take the powerful Weichselmünde Fortress ended with heavy losses when a gutsy captain broke through a provisional bridge across the Vistula with his ship, leaving several hundred of the king's German mercenaries stranded on the right bank. Danzig's forces almost completely wiped them out.

Alarmed by Tsar Ivan IV's invasion of Livonia, Báthory finally lifted the siege in September 1577 and began peace negotiations with the city. Danzig's citizens used their newly won freedom to punish the city of Elbing for its support of Báthory (as well as its trade rivalry). A large fleet sailed from Danzig into the Vistula Lagoon, pillaged Elbing's storehouses, raided around sixty ships, and returned proudly home two weeks later.

After the city council and citizenry of Danzig had reached an agreement, a German prince finally mediated peace in December 1577. Danzig apologized, paid 200,000 guilders to the king and 20,000 to the Oliva Monastery, and released its mercenaries. Báthory lifted the ban, validated Danzig's privileges, and ensured religious freedom. Eventually, in 1585, an agreement was also reached concerning the anchorage dues, half of which would go to the king. Despite the great financial cost and many lives lost, the war was ultimately a triumph for the city, which preserved its privileges in their entirety and avoided punishment for its opposition. Danzig's heyday would last into the mid-seventeenth century, particularly because the social turmoil had settled and the patriciate had again secured its dominance.

The conflicts of 1576/1577 have preoccupied ensuing generations, who have seen them, depending on the period and perspective, as evidence of a city's grand ascendancy against an entire nation, of Protestant civic society against Catholic overlords, and of "upstanding" Germans against "devious" Poles. Poems, novels, and dramas have celebrated the events. In the early twentieth century, for instance, schoolchildren in Danzig memorized a 1577 song written by Hans Hasentödter:

> O Danzig, hold fast,
> Thou city far-renowned,
> Discern thy best course
> And council not too long.
> With much negotiation
> Things will not be set right.
> The enemy hopes to vex thee,
> Cease therefore thy squabbling
> And take manly courage.[16]

Life in Danzig between Regulation and Celebration

Society in Danzig was anything but homogeneous. Not only did the city house rich and poor, merchants, artisans, and beggars, but also speakers of diverse languages. The vernacular was German, of course, and integration into the citizenry was only possible for those proficient in it. Yet many who had relocated there—mostly servants and suburban residents—had spoken Polish (or Kashubian) from birth. Clergymen held Polish sermons in some of Danzig's Protestant churches. Low German (Plattdeutsch) was prevalent, even if it was increasingly becoming a language of the lower classes.

Life was especially multilingual in the harbor and the merchants' branch offices, where Polish nobles and Dutch and English traders streamed in and out, crossing paths with Swedes, Danes, and Italians. Jews also came to Danzig, even if they, like many other foreigners, generally could not obtain a right of residence—the citizens had reserved that for themselves in the privileges of 1454 and 1457 in order to keep unwanted competition at bay. Jews were permitted to settle outside the city in the areas not belonging to Danzig—for instance, to the south in Alt Schottland (Pol. Stare Szkoty), the village founded by Scottish linen weavers in the fourteenth century.

Despite numerous disputes, religious life in Danzig following the Reformation was generally marked by tolerance, as it was in all of the Polish-Lithuanian Union. Already by the mid-sixteenth century, Protestants far outnumbered Catholics, which the king ultimately also sanctioned in 1557 by granting the religious freedom that Stefan Báthory would reaffirm in 1577. Around 1650, approximately 87 percent of Danzig's residents belonged to the Lutheran confession, almost 6 percent were Calvinists, and about 7 percent were Catholics. As of 1557, Lutheran worship services took place in nearly all of the city's parish and hospital churches, while the Calvinists congregated in the Church of St. Peter and Paul, as well as in St. Elizabeth's Church and occasionally in the Church of the Holy Trinity. Lutherans began to find themselves in bitter disputes with the Calvinists, who had grown stronger near the end of the sixteenth century through immigration from the Netherlands and Scotland and who counted many councilmen among their ranks. Under the pressure of the Counterreformation, these conflicts developed into a complex confrontation between citizenry and city government and did not abate until 1612, when a royal order—which nevertheless was not always enforced—allowed Lutherans to hold public office.

It was not enough that the Protestants quarreled among themselves; the Catholics also tried to win back lost ground. Although they had found themselves on the defensive in Danzig since the Reformation, they had powerful advocates

Figure 4.3 One of the most famous works of Hans Holbein the Younger is a portrait of the Danzig merchant and councilman's son Georg Giese from 1532. The painter portrayed him in the Hanseatic League's London Kontor, called the "Steelyard." Wikimedia Commons.

among the Polish kings, whose visits to the city normally accompanied solemn worship services and efforts to strengthen the position of the Catholic Church. There were still several monasteries in Danzig, and even the Jesuits tried to gain a foothold, though ultimately without success. Until well into the nineteenth century, Catholicism was largely unable to increase its influence and number of adherents.

The most important building block of Danzig's late medieval and early modern society was the family. In many matters, sons followed their fathers as councilmen, artisans, or proprietors of commercial enterprises. The burgher women oversaw home and hearth. Members of the middle class made diverse attempts to insulate their world against the poorer population. Home, clothing, and family celebrations—baptisms, engagements, weddings, and funerals—all lent themselves to a demonstration of affluence. Yet over the centuries, the city's rulers strove to restrict such displays of social polarities. Until the eighteenth century, an ever-increasing number of local laws regulated the breadth of houses, the size of craft enterprises, acceptable clothing for the different classes, and even celebrations, at which only a certain number of guests were permitted, only certain foods consumed, and only certain music played. For engagement parties, by way of example, a 1590 city statute recorded this:

> Furthermore at such a betrothal, and only on the one and same day, shall bride and groom have one table of as many as twelve persons and no more. Thereupon shall also string music and honorable, chaste dances be granted and allowed. The distribution of free beer and other festivities at such betrothals are nevertheless to be entirely restricted and forbidden, all under penalty of ten good marks.[17]

For decades, the motives behind such strict regimentation of bourgeois daily life in the early modern period has been discussed under the heading of social discipline. On the one hand, religious-moral grounds were important for the restrictions, which, according to the Danzig Clothing Statute of 1642, were necessary "for the inhibition of destructive haughtiness and undue pomp in clothing and jewelry," in order to avert "God's punishments from this city."[18] In addition, legislators hoped to stabilize social order and curb individual disorder and even debt among citizens.

Numerous other civic rules and institutions, such as the rigid parochial organization and the guilds, had a disciplinary effect on the society. Infringements were punished in court. The judicature (chiefly the lay judges), however, was busy with entirely different offenses like murder and manslaughter, theft, adultery, blasphemy, and much more. Those convicted of the worst crimes faced public execution, usually by decapitation by sword or hanging from the gallows outside the city. Offenders in less serious cases were banned from the city, corporally punished, sentenced to incarceration and forced labor, or, if only seldom, pilloried.

Like so much else in Danzig—as in contemporary Central European cities in general—clothing was also regulated. According to the Clothing Statute of 1642, laborers and servants were permitted to wear only the lowest priced fabrics; journeymen were at least allowed to decorate their cloaks with a silken cord and display silver keychains; and fabrics costing up to seven Polish marks per

Danzig ell (about 22.75 inches) were permitted to master craftsmen, shippers, and retailers, as well as their wives, who were also allowed to wear modest jewelry. Velvet trim, satin capes, and sable and ermine fur coats were stipulated for brewers, artists, traders of cloth, silk, and spice, and some others. Wholesale merchants had the right to wear the most expensive cloth (up to twelve marks per ell) and gold jewelry. Only councilmen and their families were exempt from such restrictions. Whether on the street or in church, therefore, a Danzig resident's position in the social order was quite simple to distinguish.

In spite of stiff regulation, life in Danzig was by no means marked by tribulation. By contrast, there was always cause for joy and amusement. Things were especially festive when the Polish kings—usually every few years—visited the city. Grand, luxurious, and received with great sympathy by the entire population, they arrived with their large retinue and took up residence in Danzig. Their visits awakened a gregarious vitality seldom seen in the bourgeois city, and the accompanying tournaments, festivals, and musical performances offered plenty of opportunity for interclass socialization between Polish nobility and the wealthy citizens. Things were similarly festive at the annual St. Dominic's Fair (referred to locally as the "Dominic") each August.

Organized into seven fraternal societies (*Bankenbruderschaften*), the upscale bourgeoisie met for celebration and carousing in the widely famous Artus Court, which foreigners also enjoyed frequenting. In 1580, the councilman Salomon Brandt wrote "that for many, especially for seafaring and commercially trading visitors as well as for other prominent people, this house, the praiseworthy Royal Arthur Court, is far preferred and praised above all other drinking rooms and meeting places in almost all of Europe."[19] Soon, the company was no longer exclusive enough for the refined Brotherhood of St. George, which relocated to the newly erected St. George's Court in 1494. Less affluent citizens visited the guild lodges and taverns. The fencing school enjoyed great popularity, as did the marksmen's competitions. Traveling theater companies, which came to the city more frequently—especially to the Dominic—drew large crowds; some troupes even came from Elizabethan England. For the citizens, however, a knowledge of English was less important than a proficiency in Polish, due to the many contacts with Poland in trade and politics, as well as in the private sphere. Parochial schools therefore offered not only Latin, but also Polish instruction, as did the Danzig Secondary School beginning in 1589.

The Secondary School was founded in 1558, began calling itself the "Academic Secondary School" around 1643, and attained a high standard of excellence under notably prominent schoolmasters starting in the late sixteenth century. Almost 6,000 students attended the school between 1580 and 1655, half of whom came from outside Danzig. The school's teachers greatly enriched the merchant city's intellectual life. The Jesuit College, founded in 1621 outside

(a)

Matronæ plebeiæ obsonantes.
Hoc obsonatum pisces carneiq, macello
It plebeia, laris provida, Gdana modo.

Gemein Handwercks Frawen.
Die Handwercks Frawen auch also/
Hertretten in Communio.
Gehn Fleisch vnd Fische zubestellen/
Damit gespeist werd Knecht vnd Gsellen.

Figure 4.4a, b, and c Clothing in Danzig was subject to strict rules. These drawings are by Anton Möller, one of the most important artists in early modern Danzig. From Anton Möller, *Der Dantzger Frawen und Jungfrawen gebreuchliche Zierheit und Tracht* (Danzig, 1601), pages 14, 16, and 24.

Common artisans' wives
Thus the artisans' wives also
Promenade together.
On their way to buy meat and fish
To feed servants and journeymen.

(b)

Matronæ contionem adeuntes.
Templa viasq́, simul Baptismi sacra lavaera
Matrona est longâ Gdana videnda stola.

Frawen zur Kirch gehende.
Zur Kirch vnd Straß die Erbarn Frawn/
Thut man in Danzigk also schawn.
Vnd auch wann sie zu Gvatter stehn/
Sein Erbar gziert so einher gehn.

Ladies on the way to church.
In Gdańsk we see at church and in the streets
Honorable ladies like these.
Likewise when they stand as godmother
Walking refined, decent, and dainty.

(c)

Ladies on a stroll.
Let us go to the new garden
And see how our little roses fare.
We'll gather the rosemary and herbs
And bring home lettuce and cress.

the city in Alt Schottland, likewise contributed to Danzig's growing reputation as a center of education. Wittenberg, Heidelberg, and soon Königsberg also became popular university locations for urban youth after the Reformation.

Danzig was Poland's largest city and had great appeal to the Polish-Lithuanian dual kingdom's population. Visitors from a Central Europe primarily shaped by nobility and a rural peasant society had the opportunity here to become familiar with middle-class lifestyles, to access crafts (and other services) of the highest quality, and to purchase luxury goods. For their part, Danzig's citizens (but also their Dutch, German, or English visitors from the west) mingled with the nobility of the Polish-Lithuanian "Noble Republic" and adopted certain behavioral patterns from the arriving guests dressed in their *kontusze*, the traditional robes of Polish nobility.

Danzig and the Struggle for Sweden

Although Danzig had successfully preserved its exceptional status under Stefan Báthory, political circumstances shifted dramatically after his death in 1586, when Sigismund III Vasa, the son of the Swedish king John III, prevailed in the ensuing election. Reaching the Gulf of Gdańsk with his fleet in late September 1587 and shortly thereafter taking his oath in the Oliva Monastery according to the conditions of the Electoral Diet, he ceremonially arrived in Danzig by boat on October 8 along with his court, entering the city through the Green Gate and accompanied by the thunder of cannon fire. The city wished to show off its best side to the young king, gave him a considerable purse of money upon his departure a few days later, and sent 300 equestrians to accompany him from the city to Praust (Pol. Pruszcz).

The election of a member of the House of Vasa would decisively influence Northern European politics in subsequent decades. The Polish members of the family tried to enforce their claim to the Swedish throne, while the Swedish rulers did everything they could to weaken their Polish cousins. Confessional disputes made matters worse, and as the center of trade, Gdańsk had to weather expectations and demands from all sides.

Raised by Jesuits, the Catholic Sigismund III was heir to the Swedish throne, yet he had to deal with considerable resistance in his already largely Protestant homeland. He gained this inheritance when his father died in 1592, but he had to appoint his Protestant uncle Karl of Södermanland as regent in Sweden and return to Poland. A civil war soon raged between the two parties in Sweden, with Sigismund suffering a disastrous defeat in 1598. Karl was elected king of Sweden in 1604, and hostilities shifted to Polish-owned Livonia, which Sigismund was able to defend against Sweden—until he ensnared Poland in wars with Russia.

Multiple conflicts arose during Sigismund's occasional visits to Danzig during these years. A dispute over St. Mary's Church broke out in 1593, when Hieronim Rozrażewski, bishop of Włocławek, brought the city to trial for the church's return to the Catholics. On his way to Sweden that summer, Sigismund stayed in the city for several weeks and, swayed by the bishop, he demanded Catholic masses in his presence in the main parish church. The city's three civic

Orders unanimously refused, but the citizenry, fearing further restrictions for Protestants, became so stirred up that a harmless quarrel between two of the king's servants—one Polish and one German—escalated into a massive riot; shots were fired, and bullets even whistled through the windows of the royal residence on Long Market.

But the judicial proceedings continued, and at the end of 1594, a royally validated verdict was issued that the city surrender the church to the bishop under threat of a penalty of 100,000 florins. The residents of Danzig appealed the decision to the Polish parliament and accused Rozrażewski of breaching the freedom of religion established in Poland. While these efforts were unsuccessful, they found support among Protestant nobles as well as with the papal nuncio in Poland, who reciprocated for grain shipments from Danzig that had greatly aided the Papal State in the midst of a crop failure years earlier. Ultimately, Danzig's skillful maneuvering repeatedly postponed the surrender of St. Mary's Church long enough for the issue to simply fade away.

The citizens fought just as fiercely against another of Sigismund's wishes, namely, to establish the Jesuit Order in Danzig. For many years, they did everything they could to impede the king's decreed transfer of the Bridgettine convent to the Societas Jesu, fearing that this key player in the Counterreformation would also endanger Protestantism in their city.

While conflicts intensified over control of Sweden and the Baltic Sea, the lack of a Polish navy proved a great disadvantage in the face of Swedish dominance on the high seas. As Poland's largest port, Danzig would always play an important role in the king's aspirations for a fleet; yet to protect its commercial interests, the city did its best to remain as neutral as possible in political and martial affairs. In 1598, the king (with the city council's endorsement) confiscated about sixty foreign ships in the harbor for his passage to Sweden. At the beginning of the seventeenth century, he had new ships constructed in Danzig for a fleet, and Polish and Danish privateers were also active in the harbor. All of this attracted more Swedish warships, to the detriment of the city's commerce.

In 1623, after years of cease-fire, conflict rekindled. Meanwhile Gustavus Adolphus had inherited the Swedish throne. Just as Sigismund arrived in Danzig with his large entourage in late June, his Swedish cousin appeared on the Gdańsk Roadstead with twenty ships and 4,000 soldiers. The frightened city feared for its free trade and tried to prevent the formation of a Polish fleet.

Gustavus Adolphus captured Pillau (present-day Baltiysk, Russia) outside of Königsberg in summer 1626 before marching from there toward Danzig. He continued to demand strict neutrality from the city, and when Danzig hesitated, he had his troops plunder the delta and local rural areas as well as capture the Weichselmünde Fortress. This even embittered the Swedish king's supporters in Danzig, and when the city declared an end to negotiations, Gustavus

Adolphus declared war. In anticipation of further hostilities, Danzig improved its fortifications, enlisted mercenaries, and asked Sigismund for help.

The Polish king actually came to Danzig, but only to appoint a royal naval commission (without the city leaders' knowledge), whose goal was to create a fleet in Danzig's harbor. Although the city again responded with a delaying tactic, a fleet ultimately formed under the leadership of Arndt Dickmann, a Danzig merchant who had been appointed admiral. The fleet even celebrated a victorious battle against a Swedish squadron near Oliva on November 28, 1627.

The Polish-Swedish war in the Vistula estuary region wore on unresolved until 1629. Pressured by Danzig (and others), whose trade suffered heavily from the battles, both warring parties finally held negotiations and signed a cease-fire on September 26 in Altmark (Pol. Stary Targ) near Stuhm (Pol. Sztum). The agreement stipulated, among other things, that a port tariff of 5.5 percent would be imposed in Danzig, 3.5 percent of which would go to the Swedish crown as well as 1 percent each to Danzig and Poland; additionally, Swedish troops would remain stationed in the Vistula delta. The tariff revenues Sweden had negotiated for itself made up more than half of the Swedish state income over the following years, yet they were ultimately not high enough to substantially hinder trade in Danzig.

When Sigismund III died in 1632, his son Władysław IV succeeded him on the Polish throne. Danzig did not object to the election, especially as the city was in a good position to exploit the king's financial woes for its own gain. The young monarch first prepared to resume the war with Sweden, and during his stay in Danzig at the end of 1634, he emulated his predecessors by setting about constructing a Polish fleet. The "Commission for Sea-going Vessels" soon controlled ten ships but was reduced first to inaction when a Swedish fleet blockaded the port, and then to irrelevance when Sweden and Poland extended the cease-fire by twenty-six years on August 15 in Stuhmsdorf (Pol. Sztumska Wieś), not far from Danzig.

This treaty did not mention the matter of the tariffs in Danzig (which had expired in 1635), yet these tariffs would define the political relations between Poland and its most important port city over the next two decades. Władysław could not resist the temptation and in early 1636 established a tariff of 3.5 percent, but when all three of Danzig's civic orders expressed their outrage, the Polish king ultimately (and for a large sum of money) decided against the lucrative source of revenue. Yet already in 1637, Polish nobles, hoping to avoid higher taxes themselves, imposed a new nautical toll to be collected beginning in autumn by three ships posted outside the Danzig harbor. Danzig's furious citizens closed the harbor, sent embassies abroad to request assistance, and prepared for a siege; but on December 1, four Danish ships entered the Gulf of Gdańsk, and their crews effortlessly overpowered the three ships, thereby essentially abolishing the new tariffs. The calm would not even last twenty years, though. The disastrous war between Sweden and Poland that would break out in 1655 would prove an enormous hardship for Danzig and usher in the proud merchant city's decline.

Nerve Center of Arts and Science

In the two centuries that elapsed between 1454 and 1655, Danzig transformed from a medieval city into an early modern metropolis, into a hub not only of economic life, but also of the arts. Rich, mighty, and proud, Danzig stood at the pinnacle of its development. As the largest city far and wide, it dominated economic activity while also playing a preeminent role for the entire region as a facilitator for transferring cultural and artistic innovations from the civilizing centers of the time (primarily Italy, the Netherlands, and German lands) to Eastern-Central and Northeastern Europe.

Council and citizenry alike were well aware of Danzig's prominent position. They endeavored to demonstrate their power and wealth symbolically, for which purpose the arts, particularly architecture, were best suited. The great public buildings erected in the late sixteenth and early seventeenth centuries sent a clear message. In the style of the Dutch Renaissance (also known as Nordic mannerism), they projected affluence, civic pride, and self-assurance. Danzig, where numerous Dutch builders were active and graphic models from the Netherlands were diligently studied and copied, became a unique center for this style within a few decades.

To approach the city around 1650 was an impressive experience, whether from the north, west, south, or east; the walls that had surrounded it on all sides had long been removed and replaced by green ramparts, even if work was still under way here and there in anticipation of new wars that the citizens saw approaching. Only four gates embedded in the ramparts allowed entry into the city, the most important of which was the monumental High Gate located in the west. Constructed in the 1570s by Hans Kramer, it was richly ornamented in 1588 by Dutchman Wilhelm van den Blocke, who based the design on styles from Antwerp—a clear signal to any Polish king entering the city through this gate when he came in representation of the Noble Republic. Elaborate coat-of-arms reliefs above the three openings greeted visitors: angels held Poland's coat of arms in the center; on the right, Danzig's coat of arms was borne by lions; on the left, supported by unicorns, was that of Royal Prussia. This trio was prevalent in Danzig and symbolized the city's three loyalties, while the attached Latin inscription expressed its desires. From Poland, for instance, the city expected justice and piety (*Justitia et pietas duo sunt regnorum omnium fundamenta*), and

Danzig itself was to strive for peace, liberty, and harmony (*Civitatibus haec optanda bona maxima: pax, libertas, concordia*).

Upon passing the High Gate, visitors came to a sight that dominated the cityscape: the Prison Tower and Torture Chamber. While at its core still medieval, this complex was developed in Renaissance style in the late sixteenth century and served as a prison. Beyond these, visitors pass Coal Market to the left and cross the magnificent Long Street Gate (today's Golden Gate), built between 1612 and 1614 by Wilhelm's son Abraham van den Block(e) in the place of a Gothic gate that no longer struck the city fathers as prestigious enough. As of 1648, the ornately designed façades furnished with columns bore eight allegorical statues: those on the western side symbolized peace, liberty, wealth, and glory, as the city most wished to represent itself outwardly; those on the eastern side, facing into the city, exhorted the citizens to prudence, piety, justice, and harmony.

Over the course of the previous two centuries, the Main Town had largely transformed into a city of stone. To protect the city from fire, the 1455 edition of *Danziger Willkür* decreed:

> Also shall nobody make buildings in a manner other than cementing with lime or laying of bricks; whosoever has constructed walls or gables with boards, though he has already completed them, shall tear them down and pay five good marks.[20]

The townhouses in Danzig, such as those lining both sides of Long Street just behind the Long Street Gate, mostly followed a certain pattern. Larger homes had three window axes while the smaller houses had two. Façades were austere in the Gothic period but decorated with miscellaneous ornamentation in the Renaissance. The terraces (*Beischläge*) in front of the buildings evolved into splendidly arranged decorative pieces with fanciful gargoyles and elaborate works from stonecutters and smiths.

Grand Renaissance apartment buildings arose on Long Street, one of the city's most prominent thoroughfares. Among these were the Adam and Eve House (1560) with its allegoric reliefs, or the Lion's Castle (1569) which boasted lions crowning the entry into its lavish interior. Entrance halls, illuminated through windows that frequently reached over fifteen feet in height, were usually located behind these buildings' façades. Curved staircases led to the higher floors where the apartments were located, while commercial branches took up the ground floor.

The Main Town's city hall still stood at the end of Long Street, at the corner of Long Market. Shortly after Danzig's transition to Poland in 1454, construction began on the eastern gable, which has remained until the present, and this was soon followed by a tall tower. The edifice was expanded, partially in Renaissance style, after a fire in 1556; the impressive slender cupola still marks the skyline today.

The city hall's interior also underwent significant changes. Inspired by Venice and other Italian cities, influential citizens implemented a redesign of the representatives' chambers, which began in 1593. For the Red Room, where the council met in summer, Wilhelm van der Meer constructed a magnificent fireplace. Hans Vredeman de Vries began decorating the walls and ceiling in 1594, but soon the Flemish painter's work was no longer good enough for the civic elite, who commissioned Isaak van den Blocke in 1606 to create the ceiling artwork. He presumably drew from the ceiling of the senate chamber in the Venetian Doge's Palace as a model: on each ceiling, smaller images and richly carved borders surround the central painting, an oval apotheosis of the respective city. In the center of this painting in Danzig, the city's silhouette is visible on a triumphal arch. In the foreground, a local merchant and a Polish noble shake hands in the midst of a large crowd in front of the stately Artus Court. River barges loaded with grain float down the Vistula River toward Danzig from the right, while seagoing ships leave the city to the left. This picture, also called *Allegory of Danzig Commerce*, portrays the city's wealth, as well as the sources of that fortune—the Vistula, the harbor, an amicable understanding with Poland, and the self-assured citizens, but also the goodwill of a higher power: a provident hand reaches out of the clouds to surround the city hall's cupola.

Neptune's Fountain, constructed in 1633 outside the city hall on Long Market, also followed Italian models and attests to the city's sought-after connection with antiquity, since such monumental fountains from the time are regarded as direct influences from the ancient world. The fountain would become another of the city's emblems and is located in front of the Artus Court, which after a fire in 1476 was reconstructed with a grand hall supported by columns. It received a Renaissance-style façade in the mid-sixteenth century, along with an interior adorned with numerous works of art, including large paintings, statues, wood carvings, and model ships. The nearly forty-foot-tall Renaissance cockle stove built in 1545 has gained particular fame. At the beginning of the seventeenth century, Mayor Johann Speimann commissioned the construction of his splendid, luxuriously decorated house—known both as the Steffenshaus and the Golden House (Polish: Złota kamienica)—directly adjacent to the Artus Court.

Sometimes referred to as a total work of art (*Gesamtkunstwerk*), Long Market was the most important public space in the city and served to display the power of the middle class. The city's construction program also included the Green Gate, built at the end of the market between 1564 and 1568; as the old, Gothic-era Cog Gate at the same location no longer represented the city authorities' prestigious aspirations, it was replaced with the newer gate, which was the first local large-scale Renaissance construction. Behind the Green Gate, the Green Bridge crosses to the densely crowded storehouses on Granary Island.

Running parallel to the most significant urban thoroughfare of Long Street and Long Market were other major streets, lined partly with opulent, ornamented patrician houses, and partly with narrow houses of less affluent citizens. Although some of the homes still bore Gothic features, they more often boasted cambered Renaissance gables. From the sea of houses rose the churches,

Figure 4.5 Danzig's Apotheosis, also called the "Allegory of Danzig Commerce," is a masterpiece by Isaak van den Blocke from the beginning of the seventeenth century. It clearly depicts the sources of local wealth: the procurement of goods and services between Poland and the Western world. This section shows the Motława's influx into the Vistula. From Herder-Institut, Marburg, Germany.

the most prominent of which was St. Mary's. The city's most significant church underwent substantial expansion in the second half of the fifteenth century. Furnished with larger side aisles, a taller tower, and magnificent arches, it was the pride of the citizens for centuries. In his description from the early seventeenth century, Dominican monk and Danzig native Martin Gruneweg ranked it alongside St. Mark's Basilica in Venice:

> As glorious, then, as the Venetian parish church is, not far behind it is Danzig's, which the people in Poland and other lands know to call simply the Great Church, and which they, like all others, deem beautiful and rich ... [a] virtuous earthly paradise.... Where can one see fairer carvings than on her high altars? ... Where are lovelier crucifixes and monuments on display than in this church?[21]

Truly, Danzig went to great lengths to furnish the interior of this house of prayer. The construction of the high altar "abounding with gold and rich in forms"[22] between 1510 and 1517 under the direction of Master Michael von Augsburg was especially painstaking. A great many other altars, a Crucifixion group, headstones, and the astronomical clock created between 1464 and 1470 by Hans Düringer all complemented these fixtures.

Similar to St. Mary's, other churches also changed in appearance. While some changes were exterior (St. Bridget's Church gained a lovely tower and the Church of the Holy Trinity was enhanced with filigree western gables), most were interior: St. John's Church acquired a sandstone and marble high altar designed by Abraham van den Blocke along with a valuable organ and an equally prized pulpit. Additionally, a gilded high altar graced the Catholic monastery's Church of St. Nicholas, and many churches' naves became vaulted in the late fifteenth and early sixteenth centuries.

In addition to fortifications, Danzig also needed weapons for its defense. For storage, the city constructed the Great Arsenal between 1601 and 1609. With its lavishly decorated façades, it is a masterpiece of Nordic mannerism. Whereas the arsenal only provided storage, the Weichselmünde Fortress was a quintessential defensive structure. Developing from a brick tower built north of the city center in 1482, a large fortress secured by ramparts and moats grew just upriver from the Vistula estuary over the next two centuries.

Yet life in Danzig was not all sunshine and roses. The narrow lanes were loud and overcrowded, wastewater flowed in open ditches to the Motława with the lingering stench of refuse and sewage, handicraft businesses polluted the air, and there was not much visible greenery. Infectious diseases, especially during the warm season, were a substantial danger to the populace. Danzig's wealthy families therefore took to travelng to the surrounding areas during summer months. Whoever could afford it acquired a summer residency—for instance, in villages bordering the city to the north, such as Langfuhr (Pol. Wrzeszcz), Strieß (Pol. Strzyża), Oliva, and Zoppot (Pol. Sopot); many patrician families leased entire royal estates. Mayor Konstantin Ferber, who had inherited his father Eberhard's inclination toward a luxurious lifestyle, was no exception, and since he was especially rich, he purchased an especially large area of land. In 1555, he even founded his own village south of the city (present-day Niegowo), which he named Konstantinopel (later shortened to Nobel by inhabitants).

By no means was artistic life in Danzig expressed solely in ambitious construction projects, though. Initially, the visual arts mainly subsisted on ecclesiastical commissions, as is still apparent today in the city's great altars but also in the gold and silver monstrances (liturgical vessels) and countless paraments (valuable liturgical hangings). The well-known artists in Danzig included the Flemish van den Block(e) family of artists, whose members made names for themselves in Danzig as sculptors and painters; painter Hans Vredeman de Vries from Friesland, who spent some time in Danzig; and Hermann Hahn, who gained recognition primarily because of his works for the Oliva Monastery and the Pelplin Abbey. Painter Anton Möller also won notable fame. He spent almost his entire adult life in Danzig and created great paintings while also recording scenes from everyday life in his *Danziger Trachtenbuch* (Danzig fashion book).

The skilled crafts also flourished, with a peak extending even past the mid-seventeenth century. Goldsmith Peter van der Rennen, for instance, received the assignment of a lifetime when commissioned to create a shrine for the reliquaries of St. Adalbert, the patron saint of Poland, in the Gniezno Cathedral. Medal engravers Johann Höhn (father and son) were also among the most esteemed representatives of their craft, and their memorial medals honoring the Polish kings remain highly sought-after collector items. Amber turners, bell founders, metalsmiths, and organ builders also earned great recognition.

The city held music in high esteem; many outstanding musicians worked for the church orchestras, composing as well as performing musical works there, in the Artus Court, in the guild lodges, or at family celebrations. The orchestra of St. Mary's Church was particularly important, as it both played sacred music and performed for the city at official events. As early as the mid-sixteenth century, the city council appointed eminent musicians as choirmasters in St. Mary's Church, including Andreas Hakenberger, whose motets and madrigals still enjoy high regard.

The prosperous city was uniquely attractive for intellectual life in Eastern-Central and Northeastern Europe. Many of the citizenry's sons had notable careers, like humanist and poet Johannes Dantiscus, who rose to serve as an advisor to Polish kings and became the bishop of Chełmno and Warmia. The city council sought to place well-educated men in its employ to be prepared when the city needed delicate political negotiations. Among these was Caspar Schütz, who began his service as council secretary in 1564 and, shortly before the end of his life, wrote a chronicle of Prussia, the *Wahrhafte Beschreibung der Lande Preussen* (Authentic account of the Prussian lands). Reinhold Curicke was also the secretary for the city council; he wrote his groundbreaking work *Der Stadt Dantzig historische Beschreibung* (Historical account of the city of Danzig) between 1638 and 1642, but it could not be published until 1687 due to the council's concerns that the book could exacerbate the religious tensions in Danzig.

Many writers and scientists were teachers in the Danzig Secondary School, such as theologian Bartolomäus Keckermann, as well as Joachim Pastorius, who had garnered recognition with his historical works. Because the chaos of the Thirty Years' War did not engulf Danzig, the city was also an attractive residence for such a highly regarded poet as Martin Opitz. This imperial poet laureate from Lower Silesia settled there in 1636 as secretary and historiographer for the Polish king Władysław IV. While Opitz escaped the war, though, he was not able to avoid the plague raging in the area, to which he fell victim in 1639. The Secondary School drew many gifted students to the city, such as Andreas Gryphius (in Danzig from 1634 to 1636), who would later become a celebrated poet and playwright, and the poet Christian Hoffmann von Hoffmannswaldau, who received his secondary education there between 1636 and 1638.

Literary life in Danzig was not limited to these few authors but consisted of a large number of writers who took up their quills for the most diverse reasons. When visiting the city from time to time, Polish monarchs received stacks of poems greeting and praising them, and occasional poetry was composed for weddings, birthdays, and the deaths of significant local personalities. The printing presses generated countless fliers, leaflets, calendars, and books, as well as—beginning in 1618—newspapers that filled the shelves of Danzig's municipal library. The library was founded in 1596 after Giovanni Bernardino Bonifacio, the Neapolitan marquess d'Oria who had become stranded in Danzig after a shipwreck, donated his books to the city. At times, the activity of authors and printers, combined with the development of the library's collection, made Danzig the most important news hub in Northeast Europe.

When the baroque poet Georg Greblinger came to Danzig in 1646, he wrote an extensive poem about this city at the height of its power. He named his composition "Das blühende Danzig" (Danzig in bloom) and concluded it with the following four sanguine lines:

> Now fare thee well, O Danzig, continue in thy blossoming,
> May God in grace deter all that would hope to obscure thee
> As would a cloud, and may God keep in thee a place
> Where, with delight, one may obtain a refuge sure.[23]

Amid this flourishing urban culture, almost nobody could have suspected how rapidly Danzig's prosperity would end.

5

Fading Hues, 1655–1793

Earlier, Herr Schmieden said, the sky over our city was still strong and blue, and there was a lush green around the city, and the red was so bright. But now, he went on, as you have said (and rightly so), to you, there seems to be no more luster in Danzig.

He paused in silence.

Earlier, Schmieden then continued, every new year was a year of sunshine, and every new year seemed to increase fortune and wealth; but now, every new year is a year of clouds and storms, and the rain washes away the colors, and the frost crumbles the plaster until it falls from the façades, and thus you perceive that which you have already expressed and which, as you have seen, so aggrieves me: proud Danzig is fading.

The Centuries Subsist on the Golden Age

Danzig's "golden age" came to an abrupt end in the second half of the seventeenth century. While the radiance faded, it would continue to color the populace's memories until the present. The magnificent edifices from the Gothic and Renaissance periods remained in citizens' minds, as did the Renaissance and Baroque townhouses that lined the great streets of the Main Town and Old Town. After its harmonious development in the Middle Ages and early modernity, however, this image of the city was becoming increasingly jeopardized by demolition and modernization in the nineteenth century, and then by ruin and obliteration in 1945. In the 1930s, German historic preservationists made efforts to dismantle the architecture of the preceding century to enable the presentation of Danzig as "an archetypal medieval German city."[1] When this "archetype" had been reduced to rubble, Polish architects of the post-war reconstruction had a similar objective, namely, to rebuild "the old Gdańsk from the time of its bloom in the sixteenth and seventeenth centuries, when it was at its most beautiful"[2]—and when the city belonged to Poland.

The impressions left by this "golden age" are still clear in the city and its elite today. In 2009, the city's official web page proclaimed, "Rich and prestigious Gdańsk—a city of many nationalities, diverse cultures, religions, and languages, the most international city of the Polish-Lithuanian Republic—was a community of singular diversity." The city has continued to regard itself precisely within this same continuity: "History has come full circle. Today's Gdańsk pulses with life as it did then and continually refines its own identity in commemoration of its past."[3]

Today, moreover, when the mayor and council members don their early modern robes for ceremonial events, they would happily turn their gaze to the past and cite the Baroque author Johann Rist, who wrote of Danzig in 1662:

> If one furthermore diligently considers the breastworks of this royally glorious city and its walls and ramparts, the notable houses of its citizens and the public buildings together with the abundant artistry and craftsmanship used in their creation, and likewise the broad and mighty harbor with the great number of ships found there at all times, and when one also diligently considers the well-ordered political and civic government along with the great stock of gunpowder always found there, then Danzig may well be counted one of the seven wonders of the world.[4]

End of the Heyday: Sweden's War against Poland

A commercial city like Danzig relied on peace, for only in peacetime was an unhindered movement of goods possible and mercantile risk manageable. Military conflict certainly presented individual merchants with great opportunities for profit, but the city and the bulk of its citizens suffered. The people in Danzig were especially glad that their city, in contrast to neighboring Pomerania, remained largely spared from the Thirty Years' War. The citizens all anxiously followed the events that began to develop in the distant southeastern lands of the Polish-Lithuanian Commonwealth in 1648. The uprising of the Zaporozhian Cossacks against their Polish overlords grew into a destructive war in which Cossacks and Tatars fought fiercely against the Polish army. Neighboring powers did not stand by idly but rather exploited this weakening of Poland. Russia occupied large regions of Lithuania in 1654, and the new Swedish king Charles X Gustav shortly thereafter deemed the time right to redefine Sweden's Pomeranian and Livonian assets and permanently shake Poland's position as an Eastern-Central European great power. When Sweden marched into Lithuania and Poland in 1655 and unleased the First Northern War, the Polish army offered hardly any resistance, and King John II Casimir Vasa fled the country at the end of September.

But Danzig remained steadfastly on the side of the Polish-Lithuanian Noble Republic, to which it owed over two centuries of wealth. Having recruited soldiers and perfected its great wreath of defensive walls under the direction of a Dutch fortress architect, the city was well prepared as the Swedish king invaded and largely occupied Royal Prussia with the help of troops from the Prince Elector in Brandenburg. The much-feared siege of Danzig did not occur, but as a precaution, the city council had the suburbs not belonging to the city burned down—this was, from the perspective of many citizens (and especially artisans), also one of the war's positive side effects in that it rid them, at least temporarily, of unwanted competition. Charles again neared Danzig in mid-1656 and began preparations to besiege the city, but the citizens flooded the delta to the southwest, forcing the attackers to retreat. All the same, the Swedes possessed numerous points of strategic importance, including—as of 1626—the headland at Danziger Haupt.

Danzig could rely on foreign support, and a Dutch-Danish fleet accordingly lifted the Swedish blockade of the harbor in 1656. This cooperation grew tenuous as Danzig merchants wished to protect themselves from their Dutch competitors and were unwilling to concede privileges to them in the city. Yet Danzig's own forces also proved sufficient; the city still possessed the financial means to sustain a force of up to 12,000 armed men composed of mercenaries and citizens.

Strengthened by an alliance with the Crimean Tatars, a cease-fire with the Cossacks, and Russian attacks against the Swedes in Livonia, Poland had meanwhile regained control of a large part of the Commonwealth. The Polish king made his way to Danzig in mid-November 1656 and stayed there through the following February. Emboldened by the royal attention, Danzig's troops sallied forth on several campaigns in 1657, including across the frozen Vistula Lagoon to Frauenburg (Pol. Frombork) and Tolkemit (Pol. Tolmicko). The Swedes retaliated with an attempt to direct the Vistula floods into the city. The situation worsened again in 1659, when a Swedish army marched into Royal Prussia and approached Danzig. Polish and Austrian troops, as well as forces from Brandenburg and Danzig, effectively repulsed the attack, and Danzig's soldiers were even able to reconquer Danziger Haupt shortly before Christmas. Peace negotiations began soon thereafter in Oliva, and—hastened by the death of Charles—they concluded with the Peace of Oliva on May 3, 1660. This settled relations between Poland and Sweden and confirmed the sovereignty of the Prince Elector of Brandenburg in the Duchy of Prussia, which had hitherto been a Polish fiefdom.

It was a dearly purchased peace, for both the Commonwealth and Danzig. Trade had been severely impaired and revenue cut off through the occupation and destruction of the surrounding country, and the city had to take out loans to cover the considerable costs of fortification efforts, mercenary upkeep, and acquisition of military equipment. The war expenses have been projected at the enormous sum of 5 million guilders, 3 million of which had to be drawn from the local money market. The king and parliament promised to reimburse this amount to the city, but although Danzig repeatedly brought up the issue, the Polish state was in chronic financial straits and never in a position to pay.

Danzig's Position in the Land

Danzig's political status remained complicated until the end of the eighteenth century, a period that has never received comprehensive scholarly attention. As the Noble Republic's largest city and a proud middle-class community, Danzig relied on shrewd politics vis-à-vis the central powers, in particular the king and the parliament. As long as the city's financial situation was bright, it had more than just good arguments at its disposal. With earnings in good years rivaling those of the crown and the entire Commonwealth, Danzig was often able to influence decisions in its favor through payments to the king and important representatives of church and state, as well as gifts such as wine, oysters, oranges, lemons, fish, and gold jewelry to Warsaw.

Danzig honored newly elected kings with bell-ringings, sermons, fireworks, addresses, and poems; it pledged allegiance to them, however, only after it had verified its city privileges. For this cause, royal commissaries traveled to the Motława to receive the oath of allegiance from the three civic orders in the city hall, whereupon the assembled citizens on Long Market would remove their hats, raise their arms, extend two fingers on their right hands, and repeat the oath. As a rule, kings visiting the city were solemnly greeted with parades, triumphal arches, poems of praise, church services, and festive meals; for a king's first visit, the city minted memorial coins. Some kings came multiple times, while others kept their distance. The kings had the right to intervene in Danzig's inner workings and to pass laws.

The king's representatives in Danzig were the burgrave (still little more than an honorary office); a commissary overseeing tariff revenues in the customs house; a Polish-Saxon ambassador (beginning at the turn of the eighteenth century); and later, a commissary general. For its part, Danzig had a clerk in Warsaw who resided at the "Danzig Court" belonging to the city, informed the council about events in the capital, and advocated the city's interests. The king did not possess a palace in Danzig, but three buildings on Long Market were placed at his disposal for the duration of his visits.

Over time, the king began to engage more frequently with events in Danzig, especially as conflicts arose among the citizens in the seventeenth and eighteenth centuries. The parliament, on the other hand, only rarely concerned itself with affairs there. Danzig continued to abide by the conviction that it was subject only to the king and not to the Noble Republic itself (and thus the parliament). In his work *Ius publicum civitatis Gedanensis*, which highlighted local inherent rights in particular, Danzig's great eighteenth-century lawyer and historian Gottfried Lengnich nevertheless admitted: "Whether or not Danzig is able to recognize the Polish Republic's sovereignty, the city is still united with the republic and stands in a certain obligation toward it."[5] Danzig was thereby entitled to take part in the royal elections at electoral assemblies, a right that the city made a point of holding, even if it seldom exercised it. Still, the city leaders in Danzig closely followed political developments in the Noble Republic, and the city was usually represented in parliament by a syndic or sub-syndic. Yet Danzig also developed its own pride in its freedom, a veritable ideology of liberty to which the city would cling even more tenaciously the weaker it—and Poland—became.

The political situation in the province of Royal Prussia changed after 1569, when its cities lost their autonomous rights. With two permanent representatives in Royal Prussia's highest administrative body, the Prussian Council, Danzig had until then held significant sway and was determined to retain its influence under the altered conditions of the real union between Poland and Lithuania. Danzig (like its Prussian sister cities Thorn and Elbing) was present with two emissaries at the General Diet, the assembly composed almost entirely of nobles and usually convoked in Marienburg or Graudenz (Pol. Grudziądz). Occasionally—such as in 1658 or 1710—the General Diet even convened in the city on the Motława. Danzig also influenced political life in the Polish-Lithuanian Commonwealth by electing delegates (*Landboten*) to represent its interests in parliament. Yet collaboration with the far more numerous nobles in the parliament was not always easy. As with the Polish parliament in the eighteenth century, the Prussian General Diet often came to an abrupt end due to the objection of only a few delegates (*liberum veto*), and as it therefore frequently could not reach a proper resolution, the Diet's potential for political instrumentality suffered.

Social Protest and Political Reform

Sweden's war against Poland, the First Northern War, had economically crippled Danzig. The golden age was lost beyond recognition as stagnation replaced prosperity. Population growth ceased, and the number of inhabitants settled at around 60,000 for the next century. Beginning in the 1670s, the waning economic activity and the implementation of necessary new levies and taxes in light of regressing public revenue gave repeated rise to great vexation, protest, and uproar on the part of artisans and merchants.

As always, the city's population was distinctly stratified. There was, for one, the division of residents with civil liberties from those without them. Whoever hoped to become a citizen had to "be born free and within wedlock, and must verify both, if he seeks citizenship."[6] Yet only about one-tenth of the population possessed this citizenship. Beginning in the second half of the seventeenth century, distinctions arose among the civil rights for merchants, artisans, and laborers. Obtaining citizenship meant reaching deep into one's pockets; it was the most expensive for merchants (the cost of citizenship from 1644 onward was between 1,000 and 3,000 guilders), but they were also the only people who pursued a career profitable enough to afford it. Due to their office, some residents were entitled to honorary citizenship; these included preachers, professors at the Academic Secondary School, physicians, civil officers, and certain other professional categories. Harbor workers, servants, journeymen and apprentices, and beggars and transient workers generally did not possess citizenship.

Only citizens enjoyed rights of political participation, and even then only indirectly by means of the guilds, the assemblies of the four city districts, or the Third Order. The First Order, the council, consisted in the eighteenth century of twenty-three councilmen (*consules*) and four mayors (*proconsules*): the presiding mayor, the deputy mayor, the chief constable, and the wartime mayor. Each mayor was also responsible for a part of the municipal territory. Moreover, every councilman oversaw a specific sector of the administration. In addition to a stately base salary, these lucrative offices offered numerous means of further revenue and contributions: the member overseeing the rural areas belonging to the city, for instance, could expect regular gifts of fresh poultry.

The council usually co-opted its members from the Second Order, the committee of lay judges, with a judge belonging to the council presiding over this group of twelve members. The lay judges administered justice at their assemblies in the Artus Court, but only for the Main Town; a separate court of lay judges existed in the Old Town. Some legal matters fell into the mayors' jurisdiction, and the court of arbitration handled infringements of police regulations. The Third Order was made up of 100 lifetime members appointed by the council, although its composition became the object of acrimonious debate; the annual day of selection in March, when seats that had become vacant from councilmen's deaths were newly filled, was regarded a city holiday. The Third Order was subdivided into four quarters: the Cog Quarter, the High Quarter, the Broad Quarter, and the Fishers' Quarter. But civic business was not administered exclusively by the three Orders; professional civil officials did that as well. Paid barely enough to get by, between six and eleven clerks serving under each syndic looked after Danzig's ongoing affairs.

Protests arose repeatedly against the city's rigid distribution of power. Artisans demanded better representation in the Third Order; merchants wanted greater agency in the council; all citizens envied the lordly incomes of the councilmen while simultaneously working to safeguard their own civil privileges from non-citizens inside and outside the city. Internal and external disputes presented opportunities to sway the council to concessions, as seen during the war against Sweden in the 1650s, when, in order to obtain the citizens' approval of the massive expenditures to finance the military, the council conceded to allow participation in the administration of the city and its resources to all three civic orders. Also hoping to benefit from the situation, the guilds, whose members were suffering under the difficult financial circumstances, sought support from the king and petitioned the council to put a stop to the activities of so-called bunglers, or workers not belonging to the guilds, and other such nuisances. The guilds also desired the right to trade their own finished and semi-finished products, a privilege which until then had been reserved for the merchants alone. However, the skilled laborers saw only limited success in these initial attempts.

Social tensions in Danzig increased anew beginning around 1673/1674, intensified by confessional disputes known as the "Strauch Religious Quarrels." These quarrels were sparked by Aegidius Strauch, who had come from Wittenberg and served both as the Lutheran pastor in the Church of the Holy Trinity as well as headmaster of the Academic Secondary School. Strauch's harshly anti-Catholic sermons evoked the outrage of the Catholic nobility in Royal Prussia, who in turn went so far as to call for the Protestant zealot to be burned at the stake. The council therefore removed him in late 1673 as a precautionary measure, but this generated major unrest within the city, since the pastor enjoyed great approval among the common citizens. When Strauch was called to Greifswald as a professor in 1675, the artisans, who saw him as a key proponent of their interests, hoped to hinder his departure; they held out in front of the city hall for two days and forced new concessions from the council. Strauch eventually left the city in October 1675.

Both sides—the council and those artisans not represented in the Orders— hoped to receive help from John III Sobieski, crowned king in February 1676. He first verified Danzig's privileges, whereupon the city took its loyalty oath; yet it was not until May 1677 that the monarch boarded Vistula barges with his court and, after a leisurely trip, arrived in the city on August 1. Received in a great celebration, with an entrance into the city lasting a full three days, Sobieskt soon attended to issues as chair of the Royal Assessorial Tribunal. The king was most interested in the position of Danzig's Catholics, but this was precisely the matter in which the council was unwilling to make concessions. The quarreling between two parties—council and guilds—thrilled the Third Order, which achieved a greater share in decision making regarding the acquisition of nascent seats within its ranks. Pursuant to Sobieski's decrees of January and February 1678, the council was also required to render greater authority to the Third Order, whose representatives, along with the two other Orders, gained influence in numerous areas of public life, from appointing positions in the treasury to horse fees and the "examination of the bushel and of other measurements." The taxes were reduced, as were the city's military expenses. But the king took no measures against the guilds' unwanted competition, and even after the council offered him a great sum of money (the payment of which, however, the council never took very seriously), Sobieski even abstained from strengthening the council's privileges in the city. He left Danzig in mid-February 1768, after a stay of more than a half year. Even the Catholics had hardly gained anything—violent conflicts arose on the edges of a parade in early May with the Lutheran populace, which stormed a monastery and a church. For the council, this was a welcome occasion to tighten the reins; the ringleaders—predominantly journeymen and servants—were arrested, and some of them sentenced to death. When one of them was actually beheaded two years later, renewed riots broke out and claimed more casualties, whereupon the king once again restricted the guilds' liberties at the council's request. The system of power in the city had undergone a change, but the patrician families were ultimately able to retain their privileges, and it would be some decades before discontent with their rule would again erupt.

Danzig in the Great Northern War

A number of relatively quiet years passed before the 1696 death of Jan III Sobieski stirred up new commotion in the land. A double election occurred in 1697; François Louis, the prince of Conti, received the most votes, but Prince Elector Frederick Augustus of Saxony arrived in Poland more quickly and began his reign as Augustus II. Danzig also acknowledged him, even though the French prince was already sailing to the city with a small fleet that anchored at Oliva in September. But as Saxon and Polish troops approached Oliva, François Louis lost his taste for adventure and returned to France.

Augustus II entered his key port and commercial city for the first time in mid-March 1698, greeted in the same manner as his predecessors, and a few days later verified the city's privileges and received the loyalty oath. That the monarch would soon plunge his country into a devastating new war could not be foreseen. His plan to reconquer Livonia from Sweden led to the Great (or Second) Northern War in 1700, which Augustus incited together with Russia. The Swedish king Charles XII delivered one defeat after another to Poland and Saxony, and his army established itself in Royal Prussia in 1703. To make matters worse, Stanisław Leszczyński, a rival king whom Sweden hoped to place on the Polish throne, appeared on the scene. While the Swedes did not besiege Danzig, they repeatedly demanded large sums of money in return, which the city was only narrowly able to produce. There was not even peace after Augustus yielded the Polish throne in 1706, with Russian troops still operating throughout the country. When the Russians soundly defeated Charles XII at Poltava, Augustus returned to Poland. He accused Danzig of having favored Leszczyński, but after a gratuity of 600,000 guilders changed his mind, he visited the city in 1710. Thereafter, he was only able to maintain his rule with Russian aid. For many years (the war did not end until 1721), the area around Danzig was still afflicted by Russian and Polish troops quartered there and eager to help themselves to local resources.

Tsar Peter I, who intently sought to open Russia to the West, had a great interest in Danzig as a supply base for his fleet. He came to the city in 1716, and, diverted by all sorts of merriment, stayed for almost three months. Many anecdotes from this time became local legend, such as the account of when Peter became cold while attending a service at St. Mary's Church. Next to him sat Danzig's mayor, whose splendid official wig appeared so nice and warm that the tsar swiped it from the dumbfounded mayor and placed it on his own head.

Still, Peter did not particularly appear to favor the city. Shortly after his departure, he demanded that for the war's duration, Danzig "produce five frigates with twelve to eighteen cannons,"[7] receive and accommodate Russian crews, and cease trade with Sweden; to refuse would mean risking war with Russia. Even Augustus II, who was staying in the city, could not do much to help Danzig, which began the construction of the raiding ships. Despite the ever-worsening economic situation, the city was still widely perceived as rich and thus encountered persistent demands for money—for instance, in 1717, when the Polish parliament under Russian guardianship reformed its military financing and obligated Danzig to make substantial payments. Polish soldiers marched to Danzig to enforce these demands but were driven away after several skirmishes. The city was nevertheless unable to forgo the financial obligation entirely.

With the great powers' interposition in Polish-Lithuanian internal affairs, Danzig increasingly found itself in jeopardy of becoming the plaything of foreign interests; since the city was no longer able to buy itself favor with great sums of money as it had earlier, its lofty special status was in jeopardy. Beginning at this point, the municipal government placed even greater focus on preserving the city's rights and privileges.

Trade and Craft—Danzig Becomes Poorer

Danzig's economic development stagnated beginning in the mid-seventeenth century. The decisive factor was the long-term recession of trade, and particularly that of grain, which until then had guaranteed the city's wealth. Between 1655 and 1660, profit margins plummeted as the grain trade fell to less than one-tenth of the amount averaged over the previous five years. Although it increased again after the end of the war, it never attained its earlier levels for any length of time.

Chiefly caused by the many wars that plagued Poland, this decline battered the country's entire basis of production (as established in the *Fronhof* system) and disrupted traditional trade relations. Crop yields sank with the destruction of large areas of cultivatable land, and small producers often lost any opportunity to raise grain for export, while year after year, the large landed estates belonging to the magnates and mostly located in southeastern Poland continued to send large numbers of Vistula barges to Danzig loaded with rye and wheat. There were other reasons for the decline, as well: Dutch merchants could realize greater profits elsewhere; trade procedures shifted simply due to the increasingly popular payment method of promissory notes; acreage and yields in Europe's developing regions saw significant increase; and the monetary crisis of the seventeenth century led to a coinage debasement in the Polish-Lithuanian Commonwealth, resulting in inflation and diminished trade.

Epidemics also adversely affected the situation, especially the great plague epidemic at the beginning of the eighteenth century, which compounded the devastation of the Great Northern War. Finally, Danzig's competition increased. Whereas more than 25 percent of all ships sailing west through the Sound had set sail from Danzig in 1660, this had fallen to 16 percent around 1700. Meanwhile, ports like Königsberg, Riga, and eventually Stettin (Pol. Szczecin) increased in significance.

Yet Danzig remained the Commonwealth's primary trading hub, and despite all of the problems with production, grain was still the country's most crucial export. In second place were wood and wood products, whose demand was on the rise in England as well as among Bordeaux vintners for barrel staves. The major import that came through Danzig into the Polish hinterland was salt. Sugar, spices, tropical fruits, wine, and saltwater fish increased in importance, and nobility traveled to the Motława to buy Danzig liquors, fine cloth, amber products, or Danzig furniture. Coffee, tea, and tobacco quickly became sought-after merchandise in the city in the 1720s and 1730s.

Ship traffic in Danzig's port sank parallel to the declining turnover. Between 600 and 1,000 ships docked annually around 1750, many of which were small and of little significance. Dutch merchants still dominated the harbor, but the

Figure 5.1a and b During his visit to his hometown in 1773, Danzig native Daniel Chodowiecki captured numerous people and scenes with his pen, including the rich merchant and shipowner Franz Gottfried von Rottenburg and the Mennonite banker Abraham Dirksen. From Daniel Chodowiecki, *Die Reise von Berlin nach Danzig: Die Bilder*. Edited and annotated by Willi Geismeier (Berlin, 1994), pages 49 and 63.

rapidly industrializing England, whose trade Danzig especially privileged in the early eighteenth century, made major gains. Based on the aspirations of prominent merchants who recognized that a purely passive role would be damaging in the long run, attempts were made to expand Danzig's little fleet. Already at the turn of the eighteenth century, more than 200 local merchants and shipowners with about 150 of their own ships were involved in maritime trade. The city even produced a ship magnate and major shipbuilder in Johann Philipp Schultz, who had over fifty ships constructed between 1726 and 1750, including the great frigate *Augustus III Rex Poloniae*, which Algerian pirates unfortunately raided on its maiden voyage.

Because ships were becoming larger, it was crucial for Danzig to improve access to the Motława harbor. To make navigation easier, a lighthouse was erected in Hela (Pol. Hel), the small town on the peninsula of the same name belonging to Danzig. Sand banks frequently formed at the Vistula estuary, necessitating regular maintenance of the waterway. Captains always had to seek new paths, especially after storms, and compulsory pilotage was enacted in 1706 for this reason. A massive sand bank later known as the Westerplatte formed over the decades and threatened the northern channel, so beginning in 1716, the western channel Neufahrwasser (Pol. Nowy Port) was expanded and outfitted with two lighthouses in 1757/1758.

All of these upgrades nevertheless proved insufficient to hinder the inexorable commercial recession in Danzig's harbor. Since trade was of key importance to the citizens, and the city obtained a considerable portion of its revenues from port dues, the years of splendid riches were soon past. Whereas the city's income from taxes and extraordinary items in the 1720s still averaged 119,000 guilders, for instance, they amounted to only around 39,000 guilders in 1755.

Danzig's craft industry fared about as well as its commerce. Decreasing membership in the guilds reflected the general economic recession, with the only exceptions being those crafts dealing with ship construction as well as textile work, which at the close of the seventeenth century sustained up to 5,000 people in Danzig. Overall price erosion accelerated, however, which is why local artisans found themselves more and more at pains to force competition from the market—for instance, from the city's monasteries or the suburbs not belonging to Danzig, where Mennonites and Jews were settling in increasing numbers. In 1745, sixty brewers were purportedly producing beer in the suburb of Stolzenberg (Pol. Pohulanka) alone.

Work in the handicraft business was difficult. Journeymen and apprentices had a hard life with long work hours and meager earnings. Becoming a master artisan often meant a lengthy wait, unless a master's daughter married a journeyman. Supposedly as a measure meant to prohibit significant inequalities, the guilds regularly strove, as they had in times past, to keep particularly ambitious artisans in their place. In practice, though, individual masters enjoyed differing degrees of access to the sparse resources; high-quality raw materials were rare (as were qualified workers), especially as Danzig was continually losing its allure for journeymen and apprentices from outside the city.

Danzig Fights, the King Flees: The Siege of 1734

When Augustus II died in the early morning of February 1, 1733, the Polish high nobility wished to replace him with a native monarch. The French King Louis XV supported his father-in-law Stanisław Leszczyński, who had briefly ruled Poland as Stanisław I before Augustus II was reinstated in 1709. Leszczyński was elected king, but Russia feared for its influence in the region and favored the son of Augustus II, Augustus III, who was also elected king, albeit by a minority of nobles and shortly following Leszczyński's election. Yet who was in the majority made little difference, since a powerful Russian army marched into Poland and presented the country with a fait accompli. Leszczyński, in possession of no such military aid, retreated to the well-fortified city of Danzig, which supported him. Poets sang of the king's arrival:

> How, upon thine arrival, loyal Danzig did greet thee
> With one thousand hails, and how it did receive thee,
> Yea, not only thine own country loves and honors thee,
> So also does nearly the world, thou unvanquished hero.[8]

The city remained on Leszczyński's side, even as the dispute over the throne escalated into the War of the Polish Succession. Things were simplest for Russia, which already had troops positioned in the country. The Polish nobles quickly defected to Augustus in light of the prevailing power relations, and approximately 30,000 Russian troops slowly marched toward Danzig. Versailles, on the other hand, did not wish to become involved in distant Poland, even though the French gave the impression that they intended to send military aid at once. This at least forced the Russian troops to stay near Danzig, and they were consequently unable to intervene in the rest of the war, which was primarily fought between French and Austrian forces. The reinforcement that Danzig finally received, however, was far too little and much too late.

Danzig prepared itself for the impending defense, enlisting mercenaries and repairing the fortifications. Together with the militia and Polish units, around 14,500 armed men stood ready in Danzig. The first costly battles occurred outside the city in mid-March 1734, and the Russians quickly captured the fortress at Danziger Haupt. On April 30, Russian attackers under the command of Field

Marshal Burkhard Christoph Graf von Münnich began shelling the city from the hills to the west and south. The lowlands to the east had been flooded, and there was consequently no threat from that direction. The Main Town, Old Town, and Old Suburbs lay for weeks under a volley of grenades; only Long Gardens east of the Motława was safe from the bombardment, which is why not only Leszczyński and his court but also many citizens sought shelter here.

The ring tightened around the city as one stronghold after another fell, even if the Russians also suffered a heavy defeat in nighttime combat at Hail Hill on May 9, in which around 1,000 attackers lost their lives and many more were wounded. This area still bears the name "Russian Grave" today, and a memorial has stood since 1898 to commemorate these battles. Shortly after this bloody engagement, a French flotilla arrived with three regiments, but they failed in all of their attempts to access the city from their camp on the Westerplatte. The situation became hopeless when a Russian fleet carrying massive reinforcements reached the Gulf of Gdańsk in mid-June, and on June 25 Danzig's city council decided to begin negotiations with the Russians. Among other things, Field Marshall von Münnich demanded Leszczyński, yet the fleeing king saved himself. Disguised as a peasant, Leszczyński escaped through the flooded regions east of the city in the night of June 28 and arrived a week later in Marienwerder (Pol. Kwidzyn) in the Duchy of Prussia; he would never again enter Poland.

Outraged at the king's escape, von Münnich briefly renewed the bombardment, but negotiations soon resumed, and the agreement of surrender was signed on July 7. Danzig was required to acknowledge Augustus III as king and pay Russia 1 million thalers in reparations, but the city was able to avoid occupation and billeting. Augustus III traveled to Oliva a little later and pardoned Danzig, but he demanded a large compensation payment, and neither at this time nor later did he ever set foot within the city's walls.

During the 145 days of the siege, 4,430 cannonballs had been fired into Danzig, 1,800 houses were destroyed, and 1,500 residents were killed or wounded. A great part of the city's villages had gone up in smoke. The total costs of defense and reparation added up to the horrendous sum of over 6 million guilders, a quarter of which went to France. This forced the city to take foreign loans that would require twenty years to repay. Yet the cost of their loyalty was not only financial in nature. For the first time, Danzig's citizens clearly realized how weak their political standing had become. The days of a republican Danzig were numbered.

Later generations mired in national paradigms either regarded the events of 1734 with great pleasure or struggled mightily with them. German historians found themselves at pains to explain why the "German" city of Danzig so fiercely defended the Polish Leszczyński against the "German" King Augustus III, whereas Polish historiography praised Danzig's stance as glorious evidence of

Figure 5.2 The Siege of Danzig in 1734 signaled danger. For the first time in memory the city was successfully brought to its knees by force of arms. Appearing in 1734 under the title "DANTZIG from the Vistula side, under the Russian/Saxon siege in 1734," this drawing by Daniel Schultz illustrates the bombardment's devastating effects. Germanisches Nationalmuseum Nürnberg, item number HB 13766.

the port city's Polish self-awareness. Yet as is so often the case in history, the truth is much more complex.

Restive Times: Social Protest and Prussian Greed

The middle of the eighteenth century in Danzig was marked by social protest but also by social awakening. While the Enlightenment took hold on the Motława, on the one hand, the discontent of the masses was rising, on the other. The economic situation had again worsened because of the siege of 1734: the financial stress on the city was mirrored in increasing taxes, whereby many citizens' real income sank. Additionally, despite the efforts of 1678, the civic elite had further insulated itself from the remainder of the populace. Certainly due in part to the ever-increasing demands of administering a great city, the connection had slackened between the patricians, most of whom had enjoyed an academic education, and the local commercial bourgeoisie; the elite were even derisively referred to as "scholars" and accused of indifference toward middle-class interests.

Tensions reached a peak in 1748. The brewers complained at court about the council, which they claimed was imposing excessive taxes upon them, and the merchants represented in the Third Order once again demanded a crackdown on unfair competition. When, on top of this, spokespeople for the merchants, shopkeepers, and storehouse proprietors appeared in person before Augustus III in Dresden, the king appointed a commission with the task of investigating the disputes onsite. The royal delegates arrived in March 1749 to discover a large middle-class opposition to the council. The king heeded the delegates' recommendations and in mid-1750 mandated, against vigorous resistance from the council, the election of a number of merchants to the First and Second Orders. He also increased the voice of the Third Order in all areas of the city's administration. The rights of Mennonites and Jews were restricted, and the guild system was strengthened. While some excise taxes were lifted, the king introduced a small wealth tax of 0.125 percent to be paid semi-annually.

When the council stalled in an effort to delay the implementation of these changes, the situation deteriorated further, kindled by numerous pamphlets and leaflets from both sides. By now the journeymen, who—together with the apprentices—stood at the bottom of the social ladder and whom the city's economic problems especially affected, had had enough. In May 1751, the journeymen shoemakers held a strike and protested outside city hall with the support of many other journeymen, which caused the council to give in to them and punish a number of master artisans. Yet when the journeyman carpenters demonstratively refused to offer their services and marched out of the city in August, thousands of journeymen and members of the poorer classes again took to the streets.

In light of this dangerous unrest, the council had a group of journeyman lumber mill workers arrested and sentenced to harsh punishments; yet this did not prevent the royal court of assessors summoned to Danzig from publicly announcing and implementing the king's 1750 mandate. Thus reconciled, the council and the Third Order took combined action against further journeyman unrest in April 1752. After some other financial issues were resolved and the king had received an additional 780,000 guilders, peace returned to Danzig. Appreciative of their victory, the grateful merchants erected a monument honoring Augustus III; dedicated in 1755, the marble statue in the Artus Court made up for the fact that the monarch himself never personally visited the great port city.

While Danzig enjoyed peace for the time being, new misfortune gathered beyond its borders. Zealously at work on his nation's ascent to the status of a major European power, the Prussian king Frederick II greatly desired to connect his hitherto separate regions of (East) Prussia and Pomerania/Brandenburg through the acquisition of Royal Prussia. He had already written in his political testament of 1752:

> I do not think that the best way of adding this province to the Kingdom would be by force of arms. . . . Poland is an electoral Kingdom; when one of its Kings dies it is perpetually troubled by factions. You must profit from these and gain, in return for neutrality, sometimes a town, sometimes another district, until the whole has been eaten up. . . . I think that in making the pacific conquest of Prussia, it would be absolutely necessary to reserve Danzig for the last mouthful, because this acquisition would raise a great outcry among the Poles, who export all their wheat through Danzig.[9]

This would be the actual sequence of events, albeit with some obstacles, since Frederick had not exactly foreseen the course of the Seven Years' War (1756–1763). The Russians occupied Königsberg in 1757 and marched to Danzig, which was once again just able to avert a Russian occupation, only to see the Prussian army approaching soon thereafter.

Elected as the Polish king in 1764 after the death of Augustus III, Stanisław II August Poniatowski wasted no time confirming Danzig's privileges, possibly because he knew the city so well. As the son of a powerful Polish noble house, he had come in late 1733 with his family, who supported Stanisław Leszczyński. He witnessed the siege of 1734 and spent five more years there under the tutelage of Gottfried Lengnich and others. The new king faced a daunting task: he was a proponent of fundamental state reform, yet he simultaneously also had to navigate between Poland's powerful neighbors Prussia and Russia. The Noble Republic's problematic position was apparent in Danzig's immediate surroundings, as well, as Russian troops were again stationed in Royal Prussia, demonstrating what St. Petersburg was capable of inflicting on Poland.

Nor did Prussia hold back in its tireless efforts to debilitate its neighboring kingdom. In 1765, Poland implemented a general toll to improve its financial situation, but Danzig objected, fearing for its trade. Frederick joined Danzig in protest, shortly thereafter establishing his own customs house under military guard in Marienwerder, where Prussia bordered Poland along the Vistula. Though Prussia soon had to close the station at Russia's insistence, Stanisław August was also compelled to lift the general toll.

Prussia and Russia sought other ways to increase their influence in Poland and impede its reform efforts, and local confessional conflicts proved to be just the thing. Action against religious tolerance in Poland had intensified in the eighteenth century and, despite resistance in Danzig, had led to the loss of a number of Protestant rights. In March 1767, dissident nobles formed a confederation in Thorn, joined by the province's three large Protestant cities, and while hopes of restoring Royal Prussia's autonomy were disappointed, the Polish parliament nevertheless ruled in favor of the Protestant dissidents' equality. This confederation produced arguments, however, which Russia, Prussia, and Austria would exploit to justify the First Partition of Poland in 1772, as did the Catholic-conservative, anti-reform Confederation of Targowica founded in 1768, toward which Danzig remained indifferent.

Hoping to protect itself amid this precarious international situation, Danzig had in March 1767 obtained a guarantee of protection from Empress Catherine the Great, who wished to do all she could so that the city "may be preserved without reduction in its existing rights, liberties, privileges, etc., especially in the possession of its lands and territories, in its maritime, commercial, and harbor rights, minting privileges, and fortress rights."[10] With this guarantee, Danzig thought itself able to withstand Prussian coercion, which vehemently demanded that the city extradite Prussian deserters while enforcing—for instance, in Prussia's occupation of Danzig's villages—its right to recruit soldiers on the city's land. The citizens soon came to fear the absolutist aims of the Prussian military state and saw their misgivings confirmed when Prussian troops drew close to the city in early 1772 under the pretense of conscription. Rumors of an imminent partition of Poland made the rounds, and nobody was surprised in August 1772 at the partition agreement between Prussia, Russia, and Austria, following which Poland lost one-third of its state territory. The Prussians took almost all of Royal Prussia into possession, and only Thorn remained part of Poland. Russia, fearing the excessive expansion of Prussian power, had taken a stand against a Prussian occupation of Danzig. Twenty hard years lay ahead for the city.

Tradition and New Fashions: Everyday Life in the Old City

Society in Danzig reflected the city's economic hardships and sinking political significance. The total population stagnated due not only to wars but also to heightened death rates in particularly cold years around 1700. During some winters, the entire Gulf of Gdańsk froze over, and in 1709, the harbor was not free of ice until early May. Yet local elation at the spring did not last long that year, since a plague epidemic took well over 30,000 lives in Danzig over the following months.

Existential worries, economic strain, and increasing prices made Danzig's citizens become more conservative; they vaunted what they possessed and were less and less willing to give up their cherished mores. Even at the end of the eighteenth century, an observer wrote that "in a manner of speaking, Danzig still lives in the seventeenth century; convention is all-powerful."[11] Such willful retreat into its own history would persist in the city into the twenty-first century.

One outward indication of this rigid insistence was the richly embellished, heavy Danzig furniture that not only decorated many citizens' homes in the city but also found consumers throughout Eastern-Central Europe.

This is not to say that the citizens cloistered themselves from innovation; if anything, they were hardly able to fend off new trends. Thus, in the seventeenth century, the collared clothing fashioned after Spanish models yielded to more comfortable French garments, and powdered wigs enjoyed increasing popularity. As before, the administration issued statutes in an attempt to curtail the display of luxury through clothing. Other regulations restricting extravagance were also tightened, and spies—referred to as "instigators"—monitored their observance; infringements were punishable by fines or imprisonment. Weddings, baptisms, and funerals thus became—as in many Central European middle-class cities— strictly regimented ceremonies, but also exercises in the art of outwitting the authorities where possible. At the same time, these regulations illustrate the material pressure on a large portion of the middle class, which passed strict rules as precautionary measures against excessive spending.

Social life changed gradually. The medieval institution of the Artus Court lost its allure, and the fraternal societies increasingly struggled to attract new members, avoided expensive feasts, and even sold pieces of their valuable tableware. They finally moved out of the Artus Court in 1742, henceforth to meet only occasionally as charitable organizations. The stock market, which until then had taken place in the open air on Long Market, moved into the Artus Court instead. New forms of socialization included associations and societies, as well as Masonic lodges, which gained importance particularly due to the influence of the Enlightenment. The first such lodge in Danzig, called Zu den drey Bleiwagen (The three plumb levels), was founded in 1751. Admittedly, men were prominent here while the middle-class women's activities were mostly limited to domestic life and maintaining the household; their role in public life would not increase until the nineteenth century. Incidentally, women in the lower social tiers were particularly disadvantaged, being restricted from managing handicraft businesses; at best, they could assist or hire themselves out as laborers.

Danzig was still a predominantly Protestant city, but by the end of the eighteenth century, the evangelical portion had sunk to below 80 percent of the city's population, with Calvinists making up a mere 2 percent. Catholics had increased from about 7 percent in 1650 to more than 20 percent in 1800 because of heightened immigration from the city's largely Catholic surrounding regions. Attending Sunday worship services was not only a moral obligation but was also required by law. Restrictions for Mennonites and Jews were tightened in the mid-eighteenth century. Mennonites were only allowed to reside in the city after paying protection money, and legal provisions in 1752 and 1763 required Jews to purchase passports to the city for periods ranging from eight days to four weeks; nevertheless, there were already some permanent Jewish residents in Danzig by that time. Not much changed linguistically; Low and High German were spoken everywhere. Polish was heard occasionally (although almost never among citizens), and the city never lacked foreigners from other countries.

Amid all of their difficulties, Danzig's citizens still fared relatively well. In 1769, they consumed 10,000 oxen, 13,000 calves, 42,000 sheep, 14,500 pigs, and a large amount of poultry, all of which—as assiduous historians have estimated—amounted to a daily average of about six ounces of meat per person. Many citizens' homes still bespoke affluence: the centerpiece was usually a large foyer cabinet called a *Spind*, in addition to particularly elaborate bedsteads, mirrors, and clocks, with the latter valued at up to 500 guilders in estate inventories—more valuable than many poorer families' entire estates.

Danzig readily participated in the new trends. Since the city still possessed immense importance for the transfer of merchandise, cultural goods, and news both to and from Poland, the merchants were the first to note what the nobility currently considered fashionable. It is even likely that local fashion actually generated interest and demand among the nobility at times. In any event, tea, coffee, and new parlor games soon became favorites in Danzig, and many families expanded their possessions with tea and coffee sets, sugar bowls, smoker's requisites, and gaming supplies, all of which influenced the shifting forms of sociality. Music was performed more often, salons appeared in the second half of the eighteenth century, and an occasional ball was arranged. The people also enjoyed stepping out into public. Alongside the traditional taverns, public coffeehouses gradually took root; the most famous belonged to the Mennonite Anton Momber and opened around 1700, offering French, German, and Dutch newspapers, as well as an inviting little garden in the summer.

Many of the same old problems persisted, though. Hygienic conditions, for instance, were still poor. Street sanitation was the responsibility of the homeowners, and the administration only occasionally had public spaces cleaned. Wastewater in the Main Town ran through trenches along the streets until it reached the sumps outside the gates on the Motława, where it was sanitized by the executioner's blackguards, who also incidentally caught and killed stray dogs. Odors drifting through the streets were certainly not always aromatic. Those taking evening strolls had to exercise caution against a misplaced step on darkened streets. People out late lit their way with kindling or lanterns. It was not until 1767 that the council brought itself to have 808 glass streetlights installed, albeit only initially in the Main Town; this also provided jobs for eight streetlight inspectors and twenty-one streetlight guards.

Increasing carriage traffic led to crowding in the streets, since the lanes between the large terraces (*Beischläge*) were narrow, and pedestrians had "enough to do merely to keep their limbs intact,"[12] according to Johanna Schopenhauer, mother of the philosopher Arthur Schopenhauer. While the terraces disturbed traffic, however, they were also an important place where citizens could enjoy tea and let their children play. Near the end of her life, Johanna Schopenhauer recalled her youth in the 1770s with a nostalgic longing for the city:

> And the terrace supplied the children with such a playground in my youth! So safe, so cozy! Under the watchful eye of their nearby mother, who sat sewing and knitting at the window above, sometimes not disdaining to also enjoy the mild evening among them. In tolerable weather, we spent all our free hours with our playmates in this haven.[13]

The city's dwindling economic power also left an impression on local imagination. Vacant buildings and dreams of big money were widespread during the time of Danzig's decline and still lingered in the nineteenth century when attempts were made to record (or invent) local folklore and legend. The tales of the Adam and Eve House in Danzig, for example, may have their roots in this period. This apartment house on Long Street stood empty for a long time, allegedly because it was haunted. All attempts to renovate the building and its grand façade failed, consistently ruined by the building's ghosts, and people who dared to sleep there often met a "swift death."[14]

As the economic situation led to an increase in the number of the needy and unemployed, contemporaries continually faced the question of what could be done for beggars. One answer was the establishment of an orphanage for poor youths, on which construction began in 1698. People also collected for the poor outside of the churches, and there were charitable foundations as well, but caring for the formidable number of people in need of support (3,400 as documented in 1734) was not so simple.

From Baroque to Enlightenment: Art and Science

With Danzig's gradual economic decline, the city's artistic significance also faded. Hardly any great architecture, for example, was created after the mid-seventeenth century, and the great churches and towers loomed above the houses like monuments of an ever-receding past. The only important public structure built was the Royal Chapel, erected between 1678 and 1683 at King John III Sobieski's special request for a parish church to serve the local Catholics; the young sculptor and Danzig native Andreas Schlüter likely received the commission to create the façade. For the entire eighteenth century, a rococo portal for the Main Town's city hall is the only notable construction. The city's fortifications were not expanded but merely adjusted and modernized as

Figure 5.3 As drawn in 1773 by Daniel Chodowiecki, Long Street was an idyllic street with many trees. From Daniel Chodowiecki. *Die Reise von Berlin nach Danzig. Die Bilder.* Edited and annotated by Willi Geismeier (Berlin, 1994), page 29.

needed. As a contribution from Mayor Gralath, 1,416 Dutch linden trees were planted lining a double avenue leading to the suburb of Langfuhr in 1768.

Even if the great civic and religious buildings were dated, Danzig still presented itself quite handsomely. Citizens took understandable pride in the city's skyline and splendid landmarks, and for this reason, they were especially glad whenever visitors from out of town concurred with poet and theologian Johann Timotheus Hermes, who wrote in 1776: "This city is incomparable."[15]

The bourgeois townhouses especially factored into such opinions. Although hardly any new homes were built, existing houses were sometimes rebuilt with new façades, first (beginning around 1680) with flowing Dutch gables in the Baroque fashion, and later (after the mid-eighteenth century) in a simpler style, but with rococo touches. In 1776, the merchant Johann Uphagen had one of the few new houses built on Long Street; today a museum, it attests to the lifestyle of Danzig's wealthy citizens from that period.

Artists found fewer and fewer commissions in the city. If painters like Jakob Wessel were not content to settle for portraits, or engravers like Mathäus Deisch for cityscapes, they needed to leave Danzig. Among such artists were Andreas Schlüter, as well as Daniel Schultz, who was influenced by Rembrandt and sometimes worked at the royal court in Warsaw. Danzig's most famous artist of the time likewise did not stay long in his hometown: at an early age, Daniel Chodowiecki went to Berlin, where he made a name for himself as an illustrator. Only once—for two months in 1773—did he return to Danzig, a trip that he

Figure 5.4 Within middle-class homes, time appeared to have stood still for centuries. Here, Chodowiecki visits his childhood home, whose halls are dominated by heavy cabinets and an intermediate story. Edited and annotated by Willi Geismeier (Berlin, 1994), page 31.

illustrated with 108 drawings. On the other hand, almost nothing survives of the many portraits of local personages he produced during his stay. Chodowiecki records in his travel journal that civilians as well as Polish dignitaries frequently asked him to draw them, and he had soon gained such recognition that, even at night, patrons were reluctant to let him leave: "When I left," he writes in his description of a social evening, "Herr Ledikowski took me to his home to draw his wife. She had already undressed and undone her hair, yet she received me quite amicably; we exchanged a great deal of pleasantries without listening to one another, and she eventually removed her nightcap and took her place to sit for me."[16]

The center of musical life was in the great churches. Two of the most important conductors in St. Mary's Church were Johann Valentin Meder, who held the office between 1687 and 1699, and Johann Balthasar Christian Freißlich, who wrote around 100 cantatas, including one performed at the unveiling of the monument for Augustus III in the Artus Court. The position of kapellmeister was so well endowed that it was attractive even to Johann Sebastian Bach, who in 1730 asked a friend living in Danzig "to lodge a most favorable recommendation for me" there, which nevertheless remained fruitless.[17] Yet in the second half of the eighteenth century, the old forms of music cultivation—such as the music in the Artus Court or festive occasional songs—decreased in significance, while weekly concerts and private concerts increased in popularity. Theater also had a great deal of enthusiasts; travelling companies like those of Konrad Ernst Ackermann and of the Schuch Family regularly came to Danzig, where they performed in the former fencing school, which in 1730 had been converted into a ramshackle theater.

Public and cultural life changed in the eighteenth century under the influence of the Enlightenment. Literary and scientific societies formed, such as the (albeit short-lived) Societas Litteraria in 1720, whose membership was made up of patricians, physicians, and merchants who kept abreast of diverse literary and scholarly news. Many more academic associations and reading societies followed soon thereafter. The Danzig Research Society (Naturforschende Gesellschaft) bore lasting significance for scientific life in Danzig from 1743 until 1945.

Danzig had developed an excellent cultural and educational infrastructure in its prime; this would sustain it for some time thereafter, and the city was still able to maintain its extra-regional significance in a number of areas. At the center stood the Academic Secondary School with its outstanding instructors, such as the philosopher Samuel Schelwig, who also directed the school for three decades. Instruction took place according to the familiar formula: in addition to the seven professors (teaching the subjects of theology, law and history, physics and medicine, philosophy, eloquence and poetry, Greek and oriental languages, and mathematics), a lecturer also taught the Polish language here. Yet even the Secondary School's star was in decline, with only sixty-five students attending in 1765. The parish schools, which poor children could attend in designated pauper classes, likewise underwent a slow downturn until the parish school system was reformed around 1720 through the opening of three large "free schools."

As a trade hub, Danzig also continued as a relevant news center, even though the significance of maritime traffic as a transmitter of news sank as land routes improved. Especially in times of crisis, local presses released an abundance of leaflets, such as on the occasion of the siege of 1577, during the Thirty Years' War, following the conflicts with Elbing in 1656, or during the siege of 1734. The publications bore cumbersome yet informative titles such as "Brief and summary document in which the innocence of the Royal City of Danzig is concisely presented against its adversaries' unfounded and invented accusation in these sorrowful and abstruse affairs (1577)," or "Brief yet thorough report of what occurred during the siege of the City of Danzig, and how the same siege was concluded: composed without bias by a lover of truth (1734)."

From early on, the news was distributed in regularly appearing newspapers in Danzig. While the first such papers were handwritten sheets with small circulations, printed newspapers also existed in Danzig beginning in 1618, such as the *Wöchentliche Zeitung* (Weekly tidings). This tradition came to an end after 1705, an indication of the city's gradual provincialization; Danzig would not have another newspaper until 1781. In addition, periodicals like the *Polnische Bibliothek* (Polish library), edited by Gottfried Lengnich, appeared in Danzig, and beginning in the mid-eighteenth century, numerous moral weeklies were published, the first of which bore a title that clearly recalled the pedantic influence of the famous contemporary literary critic Johann Christoph Gottsched and sounds quite awkward today: "The Operose Observer of Human Deeds." An advertising paper that also featured articles and poems began circulation in 1739 and appeared for nearly two centuries before being discontinued in 1921. Danzig was a site of significant book production; at least 250 printings emerged from the city council's press between 1658 and 1694. Not only did the council's library, which included 26,000 volumes at the end of the eighteenth century, accumulate books, but so too did private citizens. Heinrich Wilhelm Rosenberg, for instance, possessed nearly as many books as the council.

Although the city's artistic life no longer soared to its former heights, the sciences were quite active. The city was still wealthy enough that there were patrons—as well as somewhat whimsical and well-educated citizens—who indulged themselves in their eccentric scientific hobbies. Among the latter was Johannes Hevelius, who pursued studies in the Netherlands, England, and France before returning to his hometown to make his fortune as a merchant and brewer, as well as a member of the Old Town's city council. Yet his real interests lay in the firmament, which he observed nightly from his observatory on the roofs of his three houses in the Pepper Town district using astronomical devices of his own devising. He published detailed lunar maps and findings on new constellations in splendid works like *Selenographia* (1647) or *Machina coelestis* (1673). Everybody in Danzig talked about the learned brewer, not just for his discoveries, but also his parrot. When his house caught fire in 1679, his feathered friend is said to have been the first thing he saved while many of his scientific works burned.

Although some names have been forgotten outside of Danzig, such as physician and astronomer Nathan Matthäus Wolf, who had an observatory built in his native city, others are still known. Johann Reinhold Forster, who worked as a pastor in Nassenhuben (Pol. Mokry Dwór) and his son Johann Georg were famed natural scientists; they explored Russia in 1765 and accompanied Captain James Cook on his second voyage around the world from 1772 to 1775. One of Danzig's native sons who attained fame and honor only spent his youth in the city: Daniel Gabriel Fahrenheit, who invented the mercury thermometer and whose temperature scale is still used in the Anglo-Saxon world today. A monument on Long Market—a thermometer—commemorates him.

Also of note were the historians active in Danzig, such as Joachim Pastorius, who produced works on the history of Poland as the court historiographer to King John Casimir, or Gottfried Lengnich, a city syndic who engaged in numerous studies in the law and history of Danzig, Royal Prussia, and Poland. Yet much time would pass before the first modern, comprehensive history of the city would be written, not least because the council jealously guarded the archives to prevent political opponents from using city documents to their advantage. Between 1789 and 1791, the professor at the Secondary School and son of a patrician family Daniel Gralath the Younger finally wrote his *Versuch einer Geschichte Danzigs* (Attempt at a history of Danzig) in three volumes; it was something of a swan song for the doomed municipal republic.

The city had other eulogists in its poets. Their home was the Secondary School, whose teachers supplemented their income with occasional poetry in German and Latin, even though, due to luxury constraints, there were fewer and fewer commissions for nuptial or funerary poems. Poems honoring the Polish monarchs were still in demand, though, and the city itself occasionally served as a literary inspiration—for instance, in this anonymous verse dedicated to Danzig's coat of arms:

> The crown in thy crest shows
> That thou art Prussia's crown.
> The crosses let us know
> That thou wilt stand with Christ.
> To what do the lions bear witness?
> A lion's nature and courage in thee.[18]

Among others, the Polish lecturers in the Secondary School created local works in Polish. Overall, however, the city lacked literary personages who attained major importance outside the region, at best with the exception of Luise Adelgunde Viktoria Kulmus, the wife of Johann Christoph Gottsched, although she left the city at a relatively young age. Her play *Die Pietisterey im Fischbeinrocke* (False devotion in a hoopskirt) is set partly in Danzig.

Encircled, Enclosed, Engulfed: Danzig Becomes Prussian

The First Partition of Poland in 1772 was a jolt that unleashed new forces of reform. For Danzig, though, the partition was a drama. As a Polish exclave surrounded by Prussia and its customs frontiers, it was condemned either to a speedy economic downfall or a voluntary secession from Poland. Fearing the severe Prussian regiment, the citizens nevertheless chose loyalty to Poland, especially as they hoped that French, English, and Dutch pressure would soon enforce the partition's retraction.

Yet Frederick II was determined to maintain what he had gained; moreover, he also hoped to soon acquire Danzig by tormenting it however he could. The three partition powers of Prussia, Austria, and Russia had actually arranged to leave Danzig and its entire rural environs to Poland, while all suburbs belonging to the bishop of Włocławek or to the Oliva Monastery were to be occupied, including those directly bordering to the south and west—Alt Schottland, Stolzenberg, and Bishop's Hill—as well as Oliva to the north. But the Prussians could not leave well enough alone, and they also marched into a number of locations belonging to Danzig, particularly Neufahrwasser, from which they controlled the harbor entry and were in an excellent position to torment the city; ships traveling to Danzig soon had to unload their wares here for inspection. The city appealed to all of the European powers but was just as powerless to stop this as it was against the customs checks directly outside of the city's borders, as well as on the Vistula River in the town of Fordon (now part of the Polish city of Bydgoszc), near Thorn. The tariffs collected here beginning in 1772 were nominally 12 percent; in actuality, they amounted to between 30 and 40 percent for wares traveling to Danzig; this plan, meant to steer Vistula commerce to the once again Prussian city of Elbing, bore fruit. By 1784, Danzig's smaller sibling enjoyed a nearly equal share of the grain trade. The lumber trade still largely ran through Danzig, whose merchants tried to make headway against this inclemency with their own fleet of about seventy ships, but they were unable to accomplish much in the new geopolitical circumstances. Imports decreased in value by two-thirds between 1770 and 1791, and exports by about half. Many companies and business went bankrupt, and the skilled workers no longer received contracts. Within these twenty years, the total population fell catastrophically from almost 60,000 to around 35,000.

Not only was trade severely disrupted, but so too was the everyday life of the citizens. Gotthilf Löschin, one of Danzig's most important historians from the nineteenth century, wrote:

If Danzig's citizens wished to visit their houses located in Langfuhr, Pelonken, Oliva, and so forth, then every piece of meat and every drop of wine that they took with them had to be taxed; and the inspection that went along with it—even ladies were compelled in the most objectionable manner to disembark—became so disagreeable, that many families preferred to do entirely without the pleasure of their lovely summer homes.[19]

Even many decades later, Danzig residents would remember the Prussian customs inspectors, also known as coffee sniffers, since they stuck their noses everywhere in search of taxable goods.

There was no end to the chicaneries. Prussian troops demanded the extradition of those liable to military service in Prussian recruiting districts; goods arriving by land from Poland were frequently and forcibly unloaded before entering the city and offered for sale; the "Royal Prussian Independent City of Stolzenberg" was founded from a number of suburbs outside city limits, whose market and artisans were meant—although without substantial success—to create competition for Danzig. While the city council in Danzig was repeatedly willing to compromise with the Prussians, the Third Order and the merchants took a stronger stance. In 1785, though, nobody was able to avoid a rather obsequious agreement granting the Prussians free transport through Danzig's territory. Prussian politics did not change, even after Frederick's death in 1786.

The year 1788 saw further commotion in external politics. Prussian statesman Ewald Friedrich von Hertzberg suggested that if it received Danzig and Thorn, Prussia would respect Poland's territorial integrity. Poland would not hear of it, yet it nevertheless entered a defensive alliance with Prussia against Russia in 1790, in order to secure its planned state reform. The members of the nobility who had been working on a comprehensive reform since 1788 were well aware of the significance that Danzig bore for Poland, and representatives in Warsaw also assured Danzig's chargé d'affaires of the same sentiment:

> What? Poland relinquish Gdańsk? That will never happen. For Gdańsk is the sole window through which the more distant powers now look in upon us. If we lose this window, however, then we will remain here in the wilderness, as it were; no longer will foreign nations be able to look in upon us, and we will find ourselves abandoned to the view of only those powers surrounding us.[20]

Yet no further help could be expected from Poland. The attempt that a number of citizens made to arouse compassion in Stanisław August and stir him to intercede on Danzig's behalf was likewise doomed to fail:

O Sire! If we could guide Your Majesty's heart, ever receptive to your people's sufferings, into the homes of many who despite outward wealth suffer secretly... it would stir Your Majesty.[21]

Occupied with reform and his neighbors' lust for power, the king was unable to come to the aid of his port city in its distress, especially when events began to unfold rapidly. Prussia, which had achieved little for itself through the negotiations with Poland, spoke again with Russia, and increasingly so after Poland adopted a constitution on May 3, 1791, as the basis of a comprehensive reform package; Russia marched into Poland the following year. Partly for fear of a revolutionary movement, Prussia and Russia arranged for the Second Partition of Poland, the agreement for which was signed in St. Petersburg on January 23, 1793. Along with Thorn and the province of Greater Poland, Danzig was to become Prussian.

Informing Danzig at the end of February of the need to "reassure" himself concerning the city's loyalty, the Prussian king Frederick William II supplied a few sanctimonious excuses as pretense. Danzig, he suggested, had "for a long series of years born very little friendly sentiment toward the Prussian state," which was understandable, and "even now there nests among you that malicious and savage mob which proceeds from outrage to outrage," which was only correct insofar that all those who wanted nothing to do with Prussia considered themselves safer in a Polish Danzig.[22] Prussian troops gathered outside the city, and they moved up to the outer gates and blockaded the city bright and early on March 8. The city council armed the citizens and positioned them on the walls before finally accepting the Prussian conditions, upon which it found itself confronted with an outraged mass of common people unwilling to submit, if only because many men feared immediate conscription into the Prussian army. Yet the three civic orders, the merchants, and the guild aldermen recognized that opposition was pointless. The populace finally agreed to a Prussian entry into the city on March 28, but not before ensuring that none of the city's residents would be conscripted. Still, much of the populace distrusted these promises. As the Prussians prepared to march into Danzig, numerous city soldiers mutinied against their officers and banded together with sailors; they fired their rifles at the hated Prussians from the outworks and even seized a number of cannons by force, which they fired into the Prussian columns. The city, whose authorities were powerless, erupted into commotion. The Prussians counterattacked, and the battles and skirmishes lasted all day. It was not until April 4 that the victors could enter the city. They were all the more careful to leave their mark quickly and clearly: only a few days later, the Prussian eagle was mounted on the main gates where the crests of Poland, Royal Prussia, and Danzig had previously hung in resplendence.

On May 7, Danzig pledged allegiance to the Prussian king. The councilmen had already removed their official robes and wigs and dressed in black to express their sorrow at the Prussian seizure of the city. Gathered in the Main Town's city hall, in the great courtroom with its paintings of the Polish kings still hanging, it was clear to them that this hour marked the end of a 339-year history. The portrait of the Prussian king, displayed along with a symbolically empty throne, certainly did not alleviate their bitter moods. They would not have dared dream that the wheel of history would be turned back again only fourteen years later.

6

Prussian Blue

Fall and Rise in the Nineteenth Century, 1793–1918

The button shines in the sunlight and casts a little shadow on the fabric. The Prussian blue of the uniform stretches across the soldier's chest and shoulders. Annoyed, he swats at a few flies that buzz stubbornly around the bright jacket. He must patrol the ramparts for a few hours still, back and forth with the city now to his right, now to his left, then once again to his right, then left. He is proud. For it is he, a poor fellow from Pomerania, and not the king in distant Berlin, who rules the bourgeois city.

The soldier looks down at himself, then lifts his gaze and lets it wander. Soon it appears to him that the sky arches Prussian blue, that the sea is Prussian blue, that the surging forest, the steaming city, the looming towers are all Prussian blue, as if someone has painted the entire world Prussian blue. His heart is glad, and he finally laughs aloud, recalling how Prussian blue he was yesterday, down in the city after duty.[1]

Danzig meanwhile still sees itself brick-red and wheat-blond, even if faded.

Grieving or Glory: Divergent Opinions on the Year 1793

A long chapter of Danzig history ended in 1793. Depending on the viewer's perspective—whether economic or national, localist or constitutional—Prussia's "unfriendly takeover" of the city has evoked varying reactions from contemporaries and posterity. Well into the nineteenth century, many in Danzig would long for the city's former and, in reality, already long-receding glory. In 1871, when Danzig became part of a German empire for the first time in its history, the old sectionalism would fade from memory.

The 1893 celebration observing the 100th anniversary of the transfer to Prussia—a great festival with a worship service, a parade, popular entertainment, and an evening reception—was a display of German imperial and Prussian solidarity. As conservatives cheered the successful integration of the city into Prussia, the national-liberalist lord mayor proclaimed in his speech: "Indeed... Danzig has always been a German city, and Danzig will remain a German city forever."[2]

From the Polish point of view, however, Danzig was simply forced into the Prussian state, had never become a German city at heart, and longed for new liberty. In 1919, when a political struggle ignited over Danzig's national future, the city's daily Polish newspaper wrote that Danzig's citizens had defended themselves from the annexation "by force of arms," until the "Revolution of Gdańsk" was brutally quelled.[3] While the term "revolution" was excessive in this case, the city's small Polish minority—organized since the late nineteenth century—was clear in its thinking: the city's "long" Prussian century was a period of foreign domination. This perspective drew great resonance among Polish observers from outside the city, particularly in their efforts to eliminate all "Prussian-German" character from Gdańsk after the Second World War. In reconstruction efforts, they were in fact anxious to turn back time and return the Main Town to an ideal condition from before 1793, when the city had still belonged to Poland. Even after the political turning point in 1989, it would take some time before the civic society rediscovered—with fascination—the forgotten and supposedly foreign Prussian Danzig.

Will It Get Better? Fourteen Years in Prussia

The year 1793 meant a drastic shift for Danzig: whereas the city had largely governed itself previously, it would thereafter be ruled. New economic ties, a new king—where would it all lead? Hope and doubt counterbalanced each other.

Even before Danzig's obeisance, the administration was delegated to a deputation composed of eighteen members of the three civic orders, which soon became an "interim police magistracy." Since all four previous mayors refused to cooperate, Johann Christian von Lindenowski, the former Prussian envoy in Danzig, assumed the position of lord mayor and marshal.[4] The city retained some of its traditional rights, though under a different organization. Led by a "city president," a mayor, and a magistracy made up of ten councilors, Danzig was directly subordinate to Prussia's War and Domains Chamber in Marienwerder. Subjection to an authority located in this small town located not sixty miles up the Vistula River evoked anything but pleasure in Danzig's proud middle class. The city council initially had a severely restricted voice, and not until 1805, following years of protest, were they granted greater influence in city affairs.

Danzig kept all of its land, even if it had to concede a good deal of special privileges to Prussian authorities. For the time being, Danzig's residents were free from military service. The Main Town was exempt from quartering Prussian troops, a concession that the patricians living there had skillfully negotiated, while the Old Town and Old Suburb were required to accommodate one infantry regiment each. The strong military presence would leave its stamp on the city for over 100 years: the mercantile city became a bureaucratic garrison town.

Not all residents were willing to resign themselves to the political changes. Impressed by the revolutionary events in France, a small group of the Academic Secondary School's students and former students took up liberal ideas. Under the leadership of an artisan's son named Gottfried Benjamin Bartholdy, the secret society of the "Free Prussians" was organized in 1794 and ventured a rebellion against the Prussian rule on April 13. Yet their plan—offering liquor to entice dockworkers to join their revolutionary cause—backfired. In seeking out Bartholdy's revolutionaries, these would-be allies drew a large crowd and aroused the attention of the police. Bartholdy fled across rooftops and was arrested two days later. Though the attempted revolt was hardly more than a farce, the authorities were alarmed. The city's gates were closed and a company of guards was posted. Friedrich Leopold von Schrötter, governor of the province of East Prussia, reassuringly reported to the king:

> The conspiracy, in fact, consists merely of a small number of reckless young people, of whom not even one has reached the age of maturity. The actual citizenry express their abhorrence at the absurd endeavors of these blundering youth.[5]

The revolutionaries were soon sentenced. Bartholdy was initially condemned to death, later to life in prison, and eventually set free. He died in Danzig as a private tutor.

In spring 1798, Frederick William III became the first Prussian monarch to visit the city, even if he spent only three days there. The difference between his reception and the rituals that had traditionally accompanied visiting Polish kings was striking: it was not the council and artisans who greeted the king but rather a military parade from his own army. Provincial authorities held the reception, not in Danzig itself but outside city limits in Oliva. Nevertheless, the king participated in a ball held in the Artus Court and granted nobility to a number of people from the patrician families, a measure meant to reconcile them to the new political conditions.

Economic circumstances improved rapidly. Rid of the cumbersome Prussian customs borders, Danzig profited from Prussia's tremendous expansion, which as of 1795 reached as far as Warsaw and came close to Vilnius and Kraków. In the city's best year (1802), the volume of grain and wood shipped through the harbor was equal to amounts handled in the mid-eighteenth century. The largest consumer was England, whereas the importance of Dutch trade was in sharp decline. Other important export goods were wool, hemp, and linen. Over 1,700 ships sailed into the harbor in 1803 and again in 1804, and Danzig's fleet expanded to 111 ships.

While the Vistula thus resumed its familiar role, the country roads were also improved. Starting around 1800, postal services ran twice weekly from Danzig to the major Prussian cities of Königsberg, Warsaw, and Berlin; the stagecoach required five days for the route to Berlin, while courier mail accomplished the journey in three. Things also improved for the manufacturing industry, with textile producers enjoying notable success. Due to the economic boom, the city was able to fully pay off its debts from before 1793.

All of this inevitably had an impact on the population, which grew from almost 37,000 to 44,000 between 1794 and 1806, not including Prussian military and their families, who made up an additional 6,000 people. Commercial success enabled merchants and shipowners to raise their status in the city. Some pursued great careers, such as the harbor foreman Matthias Broschke. He became so rich through the grain and wood trade that he was able to build a toll highway to Neufahrwasser at his own expense. Over time, however, he drew the ire of all of the city's other merchants and eventually had to leave town.

Napoleon's Meddling: The Siege of 1807

This prosperous period was to end abruptly, however. "Danzig was never unhappier than during the seven years from 1807 to 1814," declared Abraham Friedrich Blech, a fervent historian and clergyman in St. Mary's Church who produced a great work on this "seven-year suffering" shortly following Danzig's first tenure as a free city.[6] Blech's assessment summarizes a tragic period from which the city would not recover for a long time.

The city's strong development under Prussian rule ceased with the outbreak of war between France and Prussia in 1806. On October 14, the French army routed Prussian troops at Jena and Auerstadt and marched into Berlin two weeks later. It was only a matter of time before they would advance farther east. Napoleon showed particular interest in Danzig and hoped to exploit the city's financial power for his own military purposes.

Danzig prepared itself for a siege lasting many months, stockpiling food provisions to support not only the population, but also the nearly 22,000 soldiers who had gathered by March 1807 under the command of General Friedrich Adolf Kalckreuth. Tensions mounted.

In the morning of Saturday, March 7, the universal cry rang out: "The enemy is at the gate! He is attacking at the Lowland Gate and the *Holzraum*."[7] It was market day! The people were running wildly into each other. The drums sounded ceaselessly; the goods at the market were sold helter-skelter.[8]

As the siege tightened, the order was given to burn the city's outskirts to impede the enemy's approach. The attacking forces, consisting mainly of Polish units alongside soldiers from France, Baden, and Saxony, amassed in increasing numbers and brought their cannons into position.

Bombardment with fireballs, bombs, and grenades—a ghastly spectacle—commenced in the night of March 23 and 24. Theodor Behrend, the eighteen-year-old son of a wealthy merchant, later recalled:

> I had gone to my uncle's that evening . . . to spend some hours there, when the servants crashed trembling and weeping into the room to inform us of the fiery orbs being launched at the city from all sides. We hurried to the door and saw for ourselves the glowing masses arcing high through the air. . . . Only one of these appeared unlikely to overshoot the marketplace. How great our fright when it fell about forty paces from us, bursting with a dreadful crash and dashing its glowing contents all about. I had sunk to my knees in terror. Hundreds of windows had shattered in the detonation and fell clattering onto the cobblestones.[9]

The first casualties fell. Everyone who had been able to had fled the previous night across the Motława to the districts of Long Gardens and Lower Town, and many people spent weeks living in basements. Yet Napoleon was implacable and even observed the siege's progress himself for a time. From the hills west of Danzig, the attackers under the command of Marshal François-Joseph Lefebvre were treated to a dazzling panorama of the great city enclosed in its green ramparts.

The bombardment lasted several weeks, with Prussian diversionary attacks proving fruitless. The western fortifications of Bishop's Hill and Hail Hill were in increasingly dire straits, the island of Holm (Pol. Ostrów) in the Vistula River north of the city toward the sea was lost at the beginning of May, and communication with the Weichselmünde Fortress and the Westerplatte could only be maintained by means of an optical telegraph, which would later become famous as a major technical innovation. A Russian attempt to provide relief failed, and as the city's population, plagued by food shortage and inflated prices, watched

Figure 6.1 Danzig held great strategic significance for Napoleon. For this reason, he personally oversaw the siege of the city in spring 1807, as depicted among his officers in this contemporary drawing. Biblioteka Gdańska Polskiej Akademii Nauk.

its last hopes dissolve, an English three-master with full sails attempted to reach the city on May 15.

> Thousands sallied onto the ramparts. The strongholds, both Prussian as well as French, all thundered with the frightful fire of small arms. Fumes and smoke veiled the city. Everyone yelled: victory, we have retaken Holm. The ship fired three rounds, then—suddenly—silence. We have taken it, they cried, while others argued to the contrary. Wild disputes arose. Yet alas, the ship and all of its supplies, money, powder, and dispatches were already in the besiegers' hands at six o'clock.[10]

Their defensive spirit broken under the impact of these defeats, several thousand Prussian soldiers deserted, and Napoleon himself attentively monitored the surrender negotiations that soon followed. Without their weapons, the Prussians left Danzig on May 27, and the French entered the city. Around 2,700 soldiers had lost their lives, as had twenty citizens.

Free City—What Now?

When Napoleon visited Danzig on June 1, he made no secret of his agenda. At a meeting with prestigious merchants, he asked curtly: "Eh bien, Messrs., quel est le plus riche (Well, gentlemen, who is the richest)?" The reticent merchants were hesitant to answer, but they finally indicated Theodor Christian Frantzius after the emperor asked more harshly. "Aha, c'est vous? Combien de millions (Aha, it's you? How many millions)?" In fear, Frantzius responded: "Oh, Sire, pas un seul (Oh, Sire, not a single one)." Napoleon announced his intention to find means and ways to open the city's buttoned purses.[11] He would prove successful, and ten years later, Frantzius was not the only one left bankrupt.

After appointing Lefebvre as "Duke of Danzig," the relentless Napoleon demanded a horrendous contribution of 30 million francs from the conquered city. In the Peace of Tilsit between Prussia and France on July 9, he declared Danzig a free city: "The city of Danzig, including an area of two leagues in radius, shall be restored to its previous independence under the protection of the kings of Prussia and Saxony and shall be ruled according to those laws which it had at the time that it ceased ruling itself."[12] He appointed General Jean Rapp governor in Danzig.

The populace's reaction to this restoration of the old glory was by no means unanimously joyful. On the one hand, leading patricians again considered themselves the lords of Danzig and dreamed of the old prosperity, while many people rejoiced in the "long lost freedom."[13] Yet other residents expressed skepticism. Their doubts would prove well-founded, for it very quickly became clear that the emperor had nothing other than his own benefit in mind with the founding of a free city.

Immediately following the occupation, the French rulers formed a new city council that faced nearly irresolvable tasks: how could they ever pay France the unbelievably high contributions demanded of them, especially as the citizens were burdened with billeting the French soldiers, and the Continental System restricted merchants to almost complete inactivity? And what was to be the extent of the city's area? With some restrictions, Danzig ultimately reacquired its old territory, as well as the suburbs whose possession it had unsuccessfully sought for centuries.

The practical formation of a city constitution likewise faced difficulties. A delegation from Danzig stayed in Paris for months to reach an agreement with Napoleon; eventually they effectively returned—at least on paper—to the old conditions. The city government again consisted of three civic orders, though the council was renamed the senate. It quickly became clear who had the say in the city, as Jean Rapp selected all of the senators. Karl Friedrich von Gralath became the city president, and the Free City of Danzig was solemnly proclaimed on July 21, 1807.

It soon became apparent that in its large-scale thinking, the French leadership was hardly concerned with Danzig's citizens. When the relaxed administration failed, despite imperial demand, both to implement the Napoleonic Code and to pay the stipulated contributions within about a year, Rapp lost patience and replaced Gralath as president with Gottlieb Hufeland, a Danzig native and law professor active at the time in the Bavarian city of Landshut. Further measures taken by Rapp included the disempowerment of the Third Order and the establishment of a finance committee tasked with expediting payment of the required contributions.

At first, an enthusiasm about the future prevailed in Danzig, seen for instance in this call to fight for Napoleon in "Song for the Fatherland" by Johann August Arnewald:

> Up, sons of Danzig, why do ye tarry?
> Give yourselves to the flag of your Fatherland!
> The two crosses wave from the lofty banner,
> Beckoning you to the virtue of your ancestors.[14]

The two crosses refer to Danzig's coat of arms, though in his republican zeal, the poet wisely chose to omit the accompanying crown.

Through exposure to the billeted French population in the city, the residents of Danzig became familiar with new, looser forms of etiquette. The French constantly arranged dances and almost completely monopolized the theater, inviting the citizens and their wives and daughters in particular. An anonymous author later recalled this time with disgust: "Church was attended more seldom, the dancefloors more frequently; little half-French children filled the orphanages, while girls afflicted with malign diseases filled the hospitals."[15]

As the Hanseatic morals loosened somewhat, the city's rulers were ill at ease, faced with financial hardships, onerous billeting, and a constant influx of French demands. "The magistrates' affairs are now chiefly confined to nothing else but the procurement of money," the Prussian ambassador wrote from the Free City in 1808.[16] In order to suppress unwanted contact with Prussia or enemies of France, as well as anti-Napoleonic sentiments in the city itself, a strict postal and press censorship was instated.

There was sufficient cause for bitterness in Danzig. The garrisoned French (at least 11,000 men in 1811) enjoyed themselves at the expense of the city and its citizens, while the flow of trade ground almost entirely to a halt. Whereas 1,194 ships had come into port in 1805, only thirty-two arrived in 1808. Most notably, the ban on trade with England impaired economic life; every violation of the continental blockade drew harsh penalties, although inventive merchants found ways to avoid punishment. The self-made man Friedrich Hoene proudly recollected how, by formally conducting trade with England through Sweden, he resourcefully—if not entirely legally—laid the foundation for his fortune during this time:

> To the same degree that the established trading houses flinched from it, this matter . . . had for me a decisive appeal. Supplied by [my trade partner] Solly with everything required from, as well as in, England, and in possession of the French authorities' trust here through my discretion, I soon played a leading part in Danzig, and my name also became known abroad.[17]

In addition to the Continental System, the customs frontiers of Prussia and the Duchy of Warsaw further afflicted the merchants. Local trade also suffered as the French imposed multiple ceiling prices, driving many companies to ruin in the process.

Of the contributions payments demanded again and again by the French, only a small portion had been mustered by 1812. Yet Danzig's actual payment to the French—including the surrender of goods, garrison accommodations, and much more—totaled over 35 million francs by 1813. Thus, despite high unemployment, the taxes were raised, and Danzig took out eighteen consecutive compulsory loans. In April 1812, Senate President Hufeland, who had incidentally quite enjoyed himself in Danzig and left behind large debts, resigned in light of his severely limited options for action and was replaced by Johann Georg Wernsdorf.

Dream's End: The Siege of 1813

Preparations for Napoleon's campaign against Russia began in Danzig in 1811; provisions were stored and field hospitals furnished. As the easternmost outpost of the French Empire, the city played an important role in the war preparations. Beginning in 1812, parts of the Grande Armée passed through Danzig and caused quite a commotion:

> Such a throng in the streets and public squares! . . . Soldiers hurrying up and down with their rifles or packs; wagons rattling back and forth to unload their items, which were bought, requisitioned, or stolen here; now and then a line of oxen teams, the beasts practicing for the trek to Russia.[18]

Napoleon personally inspected the fortifications, which had undergone months of assiduous renovations and improvements, primarily along the city's western front on Bishop's Hill and Hail Hill. Confronted with complaints at a meeting with merchants, he brushed these aside: "Je paye tout, cela s'arrangera (I'll pay for everything. It will work out.)"[19] He could not have come across as particularly reliable. Soon thereafter, he and Governor Rapp left for the east.

Although the war at first seemed distant, its shadow soon drew closer. An English and Russian fleet began to blockade the harbor and bombard Neufahrwasser in September. News from the theaters of war were becoming increasingly alarming. Rapp returned to Danzig in mid-December, having paid for his visit to Russia with a frostbitten nose, ears, and fingers. Preparations for a lengthy siege began immediately, but the harsh winter had left local provisions scarce. When Russians and Prussians surrounded Danzig in early February 1813, about 30,000 soldiers—mainly French and Polish—were stationed in the city alongside its residents. Only half of them were fit for combat. Three thousand military personnel and civilians died from disease and exhaustion in February alone.

The actual battle for the city broke out in early March. After costly weeks for both sides, Danzig was able to enjoy a cease-fire agreed on by the warring parties. Yet because the siege itself continued, the civilian population's supply situation worsened, and food prices reached dizzying heights. The man on the street faced starvation: "His breakfast, lunch, and dinner consisted of the scantiest servings of bran, brandy (if it could be found), linseed cake, and other dishes."[20]

To ease the impact of the siege, the French ordered the residents to leave the city in mid-August. About 6,000 citizens obeyed the command before combat recommenced, and around 16,000 had already fled before then. The combat was concentrated at Danzig's western front. A hundred heavy cannons, twenty-eight howitzers, and sixty-six mortars fired into the city. Langfuhr fell at the beginning of September, and the ring around the city closed tighter. The decisive blow, however, came in the night leading into November 1, when Granary Island caught fire in the bombardment and 171 storehouses went up in flames. The heat was so great that ships on the Motława's opposite shore caught fire.

When news arrived of Napoleon's ruinous defeat in the "Battle of Nations" at Leipzig, General Rapp realized the hopelessness of the situation, and the surrender was signed on November 29, 1813, following days of negotiations. Napoleon's troops were to leave Danzig on January 1, 1814. The siege had cost over 15,000 soldiers their lives. Nearly 6,000 civilians had died as well, mostly from pestilence. Over 1,200 houses were destroyed or damaged, and a massive debt weighed down the city.

In the Shadow of the Past

In 1814, the previous seven years seemed a sinister phantom and were perceived as the city's greatest humiliation in its centuries-old history. Many long-established families were decimated, fortunes wiped out, and traditions demolished. To its citizens, the city appeared "plundered and thoroughly disorganized."[21]

For a short time, it was unclear how Danzig's national future would take shape, as Russia also showed interest in the Baltic port. But eventually, Prussia prevailed and solemnly retook possession of the city on February 19, 1814. When Prussian eagles were again placed on public buildings, they were greeted—unlike in 1793—with "shouts of jubilation from the people."[22] Wilhelm Daniel Keidel, a proponent of a Free City of Danzig, spent months traveling among the European powers to advocate the city's continuing independence from larger states and even attended the Congress of Vienna, but his efforts ultimately came up short.

With its return to Prussia, Danzig once again had to content itself with its role as a bureaucratic garrison town. Nevertheless, the city did become the seat of an administrative district, and more important, the capital of the newly created province of West Prussia, whose governor, the energetic Theodor von Schön, made decisions for Danzig. And prestigious figures contributed to the city's administration, like the great Romantic poet Joseph von Eichendorff, who worked there as the senior administrative councilor for churches and schools between 1821 and 1824. But when the provinces of East and West Prussia were combined in 1823, the governor moved to Königsberg, and Danzig lost substantial political significance.

The lord mayor from 1814 to 1850 was Joachim Heinrich von Weickhmann, a member of a long-established Danzig family. As a skilled administrator, he cared for the needs of the community, yet the strained financial situation, economic difficulties, and problems arising from Danzig's fortified nature gave him only limited options for action. He was succeeded in 1851 by Karl August Groddeck, also the scion of a notable Danzig family.

Citizen control of the magistrates was assured by the city council, which was elected according to a census suffrage initially limited to Danzig's affluent circles (in 1817 this included only citizens with a yearly income of more than 200 thalers, or a mere 2,622 people). The three-class franchise system, which likewise allowed only wealthier residents to cast votes, began in 1853. The merchant bourgeoisie thus secured its influence in city leadership until the end of the First World War; around 1900, about half of the members of the city council were still merchants.

Danzig had to return the sovereignty over its surrounding territory to Prussia in 1814, but Langfuhr, Neufahrwasser, Neu Schottland (Pol. Nowe Szkoty), and a number of other suburbs were directly incorporated into the city, as well as the "combined cities" of Stolzenberg. The city's manorial rights in its former territory expired in 1824; only the right of patronage (custody of the churches) endured longer. Through incorporation, the city would grow from an initial area of 1.5 square miles to about fifty-eight by the First World War.

Debts from the Napoleonic time were a burden for decades. Even though the Prussian state took on a considerable portion of the obligations, the debts were still not paid off until 1860. In the face of economic stagnation, Danzig gladly looked back to its heyday, recalled not only by its great buildings but also in memories and local tales. Already in 1794, only a year after the city's annexation by Prussia, an observer had written:

> You are unlikely to come across such obsolete customs in any European land anymore. Whether in Protestant or Catholic countries, you will not find the spirit of the previous century so pure and unadulterated in all public dealings, all ordinances, in politics, and in the entire constitution, as you will among us.[23]

Gazing proudly to the past, the longtime established citizens reportedly "cleaved to the old like an oyster to its shell," while looking with condescension on the Prussian officials.[24] An aversion among many in Danzig to all things Prussian lingered for a long time. At the same time, though, the people were aware that they were falling behind other cities in the kingdom and moving increasingly to the periphery of economic and political events. Thus, a poet wrote in 1836:

> In the pages of history, I read the accounts with awe
> How wondrously splendid and how mighty you once had been,
> How far over land and sea your fame's boisterous echo
> At one time resonated, with triumphant force, across the entire earth.
> ...
> Danzig, you queen of cities—those fair times, they now recede,
> Your potency now lies in ruins, your radiance has grown pale,
> Only in memory do you still live on glorious and grand—
> All which is born from the womb of time—change is its certain lot!
> ...
> Danzig, loveliest of cities! Though your commerce too is laid low—
> That of which the present robs you, the future shall restore to you;
> Destinies change eternally in the speedy course of time,
> That which is born from the womb of time is subject but to change.[25]

While efforts to draw hope from former greatness and return in spirit to the glory of their forebears would characterize the city into the twenty-first century, there were nevertheless some historical situations in which the overall environment appeared to change radically and the citizens found themselves forced into new contexts. One such situation arose in 1848. The revolution in Berlin had hardly begun, and political reform in Germany had entered the realm of possibility; Prussian Poles active in this "Spring of Nations" had just posited the possibility of restoring the Polish state to its historical boundaries, including Danzig, when the magistrates and city council drafted an address to the German Confederation. Danzig was, they wrote, a German city through and through, even if it had spent a long period under Polish "domination."

> Thoroughly German, our hearts beat for Germany's welfare and honor and foster the edifying hope that this inner harmony with our German brethren, passed down from our fathers and kept alive in our sentiment, will also find outward recognition.... At this time we are confronted by the voices of those Poles who claim Prussia and our city as belonging to their nationality. We respect their national sentiment, but only insofar as it is not misused and leaves the rights of others unoffended.... We are German and wish to remain so!

They requested the German Confederation's recognition "as descendants of the earlier German settlers and as loyal stewards of German morals and sentiments," that they might be permitted to participate in building up "the fortune and resplendence of the German fatherland."[26]

This document indicates how drastic a change the city's political consciousness had undergone. On the wave of nationalist excitement, spurred on by the Romantic concept of the nation, the citizenry's hopes for the future no longer rested in the least on Poland but exclusively on Germany. Trade connections with Russian territory gained in the Partitions of Poland had been heavily disrupted by the customs borders, and personal interaction between Danzig's Germans and Polish nobles had long shifted from rule to exception, so that hardly any residual emotional ties to the former kingdom existed.

Despite the rapidly escalating conflicts in Europe in 1848, things in Danzig initially remained calm. When censorship of the press was lifted, many new newspapers emerged, in which local as well as transregional issues were discussed. Upon returning from a lively Berlin, satirist Carl Queisner versified his impressions in one of these papers, the *Danziger Krakehler* (Danzig agitator):

> I returned, then, to Danzig, so quiet, so lovely,
> I haven't seen such conditions in any other place.
> The people here don't value hard-earned joy;
> They only want their trade and commerce back.
>
> ...
>
> They do not consider history's ominous course—
> Oh, that this coziness would never end.[27]

Still, a constitutional society was organized in Danzig, challenging radicals and reactionaries alike; a leftist "Democratic Club" and a reactionary "Fatherland Society" followed shortly thereafter. Hoping for a bright future in the new German Empire, Danzig sent delegates to the Frankfurt National Assembly held at St. Paul's Church in Frankfurt am Main, ready to offer even Lake Saspe near the Baltic Sea as a prospective wartime port for the German navy.

Yet the reactionaries reared their heads. On March 18, 1849, the Democratic Club arranged a large banquet outside of the city and marched through the streets in a great parade celebrating the anniversary of the March Revolution. Conflict arose near the Oliva Gate with members of the "lowest social classes," who, "armed with knives, clubs, and fence posts," attacked the democrats. "Their flags were ripped apart and trampled in the filth. The street fight was bloody and rancorous; thirteen were injured, the majority of them severely, and four dead were tallied on the side of the attackers."[28] Reportedly instigated by the democrats' opponents, the conflict halted the city's momentum toward political reform. Modernization would begin in other ways a short time later.

Economy: Decline and New Signs of Life

Economic life struggled in Danzig after 1815. Along with the merchants' poor capital resources, inconsistent business activity and tariffs also played a role. The situation only changed when the tariffs fell during the free trade movement in the mid-nineteenth century. Yet Danzig had to watch as port cities like Stettin, Königsberg, or even Memel (present-day Klaipėda, Lithuania) grew rapidly while its own development languished. Marked by renewed tariff protectionism and promotion of domestic industry, the German Empire's economic policies after 1879 again heavily penalized Danzig, which depended on trade. The continuing struggle against protective tariffs would define Danzig's liberally oriented merchant bourgeoisie.

Danzig's access to a large economic trading area had always played an essential role in the city's development. However, its most important transport route,

Figure 6.2 Around 1870, a photographer named Ballerstaedt captured one of the most fascinating early photographs of Danzig. Around these buildings on Wood Market are ragamuffins, merchants in top hats, and even a real *Bowke*, or transient worker, lounging on a wagon. In the 1990s, photographs like this one awakened an interest among Gdańsk's Polish population in the lost German past of their home city. From Donald Tusk et al., *Był sobie Gdańsk* (Gdańsk, 1996). Biblioteka Gdańska Polskiej Akademii Nauk.

the Vistula River, decreased in significance: low water levels and poor river maintenance impeded the use of larger barges, leading to high freight costs.

Quite unexpectedly, the Vistula, blocked by ice floes during a cold winter, spilled across a few miles of the inland portion of the Vistula Spit near Plehnendorf (Pol. Płonia) early in the morning of February 2, 1840, forming the new estuary of Neufähr (Pol. Górki Zachodnie). The previous estuary arm became the "Dead Vistula." This eliminated the threat of flooding in Danzig once and for all and ended the river's deposition of soil and materials in the harbor. In addition, following the construction of a sluice, there was a new dock located between the Vistula's main current and Danzig; this dock would be particularly important for lumber storage. From 1890 to 1895, a channel measuring over four and a half miles was dug northward to straighten the estuary. The new route passed between Schiewenhorst (Pol. Świbno) and Nickelswalde (Pol. Mikoszewo).

Yet not all of the port's problems disappeared. The old Motława harbor suffered from low water levels and increased narrowing, which resulted in the growing role of the outer harbor in Neufahrwasser, where more and more ships were unloaded. A new railway was built for Neufahrwasser in 1867, followed by a new wet dock in 1879. At the close of the century, a new harbor called the Kaiserhafen was created between Neufahrwasser and the city center. The number of ships coming to Danzig had declined sharply since reaching 3,200 in 1862, but the figure slowly climbed back to about 2,800 shortly before the First World War.

The matter of railway connections proved to be a problem. Sparking anxiety among local merchants, the Prussian Eastern Railway linking Berlin and Königsberg was constructed passing to the south of Danzig; the city obtained access in 1852 through a junction from Dirschau. Having learned from these difficulties, the merchants lobbied all the more vehemently for the Marienburg-Mławka Railway, which opened in 1877 and greatly facilitated grain transport from the Russian-Polish areas to the harbor.

Danzig prospered as the movement of goods in its harbor more than tripled between 1871 and 1913. Yet this rate of growth was minor in comparison to other cities, and not only large port cities like Hamburg and Bremen, but even Stettin and Lübeck, which overtook Danzig as the second largest German port on the Baltic Sea by the beginning of the First World War. Above all, the lucrative trade in colonial goods dwindled in Danzig, and the harbor lost its international status, even though its goods turnover was still the fifth highest of all Baltic ports in 1913, behind Riga but ahead of Königsberg.

The main export goods remained, as always, grain and wood. The grain primarily came from Prussian territory, where crop yields skyrocketed in the nineteenth century, while the Russian sector of Poland exported less grain to Danzig. The chief consumer was still England. Lumber traded in Danzig arrived mostly from Russian Poland and primarily made its way to England and the Netherlands. With advances in beet cultivation, the export of sugar grew in importance. The significance of visible trade with Prussian and German ports grew, while other, historically important economic relations—for instance, with Amsterdam—slackened. The most sought-after imports apart from colonial goods were salt and wine, but demand grew for coal and iron as industrialization accelerated. Although the volume of seaward imports initially stood far behind that of exports, this centuries-old ratio reversed itself in the 1870s, and more was imported than exported through Danzig.

Shipbuilding was still not one of Danzig strengths. There were 108 completed ships registered in the harbor in 1850, and only twenty-two in 1910. Enterprisers in Danzig purchased their first steamboats around 1840, and in the 1880s, the sailing ships in the harbor were outnumbered by steamboats, although few of these belonged to local companies.

Industrialization did not come easily to Danzig, and billowing smokestacks were still the exception along the city's skyline. The fortified nature of the city hindered not only industrial settlement, since massive structures had long been prohibited within a broad strip surrounding the fortifications, but also efficient traffic infrastructure. Until the mid-nineteenth century, industry in Danzig remained limited (apart from the Royal Firearms Factory) to several mills, major breweries, and shipyards. Danzig's more economically influential residents were mainly interested in trade, and they also lacked the necessary capital for industrial investments. Danzig thus fell behind cities like Königsberg, Stettin, and even Elbing in industrial development. In 1850, it had only three industrial enterprises with more than fifty employees; in these, two steam engines produced a mere six horsepower.

Local economic attitudes changed, if slowly. Founded in 1850, the trailblazer for large industry was the Royal Shipyard (renamed the Imperial Shipyard in 1871), which would become one of Prussia's—and later Germany's—three most important military shipyards. Growing powerful through the construction of ships and submarines for the Imperial German Navy, it provided its several thousand employees with high wages and benefits. The Schichau Shipyard in Elbing decided to build an additional facility in Danzig. Shipping lines like the Hamburg America Line (HAPAG) and North German Lloyd (Norddeutscher Lloyd) were soon commissioning ocean liners here, and the Schichau yard in Danzig would later build cruisers for Nazi Germany's navy, the Kriegsmarine. The shipyard employed over 4,000 people in 1913. Incidentally, the military not only provided the shipyard with commissions but also generated good business for the firearms factory, which employed around 1,000 people, and the artillery workshops.

Yet as the nineteenth century came to a close, Danzig was still an industrial lightweight compared with other large Prussian cities. To change this, Governor Gustav von Goßler worked with regional merchants to develop a plan for the state to foster local industrialization. These efforts foundered, however, with the collapse of the Nordische Elektrizitäts- und Stahlwerke AG (Nordic Electrical and Steel Works, Inc.) a few years later. Far from the large industrial centers, such artificially established undertakings were doomed to fail due to long transport routes and insufficient markets.

While large-scale industry had its problems, a relatively high amount of mid-sized and smaller factories—largely food processing and wood processing companies, as well as chemical firms—were able to establish themselves and manufacture for the regional market. Friedrich Heykings, who had built a factory for stairways and iron construction, recalled the entrepreneurial spirit of the times in his memoirs:

> I saw my proud wish fulfilled. I saw the beautiful factory with its tall chimney—our mansion; though burdened with debts that stretched past the chimney, it was yet fortified with pride, enthusiasm, and strength. We had reached our longed-for goal. . . . We were lawful, officially registered factory owners in the venerable, lovely old city of Danzig.[29]

Traditionally well-represented in Danzig, skilled crafts also remained vitally important through the nineteenth century. There were 1,758 master craftsmen in 1828, a figure that would hardly change. Shoemakers, cabinetmakers, and butchers were the most numerous; with the city's advancing growth, master builders became especially wealthy. While guilds decreased in importance as centers of artisan sociability, other forms of community formation gained popularity, such as the trade association, founded in 1828.

Becoming a Metropolis

In the 1850s, a jolt shot through civic society. The liberal *Danziger Zeitung* (Danzig tidings) newspaper, established in 1858, became the mouthpiece of a new generation of citizens who championed a comprehensive urban modernization that, with some interruptions, would take a half century. An external indicator of the shift was the election of a new lord mayor. Leopold von Winter, a former police chief in Berlin, took office in 1863 and was a very conscious choice—not for a native, but rather a charismatic, liberal government official. His twenty-seven-year incumbency shaped the city like none other.

With the "Danzig Affair" of summer 1863, Winter's tenure began with a bang. Known for his liberal sympathies, Crown Prince Frederick William delivered a speech in Danzig in which he openly criticized Bismarck's policies and angered King William I. This purportedly spoiled Winter's chances to return to Berlin and become governor there. What hindered his progress at Prussia's royal court would benefit Danzig, though, because he dedicated himself all the more to local issues. A storm of modernization swept through the city and its administration, first (and significantly) seizing the Main Town's city hall, which since the eighteenth century had lacked modern amenities and could not provide adequate work conditions for a modern administration. Its renovation even included fitting the old walls with a state-of-the-art hot-water heating system.

The greatest reform initiative was the development of a water supply and sewage system. The city's hygienic conditions had hardly changed for centuries. Wastewater was channeled from the streets to the Motława through small, partly open sewage canals, "and the most nauseating kitchen waste—animal innards, bones, and cod heads—sat there in the open gutter."[30] While the wealthy had fresh water brought into the city by wagon, those in the poor quarters often had to draw water from the Radunia Canal, which promoted the spread of disease.

When cholera passed through Central Europe in 1831, Danzig was the first Prussian city in which the disease took hold, and the epidemic was particularly severe in the port city. All sanitary measures—isolation of the sick, fumigation of apartments, and a military cordon sanitaire around the city—had proven ineffective, and the population lived in great fear for months. Most deaths from cholera occurred between May and November and affected primarily the poorer classes. Danzig would be afflicted with repeated cholera epidemics over subsequent decades. Since scientists had no answers to the origin of the disease, poets attempted to counter cholera in verse:

> Abominable Fury, emerged from Orcus,
> Savage! Murderess!
> Destroyer of all our springtime pleasures,
> Cholera morbus! Oh leave us in peace.[31]

Only after the disease's bacterial causes had been discovered was Danzig's problem identified as water contamination. After lengthy discussions about the financial cost, the city council decided on the construction of an aqueduct and a sewer system. Advised by English experts, an aqueduct stretching over twelve miles from the headwater region in Prangenau (Pol. Pręgowo) into Danzig was first completed by 1871, and sewers were thereafter installed in the city center. The wastewater was sanitized on large septic drain fields between Heubude (Pol. Stogi) and the Weichselmünde Fortress. With this, Danzig was the first city on the European continent to possess a sewage system with wastewater treatment. Public health improved dramatically, and the number of deaths from typhoid shrank by two-thirds.

Further reforms during Winter's time as mayor—financed thanks to favorable economic conditions, state assistance, and, above all, liberal borrowing—included an upgraded harbor, development of the school system, and a disputed adjustment of traffic routes in the historical city center to cope with the growing traffic volume.

At the same time, the political climate was changing: Prussia, and therefore Danzig, became a member of the North German Confederation in 1866. In 1871, for the first time in its history, the city became part of a German empire.

The citizenry appreciated the significance of this step, and on January 31, 1871, the council approved an address drafted by the magistrates to the new emperor, in which the municipal powers expressed their gratification that Danzig finally belonged to Germany. At the same time, they sensed an obligation to legitimize this affiliation. Since there was not sufficient common political history to draw on, they argued using other categories:

> Our city admittedly did not belong to the external union of the earlier German Empire. Yet having emerged from German colonization, as a Hanseatic city and facilitator of German trade with the Slavic peoples, as an outpost of German culture, which it boldly and triumphantly upheld even during the time when Polish rule extended to its gates, it has always adhered to Germany in an inner union.

Danzig, they wrote, was finally a "fully entitled member of the complete German Empire," closing their address "in deepest veneration" and "most obediently."[32]

The new empire stirred greater local interest in pan-German issues, and some of Danzig's citizens pursued careers in imperial politics. Among these was Heinrich Rickert, editor and part owner of the *Danziger Zeitung* newspaper, who held a seat in the German imperial parliament for the liberals beginning in 1874. Moderate liberals long dominated political life in Danzig until the National Liberals and Social Democrats gained strength prior to the First World War. Rickert and Lord Mayor Winter were integral in another of Danzig's triumphs: they advocated West Prussia's detachment from the province of Prussia, since it had often been unable to assert itself against the larger East Prussia. Danzig once again became the capital city of a province in 1878. The city's additional duties in this capacity contributed to its continuing upswing.

Even with a liberal population, Danzig was still loyal to the crown, and visits from the monarch were always cause for lavish folk festivities. When William I passed through the city while returning from his coronation in Königsberg in 1861, for instance, Danzig greeted him with decorated ships, triumphal arches, royal busts, and grand illumination. Enamored by the military, William II would make frequent appearances in the city, which was one of his most important garrisons (he was less fond of the liberal citizenry). German rulers also occasionally met in Danzig with Russian tsars, such as in 1881, when William I and Alexander III met on the Motława, or when William II invited Nicholas II to the Kaisermanöver, the military exercises held annually for the emperor.

Lord Mayor Winter resigned from office in 1890 due to serious illness. His successors were uniformly unable to distinguish themselves as he had; those who

Figure 6.3 After the early modern city walls were partially removed in the 1890s, the city changed its look. Suddenly the High Gate no longer stood between ramparts but rather between a hotel and administration buildings, all attractively built in the neo-Renaissance style. Kaiser Wilhelm I (right) kept watch in front of the gate until he was toppled from his pedestal in 1945. From Herder-Institut, Marburg, Germany, 138875.

came closest were the future imperial minister of the interior Clemens Gottlieb Delbrück (1896–1902) and Heinrich Scholtz (1910–1918). Governor Gustav von Goßler, who took office in 1891, concerned himself not only with industrial development but also with founding a university. Modern facilities continued to appear in Danzig in the meantime: a gasworks, fire stations, a slaughterhouse and stockyard, a municipal electric works, and, shortly before the First World War, a city hospital with over 800 beds.

A major issue in Danzig at the turn of the century was the abolition of construction restraints around the early modern ramparts, which led to the fortifications' removal and the city's expansion. The old ramparts had become pointless in the age of long-range artillery, and after sustained efforts, Danzig managed to purchase part of the ramparts from the state in 1895. These were leveled, enabling the construction of new, broad streets and access roads in the Main Town and Old Town; numerous new residential and commercial buildings, as well as hotels; and a set of prestigious public buildings, such as the main railway station, a branch of the empire's central bank (Reichsbank), the municipal library, and the state archives. By the First World War, Danzig finally appeared to have become a proper metropolis, as Bruno Pompecki depicted it in an expressionist poem:

> In the tangle of the metropolis,
> Smoke-enwreathed,
> Blessed by dim evening glow,
> In warm brickred
> The old gables gleam,
> Coy, covert, and overflown by crows.
> The rails drone distant on arched bridges—
> In the silent gable
> A child dozes over a schoolbook.[33]

Of Citizens, Workers, and Anti-Polonism

The city's population grew rapidly in the nineteenth century, increasing from nearly 48,000 residents in 1816 to around 70,000 in 1860, once again reaching the total from the mid-seventeenth century. The modernization and industrialization that began at this point attracted droves of immigrants, largely from surrounding areas and especially from the religiously and nationally diverse regions of West Prussia. Almost 90,000 people lived in Danzig in 1871, more than doubling to over 192,000 by 1915. Langfuhr, as well as Schidlitz (Pol. Siedlce), the Old Town, Ohra, and Neufahrwasser all underwent notable growth, developing into centers of the petite bourgeoisie and proletariat.

A good number of the residents were soldiers belonging to one of the many regiments stationed there, including a life hussars regiment (and a second by 1901), as well as the 128th Danzig Infantry Regiment, newly established in 1882. In 1891, the city became the seat of the Twenty-Seventh Army Corps and shortly thereafter received a military college to provide officer training. Danzig was also an important naval base. At times, Prussian soldiers and their families made up over 10 percent of the total population.

At first, the old bourgeois families who had built their wealth through trade set the tone in Danzig, but as the city's significance in international trade regressed, the merchants increasingly struggled to maintain their status. More than a few trading companies collapsed in the nineteenth century. The middle and lower bourgeoisie was relatively large and consisted primarily of skilled workers, retailers, and public officials. Their numbers rose steadily, although the proportions shifted. Once prominent, the artisans lost influence, while the educated middle class—physicians and lawyers, as well as teachers and higher officials—gained greater standing in the urban society.

The number of laborers constantly rose despite local industrialization's sluggish progress. About a thousand industrial workers were counted in the city in 1861, and the number had risen to more than 20,000 in 1913, with over a quarter of these employed by the three largest shipyards. Two-thirds of the laborers hailed from outside of Danzig.

The growing industrial proletariat faced the danger of unemployment during times of economic difficulty. When jobs were lost, as in 1894, when the Schichau Shipyard laid off 1,200 workers, labor conflicts arose in which increasingly better organized unions stepped in. In 1911, the workforce at the Schichau Shipyard went on strike for twenty weeks (and were shut out of the facilities), although they could not enforce their demands. As elsewhere, the Social Democrats made great strides in Danzig following the founding of the German Empire in 1871, yet not great enough to endanger the position of the middle-class parties. Nevertheless, the bourgeoisie was well aware of the increasing fragility of its rule.

A city growing as rapidly as Danzig depended on immigration. Already by the mid-nineteenth century, "old Danzigers" sometimes found themselves on the defensive. One of these, Eduard Garbe, published a desperate appeal in 1880 following the demolition of a number of revered buildings:

> There are no more Danzigers! Those now designated by this name are foreigners who have purchased the old patrician homes (often for low prices), largely stripped them of their decoration, and transformed them into mundane, modern trinket shops. Foreigners hold most public offices—the weal and woe of our city rests in the hands of strangers who by nature show interest neither in the past nor the treasures still present in a place where they were not born and whose great history they are unlikely—and even undesirous—to know or display.[34]

But nothing was to be done to stop the city's transformation, which was also reflected in the population's religious makeup. The ratio of Catholics increased markedly from 23.6 percent in 1816 to exactly one-third in 1910; Protestants, who had represented 70 percent of the population in 1816, were only 64.6 percent in 1910. In 1814, the number of Jews in Danzig had grown markedly through the integration of a number of suburbs. Even so, they still represented only 4.6 percent of the population in 1816. They competed with Christian merchants, leading in one instance to a "Jewish tumult" during St. Dominic's Fair in 1821, when a large crowd demolished Jewish booths. The Jewish population diminished over the following century and was only 1.4 percent by 1910 but they erected a large synagogue in 1887, an expression of the new Jewish self-consciousness.

Nineteenth-century Danzig was still predominantly a German-speaking city. Though Polish was always present, mostly spoken by visitors or servants, it was only sporadically heard among the civic elites. This did not change much, even when industrialization brought a surge of Polish and Kashubian speaking immigrants from the Catholic rural areas outside of the city; for the most part, migrants quickly assimilated into the German majority. Near the end of the century, however, Poles began to assert themselves: representatives of the middle class founded the first Polish organization in 1876, which they called Ogniwo (Link). A Polish daily newspaper, the *Gazeta Gdańska* (Gdańsk gazette), was established in 1891, although it was mainly read in the countryside; in 1896, there were only ninety-one subscriptions of Polish newspapers in Danzig itself.

Despite the marginal role played by Poles in Danzig prior to the First World War, the German-Polish ethnic conflict intensified in the city, especially after the foundation of the German Empire. Already in 1872, as West Prussia celebrated the 100th anniversary of its transition to Prussia, the local press focused on the value of "Germandom," of the "torch of German culture," on "Polish pretension" and a "Slavic deluge."[35] Cultivated by organizations like the German Eastern Marches Society (Ostmarkenverein) and propagated by newspapers like the *Danziger Neueste Nachrichten* (Latest Danzig news), an ideology began to dominate the imagination of mainly conservative and national-liberal circles in the city. The language of national hubris quickly became radicalized. In 1902, when the Eastern Marches Society organized a "German Day" in Danzig, the local chapter's chairman, a district judge, said in his historical remarks:

> Danzig kept the German shield bright and glorious during the three-hundred-year night of Polish barbarism that spilled across our land! It was German and remained German in the surging billows of the Slavic flood, until the German Hohenzollerns, the kings of Prussia, brought salvation both to the city and the unhappy region.[36]

From talk of "the mob of Polish agitators,"[37] it was no longer much of a leap to the assertion that "[we] here in the Eastern Marches are at war. . . . For the Fatherland, we must sacrifice our possessions and—if it should one day become necessary—our blood."[38] Even if the ethnic conflict was only superficially stoked in Danzig, it nevertheless marked the thinking of many Germans for generations.

Everyday Life, Poverty. Home?

In a city as large as Danzig, the most diverse realms of experience collided. One could spend delightful childhoods here, as the novelist Julie Burow did in the 1820s, picking flowers between the Main Town's gabled roofs in the summer.

Burow rhapsodized: "Here, by means of board fragments shoved between the roof tiles, we created authentic fairylands, arbors in which my flowers grew most merrily entwined."[39] At the same time, the city's narrow alleys stank; they were, as one contemporary described, "so dank, and they exhale[d] such loathsome fumes from the gutters, that somebody accustomed to life in airier and healthier cities would be horrified."[40]

Illuminated by gaslight only since 1854, these partly paved streets were full of noise and life, even before motorized transportation. Beggars, organ grinders, and brass band musicians drew attention. Men and women sang or called out to offer their wares and services, especially on Fish Market. And seamen set the tone in the harbor districts—as did all those hoping to squeeze money from them.

Poverty was a frequent guest in the city. The *Danziger Dampfboot* (Danzig steamboat) reported on a nighttime visit to an apartment of petty thieves in 1834:

> The ground is loose and full of pits, over which you make your way by means of rotten boards, and not without natural trepidation. But now to the room itself! Here lies a filthy couple on a meager bed of straw covered in rags, and there is another, practically on the naked floorboards; beyond these lies the lair of the old hag in charge of this rabble, who by her voice and countenance all too vividly presents the image of a witch. Upon passing more individuals, the visitor finds a layer of naked children lying on repulsive straw.[41]

Danzig was never free of poverty. Maidservants lived a very modest life working for officials' families, who for their part were able to maintain a decent quality of life only with great difficulty. Before the First World War, in fact, around 87 percent of Danzig's residents rented their homes.

The wealthy citizens led an entirely different existence. Furniture and household effects distinguished the patrician houses, while the more modern apartments from the late nineteenth century displayed the "Berlin flavor" and were increasingly illuminated with electric lighting, even before the First World War. A telephone even rang now and then: there were 734 phones in 1899 and almost 5,000 in 1913.

Most people in Danzig spoke a High German colored by Low German, and Low German (Plattdeutsch) was mainly heard among the lower economic classes. A local dialect known as Missingsch developed over the course of the nineteenth century, partially through the influence of the many immigrants.

Danzig residents spent their free time in one of the diverse associations dedicated to pastimes such as singing or mutual commemoration of military service. Social associations, pastry shops, and fraternal societies' meetings in the revitalized Artus Court were also popular gathering places, as were the Masonic lodges, bars, and dives. Free time was incidentally not available to many. Working shifts for laborers were often fourteen to sixteen hours a day until well into the nineteenth century.

People ice-skated on the frozen waterways during the winter, while forests and beaches enticed them in the summer. The public beaches came into vogue in the latter half of the century, with urban dwellers flocking to the water in Brösen (Pol. Brzeźno), Glettkau (Pol. Jelitkowo), Heubude, Westerplatte, and above all Zoppot, which rapidly developed into a glamorous health resort. Hiking was also fashionable, and citizens satisfied their cravings in Danzig's beautiful surroundings. At the same time, the notion of *Heimat*[42] emerged as a reaction to the accelerating changes in the familiar countryside: smokestacks stretched into the sky, and hammering rang out from the shipyards; threats of labor unrest loomed while Poles were purportedly disrupting the *gemütlich* German way of life. All this led to a glorification of the perceived "unmarred world" of early-modern Danzig and its supposedly unspoiled natural surroundings.

Culture in the Province

Danzig's flagging economic potency and loss of political significance stifled cultural life. The city became provincial in all respects and would not again develop greater cultural appeal until the turn of the twentieth century. It did not offer attractive conditions for important artists and intellectuals, and whoever among them—despite grander ambitions—landed in Danzig usually did not stay long. Danzig propped itself up on the memory of its brilliant past, but it was a mere shadow of its former self. In spite of all this, the city was the cultural center of a large area and still the most important urban hub between Stettin, Warsaw, and Königsberg.

The initial cessation of construction activity was particularly striking. After 1814, Danzig was primarily busy rebuilding the heavily damaged city, many of whose middle-class houses received simple, neoclassical façades. There were incidentally around 4,000 such townhomes inside the ramparts—the same number as 300 years earlier. Any major new buildings were barracks built by the military.

Even though hardly any new structures took shape, many old buildings disappeared. In addition to a large portion of the city wall separating the Main Town and Old Town for centuries, a number of medieval (and at this point functionless) city gates were torn down to improve traffic conditions. Many other historic buildings fell victim to age and negligence: the Bridgettine Convent and Dominican Monastery were torn down, and the dilapidated Renaissance gables of the Green Gate disappeared. The splendid, gothic house façade at 14 Bakers' Street received a blessing in disguise when Karl Schinkel reconstructed it on Berlin's Peacock Island at the Prussian king's bidding.

Resistance eventually began to stir against the demolition of the city's structures. A new "Association for the Preservation of Antique Structures and Art Monuments in Danzig" was founded in 1856 to oppose the "alien and intrusive blind obsession with innovation."[43] The salvation of the *Beischläge*, the city's iconic terraces, was especially disputed; owners of houses and shops particularly wanted to tear down these "old, decrepit fixtures,"[44] in order to widen streets and build sidewalks, thereby improving access to their places of business, in which large display windows could then replace the smaller lattice windows. The preservationists' struggle for this unique component of the cityscape was ultimately in vain. While between 1,500 and 1,700 Beischläge and porches had still existed in 1868, only ninety-three remained in 1910.

Near the end of the century, renewed opposition arose against the capricious treatment of the city's architectural heritage. Sculptor Rudolf Freitag advocated the preservation of the Franciscan Monastery, which was converted into both a school and the City Museum; the Green Gate reobtained its Renaissance gables in 1886; the remaining Beischläge were placed under protection soon thereafter; and finally, a new preservationist society formed in 1900.

The re-establishment of West Prussia provided an impetus for urban development. The office block of "New Danzig," an administrative district set up in the suburb of New Gardens mainly for the provincial leadership and parliament, drew from the artistic legacy of old Danzig with its neo-Renaissance architecture. The structures built after the ramparts were leveled also followed this aesthetic. Through this very late expansion of the historical city beyond the former fortifications, Danzig finally grew into a large city.

The city's inner districts progressively developed into administrative and business sectors. Many wealthy citizens chose to leave the crowded Main Town and Old Town and built mansions in Langfuhr, and later in Oliva or Zoppot, as well; those with less money joined housing cooperatives. Routes for horses and streetcars, as well as railway lines to Zoppot and Neufahrwasser, greatly facilitated urban traffic conditions. For this reason, the population decreased, particularly in the Main Town, whose residents only totaled 5,900 in 1914.

Art did not flourish in Danzig. Already in 1808, somebody wrote sarcastically that the city lacked "home-grown art, for it would be driven to starvation here. Aside from culinary and confectionary artists and the like, no artist prospers in Danzig. The people here love a roast beef or veal cutlet more than any work of fine art."[45] The muses did not entirely abandon the city, though. Theater, for instance, moved to the center of bourgeois self-conception. The building that housed theater productions until the end of the eighteenth century no longer sufficed; thus from 1798 to 1801, a corporation founded by merchant Jakob Kabrun had the Municipal Theater constructed in early neoclassical style on Coal Market. The theater, which seated 1,600 people, was soon widely referred to as the "Coffee Grinder" because of its characteristic dome. It was initially managed by private businesses, but due to Danzig's poor economic situation, the Prussian king purchased and leased the theater in 1814. One especially successful leaseholder was Friedrich Genée (1841–1854), who not only attracted many talented actors to the Motława, but also staged a number of ambitious productions.

The new theater also turned out to be too small, but numerous debates only yielded modest improvements before the First World War. Regardless, the theater was the societal epicenter of the city and even attracted the lower class, who participated in cultural life to seek access to the big wide world and opportunities for advancement. In 1890, a journalist described the scene high up in the cheapest seats, where

> the simple soldier, a robust infantryman relaxing with his darling, a common cook, eats a sausage sandwich while moved to tears at Mary Stuart's impending execution; where the apprentice boy and his friend sit on Sunday, having spent their scant pocket money to partake in the refined amusement of a Berlin farce.[46]

The theater staged 137 different works in the 1900/1901 season alone, including thirty-three operas and operettas, twenty-five comedies and farces, and thirty-seven dramas and tragedies. Like the Municipal Theater, the Wilhelmtheater on Long Garden also attracted the masses with variety shows, and for a time it was the most prominent German variety theater east of Berlin.

Literary production was thoroughly tailored for local and regional consumption. While there were many in Danzig who enjoyed wielding the pen to commit poems, prose, and even plays to paper, almost none of their work found their way outside of the city, and they could usually expect little more than publication in a Danzig newspaper or perhaps a book from a regional publishing house. Some local writers, such as satirist Wilhelm Schumacher or the moralizing Protestant Walther Domansky, achieved great fame in Danzig, and Artur Brausewetter, the preacher in St. Mary's Church, even found notable extra-regional success with his many light novels.

On the other hand, some Danzig natives who moved away early were able to write themselves into literary history: painter and writer Robert Reinick; Aaron Bernstein, who found fame with his *Naturwissenschaftliche Volksbücher* (Popular books on natural science); Johannes Trojan, who edited the Berlin satirical magazine *Kladderadatsch*[47] for many years; and the bold futurist Paul Scheerbart. Dramatist Max Halbe, in contrast, never lived in Danzig; although he was born south of the city near Dirschau, Danzig still happily claimed him as one of their own, once the sensational success of his 1893 play *Jugend* (Youth) made Halbe a major figure in literary naturalism. Flattered by the city's recognition, Halbe set the action of some of his later plays in Danzig.

The musical scene in Danzig bore only provincial significance for some time and consisted of a number of busy organists, military bands, traveling virtuosos, and the Municipal Theater with its orchestra, conductors, and singers. Home concerts were also fashionable during this period. Singing and orchestral societies gained popularity over the nineteenth century, and trained and lay musicians performed public oratorios and chamber music. The city had several music schools and an eminent music critic in Carl Fuchs.

While conditions were thus favorable for artistic re-creation, they were not so conducive to actual creation. Consequently, the fine arts were hardly thriving in an economically impoverished city; artists with more than just local appeal were not to be found in Danzig. The great historical paintings created for the Main Town's city hall at the century's end were assigned exclusively to painters from outside the city. Local painters often earned their keep as art instructors while painting genre scenes and portraits on the side. Johann Carl Schulz gained recognition with his lovely copper engravings of the old city. A major shift occurred with the 1873 opening of the City Museum, in which local artwork as well as art from important German painters was collected and displayed. The city's most distinguished work of art, Hans Memling's altar triptych *The Last Judgment*, had long been returned to St. Mary's Church after an enamored Napoleon had taken it to Paris.

Danzig's most important school, the Academic Secondary School, merged with St. Mary's Parish School in 1817 to form the Municipal Secondary School, which in 1837 moved into a new building designed by Karl Schinkel. A navigation school for helmsmen had existed since 1817, and another institution of higher education, the Royal Secondary School, was established in 1876, with other schools following rapidly. As always, the primary schools were overcrowded and in bad condition; in 1910 the class sizes in the city's thirty primary schools averaged forty-six pupils.

Individuals like Hevelius or Lengnich notwithstanding, Danzig had never been a great center of science; this changed very little in the nineteenth century, at least at first. The Danzig Research Society only had twelve members in 1812 but became very active again around midcentury, emerging as a pillar of scientific life. The Westpreußische Geschichtsverein (West Prussian Historical Association), founded in 1879, made outstanding research contributions to local and regional history. Among the major scholars active in Danzig were

Christoph Coelestin Mrongovius, a Polish instructor and compiler of valued German-Polish and Polish-German dictionaries; historians Theodor Hirsch and Paul Simson; and Hugo Conwentz, who directed the Provinzialgewerbemuseum (Provincial craft museum) but made a name for himself first and foremost as a pioneer of the natural conservation movement. Many other intellectuals from Danzig made headlines, especially philosophers Arthur Schopenhauer and Heinrich Rickert.

Drastic change came when Berlin, after longtime efforts, agreed to found the Danzig Technical University, a stately neo-Renaissance building located between the city center and Langfuhr, which the emperor personally inaugurated in 1904. The university boasted departments in architecture, civil engineering, mechanical and electric engineering, naval architecture and marine engineering, chemistry, and general sciences. The city's scientific and intellectual landscape experienced a lasting vitalization with the more than thirty professors who were called to Danzig, as well as the additional teaching staff and the students, whose numbers soon exceeded 1,000.

War and the Future

Hectic commotion engulfed the city when the First World War broke out in August 1914. The regiments stationed in Danzig were sent to the front, and many men drafted into the army departed among copious tears and flowers. The shipyards, having grown large through the empire's fleet construction policies, received new commissions. More than 6,000 workers were employed at the Imperial Shipyard in 1918, mostly with U-boat construction, and the labor shortage necessitated the compulsory recruitment of Polish workers. Trade encountered difficult times, however, as hazardous sea routes resulted in a vast increase in freight costs.

The citizenry was initially full of patriotic sentiment. In autumn 1915, new war poems were still appearing daily in the *Danziger Neueste Nachrichten*, along with the newspaper's commentary: "It is as if a rush of sublime emotion permeates us all."[48] But as time passed, enthusiasm for the war dissipated as supply problems intensified and increasing numbers of the city's sons fell; there were even strikes in the factories in early 1918. Mild unrest crept over the local elites as, in early 1917, the Triple Entente listed its terms for peace, which called Danzig's future in the Reich into question. Unrest grew in January 1918, when US president Woodrow Wilson's Fourteen Points called for a Polish state with free access to the sea. New hope emerged when peace was reached with Russia, and as late as August 1918, Lord Mayor Heinrich Scholtz even dared hope for a transport route from Danzig to the Black Sea: "The new world shaped by the great war shall also see a new German East."[49] Yet this illusion quickly dissolved; Scholz died in the influenza pandemic in early October, and the German Empire collapsed in November.

Although many things appeared possible, the people of Danzig likely could not have imagined that their city would move to the center of the world stage in the coming years and, two decades later, even provide the pretext for the next world war.

7

Against a Red Background

From the Free City of Danzig to the Second World War, 1918–1945

Perhaps, said Herr Meier as he thoughtfully regarded his pupil Ulrich, I do not know the answer to your question, for the flag has always been red, as has Danzig's crest, with its two silver Teutonic crosses and golden royal crown.

Is it blood, you ask? You know, Ulrich, and you others, too, enough blood has flowed in this city's history. And yet it seems to me that plenty may still need to flow, for the German crosses are unwilling to tolerate the Polish crown, and the red cloth drives the people berserk, blind, and wild.

Poland Discovers Danzig

In the nineteenth century, Danzig's potential return to a Polish state seemed a distant prospect, and Polish visitors to the Motława found the city entirely foreign: "There are no memorials to Polishness here; the language is not Polish, neither are the inhabitants and their names; Polish, Slavic glory and triumphs do not enliven and uplift them or awaken their pride."[1]

Danzig, which had played such an important historical role for Poland, nevertheless did not disappear entirely from the national horizon. In his 1834 epic *Pan Tadeusz*, Poland's great Romantic poet Adam Mickiewicz had a protagonist give a toast with the famous Danzig Goldwasser (gold water) liquor:

> "Here's to the City of Gdańsk!" the Judge declared,
> Raising the flask, "Once ours, and—by my word—
> Ours to be again!"[2]

With the budding hope of Poland's restitution just taking shape, the political elite focused its attention on Danzig. In particular, proponents of modern Polish nationalism like Roman Dmowski had declared since the beginning of the twentieth century that a Polish state could not exist without Danzig as its sole port, even if the city's inhabitants were chiefly German. Polish affiliation would likewise benefit Danzig, they maintained, arguing that whereas it had become a "dead city" under Prussia, the connection to a large backcountry would bring new life to the city.[3]

The Western powers considered these arguments. When Woodrow Wilson proclaimed his Fourteen Points for peace on January 18, 1918, he demanded the assurance of Poland's "free and secure access to the sea." This could (yet did not necessarily have to) mean a Polish Gdańsk after the war, and it led to a battle for the city that was fought with words instead of weapons.

The Fight for Danzig: Between Revolution and Versailles

Poland's growing interest in Danzig was no secret to the city. As the Central Powers' defeat became apparent a few weeks before the war's end, voices of warning emerged. The *Danziger Neueste Nachrichten* published the headline "Polish Assaults on Danzig" at the end of September 1918 and expounded in the familiar tones of national hubris: "The Polish assault ... remains ... the ungracious act of a people whose lessons we would do well to learn from."[4]

The mood escalated following Germany's peace offer in early October. At one of the many political assemblies during this time, a German National professor at the Technical University called for resistance to the city's last breath.[5] On October 14, the apprehensive magistrates sent a telegram to the Reich Ministry of the Interior, in which it emphasized: "Our old Hanseatic City of Danzig resulted from and grew through the strength of German culture—it is German to its core."[6] At a public demonstration a few days later, all of the middle-class parties rejected any Polish claims to the city.

Mere hours after the German emperor's abdication, revolution made its way to Danzig. Insurgent sailors stormed the city's prisons on November 10, and prominent Social Democrats proclaimed the advent of the republic at a mass rally on Hay Market. A German workers' council and soldiers' council assumed power in Danzig, and a Polish council was also formed. The garrisons became subject to the councils and, along with the militia, maintained public order. A general strike on November 11 paralyzed the city.

The insubordinate fervor soon slackened, though, and this revolution quietly ran its course in Danzig, thanks in no small part to the mitigating influence of the Social Democrats under the leadership of Julius Gehl. The food supply would remain tenuous and unemployment high throughout the coming year, so concern for their own survival likewise deterred many in Danzig from revolutionary activities. The workers' and soldiers' councils lost their sway relatively quickly, while the political right won popularity with its sappy anti-Polish rhetoric.

Poland had declared its independence by mid-November, leading to the question of its national borders. On December 25, 1918, the famed Polish pianist and statesman in exile Ignacy Paderewski arrived in Danzig aboard an English cruiser, gave an incendiary address to the Polish residents, to whom he promised the city's future within the Polish state, and traveled on to Posen (soon to be the Polish city of Poznań). His arrival incited a rebellion against the German forces there, which caused an uproar among the Germans in the Prussian provinces.

Meanwhile, Danzig took part in the January 1919 elections for the Weimar National Assembly. In the Weimar parliament, Käthe Schirmacher, a German National women's rights advocate from Danzig, repeatedly predicted the demise of German Prussia. Emotions likewise ran high in Danzig itself, and local historians felt an obligation to draw historical parallels: the Polish state, they claimed, had "never been anything more than an extorter of Danzig."[7]

Heinrich Sahm, who had formerly presided over the Deutscher Städtetag (Association of German Cities), became Danzig's new lord mayor at the end of February. At his inaugural address, the experienced executive officer standing six feet, six inches tall professed "an open and intense conviction of the Germanness of this old Hanseatic city," which "is still as German at heart today as in all bygone centuries of its proud history."[8] This speech was, as he later recalled, "an open challenge to Poland"[9] and established the tone that most of the civic elites would adopt for the next twenty years. The Polish-language newspaper *Gazeta Gdańska* expressed its disappointment, arguing that if Prussia had not torn Danzig away from Poland in 1793, the city would be home to over a million people, "and thousands of ships would be cutting across the waves in the Gulf of Gdańsk."[10]

Sahm did not have much time to acclimate himself, as the nationalist and national-liberal circles dominating the city's public opinion sounded the alarm. The Polish Blue Army, assembled in France under General Józef Haller in 1917, was supposed to enter Poland by sea through Danzig, and many Germans feared that the soldiers would use this opportunity to capture West Prussia. The danger disappeared in early April when the soldiers returned to their home country by land, but nationalist tempests continued in the city, especially as the peace negotiations in Paris neared a conclusion.

In Paris, Danzig was a topic of much discussion because of Woodrow Wilson's promise of a Poland with free access to the sea. France took Poland's side and initially gained traction: on March 19, one of the commissions in the peace conference proposed giving Danzig to Poland. To indicate how strongly the population in Danzig desired to remain part of Germany, all of the city's large parties organized two mass rallies on Hay Market in the following weeks, which drew many tens of thousands of people. Some politicians even demanded that Danzig's citizens protect their "right of self-determination with weapons in hand."[11]

British prime minister David Lloyd George eventually insisted that Danzig not become Polish. He also ultimately brought Wilson over to his side, and an idea was consequently taken up that the English foreign secretary Arthur Balfour had already brought into play in April 1917, namely, the establishment of a free city. In this way, the Western powers hoped to reconcile the Polish demands for free access to the sea with the populace's right of self-determination.

Delivered to the German delegation on May 7, the conditions of peace came as a shock to the public. As it had earlier in its history, Danzig was to become a free city. The city's largest daily newspaper summarized the public sentiment with its headline: "Death Sentence against the German People: the Entente's Inhuman, Outrageous, and Unfathomable Terms . . . Danzig as a Free State under Polish Suzerainty."[12]

Responding in late May, the German peace delegation in Paris warned, "The attempt to make Danzig a free city . . . would lead to fierce resistance and a permanent belligerency in the east."[13] They instead proposed establishing a free port in Danzig with extensive rights for Poland, but the Entente did not yield and insisted on its solution. The formation of a free city, they wrote in their response of June 16, would "preserve the character which Danzig held during many centuries and, indeed, until forcibly and contrary to the will of the inhabitants it was annexed to the Prussian State. . . . The economic interests of Danzig and Poland are identical."[14] The Polish argument thus prevailed, albeit without leading entirely to Poland's desired outcome.

After some hectic days, the Weimar National Assembly eventually agreed to the peace terms, and the Treaty of Versailles was signed on June 28. Of the treaty's more than 400 articles, numbers 100 through 108 were dedicated to Danzig. The Free City would be under the protection of the League of Nations, in a customs union with Poland, and represented by Poland in foreign affairs; Poland also gained control of the city's waterways and railway lines.

Birth of an Unpopular State

The negotiators of the peace imagined this free city as an ideal model for post-war Europe, an intelligent compromise between two irreconcilable national claims. It would become clear, however, that the time was not ripe for such a post-national solution. The Free City of Danzig—a "German" city, either threatened by Poland or posing a threat to Poland, depending on one's perspective—not only made the imperfection of the existing political circumstances apparent to both Germans and Poles but also kept the world in suspense and was soon viewed as one of the potential breaking points within the Versailles system.

How a "free city" was even supposed to function was unclear, as Danzig's municipal council unanimously declared on May 13, 1919, "We reject the formation of a Free State of Danzig, seeing it only as the precursor to Danzig's annexation into Poland. As Danzig's thought and feeling has been German for centuries, we will not now, having also shared the better times, abandon our German fatherland in its gravest hardship."[15]

Mere words could not defy reality, though. Compliance with the Treaty of Versailles was not up for debate, and despite public or private opinion, Danzig had to come to terms with its new political existence, faced as it was with the pressing need to establish the newly imposed state. The city was partially able to adopt the Prussian government offices, but these needed to be removed from the former administrative structure, and some government agencies required reorganization. Although the German sympathies of the officials—whose careers had developed in Prussian offices—were naturally beyond dispute, many soon grew fond of their new roles as key representatives of their own state as they achieved a measure of prestige that they would have never attained through a normal bureaucratic career in Prussia. This tension between private pride and open discontent at the new political environment would mark the Free City for its entire duration.

With 365,000 inhabitants, the Free City of Danzig's new territory covered over 750 square miles, and its borders with Germany and Poland were about 180 miles in length. Alongside Danzig, the territory included the cities Zoppot, Tiegenhof (Pol. Nowy Dwór), and Neuteich (Pol. Nowy Staw), as well as a part of the Vistula lowlands and numerous villages in the Gdańsk Heights to the west and southwest of the city.

When the Treaty of Versailles took effect on January 10, 1920, the area of what would soon be the Free City of Danzig was removed from the Reich and placed under the Allies' administration. Two weeks later, the German troops departed to a solemn farewell on Long Market, which was a moving and somber moment for large parts of the German population: "The past shall be our future solace.... We are headed downhill. Uphill must wait for another time," the *Danziger Neueste Nachrichten* put it.[16]

An English infantry battalion was soon dispatched to Danzig to maintain order until the founding of the new state. British diplomat Sir Reginald Tower, who temporarily oversaw the city as a high commissioner representing the League of Nations, arrived on February 11. He entrusted official functions to a state council led by Lord Mayor Sahm. The state council in turn called representatives from all parties to create a constitutional committee with the assignment of drafting a constitution by the end of September.

When elections took place for a constituent assembly of 120 members on May 27, 1920, the Social Democrats became the strongest party ahead of the German National People's Party. After difficult negotiations and public commotion, the assembly adopted the Free City's constitution on August 11, albeit with some dissent from the Social Democrats and others. Yet the League of Nations also had a say in the matter, prohibiting, for instance, the term "Free and Hanseatic City of Danzig" and insisting that the new state's official name simply be "Free City of Danzig."

The highest state authority was the Senate of the Free City of Danzig. It consisted of a president as well as seven full-time and thirteen extra-official senators who were elected every four years by the parliament (*Volkstag*); the senators not only governed the state but also served as the city magistracy, and the parliament did not have the power to remove the senate president or the full-time senators from office. The high commissioner representing the League of Nations in Danzig was primarily responsible for dealing with disputes between Danzig and Poland.

To prepare the requisite treaty with Poland, a large delegation led by Sahm visited Paris. On November 9, 1920, after many weeks and complicated negotiations, they proudly produced the great Seal of Danzig from the sixteenth century, which they had brought with them for the signing. The convention in Paris arranged for, among other things, the establishment of a "Committee for Danzig's Harbor and Waterways" under a foreign chairperson and composed equally of representatives from Danzig and Poland. The boundary issues had also been settled in the meantime, and thus the English delegate was able to proclaim the founding of the Free City of Danzig at a solemn meeting of the constituent assembly on November 15. The foreign troops left the city shortly thereafter. The constituent assembly subsequently made up the parliament and appointed the *Stadtbürgerschaft*, a local council specifically responsible for the municipality of Danzig. The senate was soon elected with Heinrich Sahm at its head; although by no means a charismatic politician, Sahm was a capable negotiator who, without belonging to a party himself, acted prudently in the interests of the bourgeois-national political center.

Whether Danzig was merely a Free City, as Poland claimed (to emphasize the city's dependence upon Warsaw), or a Free State, as its German population preferred to call it (to underscore its sovereignty and complete independence

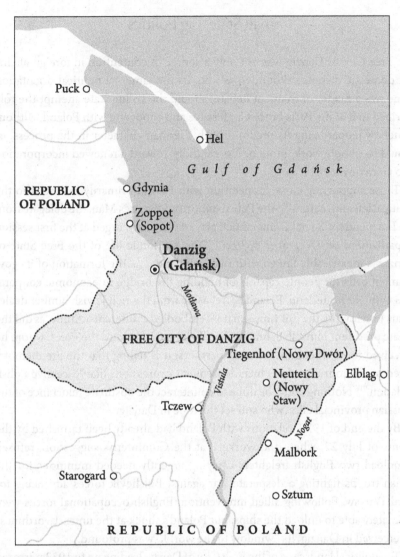

Figure 7.1 Map of the Free City of Danzig

from Poland), was a bitterly debated question for years. In any case, the Free City soon adopted many traits of an autonomous state. Beginning in 1920, much to the pleasure of the local elites, the proud Danzig coat of arms waved against a red background on flags in front of official buildings, even if the Social Democrats would have gladly removed the royal crown from the crest. Danzig received its own currency—the Danzig gulden—in 1923, and a "national holiday" soon followed, along with an anthem, "Kennt ihr die Stadt am Bernsteinstrand" (Do you know the city on the amber shore).

Small State, Big Politics

The Free City of Danzig was not only a source of contention in foreign affairs, but domestic disputes abounded as well. Its fundamental political orientation alone was a matter of frequent debate: should the young state attempt the role ascribed to it at the Paris Peace Conference and cooperate with Poland, without somehow jeopardizing its predominantly German character in the process, or should its people work, more or less candidly, toward a renewed incorporation into Germany?

Those supporting close cooperation with Poland primarily belonged to the political left and, naturally, the Polish minority. Johannes Mau, the delegate from the Independent Social Democratic Party of Germany, urged at the first session of parliament on December 6, 1920: "The economic life of the Free State of Danzig is inextricably linked with that of Poland. . . . The formation of its government calls for people capable of building the bridge to economic cooperation with our hinterland, Poland."[17] Yet aside from the rich Jewish lumber dealer Julius Jewelowski, the full-time senators embodied a different attitude, as did the senate president himself. Sahm was hardly impartial toward the Poles, whom he perceived more as enemies than as partners; it is telling that the life memoirs based on his journal entries include frequent expressions like "excessive Polish violation."[18] Nothing could be done to counteract the obstinate reluctance of the Prussian provincial elite, who still set the tone in Danzig.

By the end of 1920, relations with Poland had already been tarnished by the events of July 22, when dockworkers, at the Comintern's suggestion, refused to unload two English freighters carrying urgently needed munitions for the Polish troops fighting a desperate war against Bolshevik forces advancing toward Warsaw. Following allied intervention, English occupational forces were ultimately able to unload the ships, but Poland's shock at the untrustworthiness it perceived in Danzig, its "window to the world," was profound.

The political landscape of the Free City of Danzig leading up to 1933 mirrored the circumstances in Germany. On the one side stood the Social Democrats, whose competition on the left consisted mainly of the Communist Party, which was popular among the dockworkers and shipyard employees. On the other side were the German Nationals, from whom the National Socialists began drawing voters in 1930. A fragmented bourgeois camp took up the middle, along with the Catholic Center Party, which had a stable following and always had a hand in the government. The Poles initially had seven representatives, though this number later decreased to only two.

The political situation in the Free City was similar to that of the Weimar Republic in Germany, and it was similarly volatile. A coalition of German

Table 7.1 **Results of the parliamentary (*Volkstag*) elections in the Free City of Danzig from 1919 to 1935**

(cells indicate number of seats won as well as the percentage of vote received).

Election year	1919	1923	1927	1930	1933	1935
Voter participation	70%	81.6%	85.4%	89.1%	92.1%	99.5%
National Socialist German Workers' (Nazi) Party	–	–	0 0.8%	12 16.4%	38 50%	43 59.3%
German National Workers' Party	34 28.2%	34 28.1%	26 20.6%	10 13.6%	4 6.3%	3 4.2%
German Social Party	–	7 6.2%	1 1.2%	–	–	–
Various middle-class central parties	22 18.5%	18 15.3%	22 19.8%	11 16.1%	0 0.5%	0 0.1%
Center Party	17 13.9%	15 12.8%	18 14.3%	11 15.3%	10 14.6%	10 13.4%
Social Democratic Party (SPD)	40 33.3%	30 24.1%	42 33.8%	19 25.2%	13 17.7%	12 16.1%
Communist Party (KPD)	–	11 9.1%	8 6.4%	7 10.2%	5 6.8%	2 3.4%
Polish representation	7 6.1%	5 4.4%	3 3.1%	2 3.2%	2 3.1%	2 3.5%

The 1919 elections were for the constituent assembly. In this year, the Socialist Party of Germany was combined with the Independent Socialists (21 seats, 17.5 percent). The parliament initially consisted of 120 delegates, but this number sank to 72 beginning in 1930.

Nationals and liberals initially governed Danzig, but when the bourgeois liberal camp collapsed in the 1923 elections, there was an absence of stable majorities. A government steered by a German National minority was followed in summer 1925 by an administration comprising Social Democrats, the Center Party, and German Liberals,[19] which was only able to govern with the help of an enabling act. Reelected for four years as senate president in 1924 despite opposing votes from the Communists, Social Democrats, and Poles, Heinrich Sahm presided over the senate in all its shifting forms.

It was no wonder that Danzig did not escape external conflicts with Poland, for as Poland attempted to win greater influence in the city, all of Danzig's political groups except for Communists and Poles sought reintegration into Germany.

Nevertheless, the Versailles Treaty constrained Danzig and Poland to find a *modus vivendi*. In October 1921, after the suspicion that marked negotiations in Paris and at the League of Nations in Geneva, a delegation from Danzig visited Warsaw for the first time. The men were received with great honor: Danzig's flag flew from the city's finest hotel; the Polish head of state Józef Piłsudski invited the delegates to breakfast; and a gala was even held at the opera for the occasion. All of this impressed the provincial delegates from Danzig, even if it hardly succeeded in easing political tensions.

Misunderstandings and disputes between Danzig and Poland accumulated over subsequent years. Even the most minor tokens of Polish rights in the city or, conversely, of Danzig's "Germanness," were heavily contested, such as whether the Polish diplomatic representative was allowed to greet foreign fleets in the name of the Polish government when they visited Danzig. Much more serious was the fight for the Polish military transit depot.

After the dockworkers' strike in 1920, the Polish government had considered how to assure supplies for its army in the future. One idea posited the establishment of a military transit depot, guarded by Polish soldiers, in Danzig's harbor. In 1925, after it had resisted for some time, the senate finally had to consent to Poland's installation of an ammunition dump on the Westerplatte peninsula at the mouth of the Vistula River. Since by this time, Poland had already begun constructing its own harbor in neighboring Gdynia (Germ. Gdingen), the munitions depot was really just a matter of prestige; Poland wanted to make its presence in Danzig as strong as possible. In 1925, the League of Nations granted Poland a permanent guard detail of two officers, twenty petty officers, and sixty-six soldiers. Until then a popular beach, the Westerplatte was outfitted with bunkers and barracks.

Another conflict began on January 5, 1925, as citizens leaving their houses that morning rubbed their eyes in disbelief. Overnight, Polish postal workers had mounted ten red Polish mailboxes at various locations in the city center. What appears farcical today was, at the time, cause for an international incident. Upon obtaining the right to its own postal service in the harbor area after the war, Poland had opened a post office and telegraph office on Hevelius Plaza. Many of the city's German inhabitants perceived the red mailboxes as a sudden Polish effort to gain leverage in the city as well as to gradually yet blatantly polonize Danzig's cityscape. Feverishly contested by both sides, the mailbox controversy came before the Council of the League of Nations and was covered by international press. Eventually, the Permanent Court of International Justice in The Hague ruled in Poland's favor. The unpopular mailboxes remained in place until 1939, and Polish mail carriers conducted their business in the Free City.

Not all of the local populace supported the Danzig Senate's rigid stance against the Poles. Above all, the Social Democrats tried repeatedly to steer the state ship on a conciliatory course, as seen in an article printed in their daily paper in 1927:

> In Danzig, any indications of the countless ties that have endured for ages between the Hanseatic city and Poland have without exception met furious rejection as a challenge to the city's German character. Danzig's great merchants and artisans of previous centuries did not feel such panic, and rightly so, since there cannot be commerce with conflict, and business suffers when businessmen cannot even share a drink.[20]

The opposing winds not only blew from the German National side, but also from equally narrow-minded nationalist groups in Poland. In 1924, they had already called for a boycott of Danzig wares, and the political right's resultant indignation would hardly subside. In 1927, Danzig's Polish daily newspaper printed a sensational article, whose author claimed, among other things:

> If the people in Gdańsk have forgotten what they owe to Poland, then they should be brought to their knees, following the example set by Frederick the Great. At first they will shout, scoff, and blubber to the entire world. Let them shout, let them blubber. A small hunger diet will do them good and bring them to their senses. They will slowly quiet down and learn to behave themselves.[21]

Such nationalist rhetoric poisoned Danzig politics as well as relations between Poland and Danzig (not to mention Germany); still, the Social Democrats emerged even stronger from the November 1927 parliamentary elections. Representatives from the Center Party and German Liberals joined the dominant Social Democratic Party in the new senate with the aim of improving relations with Poland. Polish minister of foreign affairs August Zaleski's 1928 visit to Danzig led to an agreement over harbor issues and railway tariffs, and in February 1929, Polish prime minister Kazimierz Bartel even traveled to the Free City. Yet efforts toward a political détente collided time and again with vitriolic criticism from nationalists. After the 1928 agreement, for example, the *Ostpreußische Zeitung* (East Prussian tidings) newspaper ran the headline: "Treason for Railway Tariffs: Massive Political Disgrace in Danzig."[22]

The global economic crisis ultimately frustrated attempts at rapprochement, and as the port's goods turnover nosedived and competition with Gdynia intensified, confrontation seemed a better strategy. Following this logic, even the Social Democratic senate increased the pressure and tried to sway the League of Nations to force Poland into improving the harbor's turnover. The League of

Nations, under whose protection the Free City of Danzig stood, frequently had to arbitrate such stubborn disputes between Danzig and Poland well into the 1930s. Senate President Sahm himself traveled to Geneva around thirty times. The high commissioners representing the League of Nations in Danzig came from England, the Netherlands, Italy, Denmark, Ireland, and Switzerland. They alternated every three or four years, and they sympathized at times with Danzig and at others with Poland. Elegantly dressed and radiating gentlemanly flair, their role as attentive observers of the Free City's politics was matched by their active participation in the city's social life.

A consul general, who had official diplomatic duties as well as many unofficial connections between Danzig and Berlin, represented Germany's interests in the Free City. These confidential contacts were delicate, as they were not stipulated in the Treaty of Versailles, and Poland could thus protest against them at any time. Yet without Germany's financial and political support, the Free City would have been unable to survive as an autonomous state. This survival was crucial, from Berlin's perspective, in repressing Poland's influence and upholding the continuing prospect of boundary revisions, an indisputable guiding principle of German foreign policy.

In accordance with the convention between Danzig and Poland in Paris, a commissary general, who was also the primary Polish contact for Danzig's authorities, represented Polish interests in the Free City. Additionally, the office of commissary general simultaneously saw itself as the contact point for the Free City's Polish population and greatly promoted—including financially—the minority's cultural and social life.

The number of Poles in Danzig rose rapidly after the First World War. The Polish ticket received an impressive 6.1 percent in the elections for the constituent assembly, even though official records indicate that only 3.5 percent of Danzig's citizens were Polish (13,656 out of 366,730 total inhabitants, according to the 1923 census). Rather generous assessments have even estimated the Polish population at around 10 percent of the city's inhabitants, though such numbers admittedly included the many hundreds of Polish officials and their families, none of whom possessed a Danzig passport.

The largest Polish institution in the city was the railway division, which employed over 600 officials in its impressive building by the Oliva Gate. There were Polish banks, trading firms, and freelance professionals. The tight-knit Polish minority had a well-constructed network of associations. Their most important advocacy group was initially the Gmina Polska (Polish Community), and many intellectuals gravitated to the Towarzystwo Przyjaciół Nauki i Sztuki (Society of the Friends of the Sciences and Arts). The Gmina Polska dissolved in 1933, only to take form again in 1937 amid the city's increasingly anti-Polish atmosphere.

Nationalism and Confrontation

Because poor economic conditions prevented them from achieving their sociopolitical goals, the Social Democrats left the senate in March 1930. New elections at the end of the year saw the extremist parties make great gains, as had recently occurred in the Weimar Republic. In the meantime, the constitution had undergone changes, and the parliament, which had been reduced to seventy-two seats, now held the authority to dismiss all full-time senators as well as the senate president from office. Under the circumstances, the politically independent Sahm had no chance to extend his presidency. He stepped down and became lord mayor of Berlin in 1931.

The German National politician Ernst Ziehm took over the office of senate president on January 8, 1931. His administration (which the National Socialists incidentally tolerated) comprised representatives of the German National People's Party, the Liberals, and the Center Party; like its predecessor, it was largely only able to accomplish anything by excluding the parliament through enabling acts. Not one of the new senators had been born in Danzig; only Ziehm himself hailed at least from the Free City's vicinity. Hence Poland perceived Danzig, and not entirely without good reason, as a veiled offshoot of the German Reich.

Due to the global economic crisis, the nationalist parties in Germany, Poland, and Danzig enjoyed great popularity in the early 1930s. The rightwing administration in Berlin thus deemed it politically expedient to exploit German-Polish relations and engage in revisionist propaganda, to which Warsaw responded with counterpropaganda. For many Germans, Poland appeared jointly responsible for their problems, whether global or homemade, and the rashly stoked disputes also reached Danzig. When German politician Gottfried Reinhold Treviranus very openly spoke of the "unhealed wound in the east" and the "German lands yet to be won back"[23] in 1930, Poland emphasized its own claims on Danzig. Given Poland's military superiority, a *coup de main* on Danzig was not out of the question. The Western powers were alarmed; the "Polish Corridor" to the sea suddenly seemed a feasible *casus belli*. Foreign ministries and international organizations agonized over options for de-escalation, resulting in a number of adventurous ideas to surmount the separation of Danzig and East Prussia bemoaned by the Germans. Was it perhaps feasible to construct a tunnel through the Polish Corridor or a bridge across the Gulf of Gdańsk to the Free City? Could the local Poles in the Corridor perhaps be resettled elsewhere, such as the Memel Territory to the east?

The increasing confrontations had concrete repercussions for Danzig. Distrustful of and opposed to the German-National senate, Poland hindered the

Free City's trade as many political groups called for renewed boycotts of Danzig goods. Geneva again became a forum for disputes between the Free City and Poland, this time revolving around the question of whether Danzig was a Polish port, and accordingly, whether Polish warships could moor there without restriction. The city senate was unable to prevail, unlike in the case of the troop buildup on the Westerplatte. Directly following Hitler's assumption of power in the Reich, the Polish government had secretly strengthened the garrison in the munitions depot, later justifying the decision with a flimsy rationale involving threats from the Danzig SA (Sturmabteilung, the Nazi Party's brown-clad paramilitary organization). Soon thereafter, Poland's foreign minister Józef Beck had no choice but to announce the withdrawal of the additional soldiers.

Ziehm's senate grew increasingly authoritarian and even prohibited the Social-Democrat newspaper *Volksstimme* (People's voice) in 1932. While all of the city's other daily newspapers—in solidarity with the *Volksstimme*—only issued emergency editions, the largest of these, the *Danziger Neueste Nachrichten*, had already opted for political assimilation in April 1933—even before the Nazis came to power in the Free City. Danzig's path to National Socialist dictatorship appeared unavoidable. Already in 1932, Danzig's Nazis, under Hitler's instructions, were working against the senate and more forcefully toward a Nazi seizure of power. There was no way around the upcoming elections, which would take place on May 28.

Hope, Success, and Disappointment: Economic Life

For a short time, Danzig experienced the atmosphere described by Felix Scherret in his 1930 novel *Der Dollar steigt* (The dollar rises):

> A remnant of the Middle Ages still slumbered within the city's narrow lanes; the tall gabled homes, which now housed banks and exchange offices, still recalled their glorious millennial past. But life was driven by a new rhythm. The peaceful, sleepy city had become a scene of wild commercialism, a stronghold of speculation and gambling at the roulette wheel and the stock exchange.
>
> Gesticulating crowds formed on the sidewalks. Rates, markets, and dollars were their catchwords.... The narrow streets no longer sufficed for the traffic, and the hurrying messengers, brokers' assistants, and liquidators snaked between luxury automobiles and streetcars with the agility of acrobats.[24]

Figure 7.2 Danzig was seldom out of the international headlines between the wars. It also presented material for satirists, as shown in this polemical nationalist German illustration from 1932, which shows the black German eagle, an old man representing the League of Nations, and the white Polish eagle, all fighting for control of Danzig, represented here atop the iconic tower of St. Mary's Church. From *Kladderadatsch* 1932, no. 21, page 329.

Dismissed from the German state, lacking currency control (yet still using the reichsmark as its currency), and united in a customs union with Poland, the Free City became a paradise for speculators and bankers. The number of banks and savings and loans increased from nineteen in the year 1919 to 118 four years later, only to sink to half of that total by 1926. The number of companies established there grew from 214 in 1919 to 969 three years later before dropping sharply.

Whereas some resourceful individuals realized dizzying profits, the majority suffered from the inflation; on September 15, 1923, one dollar equaled 60 million reichsmarks in Danzig, and the rate was not much better for the Polish marka. The inflation led to desperation in Danzig. While there were endless banknotes, potatoes were in short supply. Agriculturally, the Free City's land area could support only one-third of its population, and Danzig was dependent on imports.

Already some weeks ahead of Germany, Danzig's financial administration decided to counter the galloping hyperinflation by introducing its own currency. Linked to the British pound and guaranteed by the Bank of England, the Danzig gulden was approved by the League of Nations and circulated on October 20. It remained stable for the better part of a decade and came under strain only in mid-1931 when the global economic crisis led to the collapse of several banks in Danzig. The Free City's central bank, the Bank von Danzig, therefore disassociated the local currency from the British pound and was able to stabilize it by backing it with gold.

Despite some successes, the economic situation in Danzig remained critical throughout the Free City's existence. "The year 1925 closes most gravely, and no less so does 1926 make its first appearance,"[25] wrote the *Danziger Volksstimme* newspaper in its New Year's Eve edition, though this financial diagnosis could have applied to almost all new fiscal years during the period. Public finances were strained, partly due to the Free City's meager industry and partly due to high pensions from Prussian times; these were largely assumed by Germany, and there were many other instances of funds making their way—often in secret—from Germany to Danzig.

Customs duties were a major source of the city's income. Already partners in a customs union, the Free City and Poland agreed that Danzig would retain 7 percent of the net earnings from customs duties collected in the city, while Poland would receive the remaining 93 percent. But the total incoming payments sank, not only because of the German-Polish tariff war that lasted from 1925 to 1934, but also because of the increasing prominence of Gdynia as a Polish port of export. The sinking proceeds and the rapid drop of the złoty, which had replaced the marka as Polish currency, led to the first severe financial crisis and high unemployment. Danzig was able to avoid worse consequences only with the help of external loans. Substantial tax increases and credits were necessary to save the Free City's budget in 1931.

While Danzig's economic structure had not been strong to begin with, conditions dramatically deteriorated under the pressure of the global crisis. In 1933, the jobless figure shot to over 30,000, an unemployment rate of over 20 percent. To combat the unemployment, the Free City founded a "Voluntary

Figure 7.3 Danzig also suffered from inflation. The Danzig artist Berthold Hellingrath created this emergency currency certificate in late 1922. Dieter Busse.

Work Service" and financed efforts to create work, such as the construction of housing districts in the suburbs.

Industry in Danzig struggled with significant problems, partially because the Entente Powers had prohibited the production of military equipment. While the Royal Firearms Factory had to close, the Imperial Shipyard, with international capital and under the direction of Ludwig Noé, became the International Shipbuilding and Engineering Co. Ltd. And expanded to repair railway cars and locomotives, manufacture machines and steel construction, and cast church bells. Around 80 percent of its output was exported to Poland, a good indicator of not only how paradoxical the Free City's frequently anti-Polish political rhetoric actually was but also the opportunities missed—by both sides—through nationalistic, parochial politics. The Schichau Shipyard survived, on the other hand, thanks solely to extensive aid from Germany, and another yard, the Klawitter Shipyard, went bankrupt in 1931. In spite of all these difficulties, the shipyards were still Danzig's largest employers.

Other factories were mostly small. These included some machine manufacturers, steel construction companies, and chemical and food-processing plants, among which were three sugar refineries as well as widely known chocolate and margarine factories. Manual trades were important for local and regional needs; in particular, the number of barbers and automobile mechanics increased rapidly. Agriculture set the tone in the Free City's rural areas, and in 1929, there were at least 70,000 cows within state territory.

In light of the difficult economic circumstances, Danzig tried to position itself as a conference venue so that it could at least attract visitors from afar. This would further enable the city to present its "dyed-in-the-wool German character" to the guests, which was consistently a high priority of the city administration. Yet attempts in the early 1920s to develop Danzig into an international exhibition location ultimately failed. Zoppot remained an attractive tourist destination with its beaches, spa facilities, and famous casino.

Unlike industry, prospects for commerce initially appeared promising, since Danzig was Poland's only seaport. The number of commercial businesses did in fact see rapid growth at the beginning of the 1920s, and the goods turnover in the harbor developed more quickly than in German ports. A decisive factor in this development was Poland's foreign trade, primarily the coal export from the Polish part of Upper Silesia, which had run through Stettin until the end of the First World War, and for which Danzig's quayside and loading equipment was significantly expanded and modernized. The ships arriving in the harbor in 1923 had already reached pre-war figures, and nearly 7,000 ships arrived in 1927. This commerce was for the most part transit trade, though, and local companies were involved to a relatively small extent in the turnover. For this reason, the Free City's shipping companies had little room for development, and only eighty-four seagoing vessels traveled under Danzig's flag in the city's best year of 1931.

To escape dependence on the politically unreliable Danzig, Poland had already resolved in 1921 to build its own port city at the fishing village of Gdynia to the north of the Free State's borders. The project developed at a truly "American rate," astonished observers noted, and its modernist architecture constituted a stark contrast to old Danzig. Gdynia had a population of 12,000 in 1926; there were ten times that number in 1939. Inhabitants of the Free City regarded this development with mixed feelings, as Gdynia's harbor grew at a similar pace, with its goods turnover exceeding that of the Danzig harbor by 1933. From the early 1930s onward, Poland's valuable piece goods trade moved predominantly through Gdynia, while the less lucrative bulk goods were left for Danzig.

Danzig was not entirely without blame for this development. In addition to the city's deep-seated reservations about its neighbor, it also lacked sufficient knowledge of the circumstances in Poland. While the Danzig Senate was thus complaining to the League of Nations about the disadvantages its harbor faced because of Poland's actions, the Poles were bemoaning Danzig's restrictions on imports from Poland: "Germany is engaging in Janus-faced politics when it compels Danzig's businesspeople to refrain from establishing ties with Poland's economy while simultaneously complaining that commerce in the Danzig harbor is proceeding so unfavorably."[26] The Free City's protest to the League of Nations resulted in an economic agreement in 1933 that enforced Poland's nondiscriminatory use of both harbors and guaranteed Danzig's harbor a minimum turnover.

The Long Road to Assimilation: National Socialist Danzig

In November 1930, Joseph Goebbels boarded a train and traveled to Danzig for a campaign rally. Visiting this city for the first time, he was impressed, as he confided to his journal:

> To Danzig! Slept, read, read, slept. Through the Corridor. The intolerable thought that this lunacy could go on forever. I'm learning to hate again on this trip.... Danzig's position is desperate. All of the treaties favor Poland.... I speak in the evenings. Through loudspeakers to six thousand people in the overcrowded halls. There is boundless enthusiasm when I'm done. They carry me through the halls. "Come again!" the people cry. An explosive rapture of populism. What a glorious movement! It will one day sweep all of Germany.[27]

Goebbels became familiar with a city in which the National Socialists had, until then, faced great difficulties. Although there had been National Socialist groups in Danzig since 1926, the group of regional organizations was fractured by constant quarreling; this network was dissolved in 1930 at Hitler's orders and placed under the direction of bank clerk Albert Forster from the Bavarian city of Fürth, who was assigned to Danzig as *Gauleiter*, or regional leader of the Nazi Party. Together with the failed sales representative Arthur Greiser, he was able to use the ongoing economic crisis as an argument against the established parties and make the National Socialists the strongest party in the city within two and a half years. The Nazis also did not shy away from brutal conflicts, in which the SA as well as the SS (Schutzstaffel, the Nazi Party's elite paramilitary unit known for its black uniforms) excelled most disreputably: in the first four months of 1931 alone, 120 people were injured in politically motivated brawls, and four were killed. Since many police officers already sympathized with the Nazi Party, criminal prosecution was far from ideal.

After the Nazi accession to power in Berlin, it seemed only a matter of time before Danzig would follow suit. With 50.03 percent and thirty-eight seats, the National Socialists attained the absolute majority in the parliamentary elections of May 28, 1933. Plagued by high unemployment, Danzig's citizens had allowed themselves to be dazzled by the prospect of a job creation program like that already initiated by the National Socialists in the Reich. The German-Polish confrontation had also driven them into the arms of the explicitly anti-Polish Nazis. Flags of the "Movement"—a black swastika in a white circle against a red background—flew everywhere in the city.

On June 20, 1933, the parliament elected a new, National Socialist-led senate which also included—if only at first—representatives from the Center Party. In the debate preceding the election, a Nazi delegate named Hans-Albert Hohnfeldt hurled threats at the Social Democratic Party: "You have issued your official decrees for the last time—you can count on that!"[28] Politically grave times were clearly approaching.

Yet matters in the Free City under the protection of the League of Nations were not as simple as Hohnfeldt fancied, and a consolidation of Nazi power was not as readily feasible there as in the Reich. Thus Albert Forster, who pulled the party strings, was not also able to become senate president; rather, the position was attained by the moderate Hermann Rauschning, a former German National with an expertise in Danzig's musical history, who owned a small manor in the delta and enjoyed the sympathies of the rural population. Immediately following the National Socialists' government takeover, the parliament passed a new enabling act, allowing the senate to take action against unpopular adversaries, political opposition, and the press. Jews were soon forced out of civil service jobs; the police and judicial system quickly fell in line with the party; and in May 1934, the Communist Party was the first political party to be banned, even if its delegates still remained members of parliament. For the time being, the Social Democrats took on the role of the Nazis' most significant opposition.

Whereas earlier administrations in Danzig had acted in harmony with Berlin, they had done so independently; in 1933, the ultimate authority in the Free City clearly became Hitler himself. Since the German chancellor wished to avoid foreign-affairs problems at the beginning of his rule, he instructed Rauschning to placate Poland. The new senate president therefore readily declared his wish for a bilateral resolution to all pending issues with Poland. In July 1933, Rauschning traveled with Greiser (who spoke fluent Polish) to Warsaw on a state visit. Danzig and Poland entered into various contracts a few weeks later, and return visits followed.

But Rauschning overshot his assigned target, proposing nothing less than a unification of the two economic markets and even founding the Danziger Gesellschaft zum Studium Polens (Danzig Society for the Study of Poland). He ran into increased resistance in Danzig with these détente politics, and even the opposition took a critical stance toward his "sellout to Poland." Following weeks of conflict, he lost the power struggle with Albert Forster and had to step down in November 1934. In 1936, Rauschning fled to Poland and later immigrated to the United States through France and England. He became one of the greatest critics of the National Socialist system, publicizing his position through his books *Die Revolution des Nihilismus* (*Revolution of Nihilism*, 1938) and *Gespräche mit Hitler* (1939, published as *Voice of Destruction* in the United States and *Hitler*

Speaks in the United Kingdom). Arthur Greiser succeeded Rauschning as senate president.

The National Socialists in Danzig had emulated their partisan counterparts in the Reich and, as advertised, launched a job-creation program. Through the construction of sewers and power plants, the unemployment rate dropped by around one-third by 1934. All of this was only possible, however, with the assistance of a foreign loan; the financial situation worsened when the repayment installments came due.

The administration kept this a secret, though, first holding elections with the assumption that it would obtain the two-thirds parliamentary majority needed to amend the constitution and finally command the Free City's political landscape unopposed. This election generated great interest at home and abroad, as for the first time since 1933, a German population could—at least somewhat freely—make its political preferences known.

Of course, the elections absolutely did not give the different parties equal chances. While the National Socialists blanketed the Free City with massive amounts of propaganda and organized over 1,300 campaign rallies, the Social Democrats and Center Party were permitted to hold only a few assemblies, which the SA and SS disrupted. Radios broadcasted exclusively in the Nazis' favor. In spite of these enormous obstacles set for their opponents, the National Socialists only received 59.3 percent of the votes and fell markedly short of the two-thirds majority in the elections of April 7, 1935, which incidentally had a suspiciously high voter turnout of 99.5 percent. Gauleiter Forster was shocked and canceled the victory parade with the SA and SS.

The Nazis' unchecked spending policies had meanwhile so unhinged the Free City's finances that a state bankruptcy loomed. Radical steps were therefore necessary after the elections. In the early morning of May 2, 1935, the Danzig gulden was devalued by 42.37 percent. Those with bank balances lost a portion of their wealth, and groceries, gasoline, and coal became much more expensive because of the rise in price for import goods. An austerity program imposed sizable cutbacks on officials and civil servants, and many retired and unemployed people were resettled in the Reich. National Socialist organizations' members abandoned them, and only with the Reich's massive financial support was the Free City's administration able to bring the situation under control.

The opposition saw its chance and united to contest the elections before Danzig's high court. Partial electoral fraud was ultimately determined and votes penalized from the National Socialists, who lost one seat in parliament as a result. An additional appeal made to the League of Nations was unable to bring additional support, though, and the opposition had to give up their efforts in mid-1936, especially as economic conditions soon improved again. Sustained by the economic revival in the Reich and in Poland, but also by immigration to

Germany and the exclusion of Jews from economic life, the number of unemployed persons sank to 534 by August 1939.

The end of the opposition came quickly. Increasingly frequent assaults left many injured and even dead, and newspapers critical of the regime were successively banned. The Social Democratic Party was dissolved in October 1936 following staged discoveries of weapons, followed in 1937 by the dissolution of the German National People's Party and finally the Center Party. The Gestapo (the Nazi Party's secret police) murdered the Social Democrat delegate Hans Wiechmann, and the parliament was ultimately consolidated following the bribing of some and the arrest and flight of many other members of the opposition; only the two Polish representatives were permitted to remain. Already months earlier, the Nazi party leaders had boasted: "There is no more parliament; that talking shop is closed. . . . Now we have grander tasks. Now the real fight begins."[29]

In reality, the League of Nations was already powerless in Danzig by this time, since it held no bargaining chips on site and Poland showed no interest in confrontation. When the Irish high commissioner Sean Lester wearily stepped down in 1936 after having taken an unsuccessful stand for the opposition, he was replaced in 1937 by Swiss historian Carl Jakob Burkhardt, who was content to limit his role to that of the lofty observer.

The Nazis had almost complete free rein, although they still proceeded more cautiously than in the Reich. The "real fight" first targeted the Jews. State-endorsed anti-Jewish sanctions took effect directly following the Nazis' assumption of power, and these became more intense after Rauschning's departure, even though Germany's racist Nuremberg Laws, enacted in the Reich in 1935 to severely limit the rights of racial minorities and particularly Jews, were—for the time being—not implemented locally in order to avoid complications in foreign affairs.

The situation shifted drastically in autumn 1937 when Gauleiter Forster marked the beginning of a new politics: "Here in Danzig as well, we must succeed in purging Jewish insolence and arrogance," he said in a keynote address.[30] A few days later, rioters damaged and partly looted Jewish homes and businesses. Further violence and harassment followed, and the party leaders' rhetoric increased in brutality: "These swine must be thoroughly smoked out," *Kreisleiter* (county leader of the Nazi Party) Werner Kampe told the National Socialist Women's League in October 1938.[31]

In the early morning of November 13, shortly after the Night of Broken Glass (Kristallnacht) in the Reich, Langfuhr's synagogues came under attack, and looters again robbed Jewish homes and businesses. The Nuremberg Laws were soon enacted in Danzig. Numerous Jews had already emigrated or simply fled the city, but it was only after the November Pogroms that the remaining Jews were fully aware of how dire their circumstances had become. In December, assembled members of the Jewish population unanimously and with heavy hearts decided to dissolve their community and emigrate en masse. To raise the funds necessary for this unprecedented course of action, they arranged sale of all Jewish property through the senate. The community's library was sent to Vilnius, the valuable art collection to New York, the archives to Jerusalem, and the Great Synagogue, the pride of Danzig Jewry, was torn down shortly thereafter. A large transport left Danzig in March 1939 and reached Palestine three months later. Through legal and illegal emigration, the number of Jews in Danzig dropped from more than 11,000 to 1,660 people by the outbreak of the Second World War.

From 1937 onward, there were no more prospects for resistance against the Nazis' machinations. Either out of conviction or resignation, Danzig's residents had submitted; those who wished to remain had to blend in or seclude themselves. Many citizens chose an easier way and joined the Nazi Party. The city's National Socialist administrative division had 4,500 members in 1937, a considerable number considering the Free City's total population of 375,000, a percentage three times as high as in the Reich. The party increasingly shaped everyday life. All German youth belonged—at least formally—to the Hitler Youth, and mass rallies served to strengthen the people's sense of unity. Only the Polish minority could publicly hold divergent opinions.

A City and Many People

Danzig was a metropolis, if only a small one. In 1925, there were 202,000 people living in the city itself and 364,000 in its entire territory. Partly due to the integration of Oliva, the urban population grew to 250,000 by 1939. The social structure was marked, on the one hand, by a strong working class, making up almost half of the urban populace, and, on the other hand, by a large number of civil servants. Emigrations eased the strain somewhat; in 1926 alone, around 1,400 locals left their homeland for Canada and Argentina.

Though men still dominated Danzig society, nine of the 120 delegates in the first parliament were women, and some women in Danzig, such as Käthe Schirmacher, Anne Kalähne, and Marie Baum, were well known outside city borders as women's rights advocates. Gradual emancipation—but also economic hardships—led to more and more women joining the workforce, and by 1936, every third woman earned her own income. But there were no women working as professors or lawyers, and after the National Socialists came to power, women were expected to restrict their lifestyle to home and family. The "Hour of the Women" would not strike until the war's end.[32]

The Free City of Danzig was not a rich city. There were certainly very wealthy citizens, such as Jewish lumber dealer Julius Jewelowski, the first minister of the economy. But his political goals of cooperation with Poland quickly brought him into the German Nationals' crosshairs, and he immigrated to London in 1838. Whereas senior civil servants, managers of a few large businesses, bankers, and wholesalers earned good money, the bulk of the population were restricted to petit-bourgeois or proletarian lifestyles.

There were bathrooms in only 12 percent and electric light in one-third of the city's apartments in 1927, with gas or kerosene lamps still illuminating most rooms. Living conditions were particularly bad in Ohra, where even in the 1930s, hardly any houses were connected to a sewer. Pressure from the Social Democrats led to the construction of large housing developments in the late 1920s, which were expanded in the 1930s.

After the chaotic years of inflation, simple provincial life quickly found its way back into the Free City; with its casino and summer beachgoers, Zoppot was the sole exception. People in Danzig observed world affairs and adopted the early season's global fashions, all with an eye on Berlin; Warsaw seemed very far away. The city's big newspapers and, since the mid-1920s, Danzig's regional radio transmitter kept citizens up to date.

Denominationally as well as nationally, the population was by no means uniform. There were great differences among the Germans alone. Alongside numerous citizens who immigrated to the city and spoke High German were the long-established Danzig residents who enjoyed conversing in the brash urban dialect of Missingsch, a mixture of High and Low German influenced by Slavic languages and the Berlin dialect. Many residents from the rural surroundings spoke Low German.

Article 4 of the Danzig Constitution stipulated the rights of the Polish minority in Danzig: "The official language shall be German. The Polish-speaking portion of the population shall have guaranteed its free racial development by the law and the administration, in particular as regards the use of its mother-tongue in the schools and in the internal administration and as well as in the administration of justice."[33] The practical implementation of these provisions led to occasional disputes, but until 1939, no senate dared tamper with them. The Polish minority was thus ever-present in the Free City's public life, visible in the Polish railway and postal officials, present in parliament and communal assemblies, and seen regularly in their societies and parades in the city. The center of minority organizations was the "Polish House" on Wall Street. One, and for a time two daily Polish newspapers circulated locally. After initial efforts to convince the Danzig Germans that they should take an interest in Poland for economic reasons, the Polish minority increasingly kept to themselves. Of course, this did not mean that they did not also visit German theater and cinema; in contrast to their German counterparts, most of the Poles in Danzig had mastered both languages.

As before, Protestants were the dominant religious community in Danzig, still making up about 60 percent of the population, although this figure was in slow decline. They belonged to the Protestant Prussian Union of Churches. After 1933, most of the clergy in office joined the regime-loyal "German Christian" movement. Although membership in the Protestant Church became less important, Catholicism's cohesiveness remained strong. The Catholic percentage of Danzig's population increased steadily, reaching around 40 percent in the 1930s. In 1925, the Catholic Church established the Diocese of Oliva, directly subordinate to the Curia in Rome. Eduard Graf O'Rourke was solemnly inaugurated as the first bishop of the Free City of Danzig in 1926 with the church of the Oliva Abbey as his cathedral. He relinquished his office near the end of the 1930s amid increasing National Socialist pressure. As O'Rourke's successor, the pope appointed Carl Maria Splett, whose attitude toward the Nazi Regime and its persecution of Poles has been the subject of controversial debate ever since. On the one hand, he was bound as an apostolic administrator to go so far as to forbid Polish as a confessional language in the Polish Diocese of Chełmno during the war; on the other hand, he also undertook numerous efforts to protect his priests from the grasp of the Nazi terror apparatus. Splett was sentenced after the war to imprisonment for collaboration with the Nazis in Poland; he was finally able to depart for West Germany in 1956.

Danzig's Jewish community had already grown strong in the nineteenth century, and its numbers tripled after the First World War, primarily because of immigration from Russia. By 1923, there were 2,500 Jews with Danzig citizenship in the city in addition to 5,000 Jewish non-citizens, and the community continued to grow. Danzig's Jews were a heterogeneous group: Zionists and assimilated Jews disputed, frequently only in broken German, as their first languages were often Polish, Russian, or Yiddish. After the First World War, however, they all quickly found themselves confronted with anti-Semitic abuse, which intensified under the influence of the National Socialists. Jewish life remained quite multifaceted into the 1930s and carried significance beyond the Free City's boundaries; several international congresses of prominent Zionist organizations, such as Hashomer Hatzair or Mizrachi, took place in Danzig. When Jews were ousted from official cultural life in 1933, a Kulturbund der Juden (Jewish Cultural Association) was created, and a Jewish theater operated for a time in Danzig, as well.

Germanness and Provincialism: Hard Times for Art and Culture

Danzig's cultural life between the wars was shaped by the city's marginality and efforts to make it appear either as Polish or as German as possible. The senate was naturally at an advantage, and its longtime minister of culture Hermann Strunk established a German cultural imperative, which he deemed necessary

> to develop the great community of the German spirit among all German people, and to gather the Danzig Germans into the greater German cultural nation alongside all other Germans, both for our sake and the sake of humanity.[34]

Such a mentality would necessarily lead to a deep insularity. If, after all, the primary objective was the frantic accumulation of evidence confirming local "Germanness," and then the population's commitment to this "Germanness," then any modernizing impulses were doomed to flounder. Felix Scherret recognized this and wrote in the left-liberal newspaper *Danziger Rundschau* (Danzig review):

> It is unfortunate that the Treaty of Versailles has imposed a prestige upon Danzig that lifts it above the level of a provincial town. Danzig should have remained a part of Germany—most ideally, of course, a part of an imperial Germany; for that was the atmosphere most conducive to quaint babbling. Whoever seriously believes that Danzig could become a global city should look at the senate and parliament. And if he does not renounce his faith by that point, then neither will God himself bring him to it.[35]

It is not surprising that Scherret left Danzig and went to Berlin shortly thereafter, for not only did the German cultural imperative make the Free City's cultural climate extremely oppressive, but so did the festering German-Polish conflict. It was not only the German side accusing the Poles of "sinister hatred against German essence."[36] Many Poles also fostered a hostile anti-German perspective. Prior to the 1933 elections, the *Gazeta Gdańska* printed the headline: "Kashubians! Poles! Every vote not cast for the Poles strengthens your perpetual enemy and disparager!"[37]

For Danzig, recognition from the greater German fatherland was politically important, and the Free City gladly supported events that shone beyond its borders for this purpose. Such occasions included the annual "German Studies Weeks," held between 1921 and 1938, and the Zoppot Sport Week. Of particular appeal was the Zoppot Forest Opera, the "Bayreuth of the north," where operas (primarily by Richard Wagner) were performed on a stage located in the middle of the forest. Financed by sources in the Reich, the Forest Opera attracted prestigious conductors like Max von Schillings and Hans Pfitzner to direct its productions.

Aside from these seasonal peaks, the heart of the Free City's cultural life was still the Municipal Theater, which the city had purchased from the Prussian king in order to have a greater say in the repertoire. Rudolf Schaper, the director until 1931, truly succeeded in reforming the institution, which performed ambitious works of spoken and musical theater as well as operettas and comedies. But Schaper remained powerless to do anything about the general audience, described here by German writer Alfred Döblin during a stay in Danzig:

> During the intermission, the people chew and suck in the corridors. A fat lady stands at the buffet, opening beer bottles; they laugh and toast. One man takes an open sandwich, egg with anchovies, bites, tears; the egg falls on his boot. They pull sandwiches out of their pockets the instant the auditorium doors are opened; then they station themselves at pillars, walls, and eat stupendously, with rustling paper in their hands. . . . Three cheese-colored adolescents walk together, discussing the singers like schoolmasters.[38]

In 1933, Albert Forster wanted to develop the theater into an exemplary Nazi playhouse, but the political propaganda plays adopted into the program were failures. The direction of Hermann Merz, beginning in 1934, stabilized the theater, which underwent a remodeling in 1935 at substantial financial costs, and thanks only to undisclosed aid payments from the Reich. Renamed the State Theater, it reopened and operated until summer 1944. While Danzig's theaters grew less important, the cinemas enjoyed a meteoric rise, with almost 3 million people attending Danzig's twenty cinemas in 1939.

The Free City's cultural politics, as established by a "State Chamber of Culture" created in 1934, dabbled particularly in the field of literature. Dramatist Max Halbe appeared to be the most suitable instrument in bringing the literary world to Danzig and drawing the Reich's attention to the Free City. Having not enjoyed success in some time, the poet was all too pleased by the city's attention and came frequently to Danzig. The city would spend several days honoring him during his visits, and it named him an honorary citizen for his sixtieth birthday in 1925. As the entire National Socialist senate paid him homage for his seventieth birthday, Halbe expressed his gratitude by confiding that he stood "in the service of a notion of homeland deeply rooted in [his] blood."[39] For his seventy-fifth birthday, the city founded a literary prize in his honor.

No other artist attained Halbe's success in Danzig. An attempt was made in the 1920s to establish the local writer Paul Enderling, who was also permitted to compose the lyrics for the Free City's anthem. In 1935, Heinz Kindermann, professor of German studies at the Technical University, strove to assemble a group of local young poets called "Young Danzig" with the aim of extolling frontier Germandom in the National Socialist spirit. Of these, only Martin Damß found any measure of success.

Yet there were also good writers who for political reasons did not enjoy such promotion: Willibald Omankowski, for instance, wrote contemplative poems about Danzig, in which he seeks islands of rest and scenes of reflection and melancholic hues in the big city—as in his poem "Frauengasse" (St. Mary's Street):

> Legends whisper forth from the stone and carry
> you to realms of childhood, that you may walk
> safe and secure, as in grace.
> Smiling, you marvel... And sleep trickles
> from the façades and seeps sweetly into your veins.[40]

The socially critical ballads of Erich Ruschkewitz took a quite different tone, as in "Ein Arbeitsloser auf der Langen Brücke" (A jobless man on Long Bridge):

> Two men cross the bridge with green huntsman's hats.
> They don't know the pains of hunger, of course.
> They carry fat watch chains on their fat bellies,
> and they surely have fat purses, too.
> And in passing they speak in fatty grunts
> of a prize for laziness. They speak of us.
> And in your rage, you'd like to give
> those fat bellies a mighty shove.
> But that won't do you any good,
> and you'd rather collect your dole.[41]

While the Jewish Ruschkewitz was deported to Riga in 1941 and presumably murdered there, other Danzig writers fared better, as long as they adhered to the "correct" faith and expressed conservative views. One of these, the poet and editor of *Ostdeutsche Monatshefte* (Eastern German monthly journals) Carl Lange, nevertheless came into conflict with the National Socialists near the end of the 1930s.

There is no known great prose about Danzig from the interwar period. Worthy of mention, at least, is the role played by Fritz Jaenicke, a journalist who composed his observations in a weekly newspaper between 1908 and 1944 in Danzig's Missingsch dialect. Although Polish writers occasionally wrote about Danzig, only two of literary significance lived in the Free City for any time: Stanisław Przybyszewski, who worked as an official of the Polish railway administration, and his daughter Stanisława, who lived out her life there sick and destitute.

Music revolved around the Municipal Theater, but music schools, organists, and orchestral and singing societies additionally enlivened local musical life. World-renowned virtuosos sometimes stopped in Danzig, but only a few musical greats came from the city; among these was the conductor Carl Schuricht, who nonetheless had to leave his hometown at a young age to pursue his career. This was incidentally the case for all artists, as the professional prospects in Danzig were anything but bright, and remaining in the city meant earning a modest living as an orchestral musician, newspaper editor, secondary school teacher, or portraitist. Great composers thus lived elsewhere. The most interesting to remain in Danzig was doubtless Johannes Hannemann, a composer of neo-Baroque works who converted to Buddhism.

Writing dejectedly of the city's artists (and likely with himself in mind) in 1927, Willibald Omankowski wondered, "Who in Danzig can sense, even faintly, the grave (or even fertile) tragedy of these people, cut off from the inspirational sources of German artistic life, persevering and hoping ... hoping in this all but hopeless city."[42] This was just one side of the coin, however, for against the meager backdrop of the provincial city, many of "these people" faced, at best, only scanty prospects of discovery, anyway.

Along with music and literature, the city's visual arts also languished under the German cultural initiative, although artists like novelist Artur Brausewetter still supported it: "Even if art bears an international imprint, the German viewpoint must be the determining factor in Danzig. For obvious reasons, we must thoroughly deny ourselves the foreign extravagance and works contradictory to German sentiments that Berlin and other cities allow themselves."[43] Fritz Pfuhle, a conservative painter of horses, thus enjoyed the greatest success. There were some artists in a position to produce nice illustrations and cityscapes, and masters from out of town occasionally came to the Free City, such as expressionist painter Stanisław Kubicki, as well as Otto Dix, who painted portraits of some of Danzig's prominent figures.

It is no surprise that architecture in Danzig also mostly languished between the wars. The focus was always toward the past, and a heated dispute raged in the 1920s over whether the city's historical streets should be carefully modernized or meticulously historicized. While one side warned that Long Street must not be permitted "to calcify into an open-air museum," many others pleaded for the "retention of the gables and saddleback roofs."[44] Beginning around the time when the Nazis assumed power in Danzig, professional conservationists successfully advocated a historical restoration of the Main Town, which at the time was facing the dangerous prospect of thoughtless capital expenditure.

That said, modern architecture had little chance in Danzig and was limited to a number of schools and administrative buildings, such as the headquarters of the public insurance company Allgemeine Ostkrankenkasse on Wall Street, designed by Adolf Bielefeldt in expressive brick architecture, as well as some residential buildings outside the historical city center. The sole large-scale Nazi construction project to reach completion was the castellated Paul Beneke Youth Hostel on Bishop's Hill, whose architectonic scheme linked the late-medieval raider's "heroic" exploits with the present Nazi period.

While the City Museum persistently displayed modern art throughout the 1920s, the primary objective of the State Museum for the History of Danzig, founded by Erich Keyser in 1927, was to amass proof of Danzig's German character and engage with the German aspect of the city's history. This brand of local history was also initially dominant in Danzig's schools following the collapse of the German Empire, with teachers making great efforts to generate a fresh sense of national coherence through notions of homeland (*Heimat*), to which curricula attached particular value. Quickly following the National Socialist's accession to power, ideologically motivated instructional content appeared with increasing frequency in lesson plans. The city possessed a number of reputable secondary schools and a well-developed primary school system, and it was obligated to offer Polish instruction, at least through primary school; there were twenty-six Polish-language classrooms in the public schools in 1936. Additionally, the Polish school association Macierz Szkolna operated its own secondary school and other schools.

Many teachers in the Free City's schools received training at the Technical University, where the department of general sciences was expanded for this purpose. There were also departments of architecture and mechanical engineering prior to the Second World War. Massively subsidized by the Reich, the Technical University was able to appoint many fine professors, including future Nobel laureate in chemistry Adolf Butenandt; yet the determining factor in the university's selection of its faculty was always their consistency with the senate's political tenets. Around 1,500 students attended the university, up to one-third of whom were Polish. Danzig furthermore obtained its Medical Academy in 1935. Yet schooling is no cure for stupidity, and many of Danzig's leading educators followed Hitler's path to a war in which the Free City would willingly play a decisive role.

The Road to War

The Second World War did not arrive unexpectedly in Danzig, as the Nazis had extolled the city's pugnacity for years: "Danzig's proud history is a surge of steady conflict through the centuries, fought on this soil to which German blood reserves a sacred right," as stated at the opening of an exhibition in 1937.[45] If Danzig had, as claimed, always fended off the supposed Polish assaults, after all, what could be more fitting than to resume—and ultimately resolve—this battle? Despite the policies of rapprochement enacted in 1933, relations with Poland were not without tensions; there were customs conflicts, disputes over Polish schooling in Danzig, and espionage affairs. Promoted in Nazi propaganda, such incidents contributed to Danzig's reputation both locally and abroad as a powder keg.

For his part, Adolf Hitler showed little interest in Danzig for some time. After the "annexation" of Austria in March and the occupation of the Sudetenland in October 1938, however, there was no doubt that he would soon demand the Free City's "homecoming." That same October, German foreign minister Joachim von Ribbentrop actually proposed a "general resolution," stipulated by Hitler, to the Polish ambassador Józef Lipski: the Free City would become part of Germany, and Germany would obtain an extra-territorial highway and railway connection through the Polish Corridor; in return, Poland would receive extra-territorial transport routes in the Danzig region; Poland would also join the Anti-Comintern Pact, and both sides would guarantee their borders.

To relinquish Danzig, a city possessing such symbolic power for the Polish public, was out of the question for any Polish administration, and nobody wanted to become the Reich's satellite state. In March 1939, once Hitler had defied all protestations by entering Prague as well as the Memel Territory shortly thereafter, the Poles no longer put any belief in his promises. Meanwhile, the greater number of Danzig's inhabitants awaited the city's return "home to the Reich." A troubled Warsaw sought support from the West but could not find widespread sympathy: "Mourir pour Dantzig?" asked Marcel Déat, the French minister in charge of the Air Force, in a newspaper article in early May—should we die for Danzig, this distant city on the far side of the continent?

The escalation could no longer be checked. Hitler—an honorary citizen of Danzig since his fiftieth birthday on April 20, 1939—had already long been planning the occupation of the Free City, and the German armed forces had been preparing since spring for the invasion of Poland. The opposing fronts dug in, and Poland responded to the German threats: a German occupation of the Free City meant war. "Danzig is a German city and wishes to join Germany," Hitler exclaimed in an address on April 28.[46] Yet Danzig was just a small step on the path to war. "Danzig is not the primary concern," Hitler said at a briefing on May 23. "For us, it is a matter of expanding our living space in the east and securing food."[47]

Events unfolded rapidly in Danzig: minor border incidents were exaggerated, Polish customs and railway officials were hindered from fulfilling their duties, and Polish students faced harassment at the Technical University. When a chauffeur for the Polish commissioner general's office shot and killed (most likely in self-defense) a member of the Danzig SA, the propaganda in the Free City and the Reich intensified further.

Not only were the Reich and Poland arming themselves, but the officially demilitarized Free City also prepared for a hostile engagement. For several years already, citizens of Danzig had been—more or less voluntarily—fulfilling their military service in the German military. Beginning in June 1939, soldiers who had come from Danzig were channeled back into the Free City with smuggled weapons to constitute a "state police regiment." This armed force amounted to around 6,500 men at the beginning of the war, not including the special SS troop SS-Wachsturmbann Eimann or the SS-Heimwehr Danzig militia, which boasted 1,500 members. Trenches were dug along the Free City's borders.

The Poles in the Free City also kept busy. They fortified the Polish Post Office and armed its employees, but above all, they reinforced the garrison on the Westerplatte with the goal of resisting a German attack long enough for the Polish army to take Danzig. Yet Poland vastly overestimated the capabilities of its armed forces. At the annual gathering of the Polish Legions in Kraków that August, Poland's Marshal Edward Rydz-Śmigły exclaimed that Poland could not exist without Danzig, which functioned as the lungs of the Polish economy.

Albert Forster referred to Rydz-Śmigły's remarks in an unmistakably menacing speech held on Long Market on August 10, shortly after Forster and Hitler had met at Hitler's retreat on the Obersalzberg in Bavaria to discuss how to further aggravate tensions in Danzig. He proclaimed that "Danzig Germans today" feared Rydz-Śmigły's cannons just as little "as their fathers [feared] the cannons of the Polish King" Stefan Báthory.[48]

The following days passed with provocations and preparations for war. A German assault on Poland appeared just a matter of time, yet the mood in Warsaw was optimistic, where they believed Poland capable of repelling a German attack. The Molotov-Ribbentrop Pact, which Germany and Russia reached on August 23, therefore came as a shock to more than just the Polish public: the Polish state could not win a war on two fronts. On the same day, Gauleiter Albert Forster decreed himself chief of state, clinching the struggle for power he had waged for years with Arthur Greiser, whom Hitler would appoint chief of the civil administration in Poznań after its capture at the beginning of the war. Warsaw issued the order for general mobilization on August 30 but abstained from launching its own attack on Danzig, an option it had been weighing for several months. Danzig units took up their field positions two days later.

On August 25, the battleship *Schleswig-Holstein*, which had been active in the First World War, entered Danzig's port for a goodwill visit and docked directly across from the Westerplatte. Some final, hectic diplomatic attempts were fruitless; Poland again rejected Hitler's renewed demand for Danzig's "return home."

The Second World War began in Danzig at 4:45 AM on September 1, 1939, as the heavy guns of the *Schleswig-Holstein* bombarded the Westerplatte and rudely awakened the city's residents. Without much resistance, the police and Gestapo seized the central railway station, the Polish railway administration, and all other Polish institutions except for the Polish Post Office, which was bitterly contested. About fifty armed postal employees defended themselves for fourteen hours against heavy assaults before finally surrendering after suffering several deaths. They were arrested, sentenced to death as insurgents a few weeks later, and shot (they would not be vindicated by a German court until 1995). In the morning hours of September 1, the Gestapo, police, SS, and SA arrested around 1,500 active members of the Polish minority who were brought to the Viktoriaschule, a middle school for girls repurposed as a Gestapo collection point. After many of them were tortured, they were transported the following day to Stutthof (Pol. Sztutowo), where they were forced to construct the future concentration camp there. Sixty-seven of them were shot in March 1940; many more lost their lives early in the war or in the following years.

By 5:00 AM on September 1, Albert Forster had already proclaimed Danzig's "reunification with the Reich," which was given legal force later that day as a "fundamental state law." Forster repealed the Constitution of the Free City of Danzig in Article 1, appointed himself dictator in Article 2, and declared Danzig's annexation into the Reich in Article 3. The High Commissioner from the League of Nations left the city. At 9:30 AM, Hitler sent a telegram informing Danzig that the law regarding the reunification was to take effect immediately. After less than twenty years, the Free City of Danzig ceased to exist. For the second time in its history, the city became a part of Germany.

But the thundering of the cannons continued. To the Germans' surprise, the Polish garrison on the Westerplatte, which Poland had increased to about 200 men, fought stubbornly. The initial advances made by a naval landing corps stalled, and attacks from dive-bombers also failed to overwhelm the defenders. Running short of supplies, the garrison under Major Henryk Sucharski finally capitulated after seven days. While the Poles lamented fifteen casualties, the German losses are said to have amounted to over 300 soldiers.

Figure 7.4 Beginning early in the morning of September 1, 1939, the German battleship *Schleswig-Holstein* bombarded the Polish ammunition depot on the Westerplatte from the harbor canal near Nowy Port. bkp/30008904.

Though doomed from the outset, the Polish defenders' heroic resistance against Germany's overwhelming military superiority quickly became the stuff of legend in Poland. In that same month, Konstanty Ildefons Gałczyński wrote in a poem that would become famous:

> In Gdańsk we stood like a wall
> And sneered at the Kraut cannons.
> Now we ascend among the clouds,
> We, the soldiers of the Westerplatte.[49]

The Last Six Years

Hostilities ceased in Danzig with the surrender of the Westerplatte. A week later, the resistance was broken in Gdynia, which was promptly renamed Gotenhafen. Enthusiastically greeted by tens of thousands on the afternoon of September 19, Hitler rode through Danzig in an open-top car before speaking in the Artus Court to prominent officials of the Reich as well as local elites:

> I stand for the first time on ground claimed by German settlers a half millennium before the first whites made their homes in the present-day state of New York. This soil has been and remained German for a half millennium longer.... Danzig was German, Danzig has stayed German, and Danzig will henceforth be German, as long as there is a German people and a German Reich.[50]

The end of October saw the formation of Reich's Danzig-West Prussia District (Reichsgau Danzig-Westpreußen) with Albert Forster ruling in its capital of Danzig as Gauleiter and governor. The city again obtained a communal "self-government," which, despite having a lord mayor in Georg Lippke, was subordinate to Forster.

Figure 7.5 On September 19, 1939, Adolf Hitler came to a "liberated" Danzig. Many citizens hailed him enthusiastically. bpk/50048100.

A new era was dawning for the "Hanseatic City of Danzig," as it was officially designated in December 1940. Its new task was to organize, in the graven image of Nazi racial policy, an area with over 2 million German and Polish inhabitants. The deportation and extermination of the district's Jews were planned in Danzig, as were the persecution, murder, deportation, or Germanization of its Poles and the annihilation of its mentally ill. Already in mid-September 1939, Forster said, "It is our duty to uncompromisingly cleanse this land of all rabble, scoundrels, Polacks, and Jews."[51]

One fundamental instrument in the implementation of these policies was Danzig's prison and labor camp in the forest near Stutthof on the former Free City's eastern edge. Construction of the camp began on September 2, 1939, and its first prisoners were primarily members of Polish intelligence from Danzig and the new administrative district. The camp became part of the National Socialist concentration camp network in 1942 and was active in the "Final Solution" to the "Jewish question" in 1944. Around 110,000 people passed through the camp over the course of the war, of whom about 65,000 lost their lives. The cruel evacuation marches in winter 1945 resulted in 18,000 deaths. Of the 52,000 total Jews incarcerated here, 35,000 were murdered.

Danzig was a control center for genocide, plundering, and expulsion. Hundreds of bureaucrats there committed crimes at their desks, and the locally stationed SS and Gestapo units diligently and brutally lent a hand in "solving" the Reich District's ethnic "problems." Yet very little of this was overtly apparent in the city itself, and the removal of Danzig's small, "racially inferior" population proceeded quickly.

Approximately 1,200 Jews still lived in Danzig in 1940. On August 26, a group of 527 of them left the city with Haifa as their destination, but British authorities sent them on to Mauritius, where they spent the duration of the war. Beginning in October 1940, the remaining Jews in Danzig had to wear the Star of David in public. By 1943, almost of all of them had been deported to the Warsaw Ghetto or the Auschwitz and Theresienstadt concentration camps. In total, twenty-two people survived the war in the Judenhaus (Jewish house), a storehouse on Mouse Street in Danzig.

Although it contradicted Reich SS Leader Heinrich Himmler, the objective of Forster's policies toward the Poles was to "Germanize," at least on paper, as many of them as possible by registering them on the German National List. What applied to the entire district also applied to the city of Danzig: while many members of the Polish minority were generally left alone following an initial wave of arrests and executions, many others continued to suffer under persecution, resettlement, or subjection to forced labor. Circumstances were hard for the Poles displaced from Danzig, as Urszula Brzezińska later recalled:

We were terribly homesick in Radom. This was not our home, after all; we had nothing.... Mama always said: "No matter what may come, we want to go home." Once I said to my mother: "Mama, is the moon also shining as beautifully in Gdańsk tonight?" Mama said: "Yes, it's also shining as beautifully there." We felt a terrible longing.[52]

Economically, Danzig also quickly integrated into the greater German Reich: the Danzig gulden was abandoned and the local industry adapted for the wartime economy. With a rapidly increasing workforce, the shipyards predominantly produced U-boats. Due to the conscription of many physically qualified Germans to military service, most factories had to resort to using forced laborers and prisoners of war. The harbor merged with Gdynia's port and now served as an anchorage for the German navy. While trade decreased because of the war, the number of ships flying Danzig's flag nevertheless grew considerably.

Albert Forster wanted to further develop and modernize his capital city and saw to the development of comprehensive urban planning. His ambitions included an entirely new organization of railway and street traffic, a connection to the Reich's autobahn network, and the construction of massive, prestigious buildings to the west of the city center. This new general development plan was presented at the end of 1940, though none of it would ever be realized.

Danzig itself remained free of direct war damage for a long time. In summer 1942, the first air raids claimed only a few casualties. Almost normal daily life still prevailed in this city far removed from all fronts. The streetcars ran as usual, and people enjoyed films in the cinemas and flocked to the beaches. Slowly yet perceptibly, though, the end drew closer: valuable works of art were evacuated from churches and museums; the final edition of the *Danziger Neueste Nachrichten* newspaper appeared on August 31, 1944; supply shortages grew increasingly severe; and younger and younger recruits were called up for military service.

Beginning in late 1944, as the Red Army advanced toward East Prussia, a steady flow of refugees streamed to Danzig. The local population, however, was not officially permitted to flee until the end of January 1945. The railway trains heading west were overcrowded. At the end of January, the first refugee ships left the harbors of Danzig and Gdynia. On January 30, a Soviet submarine off the shore of Stolpmünde (Pol. Ustka) sank the *Wilhelm Gustloff*, which had left Gdynia a few hours earlier with around 10,000 passengers, including many from Danzig.

In January 1945, the Red Army crossed the Vistula and advanced rapidly westward, pushing through Eastern Pomerania to the Baltic Sea by mid-February. Supported by a Polish armored brigade, the Soviets quickly approached the city from the west. While the civilian population had to decide between staying and fleeing by ship, the party leadership urged the people to persevere. In mid-February, Albert Forster announced in a factory in Danzig:

> Again and again, Danzig has endured and overcome times of hardship, only to emerge stronger. Without reservation, then, we too will do our part in preserving our people and, in this spirit, master these circumstances.[53]

Starting on March 9, Danzig's city center was battered almost daily in Soviet air raids and later further bombarded by artillery. These attacks claimed thousands of lives. Up to one million people were stuck in the encirclement of Danzig and Gdynia. Although the Red Army reached the Gulf of Gdańsk near Zoppot on March 23, Hitler's headquarters transmitted to Danzig two days later: "The defense of each and every square meter of the territory of Danzig/Gotenhafen is crucial."[54]

Yet words alone could not hold the front. The Red Army captured Oliva on March 26. A day later, Albert Forster fled by steamer, first to the Hel Peninsula and then, shortly before the war's end, to the West. After the war, he was sentenced to death in a trial in Danzig and later executed. Low-flying aircraft strafed the city center; the populace cowered in cellars and bunkers; and nobody could put out the fires that destroyed the historical structures. Günter Grass depicted the city's ruin in his novel *The Tin Drum* (Die Blechtrommel):

> Rechtstadt, Altstadt, Pfefferstadt, Vorstadt, Jungstadt, Neustadt, and Niederstadt, built up over the past seven hundred years, burned to the ground in three days.... Häkergasse, Langgasse, Breitgasse, Große and Kleine Wollwebergasse, were burning, Tobiasgasse, Hundegasse, Altstädtischer Graben, Outer Graben, the ramparts burned, as did Lange Brücke. Crane Gate was made of wood and burned beautifully. On Tailor Lane the fire had itself measured for several pairs of flashy trousers. St. Mary's Church burned from the inside out, its lancet windows lit with a festive glow. Those bells that had not yet been evacuated from St. Catherine's, St. John's, Saints Brigitte, Barbara, Elisabeth, Peter and Paul, from Trinity and Corpus Christi, melted in their tower frames, dripping without song or sound. In the Great Mill they were grinding red wheat. Butchers Lane smelled of burned Sunday roast.[55]

The last deserters and people who had refused to work were hanged by the SS from the linden trees on Grand Avenue, and the German military retreated to the inland portion of the Vistula Spit, which the voluntary flooding of the lowland regions had protected. The civilians who had not fled the city were meanwhile at the mercy of the Red Army soldiers and their brutal caprices. With their calls of "Uhrrr, Uhrrr" (*Uhr* is the German term for a watch or clock; Soviet soldiers used this word to demand valuables from the German civilians) and "Frau komm" (Woman come), they broke into the cellars and apartments; their agenda for several days consisted of plunder, rape, and senseless destruction. These experiences were traumatic for the victims, just as they had been for millions of people in Europe over the previous years. Christel G. later recalled: "This 'Frau komm!' will echo in my ears forever . . . and it is still impossible, even after decades, for me to depict the distress and hellish suffering which followed." And Annemarie Gerlach wrote: "I convulsively distorted my face. 'Dear God, make me look old and ugly!' "[56]

The Polish military units generally couldn't do anything about the Soviets' brutality, yet they were able, at the very least, to perform one act of symbolic significance: on March 29, a Polish soldier mounted the Polish flag on the façade of the Artus Court. The white Polish eagle stood against a red background. Danzig became Gdańsk.

8

Variations in White and Red

Gdańsk, "Fairer than Ever Before," 1945–1980

The white eagle circled above the city for some time. The trees were still bare. Dark smoke rose from blackened ruins. Wild shrieks, barking dogs, gunshots echoed from below. People hurried like shadows through the barren streets. Where were the colors?

Dread overcame the eagle: this was the place where it was to land and build its new nest? It craned its neck and cast its gaze in the distance, swooped down, quenched the fires and salved the wounds, and raised new flags and new colors: white and red now reigned in Gdańsk.

Marginalizations

Gdańsk's history is so rich and has been rewritten so often and with such contradictory interpretations that one might at times be left with the impression of numerous different cities with nothing in common beyond their name. In 1927, German National politician Heinrich Schwegemann assured his fellow party members, "The stones of our historic towers and the houses in our narrow streets preach loud and clear: this land was German, this land is German, and this land will remain German!"[1] From a Polish perspective, the matter was precisely the opposite: even before the war, "the silent stones, images, statues, and inscriptions"[2] seemed to bear witness that Gdańsk was Polish. After it had truly become Polish in 1945, the great propaganda slogan in Poland's western regions also rang out everywhere in Gdańsk: *Byliśmy, jesteśmy, będziemy*—we were here, we are here, we will be here.

For decades prior to 1945, German historians and politicians had done their best to cast Danzig in a light as German—and non-Polish—as possible, even going so far as to repaint the white Polish eagles on the city gates as black Prussian eagles. After the war, the negation of the "other" continued, but in the opposite direction: the city, it was said, had been Polish from its beginnings, its population at most only superficially Germanized. After the expulsion of the city's Germans, the government strove to remove anything that could bring German presence to mind, and many visitors to the city who were unfamiliar with the past might even have believed this new narrative.

Given this radical reconstruction of local history, much of Gdańsk's past sank into oblivion: the Prussian/German period was viewed and suppressed as an alien element. The proper point of departure for local Polish identity was 1945, the year when Polish Gdańsk's life had begun. Only many decades later would a new generation of the city's young people begin to uncover, layer by layer, the entirely unfamiliar prehistory of the world they knew.

Destruction and New Humanity

For Gdańsk, 1945 was a year of destiny. Combat and the ensuing fires destroyed around 90 percent of the historical city center. One depiction from 1945 conveys the conditions in the Main Town: "It is incredibly quiet. Everywhere there are the burned-out eye sockets of the buildings, the empty streets. Footsteps clap, echoing loudly between rubble and debris. The remains of the buildings jut ominously upward."[3] Robbed of their roofs, only the three-foot-thick Gothic church walls, the many towers, and the city gates rose silently above the sea of ruins.

The old city center was wiped out and deserted. The devastation was not as great in other districts, though. Some, such as Wrzeszcz (Germ. Langfuhr) and Oliwa (Germ. Oliva), had even survived the war relatively intact. But approximately half of the city's entire housing space and a large portion of its industrial areas were destroyed, and there was no electricity. There were nevertheless many people living in the city.

Of Gdańsk's population of around 250,000, many German residents had already fled the city before the war's end. Additionally, many of the 400,000 primarily East Prussian refugees who had temporarily stayed in the city remained for some time thereafter in the Vistula estuary region, which was still held by German troops, before traveling westward by ship from the Hel Peninsula. Several thousand Danzig Germans lost their lives during and following the fighting. By the end of June 1945, however, around 124,000 Germans (and 8,000 Poles) still lived in the city.

Soon after the Second World War had begun, all of Poland's political forces had demanded Gdańsk's postwar integration into their country, and the Allies concurred at the Yalta and Potsdam Conferences in 1945. The Danzig Germans' last hope—a reinstatement of the Free City—disappeared, and any who

Figure 8.1 Many people wandered through the burning, destroyed Gdańsk. This picture, shot by a Soviet photographer and entitled "Polish refugees return to Gdańsk after its seizure by Soviet troops," was clearly captured shortly after combat had ceased. It is much more likely that these people were German refugees, driven by their conquerors through still smoldering ruins to assembly points. Novosti/Keystone/ Keypix.de/5502527.

remained in their homes had to reckon with forced displacement. Due to the experiences of the war and the unimaginable crimes committed in Germany's name on Polish ground, but also in order to create space for Poles relocated from the eastern Polish regions annexed by the Soviet Union, the prevailing conviction in Poland was that the Germans had to leave Poland's new western territory. What the affected German population perceived as the often-traumatic loss of their homeland as well as a despotic expulsion was, for the Poles, a legitimate relocation.

The year 1945 was a year of transition. People came and went, memories departed from the city forever, new narratives arose, and for a few months, old and new, German and Polish even frequently existed side by side. Polish newcomers received homes in the same buildings where Germans were still living as they awaited their departure from Gdańsk, and the different groups by necessity came into contact and helped each other survive, as recalled by a woman relocated from Vilnius:

> When we arrived here, there were two kindhearted [German] women living upstairs.... [One of them] spoke no Polish, but we helped each

other. She taught me sewing and homemaking—I was still young, after all, and only recently married. In exchange, I would cook potatoes or something like that, which we then ate together.[4]

The Polish government had already founded the Gdańsk Voivodeship on March 30, 1945, and it sent a first group of officials to the city to organize the administration on site. Bolesław Bierut, who would become the first president of the Republic of Poland less than two years later, gained a sense of the local situation. For weeks, however, the Red Army still regarded itself as the city's lawful authority alongside the Polish administration, which led to many misunderstandings.

On May 25, Edward Ochab, an undersecretary for the Ministry of Public Administration in the Polish provisional government, declared in Gdańsk's brand-new Polish daily newspaper *Dziennik Bałtycki* (Baltic journal) that all Germans were to be resettled by year's end. But the German workforce, for the time being, still played an important role in sustaining life in the city and resuscitating its destroyed infrastructure. Yet soon, whether on their own initiative or brought in by the State Repatriation Office, Polish settlers began to arrive: there were 3,200 in April, over 4,000 in May and again in June, and the summer months each saw up to 15,000. In order to relieve the problematic supply situation and create living space for the incoming Poles, the Polish authorities were particularly keen to expel the Germans as quickly as possible, and they took action even before the resolutions of the Potsdam Conference were passed. Beginning in July 1945, many tens of thousands of people were shipped off in freight trains. They could only bring hand luggage, and they frequently fell victim to assaults and robberies during the grueling journey lasting several days through "Poland's wild west."

Owing to insufficient transport capacity, but also because the occupational authorities in Germany at times would not receive refugees, the relocation of the Germans took longer than originally planned. Beginning in 1946, they fortunately traveled in much more humane circumstances. Any former citizens wishing to remain in Gdańsk had to pass through a rehabilitation process, in which they had to demonstrate that they belonged in and were loyal to the Polish nation.

Measured against the total population of the city just a few years after the war, the number of Gdańsk's long-established residents made up only a small percentage, most of whom were Polish. In 1948, there were only a few hundred Germans in the city, as opposed to approximately 150,000 immigrated Poles, two-thirds of whom had originally come from regions still belonging to Poland ("Central Poland," mainly Lublin, Lodz, Kielce, and Rzeszów); another 15 to 18 percent had come from former Polish territories now under Soviet control.

A relatively large number of bourgeoisie and academics came from Vilnius, resulting in a particularly strong Lithuanian-Polish presence in the city's public life. It would be decades before this heterogeneous new population would coalesce.

Gdańsk's resettlement was a complex process of immigration and partial exodus: people who merely hoped to make some quick money on the coast, as well as those who simply did not like life there, did not stay long. On the other hand, the city's rapid industrial and administrative buildup encouraged many others to seek their fortune permanently in Gdańsk. There was an especially significant influx from areas long inhabited by Slavs to the city's south and west. Near the end of the 1950s, the population had again reached its prewar total; the city was home to 365,000 inhabitants in 1970 and 457,000 in 1980. Based on its population before 1918, Gdańsk had ranked twenty-seventh among Germany's largest cities; after the war, in contrast, it became Poland's fifth largest city and held a degree of esteem that it had never enjoyed in Germany.

Between Communism and Modernity: Reconstruction and New Society

The first Poles to come to Gdańsk in spring 1945 were shocked: could this city of rubble ever again become a hub of urban life? Enormous tasks lay ahead, including the organization of administration, economy, and society as well as the construction of a new city center in place of the old center's ruins—and all this in a foreign city largely vacated by its former inhabitants. All the same, the foundations of Polish Gdańsk had already been laid mere weeks after the city's capture.

In early April, after the initial Polish state representatives and security forces had arrived, the Polish old-time communist Franciszek Kotus-Jankowski, whom the government had appointed as "city president" (lord mayor), came to Gdańsk and began organizing a civic administration. At the same time, delegations from Poland's Ministry of National Education arrived to reopen the university. Physicians, city planners, and specialists for the harbor and the power plants also came; as well as a group of teachers assigned to establish a Polish school system. Politically, the communist Polish Workers' Party was in charge from the outset; it tolerated other political parties until 1947, yet members of the bourgeoisie, even those who had been active in the resistance against the Nazi occupation, quickly faced persecution. The government in Warsaw appointed the city parliament, which assembled for the first time on July 9, 1945; the first local elections took place in 1954 and exclusively with candidates from Poland's National Unity Front.

The most urgent problems were initially reactivating the city's infrastructure as well as providing food for its people; for a long time, the latter need was a critical issue and residents relied on international relief shipments. Security in the city also left much to be desired. As in many cities in Poland's western regions, looters plagued Gdańsk, helping themselves to abandoned property and often forcibly robbing both Germans and Poles. Trade in *szaber*, or looted goods, was a regular part of the immediate postwar streetscape, as was the private sale of people's last remaining minor possessions.

The streets of the destroyed city center were cleared of rubble by the end of April, with many Germans having been forced to help in the effort. But what was to be done with these empty streets lined with ruined buildings? There were numerous possibilities, since all German wealth by law had passed to the Polish state—a unique city planning situation, of which the administrations of Western Europe's war-ravaged cities could only dream.

A fierce debate soon flared up regarding the image in which Gdańsk's city center should be rebuilt. Adhering to the principle of *tabula rasa*, some politicians and architects suggested the kind of radically modernist solution that was internationally popular at the time, namely, to completely clear away the ruins, with the possible exception of some churches and the city hall buildings, and erect a perimeter block housing development or an administrative center.

Figure 8.2 Shortly after the war's end, historic Long Street was lined with rubble and burned-out ruins. Kosycarz Foto Press, mca0059z.

Another direction quickly prevailed, though. Together with architects from the Technical University, Gdańsk's vice president Władysław Czerny and the city's building authority compiled initial guidelines for architectural reconstruction. The city government buildings would be concentrated in the New Gardens area outside of the actual urban core. A residential future was envisioned for the historic city center, which was to be reconstructed in the form of the old Gdańsk and also purged of all buildings bearing "German, very German, or extremely German" features, those "traces of barbarism," as Czerny said in early September 1945.[5] In this way, the urban center was to reemerge with Polish origins and traditions and furthermore in an architectural style reflecting the nation's cultural heritage. At the presentation of a first reconstruction plan in September 1945, Czerny said, "We must rebuild our old Gdańsk, as faithfully to its spirit as we possibly can." Only then, he argued, would Gdańsk once again become a truly Polish city.[6] Poland's central authority for the protection of historical monuments ultimately supported this undertaking.

Even with the German wealth, there was the question of financing such a thoroughly historicizing reconstruction, one requiring not only historical architectural studies but also the employment of numerous skilled labor specialists. Private or communal funding was impossible in light of Poland's recent political developments. It was thus necessary to convince the communist-led government to supply the needed resources. To accomplish this, the city presented the reconstruction as national propaganda, a measure—similar to the rebuilding of the city center in Warsaw—not only to demonstrate the country's tenacity but also to manifest the Polish essence of the areas that had been "reclaimed," thereby legitimizing their place in the Polish nation. It was imperative, they argued, to rebuild the one-time German "bourgeois city" into a Polish "workers' city" and to make it more beautiful than it had ever been before.

The first phase of reconstruction began in 1948 with great vigor and was completed in the mid-1950s with the (naturally Catholic) rededication of St. Mary's Church. But idealistic notions of a reconstruction entirely faithful to the original were unrealistic. On the one hand, problems arose over which historical version of the city should serve as the model for the present. Leaders agreed upon an idealized early modern Gdańsk, but this did not rule out misinterpretation: some of the mannerist and baroque façades that were restored during this time, for instance, had first appeared only in the nineteenth and twentieth centuries. On the other hand, the area of the destroyed city center was so large that a complete historical reconstruction would have required vast resources. A compromise emerged, namely, to restore only the Main Town based on its old structure (albeit with a considerably lower building density, small apartments, and partly standardized, if also richly decorated, façades), while the Old Town's most significant historical buildings were rebuilt in a conservative modern architecture. Neglected for a long time, the Old Suburb and Lower Town gradually developed into a residential and commercial zone partly retaining their building stock from the nineteenth century, supplemented with housing blocks.

Since the housing in the Main Town was preferentially given to workers' families, the social profile of the population living in the small, standardized apartments behind the city center's splendid façades would remain problematic into the twenty-first century. Rebuilding continued between the 1960s and 1980s, for instance, with the often meticulous reconstruction of prestigious historic buildings like the Main Town's city hall, or through the further development of row houses. Despite all of these issues, no other city on the continent could boast such a thorough restoration of a similarly destroyed historic urban center.

Gdańsk's reconstruction made history, substantiated the "Polish school of historic preservation," and fascinated all visitors to the city. With West Germany's reconstruction in mind, one of the first German journalists able to visit Gdańsk after the war wrote in disbelief in 1957:

Figure 8.3 Main Town reemerged in its historical form, albeit as a worker's settlement. In this photograph, the dome to the left belongs to the Royal Chapel. Kosycarz Foto Press, z00001313.

You think you are standing before scenery on an open-air stage against a backdrop of rubble still bearing the smells of corpses and burning from those days and nights now more than a decade past. It is an overwhelming sensation, offensive and disconcerting at first, but ultimately spellbinding and enchanting.[7]

While the juxtaposition of brand-new Baroque houses and surrounding rubble was still unsettling at the time, a few decades later many tourists would be completely unaware that this city had almost been completely leveled in 1945. For the city's new inhabitants, on the other hand, the rebuilt Gdańsk was the authentic, Polish Gdańsk, not that foreign city looking back at them from ruins and photographs. The city's reconstruction thus became, in a sense, a focal point for the realization of a new local identity.

With all of its heterogeneity, Gdańsk's new Polish society still shared one characteristic: almost all of the new residents had immigrated, were strangers to their new home, and needed to discover the urban space for themselves. Most of them had few preconceptions of Gdańsk upon arriving at the Motława. Not only were the city and its history foreign to them, but so too were the traces of the former inhabitants, who had left them frequently intact public spaces, houses, and apartments—sometimes even fully furnished. This charged relationship between German past and Polish present has marked the city since the war, and the contrasts were especially stark early on. At the end of 1945, a Polish immigrant described what particularly bothered her about Gdańsk:

> This outrageous, pedantic uniformity. It is neat, it is clean, precise, smooth, and even *gemütlich*. But cramped. This place lacks a spark, imagination, the unexpected, something that could tear a cry of delight or protest from one's breast.[8]

In a process lasting for decades, the Polish population learned to appropriate their new home's foreign elements, to develop familiarity with their environment, and to adapt their surroundings to their own needs. It began with a number of symbolically powerful events: German monuments like the war memorial on Wood Market and the equestrian statue of Wilhelm I by the High Gate were toppled. In addition, Polish street names had already replaced the old German names in 1945; the names in the historical city center were mostly translated directly into Polish, while the streets in the outlying areas generally received new names. All German inscriptions were supposed to disappear via paint and chisel. For decades, though, sewer covers, business signs emerging from behind crumbling plaster, mailbox slots bearing the word *Briefe* (letters), or water faucets with "W" (*warm*) and "K" (*kalt*, cold) on them all recalled the city's lurking otherness beneath the Polish exterior.

The available housing stock and existing residential area soon became insufficient in the face of the sudden population growth. Wrzeszcz, which had suffered less devastation, became an important commercial center, while housing blocks in the style of Soviet Realism crowded the eastern side of its Main Street. Often under the direction of housing cooperatives, the post-war decades also saw the construction of completely new high-rise apartment developments that housed many tens of thousands of people, both along the flat shoreline (Przymorze, Żabianka) as well as the terminal moraine hills (Morena, Orunia, etc.). For many families, these featureless two- to four-room apartments, some of which even boasted a seaside vista, embodied an ideal of unassuming contentment, one that knew no limits if, after a long wait, the residents were able to acquire a washing machine, television, or possibly even a small car of Polish, Czech, or East German manufacture.

The city's rapid development also necessitated upgrades to the public infrastructure. Commuter railways soon connected Gdańsk to Gdynia and Nowy Port (formerly Germ. Neufahrwasser) and for a long time ran with old Berlin commuter trains delivered to Poland as reparations payments. Streetcar and bus routes were also significantly expanded. Despite material shortages that hampered the infrastructure (and other) development, the city's hospital beds increased in number, as did its schools. Decisions in these matters often came following complicated coordinated planning processes behind the scenes, since, as in other socialist countries, a dual structure of government bodies and party organs was developing in Poland. All of these were in turn under Warsaw's supervision and enforced through the voivodeship administration. The city presidents and heads of the city parliament were career executives transferred to Gdańsk; they switched frequently and hardly left a mark on the city's life at all.

Repression and Protest: Politics and Daily Life

In 1947, as Gdańsk's Stalinist period was just beginning but the communist regime had not yet fully permeated the administration, there was still unrest in the city's politics. Local leaders had planned a celebration to commemorate the city's 950th anniversary, but due to the extravagant, bourgeois nature of the upcoming event, President Bierut personally ordered its cancellation; the sole festivity was the dedication of some workers' apartments and the bestowal of honorary citizenship on the city president. The city had to submit to the Soviet Central Committee in other areas as well. The year 1946, for instance, saw a dockworkers' strike brutally quelled and a public vote rigged in the communists' favor. The parliamentary elections of January 1947 were likewise falsified when the success of the Polish People's Party (the only permitted opposition party) was reframed as a victory for the communist-led Polish Democratic Bloc. Members of the middle-class opposition could expect persecution, repression, and, for many, even prison. Formed from the 1948 unification of the Polish Workers' Party and the Polish Socialist Party, the new Polish Unified Workers' Party forcefully extended its power and built up a pervasive political apparatus; in 1956, its payroll listed more than 500 people in Gdańsk alone. The fact that only fifteen of them possessed a university degree, however, speaks to the makeup of this cadre.

Mass events, parades, and ubiquitous propaganda characterized public life during the Stalinist years. At the same time, the population faced difficulties securing consumer goods and foodstuffs. Gdańsk grew in spite of this, though, and many people in the city got along as they quietly lived their lives. Stalin's death in 1953 moved many in Gdańsk to tears, but the mood changed abruptly in October 1956. Quickened by recent labor unrest in Poznań, the Soviet political thaw set in, and the people in Gdańsk likewise began to express their criticism of Stalin's cult of personality at large assemblies at venues like the Pedagogic and Technical universities. Although Warsaw again cracked down politically just a few months later, cultural and social life remained liberal: Gdańsk's first "Miss Baltic Coast" was crowned in early 1957. In addition, though frequently suspected of separatist endeavors in the Stalin years, the Kashubians, the West Slavic ethnic group that had called Pomerania and the Pomerelian area around Gdańsk their home since before the city's first historical mention nearly a millenium earlier, could now develop freely; the headquarters of their central association was located in Gdańsk beginning in 1956.

Significant political events became scarce in Gdańsk, and the times when the city dominated the headlines of the global press seemed to be over. However, as Gdańsk made its contribution to Poland's millennial celebration arranged by the state in 1962, the entire state and party leadership came to the Motława. New memorial sites were added for their visit: an equestrian statue of King John III Sobieski created in Lviv was erected on Wood Market in 1965, and in 1967 the Monument to the Defenders of the Coast was dedicated. Erected on a hill raised specifically for this purpose on the Westerplatte, the Defenders memorial honors not only the defense of the military transit depot there but also the struggle of Poland's soldiers on all fronts in the Second World War. Embedded within a complete commemorative landscape, it soon became the central location for ceremonies on the annual anniversary of the war's outbreak.

Recreational activities increased in importance for the people in Gdańsk. The beaches were just as popular as they had been in German times, and the city soon became a sought-after vacation spot for Poles as well as foreigners. From the 1970s onward, more and more German *Heimwehtouristen* ("homesickness tourists")[9] came seeking traces of their lost homeland.

Beginning in 1954, citizens could stroll through the Gdańsk Zoo in Oliwa, which drew visitors with its animals as well as its scenic attractions. Due to the many leisure opportunities it offered in the summertime, the reconstructed Main Town was a favorite destination for excursions. "Gdańsk Days" welcomed visitors with music and street theater and was expanded in 1972 with the reactivated St. Dominic's Fair, which drew thousands of annual visitors to a Main Town enjoying much reduced inner-city traffic.

Sports also increased in significance. In 1948, the Lechia Gdańsk Football Club advanced to Poland's premiere league, the Ekstraklasa, although it would never become a top international club. Gdańsk was initially known for its boxers: Alesky Antkiewicz won Olympic bronze in 1948, and Zygmunt Chychła won Poland's first gold medal in 1952. Elżbieta Duńska-Krzesińska, broad jump gold medalist at the 1956 Melbourne Olympics, was the first national sports star who resided in Gdańsk.

The Catholic Church had special meaning for the confluence of Gdańsk's motley new population. The church acquired all of the city's Protestant houses of worship, and its old monasteries were partially reactivated. A sense of community formed among the uprooted population at Catholic Masses and large holiday ceremonies like Corpus Christi processions, and churches offered a space for the free exchange of opinions. Despite the state's attempts to exert influence, the church remained largely autonomous and was a haven for oppositional thought. In some regards, though, it pursued objectives similar to the state's: both were anxious to facilitate the western regions' quick integration into the rest of Poland. German bishop Carl Maria Splett, who was in prison in Poland until 1956, continued to hold the office of bishop in the Vatican's eyes, and a new bishop, Edmund Nowicki, was not inaugurated in Oliwa until late 1956. Lech Marian Kaczmarek then relieved Nowicki in 1971. The diocese boundaries corresponded with those of the former Free City until 1992. Having shrunk to just a few hundred people, the Protestant community assembled for worship services in a church in Sopot (Germ. Zoppot). The small Jewish congregation used the synagogue in Wrzeszcz until 1950; the Jewish Cemetery was closed in 1956, and the congregation disbanded in 1971.

The year 1968 marked the end of the relative political calm. As student protests erupted in Warsaw, Gdańsk's students—particularly those at the Technical and Pedagogical universities—did not stand idly by. The first street demonstration occurred on March 12, when about 20,000 people, including many workers, demonstrated against the communist regime three days later. The state reacted harshly: its militia brutally dispersed the protesters; around 300 people were arrested following street fights; and many students were forced out of the universities and into military service. The anti-Semitic ("anti-Zionist") slogans common in state and party propaganda caused a number of the approximately 100 Jews living in Gdańsk to emigrate. This would not be the end of the protests, though.

Ports and Shipyards

Gdańsk had traditionally lived on trade, its harbor, and the shipyards. At first, this hardly changed after the war, although the acquisition of numerous port cities presented a great challenge for Poland, whose elite had been largely wiped out in the war—there were, after all, hardly any specialists in shipbuilding or deep-sea fishing. Yet the maritime industry beckoned, and the sea offered both freedom and fascinating professional activity. Poles accordingly founded many shipping and trade companies in Gdańsk after the war. But disenchantment soon followed as these businesses were nationalized and made part of socialist central planning in 1948. This did not benefit the port revenues, and despite the (mostly) minor damage to the docks and the modernization of the loading and storage facilities, the goods turnover stagnated until 1966, when it finally reached pre-war levels. The most important products traded through Gdańsk were coal and coke from Poland's southern mining areas; lumber also retained its traditional significant role, and over time, commerce in piece goods gained in importance. Regular freight routes ran to Scandinavia, the Mediterranean, and Southeast Asia. Harbor activity focused along the Vistula between the city center and the estuary, and soon, only excursion steamers still entered the Motława harbor between the Long Bridge and Granary Island. To facilitate the unloading of large ships and tankers, the North Harbor developed between 1970 and 1975 in the Gulf of Gdańsk east of the Westerplatte. About 7,000 people worked for the port authority in 1980.

At the least, the many ships arriving in Gdańsk spread a little international flair. Foreign sailors entered the city in search of auspicious opportunities and occasional adventure, while Polish mariners brought home impressions from the West as well as items both uncommon and sought-after in Poland. Many thousands of Gdańsk's inhabitants went to sea, and the city became a vital home port for Poland's commercial fleet.

In contrast to the pre-war era, Polish Gdańsk developed into a major seat of industry, not least due to the government's corresponding economic policies. Electrical, chemical, and food processing plants were joined by large construction and printing companies, followed by an oil refinery in the 1970s. Private enterprises hardly played any role at all in the manufacturing industry, except in the skilled crafts. There were over 2,300 craft businesses in Gdańsk in 1980. Many smaller businesses were privately owned, while the larger stores belonged to the state. The first supermarket opened on Long Street in 1957.

The core of economic activity, however, was doubtless the shipbuilding industry. The shipyards were reactivated soon after the war, although the Red Army had taken a portion of the machinery with them. The former Danzig Shipyard and the Schichau Shipyard operated together under the name Stocznia Gdańska (Gdańsk Shipyard, known as the Lenin Shipyard from 1967 to 1990). As there was still a paucity of shipbuilding specialists, the shipyards initially assembled tractors and steam engines and built steel structures. In late 1948, the ore freighter *Sołdek* became the first new ship launched after the war; it is presently a museum in the Motława harbor. The year 1952 saw nineteen ships constructed in Gdańsk, which resumed its role from centuries earlier as Poland's most important shipyard site and one of the largest worldwide. In their most productive year (1975), the shipyards completed ships with a combined 306,000 gross register tons.

The largest consumer of locally built ships was the Soviet Union, but Western shipping companies also increasingly commissioned their ships in Gdańsk. The city's shipyards were not only cost-effective but were also noted for the quality of their production, thus serving Poland as major recipients of foreign money. In 1980, around 20,000 employees worked in the various shipyards in Gdańsk, which also included a large repair yard founded in 1952. Many thousands of additional jobs were created in ancillary industries.

Communist propaganda proudly celebrated the labor in the shipyards, distinguishing the best workers and even granting them certain privileges. Yet these workers also possessed a distinct self-assertiveness. Was it from their daily physical interaction with massive machinery? Was it because they came from the most diverse parts of Poland and had not yet put down roots in Gdańsk? Was it because they knew how indispensable they were to the nation's economic vitality? Or was it, as the liberal politician Donald Tusk wrote in the 1990s, the continued influence of an old local mindset, "that mixture of courage and prudence, independence and ingenuity, something arising from the sea and nearby Kashubia, which calls itself *genius loci*?"[10] Whatever the case, the shipyard workers would certainly test the state's mettle.

The Long Road Out of Provincialism

Historically, Gdańsk had never been a fertile cultural center. At most, it had served as a vital mediator of cultural developments, and little would initially change after the war. Gdańsk nonetheless found itself catapulted into the ranks of the nation's largest cities. Warsaw and Kraków, Lviv and Vilnius had always led the way in Polish cultural life, followed at some distance by Poznań. Yet Lviv and Vilnius were no longer Polish cities; the majority of Lviv's intelligentsia moved to Wrocław, while intellectuals in Vilnius divided themselves between Toruń (Germ. Thorn) and Gdańsk. Yet so dense a cultural fabric would never emerge in the metropolis on the Moława as it had in the old Lithuanian capital, and Gdańsk kept its provincial air for some time.

Still, Gdańsk soon became a cultural hub for northern Poland, which is not surprising, given its location between the marginal, working-class city of Szczecin (Germ. Stettin) and the rural Olsztyn (Germ. Allenstein). Soon after the war's end, Gdańsk's local culture revived, simply in Polish, as opposed to German. There were, of course, some mediators bridging the city's past and present. Until 1947, Erich Volmar, the city's last German curator of monuments, helped protect the art treasures that had been evacuated from Gdańsk's churches and museums. Another was the composer Helmut Hubert Degler, born in 1915, who remained in Gdańsk after the war, changed his name to Henryk Hubertus Jabłoński, and taught at the Academy of Music until 1980.

These personal continuities were not the rule, though. Many leading exponents of German cultural life had fled before the war's end, and those who remained were expelled. Most of the new Polish population could not speak German and was unable to adopt the city's cultural heritage by reading German texts. The reconstruction was therefore not based on a comprehensive study of the historical structural substance but rather occurred somewhat freeform, influenced to varying degrees by historical models, current architectural trends, and ideological objectives.

Due to the focus on reconstructing the historical city center, as well as material shortages and ideological guidelines, modern architecture made little headway in postwar Gdańsk. A number of noteworthy structures nevertheless appeared alongside the dozens of faceless residential blocks. Worthy of mention, even if it raised problematic social issues, is the Falowce in the city's Przymorze district; this gently rippling connected row of high-rise apartments housed 6,000 occupants, and its length of well over a half mile placed it among the longest residential buildings on the continent. Also of note is the green Zieleniak high-rise designed by Jansa Strzałkowska and built in 1970, which towers over the historical city center from the direction of the Oliva Gate. Planners exercised caution in the Main Town itself. Here, the Teatr Wybrzeże particularly catches the eye. Designed by Lech Kadłubowski and completed in 1966 on the former site of the old Municipal Theater, it impressed visitors with its restrained modernist architectural style, its glass front fitting in splendidly alongside the neighboring Great Arsenal. The little drummer Oskar Matzerath would have had much more glass to shatter here than before the war, when the old Municipal Theater only

Figure 8.4 Beginning in the 1960s, large suburban housing estates were built for the rapidly growing city. In this photograph from 1975, children play in front of the Falowce housing block, which stretches over a half mile. Kosycarz Foto Press, obr0555z.

had a few panes for him to destroy in a famous scene in Günter Grass's novel *The Tin Drum*.

Until 1945, architecture had benefited primarily from influence of the Technical University, but several new academies and colleges appeared and helped the city's artistic life attain unprecedented heights. One of these was the Academy of Fine Arts, located in Sopot until 1954 and then in the Great Arsenal in Gdańsk; its professors and graduates initially found abundant work in the artistic decoration of the Main Town, where they were needed to design façades and create murals. Influenced by Post-Impressionism, Colorist painting, and Social Realism, the "Sopot school" made a name for itself as its adherents—such as Józefa Wnukowa and Artur Nacht-Samborski—ascribed great importance to technical proficiency. Numerous other prominent artists were active at the Academy of Fine Arts over the decades, such as sculptor Franciszek Duszeńko and architect Adam Haupt, both of whom not only created the monument on the Westerplatte but also the striking memorial at the concentration camp in Treblinka.

Music also profited from the formation of several relevant institutions in Gdańsk alongside the Academy of Music. Most notably, the Baltic Philharmonic was located in a former sports hall on Grand Avenue and sometimes performed with the Baltic Opera. Two graduates of the Academy of Music—violinist Konstanty Andrzej Kulka and pianist Ewa Pobłocka—attained worldwide fame. Gdańsk did not become a center of compositional activity at first. Kazimierz Wiłkomirski's *Gdańsk Cantata* (1955) attracted some attention, and Henryk Hubertus Jabłoński became known for his chamber and orchestral works. Then, with the political thaw of de-Stalinization in 1956, the floodgates opened; all of a sudden, a vital jazz scene developed, and each year nationally and internationally prominent singers and pop stars enchanted the Polish public at the Sopot International Song Festival.

On the other hand, it would still take some time before Gdańsk would become a literary city. Ultimately, the founding of the University of Gdańsk was vital in this development. Up until that point, local writers had pursued one primary goal: to weave the city and its literary life into existing Polish cultural contexts. Among their ranks were poet and novelist Franciszek Fenikowski, the productive novelist Stanisława Fleszarowa-Muskat, and the crime fiction author Stanisław Goszczurny. But artistic quality often suffered as authors had to write politically acceptable texts. With few exceptions, such as the poet and director Jerzy Afanasjew or the poet Bolesław Fac, avant-garde ambitions were rare..

At first, since Gdańsk's old Municipal Theater had burned down, theater performances had to take place in other locations. In 1967, though, the national Teatr Wybrzeże was constructed on Coal Market. Smaller student theaters were also important, however, such as the Bim-Bom, where the Polish James Dean, Zbigniew Cybulski, performed, although he appeared more frequently in Gdańsk's cinemas. Film underwent a genuine boom following the reopening of the first post-war cinema in 1945; Gdańsk's citizens soon had their choice of more than twenty venues, including Long Street's Leningrad Cinema, which opened in 1953 and seated 1,200. The city was less significant as a cinematic backdrop. Stanisław Różewicz's film *Wolne miasto* (Free city) was released in 1958, and Volker Schlöndorff filmed his 1979 adaptation of Günter Grass's *The Tin Drum* in the city. Gdańsk began hosting Poland's most prestigious film festival in 1974, but the event moved to Gdynia in 1986.

The local radio station began to operate in June 1945, and a regional television station followed in 1960. The daily newspaper *Dziennik Bałtycki* began supplying the city's morning reading material in May 1945 and received some competition in the form of the party newspaper *Głos Wybrzeża* (Voice of the coast) in 1947.

Education received particular attention in the communist years, especially in order to make the often unpopular government more palatable. Numerous new schools were constructed to educate the many children born in the post-war years; in 1970, some 50,000 children attended seventy-three primary schools in

Gdańsk, most of whom went on to one of the many secondary and vocational schools. The expansive local landscape of tertiary education led to a rapid increase in post-secondary students. Only partially damaged during the war, the Technical University was reactivated as the Politechnika Gdańska; lectures began in October 1945 for the initial 1,500 students. The school developed into one of the nation's leading technical academies, first emphasizing shipbuilding and hydraulic engineering, and around 30,00 young people had graduated from there by 1980. The medical college also reopened after the war.

Since the Polish intelligentsia had suffered during the war, teacher education was a high priority in the post-war years. In 1946, the Higher Pedagogical School was founded, from which the University of Gdańsk would arise in 1976. The university first opened on its campus in Oliwa but also had institutions scattered across the city; in 1980, it enrolled around 13,000 students. There were additional higher schools for art, music, and physical education, and Gdańsk's offerings in higher education were more diverse than ever before in its history. Whereas numerous scholarly institutions devoted to technical issues (particularly with sea travel and ship construction) thrived in the city, the establishment of the humanities was organizationally weaker. Even so, the former Municipal Library, whose structure (and much of its collection) had miraculously survived the war unscathed, was invaluable for humanist scholarship.

The condition of other cultural facilities was not so favorable. The irreplaceable holdings of the Danzig State Archives could only be partly salvaged. The City Museum likewise had suffered great losses by the war's end. It was able, at least, to reopen at its old location in the Franciscan Monastery, and it was named a national museum in 1972. Its partially preserved collection expanded over time with a wealth of new exhibits including sacred and profane works of art from the city and region, as well as Polish paintings from the nineteenth and twentieth centuries. Hans Memling's *Last Judgment* altarpiece, which Soviet forces had taken with them to the USSR, also found its home in this museum after being returned in 1956.

Museums were part of the official politics of memory, which pursued the chief objective of conveying a beautified, unilaterally Polish conception of history to the local population as well as to visitors from within Poland and abroad. This began with the Archeological Museum, which opened in 1961 in the former headquarters of the Danzig Research Society; it first exhibited predominantly "Slavic" finds from excavations in Gdańsk and Pomerelia but was also soon responsible for the preservation of archaeological monuments in both the city and voivodeship of Gdańsk. The Central Maritime Museum, founded in 1962, was dedicated to Poland's nautical history, which through the eighteenth century was essentially limited to Gdańsk anyway. Since the collections of the old State Museum for the History of Danzig were destroyed in the war, there was initially no museum for local history. In 1970, the Historical Museum of the City of Gdańsk was founded in the Main Town's city hall, though for a long time, it focused mainly on reconstructing the building's historical interior space.

Museums alone were not enough to reconstruct local history, and written portrayals were urgently needed to "rectify" the image of the German Danzig in the context of the city's new circumstances. While, in a patriotic sense, postwar scholars of local history absolutely understood their research as a component of these legitimation strategies, they were also soon producing high-quality work. A preeminent milestone consisted of the first few volumes of *Historia Gdańska*, compiled by leading Polish historians under the direction of Edmund Cieślak and first published in 1978. These volumes investigated many aspects of Gdańsk's history which, until then, had lacked adequate treatment: medieval and early-modern economic and social history received just as much attention as political-historical discourse. On the other hand, owing to its meager ties to Polish history, the "Prussian" nineteenth century would still remain unexamined for a long time.

Sorrow, Longing, Hope: The Displaced Danzig Germans

Between 1945 and 1947, around a quarter million Danzig Germans lost their homes; they fled from the approaching Red Army or had to leave the city in the months and years following the war's end, most of them resettling in the German states of Schleswig-Holstein and Lower Saxony. Only some of them joined the Association of Danzig Germans (Bund der Danziger), an expellee organization founded in 1946. On the one hand, this group took up German Liberal[11] and German National traditions; at the same time, however, its members regarded themselves as the legal successors of the vanished Free City of Danzig. While German Liberals and German Nationals had ostensibly despised the Free City prior to 1933, they paradoxically sought the restoration of the little state. In reality, they had no other options: until Willy Brandt's *Ostpolitik* (eastern policy) almost twenty-five years later, the Federal Republic of Germany officially insisted upon a restoration of Germany to its borders of 1937, which had not included the Free City in the first place.

In order to legitimate the claim to Gdańsk, then, a reincarnation of the Free City's senate was created, the Delegation of the Free City of Danzig (Vertretung der Freien Stadt Danzig), elected by the Council of Danzig Germans (Rat der Danziger). The council members were appointed by the Danzig expellees via postal voting. Norbert Sternfeld, a lawyer from a Jewish family, was a longstanding director of the delegation.

Already in August 1948, the Delegation of the Free City of Danzig sent the Western powers and the United Nations a memorandum calling for a restitution of the Free City under the protection of the United Nations. The delegation argued that Danzig's incorporation into Germany carried out by Gauleiter Albert Forster on September 1, 1939, had been unconstitutional. This stance, which some incidentally still hold today, brought the Council of Danzig Germans into conflict with other homeland associations who accused it of separatism, such as the Homeland Association of West Prussia, in which former National Socialists initially played a leading role. Hermann Rauschning even spoke of "treason."[12] Yet these political turf wars became less significant over time; in 1959, the Association of Danzig Germans joined the Federation of Expellees (Bund der Vertriebenen).

Based in Lübeck, the Association of Danzig Germans had 67,000 members in 1962 and around 20,000 at the close of the 1990s. It went into an existential crisis in the early twenty-first century as it began to lose many members to old age. In 1987, it opened a small "Homeland Museum" in a renovated townhome in Lübeck. Entirely independent of the expellees' initiatives, Gdańsk had already become a permanent feature of Germany's memorial landscape, as evident in the streets and squares named after Danzig in over a thousand West German cities.

The regionally organized Danzig expellees long refused to acknowledge the city's Polish postwar history. As late as 1965, the official organ of the Association of Danzig Germans claimed that "there is no Polish history of Danzig."[13] This was even understandable from a psychological standpoint: the unexpected loss of home, the conditions of flight and expulsion, and the unsurety of their new places of residence, not to mention the frequent absence of husbands and fathers, all yielded embitterment and silence while also inciting efforts to reconstruct their lost world. An invented Danzig took the place of what had been experienced and suffered, a Danzig no longer vulnerable to contradictions arising from the reality of the post-war city.

This anxiety to idealize their lost home characterized expellees' poetry and prose. Wolfgang Federau encapsulated the bygone Danzig as follows: "The garden of my youth is sunk, just as the entire city is sunk," he wrote in 1949. "But it is still there, blossoming untouched and magnificent and wonderful as it once was, inalienable, on the soil of my soul."[14] One of his poems, "Ewige Stadt Danzig (Eternal city of Danzig)," further expressed these sentiments:

> She is not dead! Is not sunk,
> not extinguished with tower and gate.
> From fire, flames, storm, and sparks
> she has risen up like a phoenix.[15]

Danzig's resurgence could only take place in an imagined world, however, and in 1950, the official organ of the Association of Danzig Germans stated: "No power, volition, or even the most loving and devoted striving, can restore [Danzig] to its onetime splendor and glory."[16]

The Polish reconstruction of Gdańsk thus greatly irritated the Danzig Germans, overwriting their city with foreign characters and threatening to replace not only the city's image but also its very memory. Conservative contemporaries who had not been expelled similarly perceived the "loss of the German east," evident in a 1964 report by journalist Carl Gustaf Ströhm, who recorded his impressions of the Main Town in the arrogant, paternalistic style prevalent among German observers of their Polish neighbors:

> Long-haired *huligani*—Polish hooligans—lounge around on the terraces. The streets make an untidy, squalid impression. Poorly dressed, beggarly people walk through the gates. Something Galician, Volhynian is in the air—as if somebody had erected the scenery of an old Hanseatic city somewhere near Białystok in order to shoot a film. Now the extras walk across the stage without makeup—and that alone is enough to rob the audience of the illusion.[17]

In this way, many expelled Danzig Germans closed their minds from confrontation with their lost homeland. The Association of Danzig Germans did not make contact with the city government in Gdańsk until the 1990s.

But there were many Danzig Germans who thought differently. Also formed in the late 1940s, the Homeland Network for Danzig Catholics (Heimatwerk für Danziger Katholiken) was an organization of Catholic expellees. Under the direction of Gerhard Nitschke and his educational institution, the Adalbert Institute (Adalbertus-Werk), this network began establishing ties with Gdańsk in 1961 and has insisted on a policy of reconciliation and understanding through the present day. Additionally, anybody with a left-leaning political bent had an easier time with such attempts at bridge-building. Horst Ehmke, one of West Germany's leading Social Democrats, hailed from Danzig, as did Erich Brost, founder of the *Westdeutsche Allgemeine Zeitung* (West German general tidings) and one of the German Republic's post-war Social Democratic media moguls. There were furthermore many lone fighters who maintained close ties to Gdańsk and formed friendships with its new Polish residents. In 1993, for instance, while visiting his native city for the fifty-sixth time since the war, Hans Eggebrecht championed the reconstruction of the chimes in St. Catherine's Church. This kind of German devotion to Gdańsk was rewarded. In 1993, for the first time since its transition to Poland, the city granted honorary citizenship to one of its German natives: Günter Grass.

Günter Grass Rewrites Danzig

It was not through the efforts of expellee associations that Gdańsk would come to occupy a special place in many Germans' mindscapes but rather because of the work of the writer Günter Grass, who was born in 1927 in Langfuhr and lived in the suburb until the war's end. When his debut novel *The Tin Drum* appeared in 1959, literary critics agreed: here was an author who had more to write than just another piece of regionalist literature, someone who both conjured and deconstructed the notion of home with a prodigiously vivid language, who drew from an irretrievably destroyed social milieu to comment on German post-war sensitivities, and who imparted a universal quality to individual lives in Danzig.

Grass's novel needed to startle and unsettle. The childhood and life story of Oskar Matzerath, the drummer who has refused to grow, is supplemented with a familial prehistory reaching back multiple generations and comprising not only middle-class Danzig, but also the proletarian and petit-bourgeois suburbs as well as the surrounding Kashubian backcountry. Oskar's grandmother Anna Bronski is a Kashubian peasant, while his uncle (and possible father) works at the Polish Post Office. His alleged father is a shopkeeper from the Rhineland. This cast of characters alone burst all familiar paradigms; when anybody had thought of and written about Danzig before the war, the bourgeois German community and the proud Main Town had always taken center stage. Grass, on the other hand, presented the population of this supposedly German city as an ethnic mixture without local traditions. Nor did he depict the history of Danzig from the familiar perspective constructed solely by German determining factors, but rather as part of a nexus shaped in equal measure by Polish and international influences.

The sensational success of *The Tin Drum* was followed by the novella *Cat and Mouse* (*Katz und Maus*) in 1961 and the novel *Dog Years* (*Hundejahre*) in 1963; the three works subsequently made up the "Danzig Trilogy." Danzig, or more precisely the suburb of Langfuhr, became a fixed star in the literary universe of Günter Grass, a private microcosm, as a narrator of *Dog Years* observes:

> There was once a city –
> in addition to the suburbs of Ohra, Schidlitz, Oliva, Emmaus, Praust, Sankt Albrecht, Schellmühl, and the seaport suburb of Neufahrwasser, it had a suburb named Langfuhr. Langfuhr was so big and so little that whatever happens or could happen in this world, also happened or could have happened in Langfuhr.[18]

Although Grass's protagonists occasionally made their way into the historical city center, they did so without any reverence. Readers thus see Oskar, for whom it is a pleasure to shatter the windows of the Municipal Theater, that hub of bourgeois life, with his high voice:

> The box with its dome bore a fiendishly close resemblance to a senselessly enlarged, neoclassical coffee grinder, though it lacked the handle on the rounded top of its dome which, in that temple devoted to culture and the muses filled to the brim each evening, would have allowed it to grind to a grisly scrap a five-act play with its entire assemblage of tragedians, stage sets, prompters, props, and curtains. This building, from whose column-flanked lobby windows a sagging afternoon sun, steadily applying more red, refused to depart, annoyed me....
>
> After a few minutes of screams of various calibers, which however produced no results, an almost soundless tone took effect, and Oskar could report with joy and telltale pride that two midlevel panes in the left window of the lobby had been forced to surrender the evening sun and now registered as two black quadrangles in need of immediate reglazing.[19]

Günter Grass tackled Danzig's history even more radically in his grand Danzig (anti)historical novel *The Flounder* (*Der Butt*, 1977). Here he avails himself of the city's downright mythically alienated past to comment on the history of the Old World. Women are in control of history here—they cook, love, and let men wage and lose wars. Grass constructs a depersonalized history from the bottom up with women and stomachs as its most significant catalysts, as opposed to the national antagonisms that had shaped the local society since the second half of the nineteenth century.

While the literary world of the Federal Republic of Germany and the West eagerly awaited each new book by the most famous Danzig writer of all time, some circles were much more hesitant. For various reasons, only toward the end of the 1970s did an interest in Grass began to grow in Poland, including Gdańsk. Conservatives in West Germany accused Grass of what they viewed as the author's insolent advocacy for Willy Brandt's Ostpolitik, as well as writing morally reprehensible material. The Association of Danzig Germans likewise kept their distance. In 1962, an association official wrote that Grass's works were "a credit neither to him nor to us," and concluded: "Sadly we cannot feel proud of this son of our city."[20]

The author responded to the association in kind, raging in his 1965 poem "Kleckerburg":

> What says the Baltic? Blubb, pfff, pshsh …
> In German, Polish: Blubb, pfff, pshsh …
> But when I asked the functionaries
> at the assembly-weary, coach-
> and-special-train-fed gathering
> of eastern refugees at Hanover,
> they had forgotten what the Baltic says
> and made the Atlantic Ocean roar;
> I kept insisting: Blubb, pfff, pshsh …
> So: Hit him! Kill him! all yelled out,
> he's turned his back on human rights,
> on pensions, on his native city,
> on compensations, restitutions,
> just listen to his intonation:
> That's not the Baltic, that's high treason.[21]

Grass remained true to Danzig. Again and again, he traveled to the city from which he obtained so many themes for his work. Again and again he wrote about it: *The Call of the Toad* (*Unkenrufe*, 1992), *Crabwalk* (*Im Krebsgang*, 2002), and finally his great memoir *Peeling the Onion* (*Beim Häuten der Zwiebel*, 2006)—all of these books take place partly in and feed on the loved and hated city on the Motława. This was no secret in Gdańsk, and eventually the city's Polish population also discovered the writer for themselves.

First Caesura: The Worker's Rebellion of 1970

Poland's political and economic situation underwent a "little stabilization"[22] in the 1960s. The administration of Władysław Gomułka, head of the state as well as the party, also enjoyed a number of successes in foreign affairs, with the greatest triumph coming when with the Treaty of Warsaw of December 7, 1970, the Federal Republic of Germany recognized the Polish western borders. For millions of people in Poland's western regions, this signified that their hitherto provisional existence in the former German provinces appeared secured, and they no longer needed to live proverbially sitting on packed suitcases.

Bolstered by this outcome of Brandt's Ostpolitik, the authoritarian Gomułka enforced a resolution that would have bitter consequences for the population. On December 13, he announced price increases for, among other things, meat, which was bound to provoke the populace's ire so close to Christmas. The uprising began in Gdańsk. On the morning of Monday, December 14, workers at the Lenin Shipyard spontaneously laid down their tools and demanded a retraction of the price hikes as well as a boost in wages. The number of strikers grew rapidly, and by ten o'clock, there were already over 3,000 people gathered outside the shipyard's administrative building. Soon thereafter, the first workers from the shipyard marched into the city. More and more passersby joined the throng, and patriotic and revolutionary anthems echoed through the gray, December streets.

After unsuccessful attempts to pacify the workers, the regime decided to crack down. It blocked the telephone connections and traffic into the city, brought in barracked police officers, and placed the army on standby. The first violent conflicts took place that afternoon at the Oliva Gate. Yet water cannons and tear gas could not deter the protesters, who continued in street fights with law enforcement until midnight. Vehicles went up in flames, and shops were looted. The communist Security Service instigated more than a few of these attacks in an attempt to defame the uprising as criminal excesses committed by the masses. Many hundreds of protesters and oppositionists were arrested on the first day of the demonstrations, and a number of people were injured.

On the following day, the protests expanded to other professions. Shots were fired early in the morning as many thousands of workers tried to storm the militia's voivodeship headquarters, in order to free their colleagues who had been arrested the day before. One emergency meeting followed the other in Warsaw. Gomułka spoke of "counterrevolution" and sanctioned the use of firearms against the demonstrators (with the first shot in the air and the next in the leg). Around nine o'clock, about 20,000 predominantly young people had assembled outside the Workers' Party voivodeship committee headquarters on Moat Street—partly because they wished to speak with representatives from the city government and partly because there was no better target for venting their pent-up anger. Yet they had no political goals beyond that. Although the demonstrators viewed it as a beacon of hope when they succeeded in setting fire to the building, it only further infuriated the authorities against them. There were casualties as the army tried to free those trapped in the building. As the situation escalated, tanks appeared, military vehicles went up in flames, and workers drove through the city in a captured personnel carrier. Some of the main railway station's buildings ultimately burned as well. Around 500 people were arrested on this day and during the following night in Gdańsk, many of whom were brutally abused.

Powerful military units moved into the city on the night of December 15–16, occupied all of the strategically important positions, and surrounded the shipyard. Militia officers and soldiers blockaded the shipyard gates with tanks that morning. The workforce decided to resume regular shipyard operations, and when several hundred young shipyard workers tried to leave the premises to march into the city as they had on the preceding days, the army fired on them, hitting many of the protesters and killing five. In light of the increasingly dangerous

Figure 8.5 In December 1970, the workers of Gdańsk ventured a rebellion against the communist system. Tens of thousands went to the streets. Kosycarz Foto Press, wyd0086z.

situation, the workers elected a strike committee, one of whose members was a young man named Lech Wałęsa. Yet due to the massive repression and numerous casualties in Gdynia and Szczecin as well, the strikes collapsed on December 17, and the workforce was placed on leave until the year's end.

The shock in Gdańsk was profound: a government that had shot at its own citizens had irretrievably lost its validity in the eyes of many. These December events left their mark on an entire generation, including future prime minister Donald Tusk, who at the time attended a school immediately neighboring the shipyard:

> On the way to school and back home I witnessed scenes that left their impression on me for my entire life. I saw thousands of protesters singing the *Warszawianka*,[23] I saw the party building in flames, militia officers who lashed out at all and fired into the crowd, and who were then torn to pieces by the crowd. I saw a soldier who never emerged from his burning tank, shipyard workers who distributed oranges from the looted delicatessen to us children, stout women who carried off televisions and fur coats from the shops.[24]

The worker's uprising not only brought about great change in Gdańsk but also had consequences in Warsaw. The Kremlin leadership abandoned Gomułka, the opposition within the party asserted itself, and on December 20, the Upper Silesian party bigwig Edward Gierek took office as first secretary of the Polish United Workers' Party. While the new leadership was anxious to win back public trust through economic concessions, there was no legal reckoning with the events until 1990. The trials dragged on for almost a quarter century and were resolved in 2014 with two suspended sentences for participating officers, while the main defendant, Wojciech Jaruzelski, had died in the interim.

Something in the Air

The situation in Gdańsk did not calm down for quite some time following the events of December 1970; by now, resentment had spread more broadly in the society. When the new party head Edward Gierek assessed the situation in person in early 1971, he solicited the workers' trust during a visit to the shipyard, asking: "So will you help us?" Although the assembled crowd answered: "Yes, we will help,"[25] the mood remained tense. Oppositional rallies took place again and again; shipyard workers carried dissident banners at the May Day parades; and the laying of wreaths at the shipyard gate became a ritual memorializing the events of 1970. The party also occasionally deemed it necessary to mobilize its adherents, such as in 1979, when 100,000 people flocked to Long Market to hear Gierek give a speech commemorating the fortieth anniversary of the war's outbreak.

The relative peace came at a high price, as the state leadership relied on foreign credit to boost the Polish economy. Gdańsk obtained not only its North Harbor but also a large oil refinery, a partially four-lane bypass west of the cities of Gdańsk, Sopot, and Gdynia, which were slowly consolidating into the "Tricity," and a new airport near Rębiechowo on the far side of the bypass. An enormous satellite town formed on the grounds of the old airport. There were also new developments in the city center: Long Street was converted into a pedestrian zone; Gdańsk's first escalators rolled into motion at the railway station; and reconstruction continued in the historic Main Town, for instance on Bakers' Street.

Additional efforts were made to better meet the population's consumption needs. Beginning in 1973, for example, Pepsi-Cola was bottled in the Gdańsk Brewery, although the beer supply still left much to be desired. New sports institutions like the arena in Oliwa accompanied athletic triumphs: the GKS Wybrzeże Gdańsk basketball team won multiple Polish championships, and Gdańsk native Krystyna Chojnowska-Liskiewicz sailed around the earth in

420 days between 1977 and 1978, becoming the first woman to do so solo. The cautious opening to the West also resulted in a city partnership: in the first such agreement between West German and Polish cities, the two old Hanseatic cities of Bremen and Gdańsk became sister cities in 1976.

The 1973 expansion of the city, in which Gdańsk's municipal area increased not only by the inland portion of the Vistula Spit leading to the channel but also by twelve towns in the Gdańsk Heights, contributed to the city's increasing strength. It would all have been a cause for rejoicing, if not for the restrictive regime and a number of tragic misfortunes, such as an August 1975 ferry collision with an excursion steamer on the Motława in which eighteen people lost their lives. Yet for the most part, the 1970s were a time of relative prosperity and modernity in Gdańsk.

Though suspiciously monitored by security agencies, local opposition groups slowly took shape, such as the national conservative movement "Young Poland," and the Founding Committee for Free Unions, organized in 1978. Prominent among the opposition in Gdańsk were Aleksander Hall and Bogdan Borusewicz, but Lech Wałęsa, who had lost his job at the shipyard in 1976 for giving inflammatory speeches, was also making a name for himself. The first underground newspapers appeared. The economic and cultural concessions cautiously made by the ruling powers were no longer enough for many young people. In 1979, over 5,000 people assembled at the gate of the Lenin Shipyard singing patriotic songs and chanting anti-communist slogans to commemorate the ninth anniversary of the December revolts. There was something in the air, and Gdańsk was in fact only months away from shaking the entire communist Eastern Bloc.

9

Kaleidoscope

Into the Future with Solidarity and the Discovery of New Pasts

When you close your eyes, you see the city's many hues. The tighter you press your eyelids shut, the brighter the scraps of color drift across your retinas. Amber-gold shimmers by, meadow-flower green and metallic blue, scabby brick-red; strokes of grain surge blond and brown, radiant before they fade. Pinch your eyes closed until they ache, and you'll see jagged Prussian blue, silver crosses, and a crown swimming in blood. Then the white eagle wipes away the colors. You have arrived; open your eyes. The ache subsides. This is the city as it is. It pulses in many colors, if you let it; and, as with a kaleidoscope, it is up to you whether it will shine green and red or golden or blue above all others. Gdańsk is the city of such colors, and they will never leave you.

"Gdańsk Is the Most Incredible City in the World"

On January 13, 2019, Gdańsk's city president Paweł Adamowicz stepped onto a small stage on Coal Market at the end of a nationwide charity fundraiser. As the mayor spoke, nobody suspected that this would become his political credo—as well as the conclusion of his twenty years in office, during which the city had experienced a tremendous upturn: "Gdańsk wishes to be a city of solidarity.... You are all amazing. Gdańsk is the most incredible city in the world. Thank you!"[1] At that moment, a man lunged at Adamowicz and stabbed him multiple times with a knife. Adamowicz died the next day. His death marked the end of an era: after its initial decline into aimless stagnation following 1989, the city had seen dynamic growth beginning in the new millennium as it reckoned with its historical heritage, not least that surrounding the Independent Self-Governing Trade Union "Solidarity" (Solidarność).

European history truly would have unfolded differently without the Gdańsk strikes of August 1980 and the formation of Solidarity. Yet Gdańsk and Poland would not rediscover the symbolic capital of these strikes for many years. The actual watershed came in 2005 during the elaborate festivities that took place in Gdańsk to celebrate the twenty-fifth anniversary of the August Agreements, the 1980 accord reached between the Polish state and the striking shipyard workers in Gdańsk, which led to the creation of free trade unions in Poland. International statesmen and stateswomen and famous musicians arranged to meet in the city; the musician Jean Michel Jarre's concert, entitled "Space of Freedom," drew over 100,000 people to the shipyard grounds; and the various political parties that had emerged from Solidarity competed to present themselves as the true heirs of the movement's legacy. After all, everyone wanted to bask in liberty's light, which had shone out of Gdańsk into the world in 1980 and 1981.

This light appeared to falter on that January evening in 2019, as the freedom that Gdańsk had enjoyed for years seemingly turned against it. Incited by nationalist propaganda, a lone perpetrator reminded the city that one should never feel too safe, and that freedom, like the kaleidoscope of Gdańsk's history, must be protected.

Making History Once Again: Gdańsk and Solidarity

At the close of the 1970s, the period of relative peace came to a palpable end. Political unrest, social transition, and new cultural challenges, all triggered in part by a confrontation with the developments in the West, accompanied a rapidly worsening national economic situation, which was particularly crushing for broad sectors of the population. The use of foreign credit decreased the space for investment, and even though numerous sectors of the economy were ineffectual, state and party leadership were slow to enact reforms. On the one hand, the Soviet Union strove to prevent any economic liberalization in its satellite nations, and on the other hand, the worker uprisings of 1970 and 1976 had made it clear that attempts to adjust the situation—through price hikes, for instance—would only provoke social resistance. The 1978 appointment of Karol Wojtyła as pope (John Paul II) further buoyed oppositional sentiment. Independent intellectual spheres took shape in Gdańsk; as they were far away from the state government in Warsaw, they could distance themselves from the ubiquitous communist lethargy. All that was needed to bring them into action was a catalyst.

It first seemed that 1980 would be a year like many others. Most people got by, torn between apathy and a lust for life. But the poor supply situation was fostering a growing discontent that began to spread as residents talked while waiting in long lines outside city shops. When, despite all concerns, the government attempted to improve state finances by moderately raising meat prices, strikes first broke out in southern Poland and then spread elsewhere. It was the strike at Gdańsk's Lenin Shipyard, though, that would shake the very foundations of the existing political order.

The direct catalyst was the dismissal of the fifty-one-year-old crane operator Anna Walentynowicz for her activity in illegal free trade unions. Her union colleagues and parts of the political opposition were incensed. On August 14, as protest fliers made their way into the shipyard, the first groups of workers went on strike. Gaining access to the shipyard with one leap over the fence, the charismatic former shipyard electrician Lech Wałęsa, who had served on the strike committee in the 1970 rebellion and been laid off in 1976, placed himself at the head of the new strike committee and declared the occupation of the plant. Strikers initially demanded the reinstatement of Walentynowicz and Wałęsa, permission to build a monument to the casualties of December 1970, and increased wages.

Cognizant of the Gdańsk Shipyard's symbolic significance, the party and state leadership were alarmed. On August 15, meanwhile, the strikes expanded to the city's other shipyards, as well as the local mass-transit system and numerous additional operations. Authorities cut the city's telephone connections that afternoon.

The next day, a Sunday, Henryk Jankowski, the priest of St. Bridget's Church, whose parish included the shipyard, offered Mass for 5,000 shipyard workers and a large crowd of the local populace who had gathered at the shipyard's gate number two. The crowd did not leave the gate for many days, decorating it with flowers and images of the Virgin Mary while singing patriotic songs.

On the same day, an end to the strikes already seemed near: after the administration of the Lenin Shipyard had agreed to the workers' demands, Lech Wałęsa declared an end to the revolt. Yet some of his fellow protesters, as well as workers from other businesses, were not of the same mind, and a vote led to the decision that the strike would go on. An interfactory strike committee formed with Wałęsa at its helm; Bogdan Lis and Andrzej Gwiazda stood at his side as deputies. The committee presented twenty-one demands, which, written on wooden boards and hung from the shipyard's entrance, became an important symbol for the strike. The workers demanded "the establishment of free unions, independent of the party and of employers,"[2] the right to strike, and freedom of expression and of the press. In only a few days, a workers' protest had become a political movement. Prominent figures within the political opposition soon joined them, such as Bronisław Geremek and Tadeusz Mazowiecki, who arrived from Warsaw as specialists to oversee negotiations with the government.

It was this union—unprecedented in Poland's history—of workers and intelligentsia, of the industrial masses and intellectual power, that enabled the success of Solidarity in the first place.

Kept informed by Polish-language broadcasts from Radio Free Europe and the BBC, all of Poland looked to Gdańsk, and a combined 700,000 workers throughout Poland would strike by the end of August. The discipline, consistency, and Romantic-patriotic ethos displayed by the strikers also impressed the global public. Front-page stories in the world's newspapers and lengthy pieces on radio and television news were dedicated to Gdańsk and the battle that had begun there for social liberalization and political reform. The events unfolding in Gdańsk were the first clarion call for oppositional spheres in East Germany and other Eastern Bloc states.

In just days, the interfactory strike committee represented the workforces of almost 400 Gdańsk businesses and monitored a good part of the city's public life. It took until August 23, however, before initial discussions with a government delegation could take place. There were disputes in Warsaw over the regime's best response to the protests, although the Polish government certainly did not want to follow the Kremlin's recommendations of violence. In a live television broadcast on August 31, Deputy Prime Minister Mieczysław Jagielski and Lech Wałęsa finally signed an agreement in whose realization Tadeusz Fiszbach, first secretary of the Polish United Workers' Party's voivodeship committee, had played an integral role. The government expressed its acceptance of free unions, while the strikers acknowledged the Communist Party's leading role in the state. Exhausted but content, Lech Wałęsa was able to proclaim:

> We fought together, we fought for you. . . . [W]e have won the right to strike, we have obtained certain civil guarantees, and most importantly—we have won the right to free unions. . . . Starting tomorrow, life begins for our new unions. Let us take care that they always remain independent and self-administered, that they all work for all of us, for Poland, for the nation's good. I declare the strike concluded.[3]

Tens of thousands of Gdańsk's citizens cheered Wałęsa at the shipyard gate, and delegates from all of Poland founded the Independent Self-Governing Trade Union "Solidarity" with the former electrician at its helm.

Gdańsk became like a second Polish capital; the heart of the opposition beat here. Around 9 million people joined Solidarity by spring 1981, partly because they supported the political and social demands, and partly because they hoped for higher wages and improvements in the ever-worsening supply situation. In Gdańsk, too, people had to spend hours waiting outside butcher shops and bakeries, and the implementation of ration cards hardly remedied the problem.

Figure 9.1 After two weeks of struggle, victory. Lech Wałęsa celebrates after signing agreements with the government on August 31, 1980. Kosycarz Foto Press, 00016610.

Yet there were moments when the population happily forgot their daily troubles, for instance on December 16, when several hundred thousand people gathered at the shipyard gate to witness the dedication of a nearly 140-foot-tall monument designed by a Gdańsk artist to commemorate the shipyard workers who had fallen in 1970.

Known as the "Carnival" of Solidarity, the period of sixteen months leading to the declaration of martial law laid the foundation for reform across Polish civil society. The number of social and cultural initiatives and political ideas born between the Baltic Sea and the Tatra Mountains during this time would be able to sustain the country for over a decade. The sudden freedom and undreamed-of possibilities shaped an entire generation, but so did endless debates about how to proceed. Numerous local thinkers who experienced the events firsthand took an active interest in this intellectual awakening. Jan Krzysztof Bielecki, Lech Kaczyński, Donald Tusk, Aleksander Hall, Bogdan Borusewicz, Janusz Lewandowski—there is a long list of such founding Solidarity activists who would go on to play an important role in the nation's political life.

The promising signs of autumn 1980 were followed by disenchantment in 1981. The government was in no hurry to implement the August Agreements, and Solidarity declared multiple warning strikes. The May 3 procession celebrating the anniversary of the Polish Constitution of 1791 became a large oppositional demonstration when many thousands of Gdańsk citizens marched with political banners through the streets of the Main Town. The supply situation remained catastrophic during this time, and undisguised threats from Moscow placed the state and party leadership in Poland under increasing pressure to combat the "counterrevolution"—preferably through martial law.

In the meantime, the leaders of Solidarity pulled the strings from Gdańsk and, after a lengthy preparation process, organized the union's first national congress. The delegates met in the large Hala Olivia sports arena, closely observed by 750 accredited local and international journalists. The frequently tumultuous sessions lasted many days, concluding—after a two-week recess—on October 7. Moscow was infuriated by the "Message to the Working People of Eastern Europe" that emerged from the congress and professed solidarity with all who take "the hard road, the struggle for a free union movement"[4] in the communist-controlled Eastern Bloc. Prevailing against a number of more radical opponents, Lech Wałęsa was ultimately appointed chairman.

Yet tensions in the country continued to grow. While the communist government—since October 1981 under the leadership of former minister of defense, General Wojciech Jaruzelski—saw no alternative solutions to the political and economic crisis and continued its long preparations for martial law, Solidarity threatened with renewed strikes in Gdańsk and elsewhere. Students occupied the university in mid-November.

Despite many warnings, union leadership still imagined themselves safe and called a meeting of the union's national committee for December 11 in Gdańsk. But tanks gathered in the city early in the morning of December 13. Militia and ZOMO, the barracked police of the Ministry of the Interior, fanned out and arrested a large number of startled union activists, and Lech Wałęsa was taken away to an unknown destination. On the cold, gray morning of December 13, Jaruzelski appeared on television with a stony expression, declared the imposition of martial law, and forbade any union activities.

Strikes erupted immediately, but these protests—at the Lenin Shipyard, for instance—were violently crushed within a few hours. Thousands gathered at the shipyard gate on Monday, December 15, as Gdańsk businesses renewed their protests. ZOMO units finally stormed the shipyard early the following morning and arrested every protester they could get their hands on. Yet the citizens did not give up; on this anniversary of the 1970 massacre, several thousand people tried to reach the Monument to the Fallen Shipyard Workers and engaged in street fights with the militia and ZOMO. One eyewitness recalled:

> The armored militia took action against the defenseless people in the crowd, who fought back with frenzied courage, with their bare hands, with dud grenades; they wanted to fight their way through to the monument. People walked down Wall Street with candles. They approached

the militia. Only then were round, yellow tear gas projectiles fired into the crowd. The smoke lingered for a long time. When it dispersed, the street was silent and empty.[5]

The riots even carried over to the next day, but given the strong military presence, the brutal action taken by the state, and the nightly curfew, they ultimately ceased, just as the last strikes in Gdańsk's harbor came to an end on December 21. One person had been shot and killed in Gdańsk, and hundreds were injured. The carnival was over, the Solidarity revolution defeated. A widespread dejection took hold.

Between Despair and Emergence

The mood in Gdańsk was despondent. The military and militia marked the streetscape in winter 1981/1982, and as time went on, many more Solidarity activists were arrested and interned for months. Still, many citizens could not be discouraged and continued to demonstrate against the state, such as on January 20, 1982, when several thousand people rioted against law enforcement forces, or on May 1, when the counter-protest at the Labor Day parade brought together almost 50,000 people who, following Mass in St. Mary's Church, marched unchallenged as far as Wrzeszcz.

On the surface, it appeared that the communist regime had reestablished its dominance: the party licked its wounds, moderate political camps were forced out, and many new faces (mostly loyalist die-hards and opportunists) made their way into local party and government leadership. Still, society was divided, with many public figures refusing to cooperate with Jaruzelski's regime. Though robbed of almost all of its leaders, Solidarity lived on in most people's hearts. Bogdan Borusewicz, Aleksander Hall, and Bogdan Lis began to reorganize Solidarity underground and founded a Regional Coordination Committee.

Lech Wałęsa initially faced limited options for activity on his release from the internment camp on November 12, 1982, yet the global public observed him, the hero of Solidarity, quite attentively. In his first public appearance, at the shipyard monument on December 16, he called for realistic, pluralist, and transparent politics. Though blessed with great charisma and audacity, he pursued a "policy of small steps" in anticipation of a gradual, peaceful evolution of the conditions in Poland. In coming years, even despite all of the government's deceptions, he therefore consistently sought a dialogue with those in power, which earned him criticism and even accusations of betrayal from more radical members of the opposition. In hindsight, Wałęsa's proved to be the correct strategy.

At first, negotiations were admittedly out of the question, as the existing rifts were too deep. In light of the oppressive public life in Gdańsk, seemingly marginal events took on great symbolic meaning. When the Lechia Gdańsk Football Club, which had sensationally won the Polish Cup in the Third League, hosted the elite Italian club Juventus Turin in September 1985, the crowd wildly cheered for Lech Wałęsa when, despite all precautionary measures taken by the state and party, he managed to enter the stadium. On the other hand, he was not permitted to fully savor a much greater triumph when, awarded the Nobel Peace Prize that same autumn, he did not dare personally accept the award for fear that he would not be allowed to return to Poland. He sent his wife Danuta to Oslo, and perhaps not without good reason: the government had denounced the Nobel Committee's selection of Wałęsa as "anti-Polish provocation."

All restrictions notwithstanding, Gdańsk was still the center of the Polish opposition. Anyone of any distinction in Solidarity traveled to see Wałęsa in Gdańsk, and international visitors were frequent guests in his apartment in the high-rise housing district of Zaspa (Germ. Saspe). But in addition to the outlawed Solidarity, Gdańsk was home to other groups forging socioeconomic and political plans for Poland's future. Among these was the conservative Young Poland movement, which fostered Catholic-nationalist traditions. The liberal circles surrounding the newspaper *Przegląd Polityczny* (Political review) relatively quickly abandoned the Solidarity model of collective self-administration and became adherents of a moderate free-market liberal position. Donald Tusk, for instance, emerged from this movement.

Proponents of the opposition found strength and confidence in the Catholic Church. The Parish of St. Bridget in the Old Town played an important role with its energetic priest Henryk Jankowski. He supported Wałęsa and Solidarity by offering the illegalized union's representatives the use of church space, which even the martial law regime did not dare restrict.

The opposition underwent a crisis in the mid-1980s. While violent conflicts still arose between demonstrators and law enforcement each year on May 1 and 3, occasional anarchists mixing into the May Day parades infuriated the Communist Party. Large numbers in Gdańsk regularly expressed their opposition to the national political conditions on All Saints' Day as well as December 16, in memory of 1970. Weary of everyday struggles and frustrated at the lack of political prospects, however, many withdrew into their private lives, with more than a few of them emigrating to the West during these years. In 1986, the underground Solidarity Regional Coordination Committee was shattered with the arrest of Bogdan Borusewicz. Yet even though less than 50 percent of those eligible to vote cast their ballots in local and national parliamentary elections, the state's legitimacy continued to suffer as economic difficulties persisted, and it was unable to take advantage of the public social resignation.

Emboldened by the early results of the reformist Soviet perestroika movement and the government's growing openness to dialogue with the opposition, the mood improved beginning in 1987. Pope John Paul II could finally come to Gdańsk, the cradle of Solidarity, after state leadership had long feared a mass gathering of people critical of the regime. The high point of the visit was a public Mass attended by around a million people in the developing Zaspa district.

In spring 1988, a new wave of strikes rolled through the country, reaching the Lenin Shipyard in early May. With the support of Lech Wałęsa and a group of aides from Warsaw, the workforce went on strike for a week. The strike ended once ZOMO units choked off access to shipyard grounds and forced the workers to take a leave of absence, yet the resulting peace was brief. Gdańsk's shipyards renewed strikes on August 21, this time better organized than in May and heavily supported by local oppositional leaders, who had in the meantime developed greater proficiency in acting relatively openly and unchallenged. Declaring "There is no freedom without solidarity," Lech Wałęsa traveled to Warsaw and wrested the government's concession to organize a roundtable discussion for a collective solution to the political and economic crisis. The erosion of the political system was apparent.

The results of the economic stagnation also created all kinds of problems for the population in Gdańsk: ration cards accompanied them throughout the 1980s but could hardly reduce the lines that persisted outside many shops. Those in possession of Western foreign currencies were fortunate, not least because this enabled them to protect themselves from the galloping inflation. Increasingly severe problems plagued the large, state-run companies, and in 1988 it even appeared that the Lenin Shipyard faced certain closure.

Against this backdrop, it was really just a matter of time until a foundational shift had to occur in Poland's political tectonics. As the year 1989 began, the Polish United Workers' Party was ready to relegalize Solidarity, and on January 22, the trade union's National Executive Committee in Gdańsk declared their willingness to negotiate. In early February, Lech Wałęsa, Jacek Merkel, and Aleksander Hall among others participated in the roundtable discussion in Warsaw. In April, the arduous negotiations yielded partially free parliamentary elections as well as free elections for the Upper House (senate). The June elections were a rousing national success for Solidarity. From its beginnings in Gdańsk, this movement became the decisive political force in Poland and that August created the first non-communist government in the entire Eastern Bloc. US president George Bush expressed great satisfaction with the situation when he visited Gdańsk in July.

The political shift soon took place not only in Warsaw but also locally in Gdańsk, and the Communist Party slowly departed from power. Rightist youth groups stormed the party's voivodeship committee headquarters in January

1990 to prevent the destruction of documents, and the Lenin Shipyard abandoned its namesake on January 27, thenceforth to be known as the Gdańsk Shipyard. The transfer of power was ultimately possible because of a self-administered reform among the local government: in the May 1990 city council election, delegates from the Solidarity Citizens' Committee won fifty-nine of sixty seats, and Jacek Starościak was elected city president. Shortly thereafter, the government appointed conservative politician Maciej Płażyński to act as the first non-communist governor of the Gdańsk Voivodeship. Gdańsk was finally free again. It was—at the moment—the latest watershed moment in the city's thousand-year-old history.

Gdańsk, Finally Free Again

It was a paradox: Gdańsk had made the most critical contribution to the overthrow of the old system, yet Poland's secret capital quickly reassumed its familiar provincial role after 1989. As Poland was still a centrally administered country, prominent members of the former opposition left Gdańsk for Warsaw to make their mark in politics, in which they were initially successful. Lech Wałęsa was elected president of Poland in December 1990; a few weeks later, the Gdańsk liberal Jan Krzysztof Bielecki formed the government, appointing a number of Gdańsk politicians in various functional departments, including Janusz Lewandowski as minister of privatization. The so-called Gdańsk Paratrooper Commando assumed power.

In late 1991, however, Bielicki was forced to resign; his party, the Liberal Democratic Congress, lost influence and merged with the new Freedom Union in 1994. In spite of this, Gdańsk still remained a stronghold of liberalism for a long time. Due to his authoritarian tendencies, unfortunate personal decisions, and imprudent remarks, Lech Wałęsa also lost many supporters. He withdrew to the port city on the Motława in a sulk after his 1995 loss to the post-communist candidate Aleksander Kwaśniewski, who had studied at the University of Gdańsk. For a long time, Wałęsa tried—without much luck—to influence politics from Gdańsk before eventually contenting himself with his symbolic role as a living legend of the Solidarity revolution. Wałęsa's historical role would be the frequent topic of critical debate. He was accused of collaboration with the communist security service as an operative known as "Bolek" in the 1970s, but ultimately no convincing evidence of this emerged. Wałęsa was also immortalized in Gdańsk's topography when the city's airport was named after him in 2003.

Gdańsk remained the center of Solidarity, and in April 1990, the city hosted the trade union's second national congress, where Lech Wałęsa was confirmed as chair. After Wałęsa's election as Poland's president, Marian Krzaklewski succeeded him as the head of the union. Under Krzaklewski's leadership, Solidarity distinguished itself as a Christian-conservative political force and won the parliamentary elections in 1997.

Yet burdened by economic hardship, rapidly increasing unemployment, and an equally rapid development of the private sector, many in Gdańsk had little interest in politics and were simply glad that they could finally act free of political supervision. After months of hyperinflation, the economic shock therapy began to produce results: price rises slowed markedly, while the supply of food and consumer goods improved. Markets and stands popped up everywhere in the city, little shops opened in basement locations and kiosks, and many previously lifeless streets filled with bustling activity.

This systemic transformation was somewhat demanding on the population. The reforms appeared to make sense on paper, and the macroeconomic situation soon showed that the policy of economic shock therapy had by and large been the best option. Its uneven development nonetheless led to difficult living conditions on many fronts: the increasingly liberal economy collided with both a statist popular majority as well as ruling cadres predominantly shaped by socialism. Democracy and pluralism occasionally struggled to prevail against established authoritarian habits, and the catastrophically underfinanced safety, traffic, and educational infrastructure led to trepidation and unrest. Poverty was suddenly visible everywhere as beggars grabbed at the arms of passersby, while at the same time, young men able to come by quick money flaunted their large German cars with tinted windows. Gang crime began to draw attention, with the German-Polish "Godfather of Gdańsk" Nikodem Skotarczak regarded as the premier smuggler of stolen cars until his murder in 1998. For a time, petty criminals and Mafia henchmen, easy to identify by their rayon sports suits, were able to move relatively unmolested in the city.

In a time of massive privatization, though, businesses on the edge of legality were not restricted to shady dive bars. Even Franciszek Jamroż, who held the office of city president from 1991 to 1994, was moved by the prospect of an attractive secondary income to accept bribe money from a German construction firm. He was finally convicted to three years in prison in 2004. The newly elected city council, in which liberals and conservatives made up the largest contingent, selected Tomasz Posadzki as the new city president in 1994.

Resentful of the side effects accompanying the socioeconomic upheavals, the unions—with Solidarity leading the way—called for repeated strikes, which paralyzed public life in Gdańsk. There was strife in other contexts as well—for instance, concerning the privatization of the water supply and sewers as well as the year-old Market Hall, by then more than 100 years old. The Catholic Church also tried to regain property, some of which it had even lost centuries earlier. In one such effort, namely, to win back the building of the present-day National

Museum, the Franciscans ultimately had to accept defeat. One notable target of criticism was Henryk Jankowski, the extravagant priest of St. Bridget's Church and former chaplain to Solidarity, who made anti-Semitic remarks on multiple occasions beginning in 1995 and became an idol for the extreme Catholic-nationalist right wing. Repeatedly banned from preaching, he finally had to resign from office in 2009 and died the following year. In 2018, when accusations of child abuse surfaced against this former hero of Solidarity, Gdańsk decided to take down a statue of him erected only a few years earlier.

In light of Gdańsk's decreased political significance after 1990, local leaders sought out new horizons for the city's development. They first focused on symbolic politics, founding the Union of the Baltic Cities in 1991, which boasted a membership of over 100 cities within about twenty years and whose administration Gdańsk secured for itself. The city also joined another league of cities, the New Hanseatic League, whose members convened on the Motława in 1997. This date was not coincidental as it commemorated Gdańsk's 1,000-year anniversary. The city spent years preparing for its millennial celebration, which its leaders reckoned would secure it new significance on the national and international stage. Their task to draw from history to create meaning for the present while presenting perspectives for the future—was an all too familiar paradigm from the local government's long past. At least this time, though, it coincided with a burgeoning interest common to many citizens, namely, to discover the unfamiliar facets of the city they called home.

Genius loci: Discovery of the Past

Gdańsk underwent a reinvention following 1945. As the expelled German population took the city's collective memory with them, there was essentially nobody who could oppose the official reconstruction of the city's image—first in Polish-national and soon thereafter in communist overtones. After the terrible experiences suffered in the war against the Germans, the local Polish population initially had absolutely no interest in anything German, while the memories of their own native regions in Central Poland and its lost eastern areas would veil Gdańsk for a long time.

Yet having grown up among hints of foreignness and disorienting finds from an unknown past that existed, without explanation, in the Polish present, the children of these first post-war Gdańsk inhabitants thought differently. Fascinated young residents gradually began to excavate their city's buried history. In the basement of his childhood home, for instance, future novelist and literary critic Stefan Chwin found German documents that prompted him to look at old city maps. Another future Polish writer, Paweł Huelle, collected pre-war artifacts and roamed the suburbs as a boy, deciphering German inscriptions he found there.

The people were not yet fully in a position to grasp all of these peculiar traces of history, though. Not until the 1980s and 1990s did objects that had outlasted the earlier German occupants in many apartments—such as dishes, fixtures, and even books—become evidence of a hitherto unfamiliar past; before these years, they had silently accompanied the myth of a Polish Gdańsk like primeval relics. Having outlived the institutionalized lies of the communist state, these artifacts spurred on the formation of new local identities.

The works of Günter Grass formed an especially important link between German past and Polish present. Although his novella *Cat and Mouse* was released in Poland in 1964, Polish censors prohibited the publication of *The Tin Drum* for years; an underground edition finally appeared in 1979, followed in 1983 by a censored version from an official publisher. *Cat and Mouse* was also reissued at the same time. With Grass, the Polish population of Gdańsk came to know a magically alienated pre-war Danzig populated by Germans. For the first time, they could identify with that culturally alien and yet oddly familiar city. "Today the ages intermingle," a native of Gdańsk opined in the 1990s. "My two—no, my three pasts. And my three Gdańsks: Gdańsk, or more accurately the Danzig of Günter Grass, the Gdańsk of my childhood, and the Gdańsk of 'Solidarity.'"[6] Volker Schlöndorff's 1979 film adaptation of *The Tin Drum*, which was quickly available on videocassette (even though its official theatrical release did not occur until 1992), also made a great impact.

Many in Gdańsk were impressed, not least Paweł Huelle, born in 1957. With his 1987 debut novel *Weiser Dawidek*, Huelle wrote—like Grass—a magical realist story about adolescents in Wrzeszcz and Oliwa. Weiser, the exceptionally talented protagonist from a Jewish family, confronts his peers with fragments of an extinct world, namely, the foreign, unsettling German past.

Huelle's novel caused a furor and was published at precisely the right time for those striving to construct alternatives to the nationalist-communist historical narrative of party and state still dominant in the 1980s. The city's young liberal leaders enthusiastically seized on the discovery of such a literary homeland. Donald Tusk spoke in 1989 of a dream, a vision, a kind of "paradise lost," namely, the notion of a Gdańsk of "free, educated, and prosperous people," an idea whose foundations lie in the appreciation of a great regional past.[7] The city's liberal traditions, Tusk maintained, had outlasted all historical upheavals and formed the foundation of a distinct *genius loci*, a spirit that had spurred the people of Gdańsk to resistance against the Polish kings as well as revolt against the communist regime.

While popular, this interpretation was also far-fetched; this *genius loci*, after all, had not devised a way to escape either the Prussian annexation or the National

Socialist takeover. Nevertheless, Tusk's interpretation was indicative of the need for a local civic utopia whose roots the people largely sought in the reputedly metropolitan, sophisticated Danzig of pre-war times. In 1996, Tusk and some colleagues published *Był sobie Gdańsk* (Once in Gdańsk), an illustrated book of over 200 pages presenting photographs from the mid-nineteenth century up to the beginning of the Second World War. The book was a sensational success; despite its high price, the first edition sold 20,000 copies. The purpose of the book, as Tusk wrote in his foreword, was to show for the first time an undistorted, true picture of Gdańsk, but also to challenge the myth of Gdańsk's reconstruction.

The photos truly offered insights into a Gdańsk hitherto unknown in broader circles, depicting people in an urban setting whose foreignness comingled with a peculiar familiarity. Gdańsk—rebuilt, yet without history and divested of its traditions—suddenly found itself confronted with an assurance of continuity that, while unavoidable, nevertheless posed numerous problems. Was there in reality any continuity back to those Prussian merchants in their top hats, to those aproned maidservants, jaunty soldiers, manicured public parks, stately buildings—and if so, how was the current Gdańsk to fit into it? The continuity of place was indisputable, but there was no fabricating a continuity to the people and their culture without first learning to understand them.

Born in Gdańsk in 1949, Stefan Chwin made an essential contribution to this effort with his novel *Hanemann* (*Death in Danzig*), which became a literary sensation upon its publication in 1995. The novel, which takes place in Danzig/Gdańsk between the 1930s and the 1950s, portrays the end of the German city and the beginnings of its Polish successor. In addition to the eponymous protagonist who lives in Gdańsk after the war's end, the book also uses objects—furniture, dishes, and houses left behind by the Germans and discovered by the Poles—to supply continuity.

The rediscovery of the past had consequences: "Today we profess ourselves without complexes or sentiments to be Danzig's heirs and are aware that the combined work and imagination of all of its ethnic groups have contributed to what it is," as Paweł Huelle, Donald Tusk, and writer Zbigniew Żakiewicz declared in 1995.[8] Gdańsk's long postulated Polish monoculturality, like the German model preceding it, was finally and definitively broken apart; the talk was henceforth of the city's "multicultural traditions."

Gdańsk's millennial celebration of 1997 would showcase this new interpretation for the world to see. Yet 1,000 years after St. Adalbert had come to the Slavic fishing village of Gyddanyzc, the local leadership proved incapable of anything more than amassing a variegated cluster of events that often bore only minor reference to the city's history. The members of the city council appeared in early modern costumes, at least, and there were historical displays, illustrious guests, and high attendance.

The celebration's most significant outcome, however, was the revival of the city's historical discourses. The many facets of Gdańsk's history, above all of its more recent past, suddenly fascinated large sections of the population, and local identity was more stubbornly contested than ever before. Architecture and city planning were frequent areas of contention, for instance, the question of how to best proceed with the historical city center: should the city continue the work of the early modern master builders, as well as the architects of the post-war reconstruction, by filling the gaps between buildings, house by house, to create the illusion of historical intactness? Or should it show its capacity for modern development within a historical setting? Proponents of a new Gdańsk as well as keepers of the "old Gdańsk identity" quarreled over numerous prestigious projects, such as the development of Granary Island, where a first row of houses was constructed with historically idealized nineteenth-century façades on Milk Can Street in the late 1990s.

Intellectuals and architects were not the only ones stimulated by the local past. Adopting both small and large histories for themselves, many citizens began their own new discovery of Gdańsk. They developed a pride in the city's sons and daughters who bore no Polish names, like Arthur Schopenhauer or Daniel Gabriel Fahrenheit, and erected memorial plaques and monuments in their honor. Many in Gdańsk also became collectors of the city's ashtrays or clothes hangers with German inscriptions, beer bottles or coins from the Free City of Danzig—in short, things that linked their local living environment to the city's past while simultaneously radiating a pleasantly unsettling otherness. Suddenly, it was also no longer taboo to use German place and street names; on the contrary, these became a natural aspect of the local past, attesting to a plurality of local narratives and assuring an abundance of history.

Günter Grass thus also became a permanent component of Gdańsk's new identity. The city eagerly awaited his newest book (even taxi drivers were reading *Peeling the Onion*). Gdańsk happily welcomed the author during his frequent visits there and was especially proud in 1999, when he received the Nobel Prize in Literature. The city stood by him when he came under fire in 2006. Confronted for his admission of having joined the SS near the war's end and subsequently concealing this fact, the writer found himself at the center of criticism in the German media; in Gdańsk, on the other hand, he found some respite, with city president Paweł Adamowicz writing, "Gdańsk understands its son."[9] Thanks to a donation by Grass, the city established a "Günter Grass Gallery" in 2007, and further tributes followed after the author's death in 2013.

Today, the parallelism of these many narratives is a matter of course in Gdańsk, a city where Polishness and Germanness, familiarity and otherness, present and past overlap as in a palimpsest. Yet this erstwhile multiethnicity also serves to enrich the essentially monoethnic present, so that the city is at least somewhat

Figure 9.2 In the suburb of Wrzeszcz, not far from his childhood home, Günter Grass surveys the bench dedicated to Oskar, the protagonist of his novel *The Tin Drum*, in 2003. Wotjek Jakubowski/Kosycarz Foto Press, j0003830.

akin to the truly multiethnic cities of the West. The ongoing post-national appropriation of Gdańsk's many diverse histories is exemplarily reflected in a broad range of internet discussion forums, where scanned picture postcards from the Wilhelmine period (approximately between 1890 and 1918), photographs of the city's most recently discovered German inscriptions, and bits of information about post-war life in Gdańsk all create a motley potpourri. Even solely in its history (and histories), it is a fascinating city.

Breaking into the Market Economy

The economic crisis of the 1980s had led, in Gdańsk as in the entire country, to a drastic underinvestment in infrastructure. Not only did the government-owned manufactories find themselves in a deplorable state at the end of the communist era, but so did the city's plumbing, electrical, and telephone networks, school buildings, waste disposal, public transport, green spaces, streets, and footpaths. Due to financial shortages and other immense tasks facing the city government, these would see only gradual improvement after 1990. While the privatization and partial privatization of many unprofitable local businesses encountered resistance among their employees, they also greatly facilitated modernization.

The matter of transport routes had always been of great concern for Gdańsk. Since the Vistula River had long ago lost its relevance as a transport artery, ensuring the city's strong accessibility by land, sea, and air had become vital. Approach from the sea was the least problematic, as the city already possessed a large harbor that had undergone a systematic expansion after 1989. New loading facilities for (among other things) liquefied petroleum gas tankers and container ships thus appeared in the North Harbor. Additionally, a customs-free trade area was designated at the mouth of the Vistula, and a ferry terminal (primarily for routes to Sweden) was built at the Westerplatte. Over half of the harbor's goods turnover today consists of oil and oil products, followed by piece goods; grain, a longtime source of Gdańsk's wealth, plays only a marginal role. In 2019, almost 4,000 ships arrived in the city's port, which, despite competition from the harbor complex of Szczecin and Świnoujście, is responsible for almost half of Poland's maritime trade. Construction of an additional port area (Central Harbor) directly in the Gulf of Gdańsk is planned for the near future.

For quite some time, things looked much worse for land routes. While rural roads connected Gdańsk with Szczecin, Lodz, and Warsaw, the lack of expressway access following the political transition was one of the key reasons for small new industrial settlement. Already planned following the Second World War, the construction of the A1 Expressway from Gdańsk to Poland's southern border by means of Lodz and Katowice had long been local industry's greatest wish. Its construction finally began south of Gdańsk in 2005, and its junction with the important east-west route to Warsaw was completed a decade later. The construction of a four-lane expressway connecting Gdańsk with Warsaw and Kraków also began.

The Tricity already had good railway connections to the south, as Upper Silesian coal had always come rolling into local ports of export from this direction; a high-speed line completed in 2014 connects Gdańsk with the rest of the country. Many other (mostly regional) sections of track, however, are still in poor condition. Even today, for instance, the line running through Gdynia and Koszalin to Szczecin remains unelectrified and partially single-track. The condition of the trains themselves has left as much to be desired, as does the regional rail network, which has been increasingly replaced by bus lines.

Since the beginning of the twenty-first century, the Gdańsk Airport has experienced a great upturn from the boom of budget airlines, and it ultimately gained a large, new terminal. While regular flights were available to only a small number of cities in the 1990s, the number grew rapidly in the new millennium, from seven in 2000 to sixty-nine in 2020. This was partly a result of the great increase in Polish job migration, with many of Gdańsk's residents flocking to numerous European countries. More regular flights have also come to Gdańsk because of the city's attractiveness as a tourist destination. Today, there are direct flight connections to over a dozen British cities as well as to Scandinavia, Southern Europe, and Ukraine. Passenger volume multiplied from a quarter million in 1999 to over 5 million in 2019 (due to the COVID-19 pandemic, 2020 only saw 1.7 million). Bus routes have long dominated passenger travel to Germany, where many familial relationships exist from the migratory movements of preceding decades.

One of Poland's most daunting tasks on beginning its system transformation was its continued dealings with the mostly unprofitable state-owned companies. One of these was the Gdańsk Shipyard, the city's largest employer since the war, which fell on hard times after 1990. In that year, the frequently boycotted business, which moreover lost those portions of its market from former fellow Warsaw Pact countries, was converted into a corporation, 61 percent of which was owned by the state and the remaining 39 percent by the shipyard personnel. Yet operating a such a symbolically significant company, which was not only heavily indebted, but whose staff also suddenly possessed such remarkably substantial rights of participation, was not easy. Bankruptcy thus followed in 1996, but this was not the end. After long protests, a consortium under the direction of the Gdynia Shipyard took over its sister shipyard (but had to relinquish it again in 2006 after much political wrangling). Although the shipyard's future was a matter—at least for nationalist-conservative parties—of national honor, it was sold to an industrial cartel from Ukraine's Donbas region. Yet these new owners were also unable to change the enterprise's fortunes. A good 2,000 employees were still building seagoing vessels and steel structures for the former flagship company in 2010. Ten years later, once again under state ownership, the shipyard had sold large areas of its historical production facilities and mainly worked with a subsidiary company to produce wind energy plants. The repair yard, which was privatized in 2001, fared better: it has assumed operations in Gdańsk's North Harbor and, with about 2,000 employees, successfully positioned itself under the umbrella of the Remontowa Group as a yard for ship repair and conversion as well as the construction of oil rigs and other things.

Under the name Lotos, Gdańsk's oil refinery has established itself as one of Poland's market leaders; it has built an extensive network of service stations and today employs around 5,000 workers. The Lotos Group has been traded in the market in Warsaw since 2005, and the Polish state indirectly holds the stock majority. Instigated in 2018 by the nationalist-conservative government, a merger took place between Lotos and its most important inland competitor, PKN Orlen, which could potentially lead to the company's diminished economic relevance for Gdańsk.

To put an end to the agony of the centrally planned economy, the communist government began to allow the foundation of small private businesses in 1982. Especially in Gdańsk, this led to a large number of modest start-up companies, which contributed to a sustained shift in local economic mentalities and laid a solid foundation for the development of further commercial initiatives after the transformation of the communist system in 1989/1990.

Nonetheless, the democratic Gdańsk initially struggled economically, as direct foreign investments remained in short supply. In addition to the poor transport connections, the city's image at home and abroad—informed as it was by the prominent local tradition of striking—was responsible for this problem, as the notion of assertive workers willing to strike was off-putting for investors. Since 1990, the city government furthermore struggled to market Gdańsk as a corporate site, resulting in a long-term lack of large-firm settlement. The German concern Dr. Oetker caused a small stir from 1991 to 1994, when it acquired a food manufactory in Oliwa, even though this had already belonged to the firm before 1945.

Over time, though, a number of new businesses have appeared in Gdańsk and can already be seen as success stories; the clothing concern LPP (market listed in Warsaw), for example, rose to become Poland's industry leader and today employs over 20,000 people throughout Europe in a large branch network (managing, among others, the clothing brand Reserved). The greatest focus of start-up companies in Gdańsk, however, has been on the maritime economy (for instance, yacht builders) and information technology. The creation of technology parks and implementation of numerous support measures have further boosted Gdańsk's economy. As a result, several international enterprises have settled there, such as the computer giant Intel, which employed over 3,000 people in Gdańsk in 2020 and has announced further capital spending. The overall number of jobs in Gdańsk has seen a marked increase, and since the local supply of workers has been long unable to meet the demand, the number of foreign workers has grown sharply, jumping from 1,700 in 2010 to 64,000 in 2020. The unemployment rate still hovered considerably above 10 percent at the beginning of the millennium, in contrast to only 2.3 percent in 2019.[10]

No stimulation was necessary for commerce. Soon after an enormous boom (primarily in retail trade) in the early 1990s, the first foreign investors came to Gdańsk to build vast supermarkets. Backed by French capital, the first of these *hipermarkety* began to fill vacant land. Shopping malls followed everywhere, in the Old Town, the center of Wrzeszcz, and along the city's edges. These developments led to an enduring shift in the local population's shopping and consumption habits.

The local media landscape changed rapidly after the end of the late socialist period. The local newspaper *Dziennik Bałtycki* first went to a French investor and then to the publisher Passauer Neue Presse in 1995; in 2020, the state-owned oil company Orlen bought it out at the behest of the nationalist-conservative government, although the paper's print run had been continually shrinking over the preceding years. There are subsidiaries of Poland's leading private radio stations in Gdańsk along with the state-owned station Radio Gdańsk, and the state television network TV Gdańsk broadcasts from its studio next to the Palace Park in Oliwa. One of Poland's largest web portals, Wirtualna Polska, began in Gdańsk but has since relocated to Warsaw.

The city is not only a local travel destination for Poles but also attracts many tourists from abroad; tourism has thus become Gdańsk's most important source of revenue. At 40 percent today, Germans traditionally make up the largest share of foreign visitors. But as the number of Germans who spent their youth in Danzig continues to decrease over time, the tourism structure is clearly changing. Along with a growing number of English or Italian tourists, increasing numbers of new visitors (younger people, families, and short-term travelers) come for Gdańsk's active and attractive environment rather than nostalgia. The illumination of the major monuments and stylishly cobblestoned lanes in the Main Town has improved the situation, at least visually, and the city's accommodations have grown through the construction of an array of new hotels close to the city center. The restaurant trade has reached unprecedented heights. Having effectively utilized television surveillance and police patrols to stabilize its security situation (which was admittedly precarious in the early 1990s), Gdańsk is counted among Poland's most attractive tourist destinations today. The annual number of tourists visiting the city increased from about 2 million to 3.5 million between 2015 and 2019 alone.

The population in Gdańsk has plateaued at around 470,000 people. Overall, its citizens have grown continually prosperous since 1990. From 1997 to 2007, the gross national product per capita in Gdańsk more than doubled, only to nearly double again by 2019. In the economy, the average monthly gross salary in 2019 was 6,150 złoty (about 1,600 USD).

As always, there have been housing problems. There was a continuing need for low-priced housing, and never enough construction of subsidized rental apartments. As the economic situation improved for many in Gdańsk, though, a golden age began in the late 1990s for realtors and building contractors who built many new developments of housing blocks and townhomes, mainly near the bypass in the hill country west of the city center. Visitors approaching Gdańsk by plane can see how the city is expanding farther into the surrounding land and has merged with the neighboring communities.

Due to the growing prosperity and increasing familiarity of Western lifestyle habits, leisure behavior in Gdańsk has slowly changed. While the beaches naturally still drew crowds (even if the water quality was sometimes substandard), the newly emerging multiplex cinemas, bars, and discothèques increased in appeal. Civil and social engagement also grew rapidly in Gdańsk after 1989. Roughly

1,600 associations and foundations in education, youth work, culture, or sports were active around 2010, and the number jumped to over 2,300 by 2019.

The large confessional majority in Gdańsk is still Catholic, although church attendance has steadily declined since the 1990s. Along with the small community belonging to the Evangelical Church of the Augsburg Confession in Poland, other Protestant congregations have been established. There are also Orthodox churches, Eastern Catholic Christians, and an Armenian congregation. Muslims, including those from traditionally Muslim, Polish-Tatar families as well as immigrants, also live in Gdańsk; their own mosque has stood in Oliwa since 1990. The same year saw the reemergence of the Jewish community, which included about a hundred members thirty years later. In 2009, they acquired the former Langfuhr Synagogue, which had spent decades as a music school.

From a national perspective, the population in Gdańsk is also largely homogeneous. Of the city's approximately 470,000 residents in 2008, only around 5,200—little more than 1 percent—spoke a second language besides Polish in their families. The largest registered national minority in Gdańsk at that time was a few hundred mostly elderly Germans; the Kashubians living in the city do not constitute a minority (in the judgment of the Polish state), but merely speak a "regional language" and represent a regional culture. Even so, some of the Kashubians maintain that they form their own nationality and view Gdańsk as the capital of Kashubia, and the Kashubian heraldic animal—the black griffin against a yellow background—can be seen next to the proudly displayed crest of Gdańsk in many places today. Foreign immigration has sharply increased in recent years; the city's registered foreign population, of which Ukrainians and Belarussians now make up the largest part, grew from 3,700 in 2016 to 17,300 in 2019.

Culture between Günter Grass and the Underground

Regarded with mistrust by ungenerous merchant princes, restricted within national constraints, and compromised through the absence of educational institutions and financially powerful patrons, cultural life had suffered in Gdańsk for quite some time. Beginning in the 1980s, however, it began to reap the fruits of the city's post-war development, which had yielded not only the construction of numerous academies but also Gdańsk's development, as the chief city of the Tricity, into a metropolis. Clearly indicating the vitality of the local arts was the dualism marking the culture in Gdańsk during the later years of the communist system. While state institutions continued to linger, a broad, independent cultural scene simultaneously developed, making an impact and enjoying a sustained presence in the arts. Based in the artistic underground, the members of the so-called new Gdańsk school sought artistic freedom beyond the currently restrictive politics while also creating new spaces using new media like computer art, land art, and installations. Proponents of this school included (among others) Grzegorz Klaman, a student of Franciszek Duszeńko who exhibited sensational installations in the ruins of Granary Island, and the universal artist Marek Rogulski. Several galleries arose from this movement, such as the Wyspa Gallery. In the 1990s, a former public bathhouse in Lower Town became the state-sponsored center of avant-garde art known today as the Łaźnia Center for Contemporary Art. Over time, the Academy of Fine Arts has become more open to new trends. Even the shipyard grounds presented new possibilities for the city's artistic expansion. After a number of temporary exhibits were located in former production facilities, the New Art Museum (NOMUS) is now located there as a department of the National Museum.

The city has undergone an equally fascinating literary development, with authors adopting the memories of 1970 and 1980/1981 as their themes, as well as the discovery of the foreign history of Danzig. As prevailing circumstances led lyric poets like Władysław Zawistowski or Bolesław Fac to withdraw into a "new privacy," their themes became—partly due to the reception of Günter Grass— the primary concerns of a number of prose authors. With their Gdańsk novels, Paweł Huelle and Stefan Chwin wrote themselves into the center of Polish literature. Their (re)discovery of their provincial homeland influenced an entire generation of writers, and they soon became the intellectual authorities in a city still in search of a cultural core and now securing itself at least a place on Poland's literary map. Viewed for decades solely as a propagandistically shaped port city of workers and social protest, Gdańsk is taking on a new and entirely different meaning for the nation.

Faced with the all-powerful literary troika of Grass, Huelle, and Chwin, many other writers in Gdańsk struggled. Some—like Waldemar Nocny—wrote novels of the Gdańsk suburbs and thus found themselves out of their depth in waters already navigated by more formidable writers. Others tried to unlock their own poetic spaces and went on to transregional fame, such as Wojciech Wencel, Tadeusz Dąbrowski, and Jacek Dehnel, a writer at home in many genres, whose 2006 novel *Lala* was published in English in 2018.

Theater also strove to take part in the success of this new brand of regionalist literature, and thus the dramatized works of Grass and Chwin appeared on the schedule of the Teatr Wybrzeże, which had long established itself as one of Poland's greatest theaters and underwent extensive renovations in 2002. Persistent efforts began in the early 1990s to build a Shakespearean theater and thereby recall the early sixteenth-century appearance of Elizabethan actors in the city. Designed by the Italian Renato Rizzi, the Gdańsk Shakespeare Theatre finally opened in 2014; this multifunctional theatrical space housed on Old Suburb Moat Street in an expressive brick structure allows, among other things, for the faithful replication of the early modern stage.

The Gdańsk Shakespeare Theatre has not been the only notable building project of the past twenty years. Admittedly, architecture did not receive special attention after the fall of the Soviet Union, as the initial priority was by necessity to catch up rapidly with the contemporary developments in the West. After several buildings that were constructed in a postmodern-provincial style were not well received, numerous attractive projects have taken shape since 2000; and these also have been the regular subject of fierce debates, inasmuch as they concern the historical city center. The Hilton Hotel on Fish Market and the City Forum across from the central railway station are among the better examples, while some massive apartment buildings in the suburbs or on Szafarnia Street are of more questionable architectural and urbanistic quality.

New housing developments outside the city center have generally been built in a functional and restrained modern style, or else they feign tradition with their redbrick gabled roofs. A local example of successful architectural revitalization is the conversion of the former electric power station on Ołowianka Island (Germ. Bleihof) on the Motława into the home of the Polish Baltic Philharmonic.

Film has drawn international attention to Gdańsk on multiple occasions: Volker Schlöndorff's 1979 adaptation of *The Tin Drum* won the Palme d'Or in Cannes and an Academy Award. Andrzej Wajda's *Człowiek z żelaza* (*Man of Iron*), which takes place in Gdańsk during the momentous months of 1980, won the grand prize in Cannes in 1981.

The National Museum continued to subsist on the fame of its most important exhibit, Hans Memling's *Last Judgment*, while simultaneously suffering from its somewhat peripheral location, but the Historical Museum of the City of Gdańsk underwent systematic expansion. Its principal location in the Main Town's city hall was a mecca for tourists, and a growing number of historical buildings became museum branches, such as the Uphagen House, which was elaborately furnished with preserved and reconstructed fixtures and reopened in 1998, as well as the renewed Artus Court, which became a prestigious assembly space for the citizenry. The Amber Museum in the former Prison Tower attracted so many visitors that it was relocated to much larger exhibition rooms in the Great Mill in 2021. The Maritime Museum received three storehouses on Ołowianka Island and a new reception building next to the Crane Gate. Observing the latest museum trends, the city established Hevelianum, an interactive science museum with a broad range of experiments, within the Napoleonic and Prussian forts on Hail Hill.

The city owes a considerable part of its intellectual enlivenment to its institutions of higher education. Following a dry spell in the 1980s, the Technical University developed quickly in the 1990s, and the number of enrolled students there has remained between 15,000 and 20,000 for years. It ranked as the second-best technical university in the country and was one of seven Polish universities selected by Warsaw in 2019 to receive additional funding in the Polish "Excellence Initiative—Research University" program. Whereas international collaboration was initially the exception, the more than 1,000 scholars employed there today are networked in a variety of ways with foreign partner institutions. While the University of Gdańsk is not counted among the country's most renowned institutions of higher education, it regularly places in the upper midrange of the rankings. Yet deficient exchange programs with other colleges, underpaid and overworked instructors, and Gdańsk's enduring peripheral status all continue to impede local intellectual life even today, and more than a few professors have left the city when given the opportunity. Combined with the appeal of studying in Warsaw, Kraków, or even abroad, declining student enrollment in many humanities and social science disciplines has presented new challenges for intellectual life in Gdańsk.

Gdańsk in the New Millennium

As the new millennium began, Gdańsk could look back on a decade that had brought freedom and rapid development but had also not been able to resolve many of the city's difficulties. One substantial problem had to do with the urbanistic structure of Gdańsk and its neighboring cities: while the old Hanseatic city had begun a new life after the war as a city of workers and industry, the little seaside resort of Sopot had transformed into a refuge not only for artists but also for those still hoping to cling to traditional bourgeois lifestyles. After 1989, Sopot quickly became one of the richest cities in the country and attracted the wealthy and beautiful. Gdynia, on the other hand, prided itself in following the political shift as a cosmopolitan city of pragmatists. Thus, stretching across more than eighteen miles of the Gulf of Gdańsk and known throughout Poland as the collective Tricity, these three individual cities nevertheless co-existed in a constantly rekindled rivalry with each other. Although many politicians in Gdańsk dream of a large regional metropolis with a population of around 1 million, the cities' convergence is an arduous process. The year 2011 saw, at least, the founding of the "Gdańsk-Sopot-Gdynia Metropolitan Area," which also includes many surrounding rural districts, and whose members undertake numerous collective initiatives to accomplish important infrastructure tasks and planning processes.

The result of dividing urban potential into three centers has been that none of the three cities has truly attained an entirely metropolitan air. Gdynia has come the closest in terms of urban development, but Gdańsk is the most metropolitan—albeit in a negative sense—as far as the traffic is concerned. Essentially restricted to one north-south axis and one east-west connection, the massive increase in vehicles (75,000 in 1990; 260,000 in 2008; 370,000 in 2020) has resulted in frequent traffic jams stretching for miles, making the daily commute or a simple shopping trip an ordeal for many inhabitants. People have avoided travel into the city center whenever they could, contenting themselves instead with a life on the urban periphery in satellite towns and housing developments. For many, weekends have become the time to visit their retreats, ideally located in a cottage on a Kashubian lake.

The city's congested thoroughfares have also divided the city into several sections, isolating (for instance) the Main Town and Old Town from the rest of Gdańsk. As grand as the reconstruction of the Main Town had been, there was not real clarity about the role it should take under the new conditions after 1989. It no longer fulfilled any vital functions for the city, in any case; all significant authoritative bodies were located elsewhere, so all that remained for the Main Town was an existence as an open-air museum, which is overrun by tourists in the summer but bleak in the winter.

Overall, a vision for Gdańsk's future was clearly lacking at the beginning of the new millennium. The city's fixation on its own golden past had hardly unleashed developmental impetus. As in the nineteenth century, Gdańsk had looked to its history primarily to enhance its own self-assessment and find comfort in the face of a disappointing present.

Yet this outlook began to gradually change a decade after the system transformation. Whereas jobs in the local government agencies and institutions were often poorly paid and the civil service influenced by post-Soviet mentalities in the 1990s, the quality of the local government improved with time. This represented both increasing friendliness toward citizens and benefited the proper planning of complex infrastructure projects. Additionally, the competency of local politicians grew. While hardly any members of the new city council in 1990 had any notion of how to administer a large city, there were already veterans of self-government ten years later.

Under the leadership of Paweł Adamowicz of the Civic Platform beginning in 1998, Gdańsk established itself as a liberal-conservative bastion. The city government and local political elites finally began to give thought to a "vision of Gdańsk as a center of innovative development."[11] A number of factors have facilitated this development: the 1999 reform of the Polish government put an end to political-administrative centralism, demanded many competencies at the regional level, and created new, larger voivodeships; Gdańsk was now the capital of the Pomeranian Voivodeship. Furthermore, Poland's 2004 accession to the European Union opened up entirely new possibilities for local infrastructure development. Between 2004 and 2006, 560 million złoty of EU funds were circulated to Gdańsk, followed by 3.1 billion between 2007 and 2013, and another 3 billion from 2014 to 2020. Poland's economic upturn likewise proved advantageous. Overall, then, the city's revenues experienced positive developments; debt remained relatively low, and the city budget even boasted a surplus in some years.

It was under these circumstances that a strategic and determined urban development began, which, even if it did not proceed entirely without friction (and even stalled at times), nonetheless made a number of large projects possible. First among these were traffic infrastructure projects: the abysmal connections between the city's central districts and the surrounding hinterland—especially the access roads to the west bypass—were expanded or rebuilt. Begun in 2009, a new south bypass free of intersections allows east-west traffic to avoid the city center. A tunnel under the Dead Vistula in the harbor area has further relieved congestion in the city center.

Many of these projects were accelerated in the preparations for the 2012 UEFA European Championship co-hosted by Poland and Ukraine. Gdańsk successfully competed to become one of the venues, and a new, amber-colored stadium seating over 44,000 people was erected in the previously neglected district of Letnica. Not least due to the repeatedly clashing interests of the three cities in the Tricity, delays occurred in the planned expansion of public transport, particularly of a "Metrorail" leading from Gdańsk across the hills to the airport, and from there on to Gdynia. This project eventually saw completion, however, along with the construction of a number of new streetcar lines.

The UEFA Championship was not the city's only project for the future. The administration attached great importance to the creation of an entirely new city district and resolved to develop the Young Town, named after the town founded under the patronage of the Teutonic Order and destroyed in 1454. The new district was to emerge at the presumed location of the original Young Town, on the former premises of the Gdańsk Shipyard, which had transferred its operations to Ostrów Island in the Vistula delta. While numerous plans materialized for the use of this large area as a business and housing district, the financial crisis delayed development, which was originally intended to begin in 2009, and broad stretches of the land remained undeveloped even a decade later. Many investors also withdrew from the development of Granary Island's northern section, an inner-city area of ruins that had alternatively fascinated and unsettled visitors since the war's end. This last imposing evidence of Gdańsk's destruction

Figure 9.3 Panorama of Gdańsk's Main Town: Long Street, city hall, St. Mary's Church—the rebuilt city stands majestically before the eyes of its awed visitors. Kosycarz Foto Press, k00012313.

at the end of the Second World War ultimately vanished, though, as hotels, apartments, and restaurants arose in an aesthetic of glass and steel alongside the historical structures of the storehouses, bringing at least some new life in this once neglected city corner.

Although for a long time it appeared that the city did not possess the needed economic potential to bring the intended construction projects to life and that other Polish cities like Wrocław would quickly leave it in their wake, Gdańsk was able to catch up. The most recent example is the Forum Gdańsk, an immense shopping center directly bordering the historic town center, which opened in 2018 and has brought a good deal of retail activity back to the heart of the city.

Gdańsk was able to capitalize more quickly in one area where it has proven experience: history and its topical depiction in the city's interests. This effort centered around the outbreak of the Second World War and the formation of Solidarity, two events from twentieth-century European history that had gained particular symbolic power.

The creation of the European Solidarity Center, a center for exhibits, research, and events to preserve and address the memory of the movements for freedom and civil rights, was undertaken in 2007. Collectively supported by the city, the region, and Warsaw, it received an impressive building with corroded metal walls that recall the location's industrial heritage. The building stands on the former shipyard grounds, directly adjacent to the shipyard's legendary gate number two. With a permanent exhibition and numerous events, the center has developed into a hub for Gdańsk's intellectual life and attracts visitors from all over the world. At the same time, it serves the city, which has been able to maintain its influence on the center's organization and direction, as an important site for demonstrating Gdańsk's liberal, cosmopolitan attitude.

At the beginning of the new millennium, there was great outrage in Poland when German expellees requested a memorial site for victims among the displaced Germans at the end of the Second World War. Gdańsk native and Polish prime minister Donald Tusk addressed the issue shortly after taking office in 2007, proposing the creation of a Museum of the Second World War in Gdańsk. Poland's wartime experience was to find expression through a comprehensive representation of the war and its civilian victims. Crowned with a spectacular structure looming above the underground exhibition spaces, the museum has displayed its superb exhibit since opening in 2017. However, it almost didn't open; the conservative Polish government, in power since 2015, disapproved of the museum's depiction of the war, which focused on civilian suffering as opposed to Polish heroism. After lengthy political and legal disputes, founding director Paweł Machcewicz was finally able to open the museum to the public, yet opponents in the government successfully removed him from his position only a few weeks later through a series of ambiguous legal maneuvers. This incident illustrates how disputed history is in Gdańsk to this day.

The historical setting of the Westerplatte was also drawn into these quarrels: nationalist circles demanded the historical reconstruction of the old Polish defensive structures destroyed in the war, and since 2018, the annual festivities held there on September 1, which the city of Gdańsk has always organized, also drew the central government's attention. A new museum intended to depict the Westerplatte's 1939 defense is planned for construction there. Additional plans include exhibits memorializing Günter Grass and the illustrator Daniel Chodowiecki in the old orphanage, as well as a new permanent exhibit in the Gdańsk Historical Museum.

With its many new initiatives, Gdańsk has greatly elevated its status as a European city rich in museums and symbols. The visitor count in local museums and exhibits has grown from 460,000 in 2013 to 1.4 million in 2019. As impressive as these numbers are, it is also important not to rest on such "historical" laurels. The new districts near the city center must not be allowed to become concrete and glass capital expenditure wastelands or hotel monocultures but rather viewed as an opportunity to replenish the city's tattered urban fabric. This development calls for thorough, critical attention, since wherever such quantities of money circulate, there is always the danger of misuse, unlawful influence, and high-handed, investor-friendly, garden-variety architecture. The affair surrounding Stella Maris, the publisher belonging to the Archdiocese of Gdańsk, illustrates just how susceptible even supposedly upright institutions can be. The Pelpin-based operation was used for money laundering, which, once uncovered, created a public relations crisis for the diocesan administration and caused alarm among a number of prominent local citizens. City magistrates have moreover stumbled across additional minor and major affairs of this kind.

Generally, the people in Gdańsk are comfortable in their skin. Numerous surveys have determined that they make up the happiest metropolitan population in Poland. Their unique geographic position, allowing them to travel with such ease—to the sea, to the hills and lakes of Kashubia, or into a spectacular past—is certain to continue to provide rich and satisfying experiences.

According to a different survey, though, the citizens of Poland's sixth largest city have not been quite as happy with their municipal government's performance. And while Gdańsk would not be Gdańsk without its proven track record of escaping such unflattering scrutiny, not all such efforts have resulted in unmitigated success. The city was unable, for instance, to become a European Capital of Culture in 2016. Although this attempt failed, it unleashed a great deal of new cultural energy that led to the formation of several new initiatives, such as the enterprising City Culture Institute. The Culture Capital campaign also demonstrated that Gdańsk is ready to confidently shape its future without always merely conjuring up the past, as fascinating as that past is—the history of a city between nations, one that again and again has had to hold its ground and has more than once risen like a phoenix from the ashes—in other words, the quite extraordinary history of a quite extraordinary city.

Mayor Paweł Adamowicz had led the city for twenty years and had become one of Poland's best-known local politicians. However, his open, proactive manner did not please everyone; the nationalist-conservative parties criticized him, and his fellow liberal party members slowly distanced themselves from him in light of unverified accusations of corruption. These attacks, whose purpose was to conquer this stronghold of liberal Poland, intensified in particular after the national accession to power of Jarosław Kaczyński's Law and Justice Party in 2015. Yet Adamowicz prevailed again in the 2018 municipal elections and began his third decade in office as Gdańsk's president. His public murder on January 13, 2019, shocked the entire city when a mentally unstable man, recently released from prison and stirred up by state media propaganda, drove a knife into the mayor's body before grabbing the microphone and exclaiming that his deed was meant to punish the liberal party.

Even two years later, the question of whether this act can be designated a political murder had not been settled, among other things because the prosecution had not concluded its investigation. Elected to succeed Adamowicz a few weeks after the murder, Aleksandra Dulkiewicz continues her predecessor's work unabated: drawing strength from the city's history, she has positioned herself as a champion of liberal values and openness in Gdańsk. Today, the city is in a better condition than at any point in the past three centuries—as a dynamic center of the Baltic region where not only the local population but also visitors feel at home.

Epilogue

Why Gdańsk?

Repeated destruction and reconstruction, brilliant rises and sudden falls, often on everyone's mind and often forgotten: all this has taken place in the more than a thousand years of Gdańsk's history, in that center on the periphery where the Vistula feeds into to the Baltic waters.

For many generations, the residents have contemplated why their city has such an extraordinary past. Was it the Vistula and the sea, which forged self-confidence from confrontation with foreignness by bringing not only new wares to Gdańsk but also a constant flow of new ideas, ensuring that the local economy would continue to diversify and remain receptive to new shifts? Or was everything basically coincidence? Solidarity and Free City, wealth and Westerplatte—was it all just a quirk of history?

Whatever the case may be, Gdańsk is indisputably a unique place, a city with an unmistakable biography marked by ruptures and radical caesuras. How often, after all, it has been destroyed, besieged, captured, or annexed; how frequently the economic conditions of local life have changed. In 1945, the end seemed imminent. Danzig appeared to be history.

Yet history went on. Danzig became Gdańsk, which gave rise to further questions: was Gdańsk still Danzig, in spite of a nearly total exchange of its population and the annihilation of its historical structural makeup? How was the city to deal with this, the greatest rupture in its biography?

Salvation came from history: everything the generations had built up—civic structures and buildings, memories and stories, social networks—had suffered heavy damage; yet the city allowed itself to be erected anew, even if in a largely different form. Where one house once stood, there soon stood another, perhaps even on the same foundation; and often, even the walls, the furniture, and the rumors remained. Where one person once lived, there soon lived another. And this new resident likewise lived on the old foundation and was (whether willingly or not) forced to grapple with what once had been. The urban society has thus slowly sealed the cracks in its biography; Gdańsk merged with Danzig, and the same city reemerged.

It was, of course, not only the city. Always embedded within its region, state, and nation, Gdańsk has developed an intimate dialogue with its environment. People have immigrated and emigrated, rulers have interfered or acted graciously, and transnational intellectual and artistic fashions have gripped the inhabitants, molding them at times into rigid Gothic traders, at others into cheery Renaissance merchants, into wearers of top hats and petticoats, into proclaimers of proletarian traditions, generic monarchist anthems, or localist virtues, into republicans, fascists, or democrats.

So why Gdańsk, then? The city's secret is its inbetweenness. Gdańsk lives on the tension between historical wealth and relative periphery, between greatness and provincialism, between modernity and conservatism (a conflict that has often led to crippling stagnancy), between change and persistence, between boldness and faintheartedness, between captivity and aspirations of freedom.

Sufficiently removed from centers of power to defy the wills of rulers, wealthy and influential enough to go its own way, independent enough to write its own distinct biography—for many centuries, this has been Gdańsk. Coveted and wooed; at peace with itself; embedded in the beauty of its natural environment, cityscape, and history; self-assured and at times oblivious; repeatedly able to swap roles from the plaything of great powers to a major player capable of altering the course of history; the city—like its memory—has ultimately outlasted all historical caesuras, even if doing so has demanded multiple rebirths.

Appendix

NAMES OF PLACES

Localities and Topographical Designations

German	Polish
Adlershorst	Orłowo
Allenstein	Olsztyn
Alt Schottland	Stare Szkoty
Altmark	Stary Targ
Bleihof	Ołowianka
Braunsberg	Braniewo
Brösen	Brzeźno
Cammin	Kamień Pomorski
Danzig	Gdańsk
Danziger Haupt	Gdańska Głowa
Dirschau	Tczew
Elbing	Elbląg
Ermland	Warmia
Frauenburg	Frombork
Gdingen	Gdynia
Glettkau	Jelitkowo
Graudenz	Grudziądz
Hakelwerk	Osiek
Hela	Hel
Heubude	Stogi
Holm	Ostrów
Kalisch	Kalisz
Kattowitz	Katowice
Konitz	Chojnice

APPENDIX: NAMES OF PLACES

German	Polish
Köslin	Koszalin
Kulm	Chełmno
Langfuhr	Wrzeszcz
Letzkau	Leszkowy
Liebschau	Lubiszewo
Marienburg	Malbork
Marienwerder	Kwidzyn
Mewe	Gniew
Nassenhuben	Mokry Dwór
Neu Schottland	Nowe Szkoty
Neufahrwasser	Nowy Port
Neuteich	Nowy Staw
Nickelswalde	Mikoszewo
Nobel	Niegowo
Ohra	Orunia
Oliva	Oliwa
Oppeln	Opole
Östlich Neufähr	Górki Wschodnie
Pelonken	VII (Siódmy) Dwór
Plehnendorf	Płonia
Poggenkrug	Żabianke
Posen	Poznań
Prangenau	Pręgowo
Praust	Pruszcz
Putzig	Puck
Saspe	Zaspa
Schidlitz	Siedlce
Schiewenhorst	Świbno
Schlawe	Sławno
Schwetz	Świecie
Stargard	Starogard
Stettin	Szczecin
Stolp	Słupsk

APPENDIX: NAMES OF PLACES

German	Polish
Stolpmünde	Ustka
Stolzenberg	Pohulanka
Strieß	Strzyża
Stuhm	Sztum
Stuhmsdorf	Sztumska Wieś
Stutthof	Sztutowo
Swinemünde	Świnoujście
Tannenberg	Stębark
Thorn	Toruń
Tiegenhof	Nowy Dwór
Tolkemit	Tolmicko
Weichselmünde	Wisłoujście
Weißenberg	Biała Góra
Westlich Neufähr	Górki Zachodnie
Zoppot	Sopot

Streets, Districts, and Other Landmarks

English	German	Polish
Bakers' Street	Brotbänkengasse	ul. Chlebnicka
Bakers' Gate	Brotbänkentor	Brama Chlebnicka
Bishop's Hill	Bischofsberg	Biskupia Górka
Brewery Street	Jopengasse	ul. Piwna
Coal Market	Kohlenmarkt	Targ Węglowy
Cog Gate	Koggentor	Brama Kogi
Cow Bridge	Kuhbrücke	Most Krowi
Crab Market	Krebsmarkt	Targ Rakowy
Crane Gate	Krantor	Brama Żuraw
Dike (I-IV)	Damm (I-IV)	Grobla (I-IV)
English Dike	Englischer Damm	Grobla Angielska
Fish Market	Fischmarkt	Targ Rybny
Granary Island	Speicherinsel	Wyspa Spichrzów

APPENDIX: NAMES OF PLACES

English	German	Polish
Great Armory	Großes Zeughaus	Wielka Zbrojownia
Great Mill	Große Mühle	Wielki Młyn
Green Bridge	Grüne Brücke	Zielony Most
Green Gate	Grünes Tor	Brama Zielona
Hail Hill	Hagelsberg	Grodzisko (also: Góra Gradowa)
Hay Market	Heumarkt	Targ Sienny
Hevelius Plaza	Heveliusplatz	Obrońców Poczty Polskiej
High Gate	Hohes Tor	Bramy Wyżynna
Holy Spirit Gate	Heilig-Geist-Tor	Brama Świętego Ducha
Holy Spirit Street	Heilig-Geist-Gasse	ul. Św. Ducha
Hound Street	Hundegasse	ul. Ogarna
Leadyard	am Bleihof	Ołowianka
Long Bridge	Lange Brücke	Długie Pobrzeże
Long Gardens	Langgarten	Długie Ogrody
Long Market	Langer Markt	Długi Targ
Long Street	Langgasse	ul. Długa
Long Street Gate (today: Golden Gate)	Langgasser Tor	Złota Brama
Lower Town (district)	Niederstadt	Dolne Miasto
Lowland Gate	Leegetor	Brama Nizinna
Maiden Street	Jungferngasse	ul. Panieńska
Main Town (district)	Rechtstadt	Główne Miasto
Moat Street	Karrenwall	ul. Okopowa
Milk Can Street	Milchkannengasse	ul. Stągiewna
Mouse Street	Mausegasse	ul. Owsiana
New Gardens	Neugarten	Nowe Ogrody
New Town (district)	Neustadt	Nowe Miasto
Old Suburb (district)	Vorstadt	Stare Przedmieście
Old Suburb Moat Street	Vorstädtischer Graben	Podwale Przedmiejskie
Old Town (district)	Altstadt	Stare Miasto
Old Town Moat Street	Altstädtischer Graben	Podwale Staromiejskie
Oliva Gate	Olivaer Tor	Brama Oliwska
Pepper Town (district)	Pfefferstadt	ul. Korzenna

APPENDIX: NAMES OF PLACES

English	German	Polish
Prison Tower	Stockturm	Wieża Więzienna
Shout Crossing	Schuitensteg	ul. Wiosny Ludów
St. John's Gate	Johannistor	Brama Świętojańska
St. Mary's Street	Frauengasse	ul. Mariacka
Szafarnia Street	Schäferei	ul. Szafarnia
Torture Chamber	Peinkammer	Katownia
Triumph Avenue	Große Allee	Al. Zwycięstwa
Wall Street	Wallgasse	ul. Wałowa
Wood Market	Holzmarkt	Targ Drzewny
Young Town (district)	Jungstadt	Młode Miasto

NOTES

Chapter 1

1. Michael Gienger, *Lexikon der Heilsteine, von Achat bis Zoisit*, 7th ed. (Saarbrücken: Neue Erde, 2006), 173.
2. Wolfgang La Baume, *Ostgermanische Frühzeit*, 2nd ed. (Kiel: Schwentine-Verlag, 1959), 2–4.
3. Józef Kostrzewski, in *Historia Pomorza*, ed. Gerard Labuda, 2nd ed. (Poznań: Wydawn. Poznańskie, 1972), 1:174.
4. Erich Keyser, *Danzigs Geschichte*, 2nd ed. (Danzig: A.W. Kafemann, 1928), 14.
5. Otto Lienau, *Die Bootsfunde von Danzig-Ohra aus der Wikingerzeit* (Danzig: Danziger Verlag, 1934), 45.
6. Conrad Celtis, *Quatuor libri amorum secundum quantuor latera Germaniae / Vier Bücher Liebesgedichte, gemäß den vier Himmelsgegenden Deutschlands*, in *Humanistische Lyrik des 16. Jahrhunderts*, ed. Wilhelm Kühlmann et al. (Frankfurt am Main: Deutscher Klassiker Verlag, 1997), 99.
7. Wilhelm Schumacher, "Der Hagelsberg bei Danzig; oder: die Entstehung der Stadt Danzig," *Danziger Dampfboot*, Dec. 7, 1833.
8. Eduard Ludwig Garbe, *Danziger Sagen. Poetisch bearbeitet* (Danzig: A Scheinert, 1872), 12.
9. Keyser, *Danzigs Geschichte*, 17.
10. Paul Simson, *Geschichte der Stadt Danzig* (Danzig: A.W. Kafemann, 1913), 1:13.

Chapter 2

1. Komitet Organizacyjny Obchodów 1000-lecia Miasta Gdańska, *Selbstbewußt ins nächste Jahrtausend* (Gdańsk: n.p., 1997).
2. *Heiligenleben zur deutsch-slawischen Geschichte. Adalbert von Prag und Otto von Bamberg*, ed. Lorenz Weinrich (Darmstadt: Wissenschaftliche Buchgesellschaft, 2005), 62 ff.
3. Hans Prutz, "Danzig, das nordische Venedig. Eine deutsche Städtegeschichte," *Historisches Taschenbuch* 9, no. 4 (1868): 153.
4. Keyser, *Danzigs Geschichte*, 31.
5. Simson, *Geschichte*, 1:45.

Chapter 3

1. Resolution IV/54/67 of the National Assembly, File 1166/1147, Gdańsk State Archives, Gdańsk, Poland.
2. Walther Stephan, *Danzig. Gründung und Straßennamen* (Marburg: Herder-Institut, 1954), 54.

3. Simson, *Geschichte*, 3:59.
4. Otto Friedrich Gruppe, "Konrad Letzkau," in *Vaterländische Gedichte*, 2nd ed. (Neu-Ruppin: Oehmigke und Riemschneider, 1868), 340 ff.

Chapter 4

1. Friedrich Klein, "Das befreyte Preußen in dem dritten Jubelfeste," quoted in Edmund Kotarski, *Gdańska poezja okolicznościowa XVIII wieku* (Gdańsk: Wydawn. Uniwersytetu Gdańskiego, 1997), 75.
2. *Neue Wogen der Zeit* (Danzig), May 23, 1854.
3. "Eine folgenschwere Tat. Zum Gedächtnis des 11. Februar 1454," *Danziger Neueste Nachrichten*, Feb. 11, 1904.
4. "Dwie wielkie rocznice. Gdańsk—miasto historii i przyszłości," *Dziennik Bałtycki* (Gdańsk), Apr. 2, 1954.
5. Simson, *Geschichte*, 3:114.
6. Ibid, 115.
7. Ibid, 118.
8. Immanuel Wallerstein, *Das moderne Weltsystem. Die Anfänge kapitalistischer Landwirtschaft und die europäische Weltökonomie im 16. Jahrhundert*, trans. Angelika Schweikhart (Frankfurt am Main: Promedia Verlagsges. Mbh, 1986), 280.
9. Jonathan I. Israel, *Dutch Primacy in World Trade 1585-1740* (Oxford: Clarendon Press, 1989), 27.
10. Karol [Charles] Ogier, *Dziennik podróży do Polski 1635-1636*, part 2 (Gdańsk: Biblioteka miejska i Towarzystwo przyjaciół nauki i sztuki, 1953), 93 ff.
11. Caspar Weinreich, *Caspar Weinreichs Danziger Chronik. Ein Beitrag zur Geschichte Danzigs, der Lande Preußen und Polen, des Hansabundes und der nordischen Reiche*, ed. Theodor Hirsch and Friedrich August Vossberg (Berlin: J. A. Stargardt, 1855), 109.
12. Simson, *Geschichte*, 2:240.
13. Keyser, *Danzigs Geschichte*, 100.
14. Simson, *Geschichte*, 2:233.
15. Michael G. Müller, *Zweite Reformation und städtische Autonomie im Königlichen Preußen. Danzig, Elbing und Thorn in der Epoche der Konfessionalisierung (1557-1660)* (Berlin: Akademie-Verlag, 1997), 22.
16. Simson, *Geschichte*, 2:384.
17. Edmund Kizik, *Wesele, kilka chrztów i pogrzebów. Uroczystości rodzinne w mieście hanzeatyckim od XVI do XVIII wieku* (Gdańsk: Wydawn. Uniwersytetu Gdańskiego, Officina Ferberianna, 2001), 370, 8n.
18. Edmund Kizik, *Die reglementierte Feier. Hochzeiten, Taufen und Begräbnisse in der frühneuzeitlichen Hansestadt* (Osnabrück: Fibre, 2008), 403.
19. Paul Simson, *Der Artushof in Danzig und seine Brüderschaften, die Banken* (Danzig: T. Bertling, 1900), 110.
20. *Danziger Willkür* (1455), Article 39, quoted in Otto Rollenhagen, *Untersuchung und Beschreibung der Danziger Bürgerhäuser. Edition der nicht veröffentlichten Dissertation (1910-1915)*, ed. Ewa Barylewska-Szymańska et al. (Marburg: Herder-Instutut, 2008), 108.
21. Martin Gruneweg, *Die Aufzeichnungen des Dominikaners Martin Gruneweg (1562-ca. 1618) über seine Familie in Danzig, seine Handelsreisen in Ost europa und sein Klosterleben in Polen*, ed. Almut Bues, 4 vols. (Wiesbaden: Harrassowitz, 2008), 1:271-273.
22. Willi Drost, *Danziger Malerei vom Mittelalter bis zum Ende des Barock. Ein Beitrag zur Begründung der Strukturforschung in der Kunstgeschichte* (Berlin: Verlag für Kunstwissenschaft, 1938), 79.
23. Georg Greblinger, "Das blühende Dantzig," quoted in *Danziger Barockdichtung*, ed. Heinz Kindermann (Leipzig: P. Reclam jun, 1939), 230.

Chapter 5

1. August Goergens, *Mitarbeiter des Reichspropagandaamts Danzig-Westpreußen*, quoted in Erich Volmar, *Danzigs Bauwerke und ihre Wiederherstellung. Ein Rechenschaftsbericht der Baudenkmalpflege* (Danzig: Rosenberg, 1940).
2. Edmund Cieślak and Czesław Biernat, *Dzieje Gdańska*, 3rd. ed (Gdańsk: Fundacja Rew. Zabytków, 1994), 579.
3. "Historia Gdańska," City of Gdańsk, accessed December 8, 2023, https://www.gdansk.pl/turystyka-w-gdansku/historia-gdanska,a,1792
4. Johann Rist, "Zuschrift," in *Neues Musikalisches Seelenparadis*, (Lüneburg: die Sternen, 1662), (b) iiii, quoted in Hans Viktor Böttcher, *Johann Rist und die Stadt Danzig* (Lübeck: Verl. Unser Danzig, 1991).
5. Gottfried Lengnich, *Ius publicum civitatis Gedanensis, oder: Der Stadt Danzig Verfassung und Rechte. Nach der Originalhandschrift des Danziger Stadtarchivs*, ed. Otto Günther (Danzig: T. Bertling, 1900), 47.
6. Lengnich, *Ius publicum*, 113.
7. Philipp Balthasar Sinold von Schütz ed., *Die Europäische Fama, Welche den gegenwärtigen Zustand der vornehmsten Höfe entdecket* 207 (1718): 180.
8. Quoted in Edmund Kotarski, *Gdańska poezja okolicznościowa XVIII wieku*, (Gdańsk: Wydawn. Uniwersytetu Gdańskiego, 1997), 61.
9. Friedrich II, King of Prussia, *Political Testament*, trans. C. A. Macartney, in C. A. Macartney, ed., *The Habsburg and Hohenzollern Dynasties in the Seventeenth and Eighteenth Centuries* (New York: Harper & Row, 1970), 343.
10. Hans Hopf, "Danzig in der Vorgeschichte zur Zweiten Teilung Polens," *Zeitschrift des Westpreußischen Geschichtsvereins* 76 (1941): 103.
11. [August von Lehndorff], "Meine Reise in's blaue Ländchen, nebst Bemerkungen über Danzig," in *Briefen an einen Freund* (n.p.: n.p., 1799), 136.
12. Johanna Schopenhauer, *Im Wechsel der Zeiten, im Gedränge der Welt. Jugenderinnerungen, Tagebücher, Briefe* (Munich: Winkler, 1986), 45.
13. Schopenhauer, *Im Wechsel der Zeiten*, 47.
14. "Adam und Eva zu Danzig," in *Die Volkssagen Ostpreußens, Litthauens und Westpreußens*, ed. W. J. A. von Tettau and J. D. H. Temme (Berlin: Nicolai, 1837), 207 ff.
15. In his book *Sophiens Reise von Memel nach Sachsen*, quoted in Keyser, *Baugeschichte*, 428.
16. Daniel Chodowiecki, *Die Reise von Berlin nach Danzig. Das Tagebuch*, ed. Willi Geismeier (Berlin: Nicolai, 1994), 101 ff.
17. Quoted in Franz Kessler, "Das Danziger Kapellmeisteramt," in *Das Preußenland als Forschungsaufgabe. Eine europäische Region in ihren geschichtlichen Beziehungen. Festschrift für Udo Arnold zum 60. Geburtstag*, ed. Bernhart Jähnig and Georg Michels (Lüneburg: Nordostdeutsches Kulturwerk, 2000), 574.
18. Edmund Kotarski, *Gdańska poezja okolicznościowa XVII wieku* (Gdańsk: Wydawn. Uniwersytetu Gdańskiego, 1993), 293.
19. Gotthilf Löschin, *Geschichte Danzigs von der ältesten bis zur neuesten Zeit. Mit beständiger Rücksicht auf Cultur der Sitten, Wissenschaften, Künste, Gewerbe und Handelszweige* (Danzig: F.W. Ewert, 1822–1823), 2:236 ff.
20. Hopf, "Danzig in der Vorgeschichte," 126.
21. Quoted in Rudolf Damus, "Die Stadt Danzig gegenüber der Politik Friedrich's des Großen und Friedrich Wilhelm's II," *Zeitschrift des Westpreußischen Geschichtsvereins* 20 (1887): 206.
22. Quoted in Löschin, *Geschichte Danzigs*, 2:256.

Chapter 6

1. There is a double meaning here, as the word for blue (*blau*) is also commonly used to denote drunkenness in German.
2. "Danzigs Säcularfeier," *Danziger Zeitung*, May 8, 1893, evening edition.
3. "Gdańsk i Pomorze Gdańskie. Uzasadnienie naszych praw do Bałtyku," *Gazeta Gdańska*, Mar. 5, 1919.

4. From the late seventeenth to the early nineteenth century in Brandenburg-Prussia, a *Kriegsrat* (literally "war counselor") was a military officer without military authority, who was responsible for procuring financial means (through taxes, for instance) to support the army within a given territory.
5. Correspondence from Friedrich Leopold von Schroetter to the king, Königsberg, Apr. 19, 1797, File 6/314, Gdańsk State Archives, Gdańsk, Poland.
6. Abraham Friedrich Blech, *Geschichte der siebenjährigen Leiden Danzigs von 1807 bis 1814*, 2 vols. (Danzig: Carl Heinrich Eduard Müller, 1815), 1:3.
7. Literally meaning "wood space" in English, this German term is used to describe an area where the city's wood supply was stored.
8. *Tagebuch der Belagerung von Danzig. In den Monaten März, April und May* (Danzig: Wedel, 1807), 4.
9. Raimund Behrend, *Aus dem Tagebuch meines Vaters Theodor Behrend in Danzig* (Königsberg: Ostpreußische Zeitungs- und Verlagsdruckerei, 1896), 9.
10. *Tagebuch der Belagerung von Danzig*, 39 ff.
11. Quoted in Behrend, *Aus dem Tagebuch*, 17.
12. Quoted in Max Bär, *Die Behördenverfassung in Westpreußen seit der Ordenszeit* (Danzig: A.W. Kafemann, 1912), 136.
13. Contemporary statement, quoted in Erich Hoffmann, *Danzig und die Städteordnung des Freiherrn vom Stein*. Leipzig: Hinrichs, 1934).
14. Johann August Arnewald, *Spätlinge* (Danzig: Wedel, 1810), 17.
15. *Panoram der unprivilegirten Freudenmädchen in Danzig, oder freimüthige Beleuchtung eines, im Dunklen schleichenden, krebsartigen Übels* (Danzig: Louis Botzon, 1830), 14.
16. Vegesack's report (no. 13) to the Ministry of State, Apr. 10, 1808, HA III, 2.4.1., Section I, no. 2685, vol. 1, Geheimes Staatsarchiv Preußischer Kulturbesitz, Berlin, Germany.
17. Quoted from Hoene's handwritten memoirs in Almut Hillebrand, *Danzig und die Kaufmannschaft großbritannischer Nation. Rahmenbedingungen, Formen und Medien eines englischen Kulturtransfers im Ostseeraum des 18. Jahrhunderts* (Frankfurt am Main: Lang, 2009), 347.
18. Blech, *Geschichte*, 1:262 ff.
19. Blech, *Geschichte*, 1:271.
20. Heinrich Rose, *Schilderung der Belagerung Danzigs im Jahre 1813* (Danzig: A.W. Kafemann, 1940), 34.
21. Bär, *Behördenverfassung*, 238.
22. *Danziger Zeitung*, Feb. 28, 1814.
23. *Briefe über Danzig* (Berlin: F. Maurer, 1794), 53 ff.
24. Hermann Packhäuser, "Tivoli-Theater," *Patrouille*, Jul. 26, 1849.
25. H. Waldow "Danzig," *Danziger Dampfboot*, Feb. 4, 1836.
26. Quoted in "Das Jahr 1848 in Danzig," *Danziger Neueste Nachrichten*, Apr. 5, 1898.
27. "Poetischer Krakehl," *Danziger Krakehler*, Dec. 30, 1848, 126.
28. *Constitutionelles Blatt aus Böhmen* (supplement to no. 71), Mar. 24, 1849.
29. Friedrich Heyking, *Mein Leben und Wirken* (Berlin, Schlieffen-Verlag, 1933), 126.
30. Jenny Wüst, "Danziger Bilder. Kleine Pensionserinnerungen," *Heimat und Welt Beilage zur Danziger Zeitung* no. 6, Feb. 9, 1910.
31. Wilhelm Schumacher, *Verständlichste und bewährteste Belehrungen über die mit Gefahr bedrohende pestartige Krankheit Cholera morbus. Mit einem Rezepte versehen, welches das sicherste Schutzmittel wider die Cholera lehrt, und alle hierüber schon erschienene und vielleicht noch erscheinende Büchlein übertrifft und überflüßig macht. Nach den Hauptresultaten ärztlicher, in Indien, Persien, Rußland und Polen gemachten Erfahrungen sorgfältig zusammengestellt* (Danzig: n.p., 1831), 5.
32. "Bericht von der Stadtverordnetenversammlung," *Danziger Zeitung*, Feb. 1, 1871, morning edition.
33. Bruno Pompecki, "Danziger Giebel," *Die Brücke*, Nov. 1, 1919.
34. Eduard Garbe, "Danzigs alte und neue Architektur," in *Der Artushof* 26 (1880).

35. See, for instance, Theodor Kreyßig, *Die deutschen Ostmarken. Jubiläumsbetrachtungen*, a series of articles beginning on Jan. 11, 1872 in the *Danziger Zeitung* and subsequently published as a book (Danzig: 1872).
36. "Der Deutsche Tag in Danzig," *Danziger Neueste Nachrichten*, Sept. 15, 1902.
37. Editorial, *Danziger Neueste Nachrichten*, Feb. 22, 1902.
38. "Dr. Keller: Die Ostmarkenpolitik," *Danziger Neueste Nachrichten*, Nov. 20, 1911.
39. Julie Burow, *Versuch einer Selbstbiographie* (Prague: J. L. Kober, 1857), 57.
40. [Friedrich Karl Gottlieb von Duisburg], *Danzig, eine Skizze in Briefen. Geschrieben vor, während und nach der Belagerung im Jahr 1807* (Amsterdam: n.p., 1808), 35.
41. *Danziger Dampfboot*, Jan. 11, 1834.
42. The German term *Heimat* has no direct English equivalent. In addition to home or homeland, it also denotes a native space of familiarity and security, as well as a deep connection to the local natural environment. From *Heimatliteratur* to *Heimatfilme*, a large amount of cultural and artistic production has been dedicated to this concept, especially following the Second World War, when many Germans struggled with a perceived loss of homeland.
43. *Jahresbericht des Vereins zur Erhaltung der alterthümlichen Bauwerke und Kunst-Denkmäler Danzigs* (Danzig: n.p., [1857]), 1.
44. Letter to the editor, *Danziger Zeitung*, Nov. 19, 1859.
45. Duisburg, *Danzig, eine Skizze in Briefen*, 63.
46. E.[duard] P.[ietzker], "Sonntagsplauderei," *Danziger Courier*, Nov. 2, 1890.
47. The German term *Kladderadatsch* is simultaneously onomatopoeic for a crash or a bang as well as a term denoting a scandal or mess.
48. "Krieg und Gedicht," *Danziger Neueste Nachrichten*, Sept. 11, 1915.
49. "Um Danzigs Zukunft," *Danziger Zeitung*, Sept. 1, 1918, morning edition.

Chapter 7

1. August Maksymilian Grabowski, "Podróż do Prus Wschodnich i Gdańska (1844)," in *W stronę Odry i Bałtyku. Wybór źródeł (1795–1950)*, vol. 1, *O ziemię piastów i polski lud (1795–1918)* (Warsaw: Oficyna Wydawn. Volumen, 1990), 1:59.
2. Adam Mickiewicz, *Pan Tadeusz*, trans. Bill Johnston (Brooklyn: Archipelago Books, 2018, repr. 2020), 147.
3. Roman Dmowski, "Memoriał o terytorium Państwa Polskiego," in *W stronę Odry i Bałtyku*, vol. 1, ed. W. Wrzesiński (Warsaw: Oficyna Wydawn. Volumen, 1990), 212.
4. "Polnische Anschläge auf Danzig," *Danziger Neueste Nachrichten*, Sept. 24, 1918.
5. When capitalized in this text, the term "German National" denotes affiliation with the national-conservative German National People's Party (Deutschnationale Partei).
6. Reprinted in Rüdiger Ruhnau, *Die Freie Stadt Danzig 1919–1939* (Berg am See: Vowinckel, 1979), 201.
7. "Wenn Danzig polnisch wäre . . . Die Entgegnung vom Deutschen Volksrat in Danzig," *Danziger Neuester Nachrichten*, Feb. 3, 1919.
8. "Feierliche Amtseinführung des neuen Oberbürgermeisters von Danzig," *Danziger Neueste Nachrichten*, Feb. 26, 1919.
9. Heinrich Sahm, *Erinnerungen aus meinen Danziger Jahren 1919–1930*, ed. Ulrich Sahm (Marburg: Herder-Institut, 1955), 1.
10. "I sam Sahm wnet powie: niemasz Gdańska bez Polski!," *Gazeta Gdańska*, Mar. 7, 1919.
11. "Keine Polenlandung in Danzig," *Danziger Allgemeine Zeitung*, April 5, 1919.
12. *Danziger Neuste Nachrichten*, May 8, 1919.
13. Quoted in Walther Recke, "Der diplomatische Kampf um Danzig vor und in Versailles," in Albert Brödersdorff et al., *Die Entstehung der Freien Stadt Danzig* (Danzig: A.W. Kafemann, 1930), 17.
14. *Papers Relating to the Foreign Relations of the United States: The Paris Peace Conference* (Washington, DC: Department of State, 1946), 950.
15. *Protokoll der Stadtverordneten-Versammlung*, Session of May 13, 1919, 75 ff.
16. "Der Abschied der Truppen von Danzig.—Erinnern und gedenken!," *Danziger Neueste Nachrichten*, Jan. 24, 1920.

17. *Verhandlungen des Volkstags der Freien Stadt Danzig*, no. 1 (1921): 3.
18. Sahm, *Erinnerungen*, 100.
19. Members of Danzig's German Liberal Party (*Deutschliberale Partei Danzig*).
20. E. Bürger, "Danzig als Mittler zwischen deutscher und polnischer Kultur," *Danziger Volksstimme*, Jan. 25, 1927.
21. "St ... yk: Sprawy gdańskie. II," *Gazeta Gdańska*, April 24, 1927.
22. *Ostpreußische Zeitung* (Königsberg), Aug. 7, 1928.
23. Address given on Aug. 10, 1930 at the *Reichstag*, quoted in Christian Höltje, *Die Weimarer Republik und das Ostlocarno-Problem, 1919–1934* (Würzburg: Holzner, 1958), 191.
24. Felix Scherret, *Der Dollar steigt. Inflationsroman aus einer alten Stadt* (Berlin: Der Bücherkreis, 1930), 64.
25. *Danziger Volksstimme*, Dec. 31, 1925, quoted in Wilhelm Matull, *Ostdeutschlands Arbeiterbewegung* (Würzburg: Holzner, 1973), 432.
26. Henryk Bagiński, *Wolność Polski na morzu* (Warsaw: Wojskowy instytut naukowo-wydawn, 1931), 52.
27. Joseph Goebbels, *Die Tagebücher von Joseph Goebbels. Sämtliche Fragmente*, ed. Elke Fröhlich, vol. 1, *27.6.1924–31.12.1930* (Munich: K. G. Saur, 1987), 1:634.
28. *Verhandlungen des Volkstags der Freien Stadt Danzig* 17 (1933–1935), 1st Session, 3.
29. Address given by Gauschulungsleiter (district education chief) Wilhelm Löbsack in autumn 1936, quoted in Dieter Schenk, *Hitlers Mann in Danzig. Gauleiter Forster und die NS-Verbrechen in Danzig-Westpreußen* (Bonn: Dietz, 2000), 73.
30. Address given by Albert Forster on Oct. 10.1937, quoted in Schenk, *Hitlers Mann in Danzig*, 85.
31. Address given on Oct. 19, 1938, quoted in Schenk, *Hitlers Mann in Danzig*, 98.
32. This phrase is in reference to the well-known 1988 book *Die Stunde der Frauen* (*Hour of the Women*) by Christian Graf von Krockow and his sister Libussa Fritz-Krockow. The book both recounts Libussa's experiences fleeing from Pomerania in 1945 and highlights the prominent role played by women in rebuilding postwar Germany.
33. "Constitution of the Free City of Danzig," *League of Nations Official Journal* Special Supplement 7 (1922): 5.
34. Hermann Strunk, *Kulturpolitik und Kulturleistung in der Freien Stadt Danzig 1920–1930* (Danzig: A. W. Kafemann, 1930), 5.
35. Alfred Arna [= Felix Scherret], "Die Entwicklung zur Großstadt," *Danziger Rundschau*, Feb. 16, 1925.
36. Adelbert Matthaei, "Ein polnischer Angriff gegen die deutsche Kultur," *Danziger Neueste Nachrichten*, Aug. 16, 1922.
37. *Gazeta Gdańska*, May 16, 1933.
38. Alfred Döblin, *Journey to Poland*, trans. Joachim Neugroschel (London: Tauris, 1991), 262.
39. Manuscript of the birthday address, Halbe Collection, L 3128, Literaturarchiv der Münchener Stadtbibliothek (Monacensia).
40. Willibald Omankowski, *Danzig. Antlitz einer alten Stadt* (Danzig: Danziger Verlags-Gesellschaft, 1924), 17.
41. Erich Ruschkewitz, *Adlers Brauhaus bis Leichenschauhaus* (Danzig: Danzig Buchdr. u. Verlagsges. Danzig Rats-Buchh. M. Kloschies, 1929), 13.
42. *Danziger Volksstimme*, Mar. 8, 1927.
43. Artur Brausewetter, "Deutscher Kampf—deutsche Kunst!," *Berliner Börsen-Zeitung* (Berlin), Jan. 6, 1928.
44. "'Neue Baugedanken im alten Danzig.' Ministerialdirektor Kießling spricht in Berlin über Danzig. Hochschulprofessor O. Kloeppel-Danzig antwortet," *Danziger Neueste Nachrichten*, Jan. 23, 1929.
45. "Geschichte spricht zum Volk ... 'Das politische Danzig'—Ausstellung im Stadtmuseum Fleischergasse," *Danziger Neueste Nachrichten*, June 26, 1937.
46. *Danziger Neueste Nachrichten*, Apr. 28, 1939.
47. Max Domarus, *Hitler. Reden und Proklamationen 1932–1945*, vol. 2, *Untergang. Erster Halbband (1939–1940)* (Neustadt a. d. Aisch: Schmidt, 1963), 2:1197.
48. "'Danzig ist deutsch und will zu Deutschland,'" *Danziger Neueste Nachrichten*, Aug. 11, 1939.

49. Gałczyński, Konstanty Ildefons, "Pieśń o żołnierzach z Westerplatte," in *Wybór Poezji* (Wrocław: Zakł. nar. im. Ossolińskich, 1970). 128f.
50. "Die Rede des Führers," *Danziger Neueste Nachrichten*, Sept. 20, 1939.
51. Quoted in Schenk, *Hitlers Mann in Danzig*, 143.
52. "Erinnerung von Urszula Brzezińska," in *Danzig Gdańsk 1945. Erinnerungen nach 50 Jahren / Wspomnienia 50 lat później*, ed. Zenona Choderny (Gdańsk: Wydawn. Marpress, 1997), 90.
53. "Wieder sind wir Vorposten an der Weichsel. Gauleiter und Reichsstatthalter Albert Forster sprach vor den Schaffenden eines Danziger Betriebes," *Danziger Vorposten*, Feb. 16, 1945.
54. Quoted in Schenk, *Hitlers Mann in Danzig*, 260.
55. Günter Grass, *The Tin Drum*, trans. Breon Mitchell (Boston: Houghton Mifflin Harcourt, 2009), 371–372.
56. Peter Poralla, *Unvergänglicher Schmerz. Ein Protokoll der Geschichte. Danzigs Schicksalsjahr 1945* (Freiburg (Breisgau): Hogast, 1985), 10, 23.

Chapter 8

1. "Die Heerschau der Deutschnationalen Volkspartei," *Danziger Allgemeine Zeitung*, Sept. 24, 1927.
2. Władysław Cieszyński, "Fałszowanie historji gdańskiej," *Gazeta Gdańska*, Mar. 5, 1921.
3. Quoted in *Dziennik Bałtyki* (Gdańsk), Aug. 24, 1945.
4. "Erinnerung von Janina Matuszewska," in *Danzig/Gdańsk 1945*, ed. Zenona Choderny, 326.
5. *Dziennik Bałtycki* (Gdańsk), Sept. 4, 1945, quoted in Jacek Friedrich, "Gdańsk 1945–1949. Oswajanie miejsca," in *Gdańsk Pomnik historii. Część 2*, ed. Piotr Najmajer (Gdańsk: Regionalny Ośrodek Studiów i Ochrony Środowiska Kulturowego, 2001), 29.
6. "Gdańsk odzyska polski charakter. Plan odbudowy w oświetleniu wiceprezydenta inż. Wł. Czernego," *Dziennik Bałtycki* (Gdańsk), Sept. 4, 1945.
7. Horst Wilcke, "Es sind die alten Häuser, Straßen und Plätze . . ." *Die Welt* (Hamburg), June 22, 1957.
8. E. Osten Ostachiewicz, "Sto procent płci (o niemieckiej duszy na tle niemieckich mieszczan)," *Dziennik Bałtycki* (Gdańsk), Dec. 4, 1945, quoted in Jacek Friedrich, *Neue Stadt in altem Gewand. Der Wiederaufbau Danzigs 1945–1960* (Cologne: Böhlau, 2010), 52.
9. This German term refers to tourists visiting out of a yearning or nostalgia for a perceived lost home.
10. Donald Tusk, Grzegorz Fortuna, and Wojciech Duda, *Był sobie Gdańsk* (Gdańsk: Dar Gdańska, 1996), 6.
11. This term denotes affiliation with the German-Danzig People's Party (*Deutsch-Danziger Volkspartei*).
12. "Rauschning schreibt . . . wir antworten," *Unser Danzig* 2, no. 3 (1950).
13. K.[önnemann], "1945–1965," *Unser Danzig* 17 no. 6 (1965).
14. Wolfgang Federau, *Versunkene Gärten* (Hamburg: Dt. Literatur-Verl., 1949), 248.
15. Wolfgang Federau, "Ewige Stadt Danzig," in *Gedichte um eine Stadt. Eine Anthologie Danziger Lyrik*, ed. Siegfried Rosenberg (Oldenburg: Danziger Verl.-Haus, [1952]), 23.
16. "Zum 26. März 1950—zum 5. Jahrestag der Zerstörung," *Unser Danzig* 2, no. 3 (1950).
17. Carl Gustaf Ströhm, "Die Stadt hieß einmal Danzig," *Christ und Welt* (Stuttgart), Oct. 16, 1964.
18. Günter Grass, *The Danzig Trilogy*, trans. Ralph Mannheim (New York: Pantheon, 1987), 812.
19. Günter Grass, *The Tin Drum*, trans. Breon Mitchell (Boston: Houghton Mifflin Harcourt, 2009), 92–93.
20. Theodor Wallerand, "Günter Grass ein Danziger Schriftsteller?," *Unser Danzig* 14, no. 3 (1962).
21. Günter Grass, *In the Egg and Other Poems*, trans. Michael Hamburger and Christopher Middleton (New York: Harcourt Brace Jovanovich, 1977), 127.
22. The Polish term *mała stabilizacja* ("little stabilization"), borrowed from the subtitle of the 1962 drama *Świadkowie; albo, nasza mała stabilizacja* (*Witnesses, or Our Little Stabilization*) by Tadeusz Różewicz, became a popular term used to describe the situation in 1960s Poland.
23. A Polish patriotic song.

24. Donald Tusk, *Solidarność i duma* (Gdańsk: Wydawn. Słowo/obraz terytoria, 2005), 18 ff.
25. Grzegorz Fortuna and Donald Tusk, *Wydarzyło się w Gdańsku 1901–2000. Jeden wiek w jednym mieście* (Gdańsk: Milenium Media, 1999), 188.

Chapter 9

1. Quoted in "Ostatnie słowa Pawła Adamowicza: Gdańsk dzieli się dobrem," *Rzeczpospolita* (Warsaw), Jan. 14, 2019.
2. Jerzy Holzer, *"Solidarität". Die Geschichte einer freien Gewerkschaft in Polen* (Munich: C. H. Beck, 1985), 115.
3. Andrzej Drzycimski, *Tadeusz Skutnik: Gdańsk Sierpień '80. Rozmowy* (Gdańsk: Oficyna Wydawn. Aida, 1990), 433.
4. Quoted in Barbara Büscher et al. (eds.), *Solidarity. Die polnische Gewerkschaft "Solidarität" in Dokumenten, Diskussionen und Beiträgen. 1980 bis 1982* (Cologne: Bund-Verlag, 1983), 274.
5. Fortuna and Tusk, *Wydarzyło się w Gdańsku*, 234.
6. Statement of the engineer Henryk Bryll in Katarzyna Bogucka-Krenz, "Nasze Miasto," *Tytuł* (Gdańsk) no. 1 (1998): 17
7. Donald Tusk, "Gdańsk niezależny," *Pomerania*, no. 5 (1989): 27.
8. "Bunt prowincji." *Dziennik Bałtycki* (Gdańsk), Nov. 21, 1995.
9. Quoted in *Süddeutsche Zeitung* (Munich), Aug. 25, 2006.
10. Gdańsk w liczbach, accessed June 24, 2021, https://www.gdansk.pl/gdanskwliczbach.
11. Jan Szomburg, "Szanse i zagrożenia w rozwoju gospodarczym," in *Samorząd gdański w latach 1991–2001* (Pelplin: Bernardinum, 2001), 155.

SELECTED BIBLIOGRAPHY

Comprehensive Histories of Gdańsk

Askenazy, Szymon. *Dantzig and Poland.* Translated by William J. Rose. Gdańsk: George Allen and Unwin, 1921.—The first comprehensive Polish account of the city's history; representing the Polish view at the time of the Paris Peace Conference, it appeared in Polish, German, English, and French.

Cieślak, Edmund, ed. *Historia Gdańska.* 5 vols. Gdańsk/Sopot: Wydawn. Morskie, 1978–1999.— Exhaustive historical work with voluminous studies on many aspects of the city's history; the fifth volume is a bibliography of Gdańsk's history up to the reporting year of 1985. The other volumes contain many extensive sections from individual authors, which bear similarity to monographs. Notable among these are the chapters by Andrzej Zbierski (archaeology, Early Middle Ages, vol. I), Marian Biskup (history from 1308 to 1454, vol. I), Henryk Samsonowicz (political and economic history from 1454 to 1570, vol. II), Maria Bogucka (economic and commercial history from 1570 to 1655, vol. II), Edmund Cieślak (political, economic, and social history from 1655 to 1793, vol. III/1), Władysław Zajewski (Free City from 1807 to 1814/15, vol. III/2), Bolesław Hajduk (economic and commercial history from 1920 to 1945, vol. IV/2).

Cieślak, Edmund and Czesław Biernat. *History of Gdańsk.* Translated by Bożenna Blaim and George M. Hyde. 2nd. ed. Gdańsk: Fundacji Biblioteki Gdánskiej, 1995.—English translation of comprehensive history originally published in Polish.

Curicke, Reinhold. *Der Stadt Dantzig historische Beschreibung.* Amsterdam: Johan und Gillis Jansson von Waesberge, 1687.—A facsimile edition appeared in Hamburg in 1979.

Fischer, Frank. *Danzig. Die zerbrochene Stadt.* Berlin: Propyläen, 2006.—A popular history of the city but lacking consideration of the Polish specialist literature.

Gliński, Mirosław and Jerzy Kukliński. *Kronika Gdańska 997–1997.* 2nd ed. 2 vols. Gdańsk: Urząd Miejski Wydział Promocji Miasta, 2006.—Chronological list of events from Gdańsk's history.

Gralath, Daniel. *Versuch einer Geschichte Danzigs aus zuverläßigen Quellen und Handschriften.* 3 vols. Königsberg: Gottfried Leberecht Hartung, 1789–1791.—The first comprehensive history of the city.

Keyser, Erich. *Danzigs Geschichte.* 2nd ed. Danzig: A.W. Kafemann, 1928.—Fundamental German overview of the interwar years with an emphasis on German aspects of local history.

Keyser, Erich. *Die Stadt Danzig.* Stuttgart: Deutsche Verlags-Anstalt, 1925.—Methodologically innovative portrayal, albeit unevenly biased toward German aspects of local history.

Kilarski, Jan. *Gdańsk.* Poznań: Wydawn. Polskie, 1937.—Popular, richly illustrated work.

Kutrzeba, Stanisław, ed. *Gdańsk. Przeszłość i teraźniejszość.* Lwów: Wydawn. Zakladu Narodowego im. Osslińskich, 1928.—First scholarly established, Polish, comprehensive history of Gdańsk.
Labuda, Gerard, ed. *Historia Pomorza.* 4 vols. Poznań: Wydawn. Poznańskie, 1972–2003.— Vols. 1–3 (divided into 5 sub-volumes) of a major overview of the history of Pomerania, Pomerelia, and East Prussia until 1850; refer to Salmanowicz for volume 4.
Löschin, Gotthilf. *Geschichte Danzigs von der ältesten bis zur neuesten Zeit. Mit beständiger Rücksicht auf Cultur der Sitten, Wissenschaften, Künste, Gewerbe und Handelszweige.* 2 vols. Danzig: F. W. Ewert, 1822–1823.—History of Gdańsk; influential until the beginning of the twentieth century.
Pelczar, Marian. *Polski Gdańsk.* Gdańsk: Biblioteka Miejska, 1947.—Idealized presentation of the Polish aspects of local history.
Piwarski, Kazimierz. *Dzieje Gdańska w zarysie.* Gdańsk: Instytut Bałtycki, 1946.—Piwarski presents the German Danzig as a constant foreign body in the Polish state.
Prutz, Hans. "Danzig, das nordische Venedig. Eine deutsche Städtegeschichte." *Historisches Taschenbuch* 9, no. 4 (1868): 137–246.—First comprehensive portrayal following a "national cognitive interest in history."
Ruhnau, Rüdiger. *Danzig. Geschichte einer deutschen Stadt.* Würzburg: Holzner Verlag, 1971.— Biased portrayal.
Salmonowicz, Stanisław, ed. *Historia Pomorza.* Toruń: Wydawn. Poznańskie, 2000–2003.—Vol. 4 (in 2 sub-volumes); covers the period from 1850 to 1918; refer to Labuda for volumes 1–3.
Simson, Paul. *Geschichte der Stadt Danzig.* Danzig: L. Sauniers Buchhandlung, 1903.—Concise overall view.
Simson, Paul. *Geschichte der Stadt Danzig.* 3 vols. Danzig: A.W. Kafemann, 1913–1918.—For decades the most important local history, and still significant today. The author died prematurely, however, and was able to provide an account only to the year 1626.

"In a League of Its Own," so to Speak

Grass, Günter. *The Flounder.* Translated by Ralph Mannheim. New York: Harcourt Brace Jovanovich, 1978.—Günter Grass portrays Gdańsk's entire history in his fascinating novel, albeit in a heavily defamiliarized manner and supplemented with many fantastical elements.

Epoch-spanning Histories

Arnold, Udo, ed. *Danzig. Sein Platz in Vergangenheit und Gegenwart.* Warschau: Oficyna Wydawn. Volumen, 1998.
Banaszowski, Jan. *Przemiany demografi czne w Gdańsku w latach 1601–1846.* Gdańsk: Wydawn. Uniwersytetu Gdańskiego, 1995.
Bär, Max. *Die Behördenverfassung in Westpreußen seit der Ordenszeit.* Danzig: A. W. Kafemann, 1912.
Cieślak, Katarzyna. *Tod und Gedenken. Danziger Epitaphien vom 15. bis zum 20. Jahrhundert.* Lüneburg: Verlag Nordostdeutsches Kulturwerk, 1998.
Drost, Willi. *Danziger Malerei vom Mittelalter bis zum Ende des Barock. Ein Bei trag zur Begründung der Strukturforschung in der Kunstgeschichte.* Berlin: Verlag für Kunstwissenschaft, 1938.
Echt, Samuel. *Die Geschichte der Juden in Danzig.* Leer/Ostfriesland: Rautenberg, 1972.
Foltz, Max. *Geschichte des Danziger Stadthaushalts.* Danzig: A. W. Kafemann, 1912.
Fortuna, Grzegorz and Donald Tusk. *Wydarzyło się w Gdańsku 1901–2000. Jeden wiek w jednym mieście.* Gdańsk: Milenium Media, 1999.
Friedrich, Jacek. *Gdańskie zabytki architektury do końca XVIII w.* Gdańsk: Wydawn. Uniwersytetu Gdańskiego, 1995.
Jaroszewski, Marek, ed. *1000 Jahre Danzig in der deutschen Literatur. Studien und Beiträge.* Gdańsk: Wydawn. Uniwersytetu Gdańskiego, 1998.
Keyser, Erich. *Baugeschichte der Stadt Danzig.* Cologne: Böhlau, 1972.

Lingenberg, Heinz. *Oliva—800 Jahre 1186–1986. Abriß der Geschichte.* Lübeck: Verlag Unser Danzig, 1986.
Loew, Peter Oliver. *Danzig und seine Vergangenheit, 1793–1997. Die Geschichte einer Stadt zwischen Deutschland und Polen.* Osnabrück: Fibre, 2003.
Loew, Peter Oliver. *Gdańsk—między mitami.* Olsztyn: Borussia, 2006.
Loew, Peter Oliver. *Das literarische Danzig, 1793 bis 1945. Bausteine für eine lokale Kulturgeschichte.* Frankfurt am Main: Lang, 2009.
Matull, Wilhelm. *Ostdeutschlands Arbeiterbewegung.* Würzburg: Holzner Verlag, 1973.
Pompecki, Bruno. *Literaturgeschichte der Provinz Westpreußen. Ein Stück Heimatkultur.* Danzig: A. W. Kafemann, 1915.
Simson, Paul. *Der Artushof in Danzig und seine Brüderschaften, die Banken.* Danzig: T. Bertling, 1900.
Simson, Paul. *Geschichte der Danziger Willkür.* Danzig: L. Saunier, 1904.
Stephan, Walther. *Danzig. Gründung und Straßennamen.* Marburg: Herder-Institut, 1954.

Selected Literature on Individual Epochs

UP TO 1454

Arnold, Udo. "Vom Rand ins Zentrum. Danzig zwischen Deutschem Orden und Polen im 14./15. Jahrhundert." In *Danzig und sein Platz in Vergangenheit und Gegenwart,* edited by Udo Arnold, 23–32. Warschau: Oficyna Wydawn. Volumen, 1998.
Biskup, Marian and Gerard Labuda, eds. *Die Geschichte des Deutschen Ordens in Preußen.* Osnabrück: Fibre, 2000.
Hirsch, Theodor. *Danzigs Handels- und Gewerbegeschichte unter der Herrschaft des Deutschen Ordens.* Leipzig: Hirzel, 1858.
Keyser, Erich. *Die Entstehung von Danzig.* Danzig: A. W. Kafemann, 1924.
La Baume, Wolfgang: *Ostgermanische Frühzeit.* 2nd ed. Kiel: Schwentine-Verlag, 1959.
Labuda, Gerard. *Święty Wojciech. Biskup—męczennik. Patron Polski, Czech i Węgier.* 2nd ed. Wrocław: Funna, 2000.
Lingenberg, Heinz. *Die Anfänge des Klosters Oliva und die Entstehung der deutschen Stadt Danzig. Die frühe Geschichte der beiden Gemeinwesen bis 1308/10.* Stuttgart: Klett-Cotta, 1982.
Paner, Henryk, ed. *Gdańsk średniowieczny w świetle najnowszych badań archeologicznych i historycznych.* Gdańsk: Muzeum Archeologiczne w Gdańsku, 1998.
Paner, Henryk. "Archeologia Gdańska w latach 1988–2005." *Archeologia Gdańska,* 1 (2006): 11–88.
Śliwiński, Błażej. *Rzeź i zniszczenie Gdańska przez Krzyżaków w 1308 roku.* Gdańsk: Wydawn. Marpress, 2019.

1454 TO 1793

Bömelburg, Hans-Jürgen. *Zwischen polnischer Ständegesellschaft und preußischem Obrigkeitsstaat. Vom Königlichen Preußen zu Westpreußen (1756–1806).* München: Oldenbourg, 1995.
Bogucka, Maria. *Gdańsk jako ośrodek produkcyjny w XV–XVII w.* Warszawa: Państwowe Wydawn. Naukowe, 1962.
Bogucka, Maria. *Handel zagraniczny Gdańska w pierwszej połowie XVII wieku.* Wrocław: Zakład Narodowy im. Ossolińskich, 1970.
Bogucka, Maria. *Das alte Danzig. Alltagsleben vom 15. bis 17. Jahrhundert.* München: Koehler, 1987.
Bogucka, Maria. *Baltic Commerce and Urban Society, 1500–1700. Gdańsk/Danzig and Its Polish Context.* Aldershot: Ashgate, 2003.
Cieślak, Edmund. *Walki społeczno-polityczne w Gdańsku w drugiej połowie XVII wieku. Interwencja Jana III Sobieskiego.* Gdańsk: Gdańskie Towarzystwo Naukowe, 1962.
Cieślak, Edmund. *Konflikty polityczne i społeczne w Gdańsku w połowie XVIII w.: sojusz pospólstwa z dworem królewskim.* Wrocław: Zakład Narodowy im. Ossolińskich, 1972.
Cieślak, Edmund. "Miejsce Gdańska w strukturze Rzeczypospolitej szlacheckiej (XV–XVIII w.)." In *Strefa bałtycka w XVI–XVIII w. Polityka—Społeczeństwo—Gospodarka,* edited by Jerzy Trzoska, 37–50. Gdańsk: Wydawn. Marpress, 1993.

Cuny, Georg. *Danzigs Kunst und Kultur im 16. und 17. Jahrhundert. Erstes Buch. Baugeschichtliches. Danzigs Künstler mit besonderer Berücksichtigung der beiden Andreas Schlüter.* Frankfurt am Main: Keller, 1910.
Friedrich, Karin. *The Other Prussia. Royal Prussia, Poland and Liberty, 1569-1772.* Cambridge: Cambridge University Press, 2000.
Grzybkowska, Teresa, ed. *Aurea Porta Rzeczypospolitej: sztuka gdańska od połowy XV do końca XVIII wieku.* 2 vols. Gdańsk: Agencja Reklamowo-Wydawnicza A. Grzegorczyk, 1997.—Exhibit catalogue with numerous contributions and illustrations.
Heß, Corina. *Danziger Wohnkultur in der Frühen Neuzeit. Untersuchungen zu Nachlassinventaren des 17. und 18. Jahrhunderts.* Berlin: Lit., 2007.
Hillebrand, Almut. *Danzig und die Kaufmannschaft großbritannischer Nation. Rahmenbedingungen, Formen und Medien eines englischen Kulturtransfers im Ostseeraum des 18. Jahrhunderts.* Frankfurt am Main: Lang, 2009.
Hoburg, Karl Wilhelm. *Die Belagerung der Stadt Danzig im Jahre 1734.* Danzig: Theodor Bertling, 1858.
Hoffmann, Heinz. *Danzig und Rußland bei der zweiten Teilung Polens.* Danzig: Unger, 1935.
Kaczor, Dariusz. *Przestępczość kryminalna i wymiar sprawiedliwości w Gdańsku w XVI-XVIII wieku.* Gdańsk: Wydawn. Uniwersytetu Gdańskiego, 2005.
Kizik, Edmund. *Die reglementierte Feier. Hochzeiten, Taufen und Begräbnisse in der frühneuzeitlichen Hansestadt.* Osnabrück: Fibre, 2008.
Kotarski, Edmund. *Gdańsk literacki (do końca XVIII wieku).* Gdańsk: Mestwin, 1997.
Krannhals, Detlef. *Danzig und der Weichselhandel in seiner Blütezeit vom 16. zum 17. Jahrhundert.* Leipzig: S. Hirzel, 1942.
Lengnich, Gottfried. *Ius publicum civitatis Gedanensis, oder: Der Stadt Danzig Verfassung und Rechte. Nach der Originalhandschrift des Danziger Stadtarchivs.* Edited by Otto Günther. Danzig: T. Bertling, 1900—Printed edition of Lengnich's long-unpublished work from the mid-eighteenth century.
Müller, Michael G. *Zweite Reformation und städtische Autonomie im Königlichen Preußen. Danzig, Elbing und Thorn in der Epoche der Konfessionalisierung (1557-1660).* Berlin: Akademie Verlag, 1997.
Rauschning, Hermann. *Geschichte der Musik und der Musikpflege in Danzig: von den Anfängen bis zur Aufl ösung der Kirchenkapellen.* Danzig: Kommissionsverlag der Danziger Verlags-Gesellschaft M.b.h., 1931.
Salmonowicz, Stanisław, ed. *Mieszczaństwo gdańskie.* Gdańsk: Nadbałtyckie Centrum Kultury: Gdańskie Tow. Nauk., 1997.—Conference proceedings with numerous contributions focusing primarily on Gdańsk's early modern history.
Samsonowicz, Henryk: *Untersuchungen über das Danziger Bürgerkapital in der zweiten Hälfte des 15. Jahrhunderts.* Weimar: Böhlau, 1969.
Trzoska, Jerzy: "Gdańsk on the Economic Map of Early Modern Europe." *Acta Poloniae Historica* 81 (2000): 91-116.

1793 TO 1918

Bertling, Anton. *Danzigs Bürgermeister im 19. Jahrhundert.* Danzig: A. W. Kafemann, 1929.
Blech, Abraham Friedrich. *Geschichte der siebenjährigen Leiden Danzigs von 1807 bis 1814.* 2 vols. Danzig: Carl Heinrich Eduard Müller, 1815.
Dann, Eduard Otto. *Topographie von Danzig, besonders in physischer und medizinischer Hinsicht.* Berlin: Enslin'sche Buchhandlung, 1835.
Fabiani-Madeyska, Irena. *Odwiedziny Gdańska w XIX wieku. Z relacji polskich zebrała.* Gdańsk: Gdańskie Tow. Nauk., 1957.
Gliński, Mirosław. *Ludzie dziewiętnastowiecznego Gdańska.* Gdańsk: Wydawn. Gdańskie, 1994.
Hoffmann, Erich. *Danzig und die Städteordnung des Freiherrn vom Stein.* Leipzig: J. C. Hinrichs, 1934.
Letkemann, Peter. *Die preußische Verwaltung des Regierungsbezirks Danzig 1815-1870.* Marburg: Herder Institut, 1967.

Richter, Friedrich. *Preußische Wirtschaftspolitik in den Ostprovinzen. Der Industrialisierungsversuch des Oberpräsidenten v. Goßler in Danzig.* Königsberg: Ost-Europa-Verlag, 1938.
Schaumann, Elly. "Die Danziger Presse im 19. Jahrhundert bis zur Gründung der 'Danziger Zeitung.'" *Zeitschrift des Westpreußischen Geschichtsvereins* 72 (1935): 5-96.
Scholtz, Heinrich, Artur Grünspan, and Erwin Stein. *Danzig.* Oldenburg: G. Stalling, 1914.

1918 TO 1945

Andrzejewski, Marek. *Socjaldemokratyczna partia Wolnego Miasta Gdańska 1920-1936.* Gdańsk: Zakład Narodowy im. Ossolińskich, 1980.
Andrzejewski, Marek. *Wolne Miasto Gdańsk w rewizjonistycznej propagandzie niemieckiej 1920-1939.* Gdańsk: Wydawn. Uniwersytetu Gdańskiego, 1987.
Andrzejewski, Marek. *Opposition und Widerstand in Danzig 1933 bis 1939.* Bonn: J. H. W. Dietz Nachfolger, 1994.
Berendt, Grzegorz. *Żydzi na terenie Wolnego Miasta Gdańska w latach 1920-1945 (Działalność kulturalna, polityczna i socjalna).* Gdańsk: Gdańskie Tow. Nauk., Wydz. I Nauk Społecznych i Humanistycznych, 1997.
Cienciala, Anna M. "The Battle of Danzig and the Polish Corridor at the Paris Peace Conference of 1919." In *The Reconstruction of Poland, 1914-1923,* edited by Paul Latawski, 71-94. New York: School of Slavonic and East European Studies, 2016.
Hajduk, Bolesław. *Gospodarka Gdańska w latach 1920-1945.* Gdańsk: Wydawn. Instytut Historii Polskiej Akademii Nauk., 1998.
Hensel, Jürgen and Pia Nordblom, eds. *Hermann Rauschning. Materialien und Beiträge zu einer politischen Biographie.* Warschau: Oficyna Wydawn. Volumen, 2002.
Kimmich, Christoph M. *The Free City. Danzig and German Foreign Policy 1919-1934.* New Haven, CT: Yale University Press, 1968.
Levine, Herbert S. *Hitler's Free City. A History of the Nazi Party in Danzig 1925-1939.* Chicago: University of Chicago Press, 1973.
Mikos, Stanisław. *Działalność Komisariatu Generalnego Rzeczypospolitej Polskiej w Wolnym Mieście Gdańsku 1920-1939.* Warszawa: Państwowe Wydawn. Naukowe, 1971.
Mikos, Stanisław. *Wolne Miasto Gdańsk a Liga Narodów 1920-1939.* Gdańsk: Wydaw. Morskie, 1979.
Pallaske, Christoph. *Die Hitlerjugend der Freien Stadt Danzig 1926-1939.* Münster: Waxmann, 1999.
Pusback, Birte. *Stadt als Heimat. Die Danziger Denkmalpflege zwischen 1933 und 1939.* Cologne: Böhlau Verlag, 2006.
Ramonat, Wolfgang, *Der Völkerbund und die Freie Stadt Danzig 1920-1934.* Osnabrück: Biblio-Verlag, 1979.
Ruhnau, Rüdiger. *Die Freie Stadt Danzig 1919-1939.* Berg am See: Vowinckel, 1979.—Informative but biased book.
Samerski, Stefan. *Die katholische Kirche in der Freien Stadt Danzig 1920-1933: Katholizismus zwischen Libertas und Irredenta.* Cologne: Böhlau, 1991.
Schenk, Dieter. *Die Post von Danzig. Geschichte eines deutschen Justizmords.* Reinbek: Rowohlt, 1995.
Schenk, Dieter. *Hitlers Mann in Danzig. Gauleiter Forster und die NS-Verbrechen in Danzig-Westpreußen.* Bonn: Dietz, 2000.
Stępniak, Henryk. *Ludność polska w Wolnym Mieście Gdańsku 1920-1939.* Gdańsk: Wydawn. Diecezji Gdańskiej "Stella Maris," 1991.
Wojciechowski, Mieczysław: "Gdańsk w latach 1918-1920." In *Miasta Pomorza Nadwiślańskiego i Kujaw w okresie I wojny światowej oraz w międzywojennym dwudziestoleciu (1914-1939),* 7-59. Toruń: Wydawnictwo Uniwersytetu Mikołaja Kopernika, 2000.

SINCE 1945

Adamowicz, Paweł. *Gdańsk jako wyzwanie.* Gdańsk: Wydawn. słowo/obraz terytoria, 2008.
Andrzejewski, Marek. *Marzec 1968 w Trójmieście.* Warszawa: Instytut Pamięci Narodowej, Komisja Ścigania Zbrodni przeciwko Narodowi Polskiemu, 2008.

Choderny, Zenona, ed. *Danzig/Gdańsk 1945. Erinnerungen nach 50 Jahren/Wspomnienia 50 lat później.* Gdańsk: Wydawn. Marpress, 1997.

Czyżak, Bogdan. *Dylematy. Kultura na Wybrzeżu 1945–1980.* Gdańsk: Wydawn. Morskie, 1985.

Eisler, Jerzy. *Grudzień 1970. Geneza, przebieg, konsekwencje.* Warszawa: Instytut Pamięci Narodowej (Komisja Ścigania Zbrodni przeciwko Narodowi Polskiemu), 2000.

Friedrich, Jacek. *Neue Stadt in altem Gewand. Der Wiederaufbau Danzigs 1945–1960.* Translated by Heidemarie Petersen. Cologne: Böhlau, 2010.

Mażewski, Lech and Wojciech Turek, eds. *"Solidarność" i opozycja antykomunistyczna w Gdańsku (1980–1989).* Gdańsk: Instytut Konserwatywny im. E. Burke'a, 1995.

Mroczko, Marian, ed. *Gdańsk 1945. zbiór studiów.* Gdańsk: Wydawn. Marpress, 1996.

Nowaczewski, Artur. *Trzy miasta trzy pokolenia.* Gdańsk: Polnord Wydawnictwo Oskar, 2006.

Stryczyński, Michał. *Gdańsk w latach 1945–1948. Odbudowa organizmu miejskiego.* Wrocław: Zakład Narodowy im. Ossolińskich, 1981.

Tomczyk-Watrak, Zofia. *Wybory i przemilczenia. Od szkoły sopockiej do nowej szkoły gdańskiej.* Gdańsk: Słowo/obraz, 2001.

Załęcki, Jarosław. *Przestrzeń społeczna Gdańska w świadomości jego mieszkańców. Studium socjologiczne.* Gdańsk: Wydawn. Uniwersytetu Gdańskiego, 2003.

INDEX

For the benefit of digital users, indexed terms that span two pages (e.g., 52–53) may, on occasion, appear on only one of those pages.

A1 Expressway, 228
abhominabile strage, 22
Åbo (Turku), 50
Academic Secondary School, 69–72, 82, 89, 90, 107, 116, 142
Academy of Fine Arts, 199
Academy of Music, 198, 199–200
Adalbert (Bishop), 11–12
Adalbert Institute, 204
Adalbert (Saint), 9–10, 11–12, 19, 81, 225
Adam and Eve House, 77, 104
Adam and Eve in Danzig, 104
Adamowicz, Paweł, 212, 226, 236–37, 240–41
administration of Danzig
    Free City of Danzig, 148–51, 165–66
    Gdańsk, 188
    Plauen, 38
    Polish, 47, 52, 55–58
    political participation, 89–90
    Prussian, 115–16, 124–25, 252n.4
    refusal of obligations 1572, 63–65
    17th century, 88–91
    Teutonic Order, 30–32, 37, 43
agriculture, 18, 33, 93, 161
airports, 210, 228
Alexander III, 133
All Saints' Day protests, 219
Allegory of Danzig Commerce, 78, 79f
Allgemeine Ostkrankenkasse, 174
Alt Schottland (Stare Szkoty), 66, 110
amber
    Gdańsk as capital, 4
    legal rights to, 28
    Roman influences on, 5–7
    skilled trades, 81

    symbolism, 4
    Teutonic State trade in, 32–35
    trade in, 18, 55, 93
Amber Road (Via mercatorum, Merchants' Road), 5
Anti-Comintern Pact, 175
anti-Polonism, 137
Antkiewicz, Alesky, 195
aqueducts, 132
Archaeological Museum, 18, 201–2
architecture, 76–83, 104–5, 139–40, 173–74, 193, 198–99, 234
Armenian congregation, 232
artisans
    avant-garde art, 232–33
    competition, crackdowns on, 66, 86, 90–91, 98–99
    connection, 255n.42
    decline of, 93–96, 104–9, 140–41
    education, 199
    in Free City of Danzig, 170–74
    Gdańsk, 198
    production, 18, 30, 42–43
    revolt by, 38–39, 90
    Teutonic development of, 35–36
    Teutonic oversight of, 32
Artus Court, 29–30, 41, 58, 78, 81, 89–90, 102, 107, 179, 183, 234
Association of Danzig Germans, 202–3, 204, 206
astronomy, 108–9
August Agreements, 213, 215, 216–17
Augustus II (Frederick Augustus), 91–92, 96
Augustus III, 96, 97–99, 100, 111
Augustus III monument, 107
Auschwitz, 180

INDEX

autonomy. *see* privileges/autonomy

Bach, Johann Sebastian, 107
Bakers' Gate, 31–32
Bakers' Street, 27
baking trades development, 35–36
Balfour, Arthur, 148
Baltic Opera, 199–200
Baltic Philharmonic, 199–200
Bank von Danzig, 160
Bankenbruderschaften, 69
bankers, banking, 54, 134, 159–60
Bartel, Kazimierz, 155
Bartholdy, Gottfried Benjamin, 116
basketball, 210–11
Báthory, Stefan, 63–65, 73
Battle of Grunwald, 43
Battle of Nations, 123
Baum, Marie, 167–68
BBC, 215
beaches, 194–95
Beck, Józef, 157–58
beggars, 104
Behrend, Theodor, 118
Beneke, Paul, 57
Berlin, 117, 129
betrothals, 68
Bielecki, Jan Krzysztof, 216, 221
Bielefeldt, Adolf, 174
Bierut, Bolesław, 187, 193–94
Bim-Bom, 200
Bishop's Hill, 42, 48, 110, 118–19, 123, 174
black monks, 42
Blech, Abraham Friedrich, 117
Blocke, Abraham van den, 77, 80
Blocke, Wilhelm van den, 76–77
boats, 1933/1934 discovery, 6–7
Bogucka, Maria, 35–36
Bogusza (governor), 21
Bolesław I, 12
Bolesław III, 19
Bolesław the Pious, 20
Bolsheviks, 152
bombardment of Danzig 16th century, 58
Bonaparte, Napoleon, 117–23, 119*f*
bond servants, 50
Borusewicz, Bogdan, 211, 216, 219
boxing, 195
boycotts, 155, 157–58, 229
Brandenburg, Margraves of, 20–21, 22
Brandenburg-Prussia, 252n.4
Brandt, Salomon, 69
Brandt, Willy, 202, 207–8
Brausewetter, Artur, 141, 173
Bremen, 129
Brewery Street, 27
brewing, brewers, 35–36, 55, 98–99, 210–11

brick manufacture, 51
Bridgettine Convent, 139–40
Bridgettine Sisters, 42
Broad Quarter, 89–90
Bronze Age, amber's value in, 5
Brost, Erich, 204
Brotherhood of St. George, 29–30, 69
Brzezińska, Urszula, 180–81
Bug river, human settlement in, 6
bunglers, 90
burgrave, 87
Burkhardt, Carl Jakob, 166
Burow, Julie, 137–38
butchers, 63
Butenandt, Adolf, 174

Calvinism, 66, 102
Camin, destruction of, 21
Casimir III, 33
Casimir IV, 47
Casimir IV Jagiellon, 44
castle. *see* medieval castle complex
Cat and Mouse (Katz und Maus) (Grass), 205, 224
Catherine II, 101
Catholic Center Party, 152
Catholicism, 42, 59–60, 66–67, 73–74, 90–91, 100–1, 102, 136, 169, 190–91, 195, 219, 222–23, 232
celebrations, 18, 35, 69, 87, 102, 133, 193–94, 195
Center Party, 152–53, 153*t*, 157, 166
Central Maritime Museum, 201–2
charity, 104
Charles X Gustav, 85–86
Charles XII, 91–92
charter of 1466, 47
Chodowiecki, Daniel, 94*f*, 105–6, 105*f*, 106*f*, 239
Chojnowska-Liskiewicz, Krystyna, 210–11
cholera, 132
Church of St. James, 39–40
Church of St. Nicholas, 14*f*, 16–17, 80
Church of St. Peter and Paul, 66
Church of the Holy Spirit, 39–40
Church of the Holy Trinity, 66, 80, 90
Chwin, Stefan, 223–24, 225, 233
Chychła, Zygmunt, 195
Cieślak, Edmund, 202
cinema, 200
citizenship, 29, 89
City Forum, 234
City Museum, 140, 142, 174, 201
cloth trade, 18
clothing, 18th century, 102–3
Clothing Statute of 1642, 68–69, 70*f*
coal/coke trade, 196
Coal Market, 77, 140–41, 200
coat of arms, 31–32, 31*f*, 76–77
Coffee Grinder, 140–41

coffeehouses, 103
Cog Gate, 27, 78–79
Cog Quarter, 89–90
cogs, 18, 36
coinage debasement, 93
coloni, 17
commerce. *see* economic development; trade
commissary/commissary general, 87
commissary general, 156
Commission for Sea-going Vessels, 75
"Committee for Danzig's Harbor and Waterways," 150
Communist Party of Germany (KPD), 153t, 164
composers, 199–200
concentration camps, 180, 199
conflicts of 1576/1577, 63–65
Conradus Celtis, 7–9
constitutions, 61–62, 112, 120–21, 150, 157, 168–69, 177
consul general, 156
consules, 89
Continental System, 120, 121–22
Convent of St. Bridget, 40
convents, 40, 74, 140
Conwentz, Hugo, 142–43
Cook, James, 108–9
Cossack uprising, 85–86
Council of Danzig Germans, 202–3
Council of the League of Nations, 154
Counterreformation, 66, 74
Cow Bridge, 27
Crane Gate, 41, 52–53, 234
cultural life
    development of, 103
    Enlightenment effects on, 107, 109
    Free City of Danzig, 170–74
    Gdańsk, 197–202, 232–35
    intellectuals, 81–83
    literary works, 109
    music, 81
    urban modernization, 139–43
Culture Capital campaign, 240
currency, 150–51, 159–60, 161f, 165
Cybulski, Zbigniew, 200
Czerny, Władysław, 190
Człowiek z żelaza (Wajda), 234

Dąbrowski, Tadeusz, 233
Dagome iudex, 19
Damß, Martin, 172
Dantiscus, Johannes, 81–82
Danzig gulden, 150–51, 160, 165
Danzig Research Society, 107, 201–2
Danzig SA (Sturmabteilung), 157–58, 163, 176, 177
Danzig State Archives, 201
Danzig Technical University, 143, 146, 172, 174, 176, 190, 195–96, 200–1, 235
Danzig Trilogy, 205

Danzig-West Prussia District (Reichsgau Danzig-Westpreußen), 179
Danziger Dampfboot, 138
Danziger Gesellschaft zum Studium Polens, 164–65
Danziger Haupt (Głowa Gdańska), 64, 86, 96–97
Danziger Krakehler, 126–27
Danziger Neueste Nachrichten, 143–44, 146, 149, 158, 181
Danziger Rundschau, 170
Danziger Trachtenbuch (Möller), 81
Danziger Volksstimme, 160
Danziger Willkür, 30
Danziger Zeitung, 131, 133
Danzig's Apotheosis, 78, 79f
"Das blühende Danzig," 82–83
Dead Vistula, 128
death marches, 180
Degler, Helmut Hubert, 198
Dehnel, Jacek, 233
Deisch, Mathäus, 105–6
Delbrück, Clemens Gottlieb, 133–34
Delegation of the Free City of Danzig, 202–3
Democratic Club, 127
Denmark, Hanseatic wars with, 36–37
Der Dollar steigt (Scherret), 158
destruction of Gdańsk, 16, 21–23
Deutscher Städtetag, 147
dialects, 29, 66, 102–3, 136–37, 138, 168, 169
Die Stunde der Frauen (Krockow/Fritz-Krockow), 256n.32
Diet of Lublin 1569, 61, 62
Diet of Nuremberg, 55–56
Diet of Warsaw 1570, 62
diets, 103
Diocese of Oliva, 169
Diocese of Włocławek, 19
Dirschau (Tczew), 64
diversity, 85
Dix, Otto, 173
Dmowski, Roman, 146
Döblin, Alfred, 171
dockworkers' strike 1920, 152, 154
Dog Years (Hundejahre) (Grass), 205
Domansky, Walther, 141
Dominican Church of St. Nicholas, 40
Dominican Monastery, 139–40
Dr. Oetker, 230
Duchy of Gdańsk, 19
Dulkiewicz, Aleksandra, 241
Duńska-Krzesińska, Elżbieta, 195
Düringer, Hans, 80
Duszeńko, Franciszek, 199, 232–33
Dutch Renaissance, 76
Dziennik Bałtycki, 187, 200, 230–31

Eastern Catholic Christianity, 232
Eastern Marches Society, 137

economic development
  expansion, 14/15th centuries, 27, 29–30, 32–35
  Free City of Danzig, 155–56, 158–62, 165–66
  Gdańsk, 196–97, 210, 227–32
  Hanseatic City of Danzig, 181
  market economy, 227–32
  under Polish rule, 50–55, 196–97, 210
  under Prussian rule, 116–17, 127–31, 128f
  17th century, 93–96
  Teutonic State, 32–35
education, 18, 42, 69–72, 82, 107, 142–43, 174, 188, 199, 200–1, 235
Ehmke, Horst, 204
Eichendorff, Joseph von, 124
"Ein Arbeitsloser auf der Langen Brücke," 172
Ekstraklasa, 195
Elbe River, 6, 34
Elbing (Elbląg), 23, 33–34, 37–38, 56, 64, 65, 107–8, 110, 130
elections 1947, 193–94
elective monarchy, 63, 73, 88, 91
electric lighting, 138
Enderling, Paul, 172
England, trade with, 116–17, 121–22, 129, 152
Enlightenment, 98, 102, 107
epidemics, 29, 32–33, 58, 82, 93, 101, 123, 132
Eridanos river, 5–6
Erlichshausen, Ludwig von, 44
Ermland (Warmia), 56
European Solidarity Center, 239
Evangelical Church/Augsburg Confession, 232
"Ewige Stadt Danzig," 203
excavation, post-WWII, 12–13
Excellence Initiative—Research University program, 235

Fac, Bolesław, 233
factors (agents), 52, 56–57
Fahrenheit, Daniel Gabriel, 108–9, 226
Falowce, 198–99, 199f
family life, 67–68
famine, 29, 123
Fatherland Society, 127
Federal Republic of Germany, 202, 207
Federation of Expellees, 203
Federau, Wolfgang, 203
Fenikowski, Franciszek, 200
Ferber, Eberhard, 56–57, 59
Ferber, Konstatin, 61, 64, 80–81
Final Solution, 180
financial collapse 1517, 59
First Northern War, 51, 85–86, 88–89
First Order, 30–31, 89, 98–99
First Partition of Poland, 100–1, 110–13
Fish Market, 35, 138, 234
fish trade, 17–18, 28, 34
Fishers' Quarter, 89–90

fishing, 18
Fiszbach, Tadeusz, 215
Flanders, 17–18
Fleszarowa-Muskat, Stanisława, 200
Flissen/Flissaken, 52–53
flooding, 13, 48, 52–53, 62, 86, 96–97, 128, 182–83
Flounder, The (Der Butt) (Grass), 205
food trade, 50–51
football, 195
forced labor, 180–81
Fordon, 110
foreign direct investment (FDI), 230–31
Forster, Albert, 163, 164, 171, 176–77, 179, 180–81, 182, 203
Forster, Gauleiter, 166
Forster, Johann Reinhold, 108–9
forty-eight men, 59
Forum Gdańsk, 238
Founding Committee for Free Unions, 211
Fourteen Points, 143–44, 146
France, conflicts with, 147–48
Franciscan Monastery, 140, 201
François Louis, 91
Frankfurt an der Oder, battle of, 58
Frankfurt National Assembly, 127
Frantzius, Theodor Christian, 120
fraternal societies, 69
Frauenburg (Frombork), 86
Frederick II, 99–100, 110
Frederick William II, 112
Frederick William III, 116, 131
Free City of Danzig. see also Prussian rule
  administration of, 148–51, 165–66
  collector's items from, 226
  confidential political contacts, 155–56
  cultural life/imperative/politics, 170–74
  currency, 150–51, 159–60, 161f, 165
  economic development, 155–56, 158–62, 165–66
  exports, 161
  industry in, 161, 165
  Jewish purge in, 165–67, 168, 169, 180
  lifestyle, 167–69, 256n.32
  mandated military service, 116, 176
  map, 151f
  national socialism in, 163–67
  nationalism in, 150, 152–53, 155, 157–58
  Nazism in, 157–58
  parliamentary elections, 152–53, 153t, 156
  Polish minority purge, 177
  Polish minority rights, 168–69, 180–81
  Polish resistance in, 177–78
  Polish settlers in, 156
  political relationships, 152–56, 157, 159f, 164
  population, 167–69
  Prussian rule of, 124–27

reinstatement of, 185–86, 202–4
reunification with Reich, 175–83, 179*f*
taxation, 160
tourism, 162
unemployment in, 160–61, 163, 165
women's roles, 167–68, 256n.32
World War II in, 175–78, 178*f*, 181–83
Free Prussians society, 116
Freitag, Rudolf, 140
French rule, 120–23
Fritz-Krockow, Libussa, 256n.32
Fronhof system, 50, 93
Fugger family, 57–58
fur trade, 50
furniture, 101–2

Gałczyński, Konstanty Ildefons, 178
Garbe, Eduard, 136
Garbe, Eduard Ludwig, 9
Gauleiter, 163
Gazeta Gdańska, 136–37, 170
Gdańsk
 administration of, 188
 architecture, 193, 198–99, 234
 crime in, 222
 cultural life, 197–202, 232–35
 displaced Germans in, 185–88, 202–4, 239
 economic deterioration, 213–14, 215, 216–17, 220
 economic development, 196–97, 210, 222, 227–32
 geographic topography, 7, 8*f*
 historical representations of, 1–2, 184–85, 202–4
 history, rediscovery of, 223–27, 233
 housing, 193, 198–99, 199*f*, 226, 231, 234
 industry in, 196–97
 lifestyle, 193–96, 222, 231–32
 literary life, 200
 maps, xv*f*, xvi*f*, 8*f*, 14*f*, 49*f*
 millennial celebration 1997, 11–12, 225–26
 name's origin, 7–10
 new millennium, 235–41, 238*f*
 political repression in, 193–96
 population, 192–93, 231–32
 postwar integration into Poland, 185–88, 190
 privatization of businesses, 222–23, 227, 229–30
 reconstruction of, 188–93, 189*f*, 191*f*, 198, 204
 recreational activities, 194–95, 210–11
 social reforms, 210–11
 start-up companies in, 230
 systemic transformation/reinvention of, 221–23, 236
Gdańsk Airport, 228
Gdańsk Bloodbath, 21–23
Gdańsk Bloodbath memorial, 24–25
Gdańsk Cantata, 199–200

Gdańsk Days, 195
Gdańsk Festival 1754, 45–46
Gdańsk Heights, 7, 149, 211
Gdańsk Historical Museum, 239
Gdańsk Lowlands, 7
Gdańsk Paratrooper Commando, 221
Gdańsk school, 232–33
Gdańsk Shakespeare Theatre, 233–34
Gdańsk Shipyard, 220–21, 229, 237–38
Gdańsk Voivodeship, 187, 220–21
Gdańsk Zoo, 195
Gdynia (Gdingen), 154, 155–56, 160, 162, 179, 182, 208–9, 236
Gdynia Shipyard, 229
Gebietiger, 25–26
Gehl, Julius, 147
Genée, Friedrich, 140–41
General Diet, 88
George, David Lloyd, 148
Gepids, 6
Geremek, Bronisław, 214–15
German Day, 137
German Liberals Party, 152–53, 157, 202
German National People's Party, 150, 152–53, 155, 157, 166, 202
German National Workers' Party, 153*t*
German Social Party, 153*t*
Gerwin, 18
Gesamtkunstwerk, 78–79
Gestapo, 166, 177
Gierek, Edward, 210
Giese, Georg, 67*f*
Glasgow, Paul, 61
glass trade, 18
Głos Wybrzeża, 200
Gmina Polska, 156
Gniezno, 12, 17–18
Gniezno Cathedral, 81
Göbel, Kaspar, 64
Goebbels, Joseph, 163
Goldwasser toast, 145
Gomułka, Władysław, 207–10
Goßler, Gustav von, 130, 133–34
Goszczurny, Stanisław, 200
Gotenhafen, 179
Gothic murals, 41
Goths, 5–6, 7–9
Gotland, Hanseatic occupation of, 36–37
Gottsched, Johann Christoph, 108, 109
grain trade, 18, 32–35, 50–51, 52–54, 93, 116–17, 129, 228
Gralath, Daniel the Younger, 109
Gralath, Karl Friedrich von, 120–21
Granary Island, 41, 123, 226, 232–33
Grand Avenue, 199–200
Grass, Günter, 182, 198–99, 200, 205–7, 224, 226, 227*f*, 233, 239

Great Arsenal, 80, 198–99
Great Northern War, 91–92, 93
Great Synagogue, 166–67
Greblinger, Georg, 82–83
Green Gate, 139–40
Greiser, Arthur, 163
Groddeck, Karl August, 124
Großschäffer, 34–35
Grunau, Simon, 9
Gruppe, Otto Friedrich, 38
Gryphius, Andreas, 82
Gulf of Gdańsk, 18, 97, 101, 182, 228
Günter Grass Gallery, 226
Gustavus Adolphus (Gustav II Adolph), 74–75
Gwiazda, Andrzej, 214–15
Gyddanyzc, 11–12, 225

Hagel (Prince) legend, 9
Hahn, Hermann, 81
Haifa, 180
Hail Hill, 118–19, 123, 234
Hakelwerk, 28, 29
Hakenberger, Andreas, 81
Halbe, Max, 141–42, 171–72
Hall, Aleksander, 211, 216, 220
Haller, Józef, 147
Hamburg, 129
Hamburg America Line (HAPAG), 130
Hanemann (Chwin), 225
Hannemann, Johannes, 173
Hanseatic City of Danzig, 179–83
Hanseatic League
  military support of, 57–58
  trade with, 33–34, 36–37, 51
Hanseatic League privileges, 34
happiness of people, 240
harbor life, 52–54, 53*f*, 66
Hasentödter, Hans, 65
Hashomer Hatzair, 169
Haupt, Adam, 199
Hay Market, 35, 146, 147–48
Hecht, Arnold, 38
Hegge, Jakob, 59
Heimat, 139, 174, 255n.42
Henry, Earl of Derby, 42
Henry IV (King of England), 42
Hermes, Johann Timotheus, 105
herring trade, 34
Hertzberg, Ewald Friedrich von, 111
Heubude (Stogi), 132
Hevelianum, 234
Hevelius, Johannes, 108
Hevelius Plaza, 154
Heykings, Friedrich, 130–31
High Gate, 76–77, 192–93
High Quarter, 89–90
Higher Pedagogical School, 201

Hilton Hotel, 234
Himmler, Heinrich, 180
Hirsch, Theodor, 142–43
Historia Gdańska, 202
historians, 109
Historical Museum/City of Gdańsk, 201–2, 234
Hitler, Adolph, 157–58, 163, 164, 175–83, 179*f*
Hoene, Friedrich, 121–22
Hohenstaufen, 25–26
Höhn, Johann, 81
Hohnfeldt, Hans-Albert, 164
Holbein, Hans the Younger, 67*f*
Holm (Ostrów), 118–19
Holy Roman Empire, 55–56
Holy Spirit Gate, 41
Holy Spirit Street, 27, 35
Homeland Association of West Prussia, 203
Homeland Museum, 203
Homeland Network for Danzig Catholics, 204
hospitals, 133–34
Hound Street, 27
Hour of the Women, 167–68, 256n.32
housing cooperatives, 140
Huelle, Paweł, 223–24, 233
Hufeland, Gottlieb, 121, 122
human settlement
  early-medieval centers map, 14*f*
  excavation, post-WWII, 12–17, 14*f*, 15*f*
  medieval castle complex inhabitants, 17–18
  in Vistula delta, 6–7
hygienic conditions, 103

idealization of Danzig, 203–4
identity development, 2–3, 12, 55–58, 84–85, 223–27, 233, 240, 242–43
immigration, 29, 136–37
Imperial Shipyard, 130, 143, 161
Independent Social Democratic Party of Germany, 152
industrialization, 129–31, 135–37, 161
information technology, 230
instigators, 102
Intel, 230
intellectual life, 81–82, 142–43, 201
International Shipbuilding and Engineering Co. Ltd., 161
Islam/Muslims, 232
Israel, Jonathan I., 51
Ius publicum civitatis Gedanensis (Lengnich), 88
Ivan IV Vasilyevich, 61, 65

Jabłoński, Henryk Hubertus, 198, 199–200
Jaenicke, Fritz, 173
Jagielski, Mieczysław, 215
Jamroż, Franciszek, 222
Jankowski, Henryk, 214, 219, 222–23
Jarre, Jean Michel, 213

INDEX

Jaruzelski, Wojciech, 210, 217
Jesuit Order, 74
Jewelowski, Julius, 152, 168
Jewish Cemetery, 195
Jewish community, 95, 98–99, 102, 136, 165–67, 168, 169, 195
John II Casimir Vasa, 85–86, 109
John III Sobieski, 90–91, 104–5, 194
John Paul II, 213, 220
Jordanes, 6
Jugend (Halbe), 141–42
Jungingen, Ulrich von, 37
Juventus Turin, 219

Kabrun, Jakob, 140–41
Kaczmarek, Lech Marian, 195
Kaczyński, Jarosław, 240–41
Kaczyński, Lech, 216
Kadłubowski, Lech, 198–99
Kaiserhafen, 129
Kaisermanöver, 133
Kalähne, Anne, 167–68
Kalckreuth, Friedrich Adolf, 117
Kampe, Werner, 166
kapellmeister, 107
Karl of Södermanland, 73
Karnkowski, Stanisław, 61–62
Karnkowski Commission, 63
Kashubians, 17
Keidel, Wilhelm Daniel, 124
Keyser, Erich, 22–23, 174
kickbacks for council members, 89
Kindermann, Heinz, 172
Kladderadatsch (Trojan), 141–42
Klaman, Grzegorz, 232–33
Klawitter Shipyard, 161
"Kleckerburg," 206–7
Klefeld, Georg, 61
Klein, Friedrich, 45–46
Kniprode, Winrich von, 28
Kogge, Martin, 59
Kölln, Hans Winkelburg von, 64
Komeggen, 52–53
König, Ludolf, 27
Königsberg, 34–35, 93, 100, 117, 129, 130
Konitz (Chojnice), 46–47
Konrad I, 25–26
Kotus-Jankowski, Franciszek, 188
Kramer, Hans, 76–77
Kriegsrat, 252n.4
Krockow, Christian Graf von, 256n.32
Krzaklewski, Marian, 221–22
Kubicki, Stanisław, 173
Kulka, Konstanty Andrzej, 199–200
Kulmus, Luise Adelgunde Viktoria, 109
Kulturbund der Juden (Jewish Cultural Association), 169

Kwaśniewski, Aleksander, 221

labor conflicts, 99, 136, 193–94, 207–10, 211. *see also* Solidarity (Solidarność)
Lala (Dehnel), 233
Landmeister, 22–23
Landtage, 56
Lange, Carl, 172
Langfuhr, 123, 124–25, 135, 166–67
Last Judgment, The, 57, 142, 201, 234
Law and Justice Party, 240–41
Łaźnia Center for Contemporary Art, 232–33
League of Nations, 148, 149–50, 153–54, 155–56, 160, 162, 165–66
leather making, 55
Lechia Gdańsk Football Club, 195, 219
Lefebvre, François-Joseph, 118, 120
leisure, 69, 138–39
Lengnich, Gottfried, 88, 108, 109
Lenin Shipyard, 197, 207–8, 211
Lenin Shipyard strikes, 213–18, 220
Leningrad Cinema, 200
Leszczyński, Stanisław (Stanisław I), 91–92, 96–98
letters of marque, 61
Letzkau, Konrad, 29–30, 37–38
Letzkau (Leszkowy), 29–30
Lewandowski, Janusz, 216, 221
Liberal Democratic Congress, 221
libraries, 201
lifestyle
    14th century, 42–43
    16th century, 66–73
    18th century, 101–4
    19th century, 137–39
    connection importance, 139, 255n.42
    Free City of Danzig, 167–69, 256n.32
    Gdańsk, 222, 231–32
    Prussian rule, 110–13
    social stratification, 58–60, 63
Lindenowski, Johann Christian von, 115
Lion's Castle, 77
Lippke, Georg, 179
Lipski, Józef, 175
Lis, Bogdan, 214–15
literary life, 82–83, 107, 109, 171–73, 200, 233
literary production, 141–42
Little Christopher room, 41
Livonia invasion 1558, 61, 65
Long Gardens, 27, 141
Long Market
    construction of, 27, 41, 78–79
    elite housing, 29–30
    Forster's speech, 176
    German troops departure, 149
    historically, 17
    public rallies on, 87, 210

Long Market (*cont.*)
  Reformation protests, 59–60
  royal residence, 73–74
  weekly markets, 35
Long Street, 17, 27, 29–30, 104, 105*f*, 173–74, 189*f*, 200, 210
Long Street Gate, 41, 77
looting, 189
Löschin, Gotthilf, 110–11
Lotos Group, 229
Louis XV, 96
Lower Town, 190–91, 232–33
LPP, 230
Lübeck, 18, 29, 30–31, 34, 57–58, 129, 203
Lübeck law, 16
lumber. *see* wood/lumber trade
Lusatian culture, 6
Lutheranism, 59, 66
Lviv, 197–98

Machcewicz, Paweł, 239
Machina coelestis (Hevelius), 108
Macierz Szkolna, 174
Main Town
  architecture, 198–99
  city hall, 41, 77–78, 104–5, 131, 142, 191
  destruction in WWII, 185–88, 186*f*
  excavation, 13–14, 14*f*, 17
  expansion of, 26–28, 134
  fortifications, 41, 48, 64, 123, 134
  Great Mill, 14*f*, 41, 43–44
  harbor facilities, 41
  housing, 41–42, 48, 77, 191, 193
  judiciary, 89–90
  markets, 35
  population, 29–30, 48, 58, 110, 117, 135–37
  privileges/autonomy, 38
  reconstruction of, 190–91, 191*f*, 210, 236
  religious buildings in, 39–40, 40*f*, 48
  seal of, 31–32, 31*f*
  Siege of 1734, 96–97
  skilled trades development, 35–36
  submission to Polish crown, 37–38, 45–46
  support of Hanseatic wars by, 36–37
  tourism in, 195, 231
  trade with Hanseatic League, 33–34
mandated military service, 116, 176, 181
mansions, 140
March Revolution, 127
Marienburg (Malbork), 25–26, 34–35, 60–61
Marienburg (Malbork) siege, 37–38, 46–47
Marienburg-Mlawka Railway, 129
Marienwerder (Kwidzyn), 97, 100
Maritime Museum, 234
marka, 160
Market Hall, 16–17, 222–23
Masonic lodges, 102

Mattern, Georg/Simon, 56–57
Matzerath, Oskar, 198–99, 205, 227*f*
Mau, Johannes, 152
Mauritius, 180
Maximilian II, 63, 64
May Day protests, 219
Mazowiecki, Tadeusz, 214–15
Medical Academy, 174
medieval castle complex
  destruction of, 48
  excavation, 12–16, 15*f*, 26
  expansion, 14/15th centuries, 26–28
  inhabitants of, 17–18
Memling, Hans, 57, 142, 201, 234
memorials, monuments, 24–25, 194, 199, 201–2, 226
Mennonites, 95, 98–99, 102
Merkel, Jacek, 220
Merz, Hermann, 171
"Message to the Working People of Eastern Europe," 217
Mestwin I, 19, 20
Mestwin II, 20
Metrorail, 237
Michael from Augsburg, 80
Mickiewicz, Adam, 145
Mieszko I, 13–14, 19
Miss Baltic Coast, 194
Mizrachi, 169
modernization, 84–85
moedernegotie, 51
Möller, Anton, 81
Molotov-Ribbentrop Pact, 176–77
Momber, Anton, 103
monasteries, 40, 59–60, 64, 139–40
Monument/Defenders/Coast, 194
Motława harbor access, 95
Motława River, 7, 13–16, 27
Mrongovius, Christoph Coelestin, 7–9, 142–43
Municipal Library, 201
municipal proceedings, 30–31
Municipal Secondary School, 142
Municipal Theater, 140–41, 142, 171, 198–99, 200
munitions depot, 154
Münnich, Burkhard Christoph Graf von, 96–97
Museum/Second World War, 239
museums, 18, 140, 142–43, 174, 201–2, 234
music, 81, 103, 107, 142, 173, 198, 199–200
Mycenae (Greece), 5

Nacht-Samborski, Artur, 199
Nassenhuben (Mokry Dwór), 108–9
National Museum, 222–23, 234
National Socialist German Workers' (Nazi) Party, 153*t*, 163–67, 203
natural sciences, 108–9
Naturwissenschaftliche Volksbücher (Reinick), 141–42

naval commission, 61–62, 74, 75
naval raids, 57–58, 61, 65
Nazi Germany, 130, 157–58, 163, 175–83
Nazi Party, 163, 166–67
Neolithic Age, amber's value in, 5–6
Neptune's Fountain, 78
Netherlands, trade with, 33–34, 51–52, 93, 116–17, 129
Neu Schottland (Nowe Szkoty), 124–25
Neufähr (Górki Zachodnie), 128–29
Neufahrwasser (Nowy Port), 95, 110, 123, 124–25, 135
Neuteich (Nowy Staw), 149
New Art Museum (NOMUS), 232–33
New Gardens, 140, 190
New Hanseatic League, 223
New Motława canal, 27, 48
New Town development, 27
newspapers, 107–8, 126–27, 131, 136–37, 173, 181, 187, 200, 230–31
Nicholas II, 133
Nickelswalde (Mikoszewo), 128
Night of Broken Glass (Kristallnacht), 166–67
Nitschke, Gerhard, 204
Nobel Peace Prize, 219
Nobel Prize in Literature, 226
Nocny, Waldemar, 233
Noé, Ludwig, 161
Nordic mannerism, 76
Nordische Elektrizitäts-und Stahlwerke AG, 130
North German Confederation, 132–33
North German Lloyd (Norddeutscher Lloyd), 130
November Pogroms, 166–67
Nowicki, Edmund, 195
Nuremberg Laws, 166–67

oath of loyalty/allegiance, 59–60, 61–62, 87, 90–91
Ochab, Edward, 187
Ogier, Charles, 53–54
Ohra, 135, 168
oil/oil products, 228, 229–30
Old Suburb
  construction of, 27
  population, 29
  reconstruction of, 190–91
  religious buildings in, 40
  Siege of 1734, 96–97
Old Town
  administration of, 32, 37, 47
  excavation, 14f, 16, 22–23
  expansion of, 134
  Great Mill, 36
  mills, 14/15th centuries, 27–28
  population, 29, 135
  privileges/autonomy, 27–28
  reconstruction of, 190–91, 236

religious buildings in, 39–40
Siege of 1734, 96–97
Teutonic State governance, 27–28
Old Town Moat Street, 25
Oliva Gate, 16, 127, 156, 198–99, 208
Oliva Monastery, 20, 22, 43, 64, 65, 73, 81, 110, 169
Ołowianka Island (Bleihof), 234
Omankowski, Willibald, 172, 173
128th Danzig Infantry Regiment, 135
Opitz, Martin, 82
Orłowo, 7
O'Rourke, Eduard Graf, 169
orphanages, 104
Orthodox churches, 232
Ostdeutsche Monatshefte, 172
Ostpolitik, 202, 207–8
Ostpreußische Zeitung, 155
Ostrów Island, 237–38

Paderewski, Ignacy, 147
painters, paintings, 142, 173, 199
Pan Tadeusz (Mickiewicz), 145
Parerga historica (Uphagen), 5–6
Parish Church of St. Catherine, 16
parliament *(Volkstag)*, 150
Passauer Neue Presse, 230–31
Pastorius, Joachim, 109
patron saints depiction, 32
Paul Beneke Youth Hostel, 174
Peace of Tilsit, 120
Pedagogical University, 195–96
Peeling the Onion (Beim Häuten der Zwiebel) (Grass), 226
Pepsi-Cola, 210–11
perestroika, 220
periodicals, 107–8
Permanent Court of International Justice, 154
Peter I, 92
Peter von Danzig, 57
Pfuhle, Fritz, 173
Phaethon, 5–6
Phoenicians, travel to Danzig by, 5–6
Piast Dynasty, 13–14
Pierre de la Rochelle, 55
Pillau, 74–75
Piłsudski, Józef, 153–54
PKN Orlen, 229, 230–31
plague, 29, 58, 82, 93, 101
Plauen, Heinrich von, 38, 43
Plehnendorf (Płonia), 128
Pobłocka, Ewa, 199–200
poetry, 81–83, 109, 143–44, 172, 233
Poles, resettlement of, 185–88
Polish Baltic Philharmonic, 234
Polish Blue Army, 147
Polish Constitution of 1791, 216–17

Polish Democratic Bloc, 193–94
Polish-Lithuanian Commonwealth, 37, 43, 47, 52, 55–56, 62, 66, 93
Polish-Lithuanian Noble Republic, 86, 88
Polish military transit depot, 154
Polish nationalism, 145–46
Polish People's Party, 193–94
Polish postal service, 154
Polish-Swedish war, 73–76, 85–87, 88–89
Polish United Workers' Party, 193–94, 210, 215, 220
Polish Workers' Party, 188
Politechnika Gdańska, 200–1
political reforms 17th century, 88–91
political status 18/19th centuries, 87–88
Polnische Bibliothek, 108
Pomerelia
   Gdańsk Bloodbath, 21–23
   human settlement in, 5–7
   military campaigns in, 19–21
   return to Polish state, 20
   sovereignty shifts, 19–21
   Teutonic Order's administration of, 25–26, 38
Pompecki, Bruno, 134–35
Posadzki, Tomasz, 222
Posen (Poznań), 147, 194, 197–98
Potsdam Conference, 185–86
poverty, 138
Poznań, 17–18, 176–77
Prangenau (Pręgowo), 132
Praust (Pruszcz), 73
prison/labor camps, 180–81
Prison Tower, 41, 77
privateers, 36–37, 46–47, 58, 61, 74
privileges/autonomy
   under Báthory, 65
   under French rule, 120–22
   North German Confederation, 132–33
   under Polish rule, 46–47, 60–61, 87, 90–92, 100
   under Prussian rule, 101, 116
   Royal Prussia, 62
   under Teutonic State, 34, 38
   trade, 52, 66, 86, 90, 93–95
proconsules, 89
Proite, Johann, 61
Protestant Duchy of Prussia, 58
Protestant Reformation, 59–60
Protestantism, 73–74, 90–91, 100–1, 102, 136, 169, 195, 232
Provinzialgewerbemuseum, 142–43
Prussian Confederation, 43–44, 46–47
Prussian Eastern Railway, 129
Prussian rule. *see also* Free City of Danzig
   administration, 115–16, 124–25, 252n.4
   debts, post-Napoleon, 125
   decline of, 146–48

economic development under, 116–17, 127–31, 128*f*
German Confederation recognition, 126
lifestyle, 110–13
mandated military service, 116
newspapers, 126–27
perceptions of, 114–15, 125
post-France, 124–27
privileges/autonomy under, 101, 115–16
revolt 1794, 116
social unrest, 127
Przegląd Polityczny, 219
Przemysł II, 20
Przybyszewski, Stanisław/Stanisława, 173

Queisner, Carl, 126

Radio Free Europe, 215
radio stations, 200, 230–31
Radunia Canal, 41, 132
Radunia River, 5–6, 27–28
rafts, 52–53
railways, 129, 155, 156, 161, 177, 193, 228, 234
Rapp, Jean, 120–21, 123
Rauschning, Hermann, 164–65, 166, 203
rebellion of 1456, 59
Red Army, 181–83, 202
reforms 16th century, 58–61
refugees, 181, 185–86, 186*f*
Reichsbank, 134
Reinick, Robert, 141–42
religious life, 40, 59–60, 66–67, 169, 195, 232
Rembrandt Harmensz van Rijn, 51, 105–6
Rennen, Peter van der, 81
Reserved, 230
resistance to Polish rule, post-WWI, 146–48
Revolution of Gdańsk, 115
Rhineland, 17–18
Ribbentrop, Joachim von, 175
Rickert, Heinrich, 133, 142–43
Riga, 50, 93
Rist, Johann, 85
Rogulski, Marek, 232–33
Rosenberg, Georg, 64
Rottenburg, Franz Gottfried von, 94*f*
Royal Assessorial Tribunal, 90–91
Royal Chapel, 104–5, 191*f*
Royal Firearms Factory, 130, 161
Royal Prussia, 44, 46–47, 62, 86, 90, 91–92, 99–101
Royal Secondary School, 142
Royal Shipyard, 130, 197
Różewicz, Stanisław, 200
Rozrażewski, Hieronim, 73–74
Rüdiger (abbot), 22
Ruschkewitz, Erich, 172
Russia, conflicts with, 61, 65, 91–92, 96–98, 101, 112, 122–23, 176–77

INDEX

Russian Grave, 97
Rydz-Śmigły, Edward, 176

Sahm, Heinrich, 147, 149–50, 152, 155–56, 157
salt trade, 17–18, 32–35, 52, 93
Salza, Hermann von, 25–26
Sambor I, 19
Scania, Sweden, 34
Schaper, Rudolf, 171
Scheerbart, Paul, 141–42
Schelwig, Samuel, 107
Scherret, Felix, 158, 170
Schichau Shipyard, 130, 136, 161, 197
Schidlitz (Siedlce), 135
Schiewenhorst (Świbno), 128
Schiffskinder, 37
Schinkel, Karl, 139–40, 142
Schirmacher, Käthe, 147, 167–68
Schleswig-Holstein, 177, 178*f*
Schlöndorff, Volker, 200, 224, 234
Schlüter, Andreas, 104–5
Scholtz, Heinrich, 133–34, 143–44
Schön, Theodor von, 124
Schöne Madonna, 42
Schonenfahrer, 34
Schopenhauer, Arthur, 142–43, 226
Schopenhauer, Johanna, 103–4
Schörappke, 52–53
Schultz, Daniel, 105–6
Schultz, Johann Philipp, 93–95
Schulz, Johann Carl, 142
Schumacher, Wilhelm, 9, 141
Schuricht, Carl, 173
Schütz, Caspar, 81–82
Schwegemann, Heinrich, 184
sciences, 76–83, 104–9, 142–43
Seal of Danzig, 150
Second Order, 30–31, 89–90, 98–99
Second Peace of Thorn, 46–47
Selenographia (Hevelius), 108
Senate, 150, 162
Seven Years' War, 100
sewage system, 103, 132
Shaveling War (Pfaffenkrieg), 56
shipbuilding, 55, 129–30, 143, 161, 181, 196–97, 229
shoemakers, 99
Siege of 1734, 96–98, 98*f*, 107–8
Siege of 1807, 117–19, 119*f*
Siege of 1813, 122–23
Sigismund I, 58, 60–61
Sigismund II Augustus, 61–63
Sigismund III Vasa, 73–75
silk trade, 18
Simson, Paul, 22–23, 62, 142–43
skilled trades, 18, 30, 35–36, 50–55, 81, 93–96, 110, 131, 161, 196–97

Skotarczak, Nikodem, 222
Sławno region, 21
Śliwiński, Błażej, 21–22
Słupsk, 17–18
Sobiesław I, 19
Social Democratic Party (SPD), 146–47, 150, 152–53, 153*t*, 154–55, 157, 158, 164–66, 204
social discipline, 68–69
social stratification, 29–30, 58–59, 63, 67–69, 89, 138
social unrest. *see also* Solidarity (Solidarność)
    16th century, 58–65
    17th century, 88–91
    18th century, 98–101
    labor conflicts, 99, 136, 193–94, 207–10, 211
    Worker's Rebellion of 1970, 207–10, 209*f*, 214, 215–16
Societas Litteraria, 107
Sołdek, 197
Solidarity (Solidarność)
    August Agreements, 213, 215, 216–17
    formation of, 213–18
    free elections, 220
    impacts of, 213, 216, 221–22
    martial law, 216–18
    media coverage of, 215
    national congress, 217
    negotiations/resistance, 218–21
    Solidarity Regional Coordination Committee, 219
    supply shortages, 213–14, 215, 216–17, 220
    ZOMO units, 217–18, 220
"Song for the Fatherland," 121
Sopot school, 199
Sopot (Zoppot), 195, 235
Soviet Central Committee, 193–94
Space of Freedom concert, 213
Spind, 103
Splett, Carl Maria, 169, 195
sports, 195, 210–11
Spring of Nations, 126
SS (Schutzstaffel), 163, 177, 182–83
St. Anne's Chapel, 42
St. Barbara's Church, 39–40
St. Bartholomew depiction, 32
St. Bridget's Church, 80, 222–23
St. Catherine depiction, 32
St. Catherine's Church, 14*f*, 21–22, 39–40
St. Dominic's Fair, 18, 35, 69, 136
St. Elizabeth's Church, 39–40, 66
St. George's Court, 69
St. James's Church, 22
St. John's Church, 39–40, 80
St. John's Gate, 41
St. Mary's Church
    altarpiece, 57

St. Mary's Church (cont.)
  architecture, 39, 40f, 79–80
  artistic activity in, 42
  Blech's histories, 117
  Brausewetter's novels, 141
  Catholic masses dispute 1593, 73–74
  construction of, 27
  education/school in, 42
  Letzkau commemoration, 38
  orchestra, 81
  placement in Gdańsk, map, 14f, 49f
  priest appointments, 47
  rededication of, 190–91
  Reformation and, 59–60
  WWII effects on, 142
St. Mary's Street, 4
St. Nicholas' Church, 14f, 16–17
St. Paul's Church, 127
Stadtbürgerschaft, 150
Stalin, Joseph, 194
StanisławII August Poniatowski, 100
State Chamber of Culture, 171–72
State Museum/History of Danzig, 174, 201–2
Statuta Karnkoviana, 61–62
Stecknitz Canal, 34
Steelyard, 34
Sternfeld, Norbert, 202
Stettin (Szczecin), 17–18, 93, 129, 130, 198, 208–9
stock market, 102
Stockholm, Hanseatic occupation of, 36–37
Stocznia Gdańska, 197
Stolpmünde (Ustka), 181
Stolzenberg, 110, 124–25
strage magna, 22
strage maxima, 22
Strait of Baltiysk, 33–34
Strauch, Aegidius, 90
Strauch Religious Quarrels, 90–91
street sanitation, 103
streetlights, 103
Ströhm, Carl Gustaf, 204
Strunk, Hermann, 170
Strzałkowska, Jansa, 198–99
student protests 1968, 195–96
student theaters, 200
Stutthof, 180
suburbium, 14–16
Sucharski, Henryk, 177
summer residency, 80–81
Svenichen, Alexander, 59–60
swastika, 163
Sweden, conflict with, 73–76, 85–87, 88–89, 91–92
Święca family, 20–22
Swietopelk II, 16, 19–20
symbols/symbolic acts, 31–32, 76–77, 183, 192–93
szaber, 189

Tagfahrten, 56
Tatar alliance, 86
taxation
  customs exemptions, 19–20
  financial collapse 1517, 59
  under Frederick II, 110–11
  Free City of Danzig, 160
  under French rule, 120–22
  general toll 1765, 100
  market revenues, 18
  Old vs. Main Town, 32
  Order exemption from, 34–35
  oversight, 87
  port tariffs, 75–76
  poundage tariff, 18, 33–34, 36–37, 43–44
  under Prussian rule, 45, 125, 127, 252n.4
  railway tariffs, 155
  rebellion of 1456, 59
  reforms, 98–99
  wealth tax, 98–99
Tczew, 17–18
Teatr Wybrzeże, 198–99, 200, 233–34
telegraphy, 118–19, 154
telephones, 138
television, 230–31
terraces (Beischläge), 103–4
Teutonic Order/Teutonic State
  administration by, 30–32, 37, 43–44
  agriculture development, 33
  citizens, 14/15th centuries, 29–30
  coinage, 38–39
  crest, 31–32, 32f
  destruction of Gdańsk, 13–14, 16
  economic development, 32–35
  expansion, 14/15th centuries, 26–28
  fall of, 43–44, 58
  Gdańsk Bloodbath, 21–23
  lifestyle, 42–43
  privileges/autonomy under, 27–28, 34, 38
  rise to power, 19–21, 25–26
  skilled trades development, 35–36
  structural growth 14/15th centuries, 39–42
  Thirteen Years' War, 46–47
  trading/mercantile activities, 34–35
  urban vernacular/dialects in, 29
textile trades, 18, 34–36, 52, 55, 93, 196
theater, 140–41, 198–99, 200, 233–34
Theresienstadt, 180
Third Order, 61–62, 64, 89–91, 98–99, 121
Thirteen Years' War, 24–25, 46–47, 59
Thirty Years' War, 82, 85–86, 107–8
Thorn (Toruń), 33–34, 37–38, 56, 64
Tiegenhof (Nowy Dwór), 149
Tin Drum, The (Grass), 182, 198–99, 200, 205–7, 224, 227f, 234
Tolkemit (Tolmicko), 86
Torture Chamber, 77

Toruń (Thorn), 197–98
tourism, 194–95, 228, 231
Towarzystwo Przyjaciół Nauki i Sztuki, 156
Tower, Reginald, 149–50
trade
   Continental System, 120, 121–22
   Danzig harbor life, 52–54, 53*f*
   development of, 16–18, 23, 50–55
   under Frederick II, 110
   guilds, 36, 55, 90, 95–96, 98–99
   looted goods, 189
   news center, 107–8
   under Polish rule, 196–97
   privileges/autonomy, 52, 66, 86, 90, 93–95
   prohibitions on, 64
   regulation of, 52
   routes, 5, 13, 17–18, 33–34, 54, 127–28, 228–29
   sea access for Poland, 143–44, 146, 147–48, 157–58, 162
   17th century, 93–96
   ship traffic statistics, 93–95, 121–22, 129, 155–56, 162, 181
   ships, collective ownership of, 34
   Teutonic State development of, 32–35
   war's effects on, 43–44, 46–47, 61, 87, 143, 181
traffic, 103–4, 140
Trave River, 34
Treaty of Versailles, 148–49, 153–54, 156, 170
Treaty of Warsaw 1970, 207
treaty with Poland 1920, 150–51
Treblinka, 199
Treviranus, Gottfried Reinhold, 157
Tricity, 7, 210, 228, 232–33, 235, 237
Trojan, Johannes, 141–42
Tullatsch the giant, 39
Tusk, Donald, 209, 216, 224–25, 239
Twenty-Seventh Army Corps, 135

UEFA European Championship, 237
Ukraine, 228–29, 237
unemployment, 136
Ungeradin, Heinrich, 41
Union of the Baltic Cities, 223
United Nations, 203
University of Gdańsk, 201, 221
Uphagen, Johann, 5–6
urban modernization, 131–35, 134*f*, 139–43, 181, 237–40, 238*f*

Venice, trade with, 52
Victual Brothers, 36–37
Vier Büchern Liebeselegien (Conradus Celtis), 7–9
Vilnius, 197–98
Vistula delta
   draining/settlement of, 7, 13, 26, 27, 33
   geographic topography, 7, 13
   human settlement in, 6–7, 12–17
   Swedish troops in, 75
Vistula Lagoon, 33–34, 46–47, 65, 86
Vistula River, 17–18, 25–26, 110, 127–28, 228
Vistula Spit, 47, 211
visual arts, 142, 173
Volksstimme, 158
Volmar, Erich, 198
Vredeman de Vries, Hans, 78, 81

Wagner, Richard, 170–71
Wajda, Andrzej, 234
Walentynowicz, Anna, 214
Wałęsa, Lech, 208–9, 211, 213–22, 216*f*. *see also* Solidarity (Solidarność)
Wall Street, 174
Wallerstein, Immanuel, 51
warehouse district, 27
Warsaw, 117, 197–98
Warsaw delegation 1921, 153–54
Warsaw Ghetto, 180
wastewater, 103, 132
water supply, 132
waterwheels, 36
Wawel Castle, 37
Weichselmünde (Wisłoujście) Fortress, 64–65, 74–75, 80, 118–19, 132
Weickhmann, Joachim Heinrich von, 124
Weimar National Assembly, 147, 148
Weimar Republic, 152–53, 157
Weiser Dawidek (Huelle), 224
Weißenberg (Biała Góra), 51
Wencel, Wojciech, 233
Wenceslaus II, 20
Wenceslaus III, 21
Wessel, Jakob, 105–6
Westdeutsche Allgemeine Zeitung, 204
Westerplatte, 95, 97, 118–19, 154, 157–58, 176, 177, 194, 199, 228, 239
Wiechmann, Hans, 166
Wiek legend, 9
Wilhelm Gustloff, 181
Wilhelm I, 192–93
Wilhelmtheater, 141
Wiłkomirski, Kazimierz, 199–200
William I, 131, 133
William II, 133
Wilson, Woodrow, 143–44, 146, 148
Winter, Leopold von, 131, 133–34
Władysław IV, 75–76
Władysław I Herman, 19, 20–21
Władysław II Jagiełło, 37–38
Wnukowa, Józefa, 199
Wöchentliche Zeitung, 108
Wojtyła, Karol. *see* John Paul II
Wolf, Nathan Matthäus, 108–9
Wolne miasto, 200

women's roles, 102, 104, 167–68, 256n.32
wood/lumber trade, 18, 32–36, 50, 51, 52–53, 54, 93, 116–17, 129, 196
Wood Market, 16, 192–93, 194
Worker's Rebellion of 1970, 207–10, 209f, 214, 215–16
World War I, 22–23, 124, 129, 134, 143–44, 169
World War II, 12–13, 24–25, 175–78
Wrocław, 238
Wrzeszcz (Langfuhr), 185, 193, 195
Wyspa Gallery, 232–33

yacht building, 230
Yalta Conference, 185–86
Young Danzig, 172
Young Poland movement, 211, 219
Young Town
   administration of, 32, 37
   creation of, 26, 28
   destruction of, 48
   modernization of, 237–38
   population, 29
   privileges/autonomy, 28
   religious buildings in, 39–40

Zaleski, August, 155
Zawistowski, Władysław, 233
Zborowski, Jan, 64
Ziehm, Ernst, 157, 158
Zieleniak, 198–99
złoty, 160
ZOMO units, 217–18, 220
Zoppot, 149, 168, 182, 195, 235
Zoppot Forest Opera, 170–71
Zu den drey Bleiwagen, 102